TOWARDS A STRATEGIC MANAGEMENT AND DECISION TECHNOLOGY

THEORY AND DECISION LIBRARY

General Editors: W. Leinfellner and G. Eberlein

Series A: Philosophy and Methodology of the Social Sciences
Editors: W. Leinfellner (Technical Universtiy of Vienna)
G. Eberlein (Technical University of Munich)

Series B: Mathematical and Statistical Methods
Editor: H. Skala (University of Paderborn)

Series C: Game Theory, Mathematical Programming and Operations Research
Editor: S. H. Tijs (University of Nijmegen)

Series D: System Theory, Knowledge Engineering and Problem Solving
Editor: W. Janko (University of Vienna)

SERIES A: **PHILOSOPHY AND METHODOLOGY OF THE SOCIAL SCIENCES**

Editors: W. Leinfellner (Technical University of Vienna)
G. Eberlein (Technical University of Munich)

Scope

This series deals with the foundations, the general methodology and the criteria, goals and purpose of the social sciences. The emphasis in the new Series A will be on well-argued, thoroughly analytical rather than advanced mathematical treatments. In this context, particular attention will be paid to game and decision theory and general philosophical topics from mathematics, psychology and economics, such as game theory, voting and welfare theory, with applications to political science, sociology, law and ethics.

For a list of titles published in this series, see final page.

TOWARDS A STRATEGIC MANAGEMENT AND DECISION TECHNOLOGY

Modern Approaches to Organizational Planning and Positioning

by

JOHN W. SUTHERLAND
Virginia Commonwealth University, Richmond

KLUWER ACADEMIC PUBLISHERS
DORDRECHT / BOSTON / LONDON

Library of Congress Cataloging in Publication Data

Sutherland, John W.
Towards a strategic management and decision technology : modern approaches to organizational planning and positioning / John W. Sutherland.
p. cm. -- (Theory and decision library. Series A, Philosophy and methodology of the social sciences)
Includes index.
ISBN 0-7923-0245-1
1. Strategic planning. 2. Decision-making. I. Title.
II. Series.
HD30.28.S9 1989
658.4'012--dc20 89-2696

ISBN 0-7923-0245-1

Published by Kluwer Academic Publishers,
P.O. Box 17, 3300 AA Dordrecht, The Netherlands.

Kluwer Academic Publishers incorporates
the publishing programmes of
D. Reidel, Martinus Nijhoff, Dr W. Junk and MTP Press.

Sold and distributed in the U.S.A. and Canada
by Kluwer Academic Publishers,
101 Philip Drive, Norwell, MA 02061, U.S.A.

In all other countries, sold and distributed
by Kluwer Academic Publishers Group,
P.O. Box 322, 3300 AH Dordrecht, The Netherlands.

printed on acid free paper

Printed in The Netherlands

For Alban, who for so many years offered so freely the next best thing to critical inspiration -- her uncritical affection.

FOREWORD

The focus in these pages is on what the modern management, decision and system sciences can do to assist higher management authorities. For it is they who are generally charged with the responsiblity for ensuring the overall strategic 'readiness' of the organizations they serve...this a measure of the extent to which an organization is prepared to respond --in both a proper and timely way-- to whatever opportunities and perils the world may hold in store. Here then is the essence of the strategic management challenge. And here also is the core of the problem for these pages. For as things now stand, science has a great deal less to offer strategic decision-makers than it does their subordinates at the middle-echelon or line levels of enterprise.

This is just another way of saying that all of us, practitioners, professionals and academics alike, are better prepared to handle tactical or operational challenges than strategic issues. The clearest evidence of this is that the repertoire of currently available decision support instruments is still monopolized by quantitative techniques that simply cannot comprehend the essentially conceptual or 'notional' matters that are the stuff of true strategic decision exercises. We might choose to pretend otherwise. But the absolute, unarguable fact of modern managerial life is this grand paradox:

> The more sweeping and significant of the decisions taken within the typical enterprise --those of strategic import-- will be the least likely to benefit from any formal discipline or precision.

Everything that will be done in this book will be aimed at addressing this paradox.

But it will be addressed from the perspective of the technician, i.e.: from the view point of the management scientist rather than the management theorist. And this may seem to present a paradox of another nature. For if it is true that strategic decisions turn on matters of value, judgement and perspective, then how might it be that they could fall into the province of the technician?

It will be many pages yet before we can attempt to provide any really adequate answer to this question. But when it finally does appear, what we'll be looking at is a strategic management technology centered around two different but ultimately complementary sets of provisions:

> a). Formal structuring conventions that are not intended to generate solutions to problems, but rather provide analytical and procedural frameworks to help strategic decision authorities find a disciplined route to solutions of their own devising. That is, the various structured strategic management and planning/positioning platforms we'll be introducing are designed to assist strategic analysts and decision-makers in organizing, displaying, evaluating and modifying their "reasoning" about matters that are too empirically elusive to admit to any sort of neat mathematical or statistical resolution.
>
> b). But strategic matters are also too important to be left to casual speculation or raw rhetoric. Hence the requirement for a set of qualitative analysis techniques and a family of logical processing facilities...such intended to do for strategic decision exercises at least some of what traditional quantitative analysis techniqes and data processin facilities have been able to do for tactical and operational decision exercises.

The path to be followed towards a strategic management technology may thus take us through some generally ill-charted ground. And while it's a reasonably long path, it's also reasonably straight. For this book has seven chapters divided into three major parts, all hopefully following a fairly neat elaborative progression of concepts and capabilities.

Particularly, the two chapters constituting Part I will try to give a detailed indication of the rather unique perspective that the technician takes on the strategic management challenge. Central to this perspective, as will be argued in Chapter 1, is that true strategic decision exercises take place over qualitatively-disparate alternatives...over choices that are 'different in kind' rather than merely different in degree. This, in turn, suggests that strategic management practice poses some very special requirements in terms of analytical procedures and instruments relative to tactical and operational decision exercises.

We'll then go on to elaborate and defend another critical aspect of the technician's perspective on enterprise: Not all higher-management authorities may be said to have 'strategic' decision responsibilities! Rather, it's mainly a matter of the nature of the environmental/competitive context in which their organization is resident. This then leads, in Chapter 2, to the definition of several different approaches to strategic management under which contemporary organizations may elect to operate. And as a critical corollary, much discussion will be devoted to an indication of the conditions under which each would become the preferred basis for the pursuit of organizational "readiness".

Part II will take us further into the matter of strategic management technology. For there we'll be looking in some detail at the generation and use of strategic planning/positioning structures, and most particularly the following ostensibly state- of-the-art platforms:

Chapter 3: Structured Strategic Contingency Planning
" 4: Dynamic Strategic Planning/Positioning
" 5: Adaptive Strategic Management Protocols

For the most part, the technical initiatives and procedures that will be brought out in these chapters will not be readily available for any other source. For most are based on concepts that are not only of very recent origin, but which have also been confined mainly to certain segements of the modern military and intelligence communities.

In Part III we turn to a consideration of strategic analysis and decision technology. And sadly, it will become apparent that even the best that can be done with existing techniques is often not good enough. For in Chapter 6 we'll look at how and why strategic decision exercises are so extraordinarily susceptible to crippling confoundations...to conditions that can frustrate or even defeat any attempt to remain within the bounds of rationality that the management and decision sciences can now provide. Hence our concern with the prospect of a shortfall in strategic technology. It's the various symptoms of this technical 'shortfall' against which we'll target the provisions of a

Strategic Analysis Protocol to be introduced in Chapter 7. This will bring our inquiry to a close.

For those who might be thinking about joining in this inquiry, there's one encouraging point to consider. Because strategic management and decision support facilities will be more logical than algorithmic in nature --and more qualitative than quantitative in inspiration-- the arguments raised in these pages should be readily accessible even to those who are not familiar with the intricacies of modern mathematical or statistical methods. True, you'll see symbolic notations at various points in the text. But all are intended to make the lines of argument we'll be following simpler to track than would otherwise be the case. Yet while nothing much is demanded of the reader in the way of special technical preparation, the lines of argument we will be following will at times get rather intricate. For success in strategic matters --as in love and war-- may often depend on the tiniest turn of judgement and analytical nuance.

It should also be noted that, despite the pragmatic power of modern structuring conventions and qualitative analysis initiatives, they are not technical tricks. For in the strategic domain, there are really no reliable substitutes for concerted intellectual effort. Strategic insights of worth in the real world will be less likely to arise as speculative windfalls than to have been hard won.

As for whom this work is intended, it is meant first of all for my academic colleagues in the administrative disciplines. The hope is that at least some of the more speculatively-grounded conceptual and instrumental provisions raised in these pages will be considered interesting enough to be posed as items for entry into the management and decision science research and development agendas. A second audience that might be interested in what's said here would be those working professionals charged with actually carrying out strategic analysis and planning activities...or, indeed, providing any of a wide variety of technical support services at the higher-echelons of commercial, industrial, governmental or military enterprises. For the various strategic planning/positioning structures that will be discussed are available to serve as the centerpieces for the next-generation management support systems that are now being designed to take advantage of advances in distributed systems architecture and command/control configurations.

And of course, by way of a third hoped-for set of readers, there are those preparing to become strategic managers . . . particularly graduate level students in business or public administration, etc. For it's at the graduate-level where students are expected to become engaged more completely with higher-order decision issues. Moreover, graduate students will generally be more familiar with the traditional, majorally non- technical literature on higher-management. And what we will be doin here is designed to complement, not displace, advises from these perspectives. In this sense, our volume will hopefully be seen as a useful addendum to courses on strategy and policy, or the increasingly popular attempts at developing "capstone" courses designed to convey an integrated perspective on organizational management. Or it may serve as a stand-alone reference for classes that want to focus on the science vs. the art of higher-management.

Finally, there is an attribution in order. For if there was any trigger that set this book in motion, it was General Douglas MacArthur's compelling expression of the ultimate purpose of any endeavors in the strategic domain:

> Tell them that if I like, I can finish Leyte in two weeks. But I won't! I have too great a responsibility to the mothers and wives in America to do that to their men. I will not take by sacrifice what I can achieve by strategy.

There is a handsome irony in the fact that it was MacArthur, an American military commander, that perhaps best carried forward to our times the classical European insight that strategic issues are not merely tactical issues writ large. For he gave concrete moment to the realization that while strategic and tactical initiatives may generally be viewed as working complements, there are also times when it is absolutely crucial to see them as substitutes. Indeed, the first test of MacArthur's practical genius was his instinctive recourse to strategic wit as a means to compensate for his tactical disadvantage in the earlier stages of his Pacific campaign.

But MacArthur's statement provides us with second and even surer test. For when it came time to contemplate the taking of Leyte, he could if he wished have expended assets instead of intellectual effort. There are, of course, many men who owe their lives to his decision to forego force of arms in favor of finesse. Besides this, it is perhaps a small thing to note that all that follows here has been done in response to a great general's provision of of a sense of mission to a minor technician. For while it is clear that an adequate strategic management and decision technology still rests somewhere beyond our immediate technical grasp, MacArthur's message is that it is equally clear that we ought not be content to let it remain beyond our technical reach for very much longer.

Midlothian, Virginia
January, 1989

CONTENTS

PART I:

A TECHNICAL PERSPECTIVE ON STRATEGIC MANAGEMENT REQUIREMENTS

CHAPTER 1

SOURCES OF THE STRATEGIC MANAGEMENT CHALLENGE

Of the functions for which higher-management authorities are generally responsible, the most critical is Organizational Positioning. For this demands decisions as to how to best "position" an enterprise to exploit whatever opportunities and avert whatever perils the world outside may hold in store. With respect to this function then, the order of challenge devolving on higher-management authorities may be seen to derive primarily from the complexity of the context -- the matrix of environmental and competitive conditions-- in which their organization is resident. And by way of a fairly obvious proposition, increases in contextual complexity will be expected to translate directly into the demand for greater strategic sophistication from higher-management. The task for this first chapter is to provide an elaboration and defense of this proposition, and in the process introduce certain concepts effectively unique to the management science perspective on higher-management requirements.

1.1 Distinguishing the Strategic Decision Domain

What we might think of as the conventional portrait of organizational management is based on a much-cited, three-part taxonomy distinguishing between Strategic Planning, Managerial Control and Operational Control.[1] What's generally understood is that the strategic planning function is designed to answer for the long-run integrity of the organization as a whole. In contrast, managerial control is oriented towards the nearer-term and is concerned with regulating the performance of some major segment of an organization (e.g., a division) with respect to whatever goals or standards might have been set at the strategic level. Finally, operational control is concerned with managing the day-to-day activities of an individual unit (a department) in light of criteria established at the managerial control level. Thus, each of these activities in effect applies to a different level of management, i.e.:

Strategic Planning	--->	Higher Management
Managerial Control	--->	Middle Management
Operational Control	--->	Line Management

There's much in both concept and real-world experience to support this sort of distribution.

For strategic decisions are commonly taken to pertain to the most weighty matters, to committments of relatively sweeping implication in terms of ultimate effects. We all understand somehow that a strategy has great moment and significance. Strategic success is thus greatly to be wished, and strategic failure assiduously to be avoided. It thus usually follows that authority over strategic matters will be reserved to the highest-level executives in any enterprise . . . for the chief executive and directors of a commercial corporation; for the senior elected (vs. appointed) officials of a governmental agency; for the generals and admirals in the military. This, in turn, may be taken to reflect the understanding that strategic decision issues are to be resolved mainly as a matter of judgement. For there is a natural tendency to assume that the judgement of those occupying the highest-level positions in any organization --by virtue of breadth of experience and the tempering of perspective assumed to follow from their long climb to the top-- will likely be superior to those who have not seen as much or risen as high.

So under the conventional portrait of management, strategic decision-makers are charged with responsibility for the long-run welfare of the organization as a whole. Their focus thus rests for the most part on factors, agencies and effects perhaps relatively remote in space and/or time from the organization itself. It thus falls to strategic authorities to set the destination towards which the organization is to be pointed and chart the basic course to be followed towards that end.

The portrait then continues by having any determinations made at the strategic level serve to constrain the focus and latitude of the organization's middle-management functionaries. For as a rule, middle managers are assigned responsibility for some segment (aggregate of two or more basic units) of the organization, with this segment in turn charged with carrying out one or more aspects of the strategic scheme under which the organization as a whole is to operate. The middle management/management control orientation is thus somewhat more circumscribed than the strategic focus. For the middle-manager's interest in outside factors will normally be limited to those that have relatively near-term implications for his particular segment of the organization, such that much of his attention tends to be focussed within the organization (e.g., coordination of relationships with other segments) or within the segment itself (coordination of the units under his change).

Finally, the portrait closes by having middle-management choices emerge as constraints on the decision latitude allowed line management functionaries. For again, such are assigned responsibility for some still lower-order element of the enterprise, or a segment within a segment as it were . . . the overseeing of some particular manufacturing process within an industrial plant; charge of the accounts receivable department within the controller division; command of a specific naval vessel in a fleet of such; direction of a local branch office of some governmental bureaucracy. Normatively then, we expect his attention to be rather narrowly focussed in both time and space, dominated in fact by matters confined to his own immediate neighborhood within the enterprise. For example, as carried out in the typical manufacturing enterprise, strategic planning activities are aimed at providing for the extensive welfare of the enterprise by long-range assessment of future macroeconomic and market conditions, such to be followed by decisions as what proportion of organizational resources ought to be allocated to what lines of business, etc. Managerial control might then apply to the administration of a manufacturing plant or perhaps to the conduct of some basic commercial function (e.g., marketing), with operational control/line management activities generally being confined to a particular process within a plant (milling; quality assurance) or a single sub-function (advertising).

A similar set of structural dependencies is also characteristic of managerial activities as undertaken in the military sector. For example, we might think of strategic planning as being directed at the development of a theater-level war plan covering issues such as the following: Integration of land, sea, air and possibly even space assets of both own and allied forces; recitation of conditions calling for employment of nuclear vs. conventional weapons; when to adopt a defensive vs. offensive posture? Middle-echelon commanders might then be responsible for developing a Mission Plan, expressing how they intend to employ major force segments (e.g., a naval fleet, air wing or army corps) in support of the theater-level plan.

Finally, subsumed within any mission plan would be a set of Battle Plans prepared by the line-management equivalents in the military (the commander of a warship or battle group, a batallion commander, etc.) indicating how he intends to deploy his force against whatever adversary units he is to confront . . . with his battle plan paying full heed to whatever constraints --rules of engagement, etc.-- have been passed to him via the mission plan.

A typical public-sector or governmental management sequence might then begin with a strategic committment in terms of some broad Policy Platform, usually a product of congressional legislation or an executive branch edict. This would allocate program responsibilities to one or more agencies and also lay out inter-agency relational protocols, etc. The middle-management corollaries (usually high-level appointed vs. elected officials) would then be expected to formulate Agency Directives outlining how their division of government intends to carry out the aspects of the policy for which it is responsible, subject to any legislated or political constraints that have been imposed on its scope of authority or procedural latitude. In the public sector, operational control will usually be conveyed via a set of Field Guidelines that lay out usually quite precise prescriptions as to how the agency directives are to be carried out by line-level authorities (e.g., heads of field offices).

But from the perspective of the technician --say the management scientist vs. the management theorist-- the more or less automatic equation of higher-management with strategic decision responsibilities is not warranted. For rather than considering levels of decision responsibility to be a simple reflection of levels of management, the technician wants to be sure that strategic, tactical and operational decisions are distinguished in terms of the order of analytical challenge they represent. Hence the following technically-significant trichotomy of classes of decision exercises:

- STRATEGIC decision exercises will be defined so as to involve the need to formulate, evaluate and elect from among alternatives that are different in *kind* . . . i.e., that represent *qualitatively* disparate options.

- TACTICAL decision exercises will involve the formulation, evaluation and selection from among a set of alternatives that are comprehensible as variations on a singular strategic theme, and so different more in *degree* than in *kind*.

- OPERATIONAL decision exercises will be distinguished mainly in terms of the specific *quantitative* properties each exhibits, and so represent alternatives that are different in *magnitude* only.

Working through an abbreviated, somewhat apocryphal example of a decision exercise might help make these distinctions more concrete.

Particularly, what has become a classic empirical example of the tribulations that might attend a straetic decision exercise is the quandary faced by the Carter administration following the seizure of the American embassy and its personnel by Iranian populists following the overthrow of the Shah. For while there may have been some doubt about exactly what had taken place in the very early stages, this was quickly dispelled both by intelligence acquired by US agencies and information more or less freely supplied by Iranians themselves. What may fairly be said then was that a working concensus as to the nature of the event that occurred was readily at hand. Disputation was thus pretty much restricted to the issue of what to do about it. And there were at least three different strategic response options that were advanced by various parties: 1) Diplomatic; 2) Economic; and 3) Military. From an airy academic perspective, we might be tempted to view the above as initiatives to be exercised in sequence, arrayed as they are in terms of the most innocent (the Diplomatic) to the most ominous (a Military confrontation).

But in fact --and not without practical merit-- the proponents of these three positions tended to pose them as mutually-exclusive options, such that recourse to one would deny effective access to the others. Perhaps the primary reason for this recriminatory relationship was that the advocates of the several positions had in fact three different ideas about what would constitute a satisfactory conclusion. That is, while advocates of all three positions gave at least lip service to the importance of securing the return of the American hostages, each group of advocates was primarily oriented towards a fundamentally different objective, and its response preferences dictated accordingly. The result was then a multiobjective decision situation, but one where the disparate objectives were essentially *tacit.*

For example, what we might think of as the objective most valued by those arguing for a diplomatic approach was not simply the restoration of the hostages, but rather the stuff from which every professional diplomat's dreams are spun: The prospect of a secularly self-sustaining, amicable relationship between the United States and the new Iranian regime. Such was their vision of where the longer-run interests of the US lay, and hence the real (if for the most part unexplicated) reason for their urging of a negotiative posture as the only really acceptable line of recourse. In practical terms, the approach they argued for was an admixture of a conciliatory initiative (wherein the United States would admit to the possibility that certain of the aspects of the Shah's administration were not entirely to be admired), this to be complemented by reliance on the suasive authority attributed to the United Nations, certain third-party states (e.g., Algeria) and international agencies such as the World Court. At the same time, they were eloquent in pointing out that any attempt at coercion --via imposition of economic sanctions and even more obviously by any military adventure-- would merely serve to make increasingly improbable any satisfactory resolution in either the short or long run, in that it would most likely simply strengthen the hand of the xenophobic --indeed, even masochistic-- extremists in the Ayotollah Khomeini's entourage.

In contrast, the case for economic sanctions (the primary authors of which were those business firms, banks and others whose assets had been de facto appropriated) was given much credence among administration advisors perhaps because of its *realistic* orientation . . . which really meant that it aligned well with the basically materialistic preoccupation of so many of those who accede to higher government office in the United States. The formulation and defense of this strategic option was thus a wonderful example of the sort of ethnocentrism that plays such a major role in US foreign policy, this evinced by the extraordinary willingness to project our own priorities and interests upon others. The thought was that the Iranians at large would naturally make a marginal computation as to the cost of their continuing to hold the American hostages, and that eventually this price would be more than they would be willing or able to pay. At this point, not only would the American hostages be released, but there would then occur what must be seen to be the really dominant objective of those advocating economic sanctions as the singularly preferred line of reaction: There would be a popular uprising against the austerity imposed by the Khomeini regime and so a return to an administration that would again make Iran into an arena of profitable opportunity for foreign investors.

Equally clear is what we might think of as the real vs. manifest objective of those who argued for a military response (among whom we would predictably enough number representatives of the Pentagon and the more hawkish members of congress). Their end purpose was not so much to secure the release of the American hostages, but rather first of all to punish the Iranians for their effrontery, and secondly to discourage this sort of thing from ever being attempted again by others. From such a perspective, the Iranian's actions were perceived to be nothing less than a declaration of war against the United States . . . a military initiative in its own right. Therefore, the only really appropriate counter-response was to retaliate in kind, and treat the Iranians to a display of US military capabilities. Any initiatives on the diplomatic or economic front would thus be merely dilatory and a signal of US lack of resolve. Moreover, time wasted on such would simply allow the Iranians the opportunity to disperse the hostages, harden their defenses or in other ways increase the risk and expense associated with the military initiative that we must ultimately depend upon.

Note then that the diplomatic, economic and military options represent *strategic* alternatives, not just because they are themselves defined so as to take place on qualitatively disparate dimensions, but also because each is addressed more or less directly towards qualitatively unique objective. We'll say more about such matters later, but had best now suggest what the tactical and operational level derivatives might possibly look within this scenario.

To do so, we will assume --and in such an assumption follow reality-- that there has emerged a consensus at the strategic level in favor of a Military initiative of some kind. This allows us to transit to the tactical decision domain, where the choice is now to be made from among a set of action-alternatives that are all comprehensible as variations on the basic strategic theme of a military response. Just to give some indication of what might constitute tactical military alternatives, consider the following examples:

a) Use regular (uniformed) US force elements to mount a surgical assault on the US embassy with the limited and specific objective of liberating the US hostages, and then orchestrate an immediate withdrawal.

b) Use regular third-party (e.g., Israeli; Iraqui) forces to mount limited attacks against selected Iranian assets --ports; oil refineries, etc.-- with their aim of securing them as currency for an exchange.

c) Deploy a covert US or irregular force to kidnap the Ayatollah Khomeini or other important officials of the new regime and pose threats to their welfare unless the US hostages are released unharmed (with such an initiative unable to be tied directly to the US).

d) Employ regular US and/or third-party forces in an assult in strength against one or more major Iranian targets . . . i.e., attempt to seize and hold an entire region against the prospect of an Iranian capitulation.

e) Commission irregular forces (e.g., mercenaries; Iranian expatriates) to seize one or more Iranian embassies or installations and hold them as counter-hostages.

f) Deploy US naval and air forces against Iranian military assets, and prevent their reconstruction, to deprive Iran of the wherewithal to protect itself against the prospect of attack from regional adversary such as Israel or Iraq.

Finally, a transit to the Operations level would follow from the election of one or another of the tactical alternatives that had been defined. And again, once at this level, the decision choices will be mainly of parametric significance.

Let's assume that option (a) above has been elected as the preferred Tactical choice. If so, the derivative operational matters that would have to be resolved would be of this sort:

- The exact composition of the US assault team in terms of numbers, affiliation, training and special skills, etc.
- The determination of the mode of transport and route of approach and exit;

- The development of a campaign plan defining what initiatives are to be taken in what order by which elements of the force;
- The fixing of a precise time schedule for the activities, including the determination of when the assault itself is to take place;
- Determinations as to logistics, including the inventory of equipment and sorts of weapons to be made available;
- Establishment of certain *rules of engagement* that will be used to pre-define what sorts of responses US forces are to take should certain predictable contingencies occur, etc.

With such issues resolved, the analytical (vs. implementational) aspects of the decision would have come to a conclusion.

A natural question is then to ask about what would occasion the need for a strategic vs. tactical vs. operational choice? We know that the answer must have something to do with the nature of the problem at hand. To answer this question in a reasonably precise way, it's necessary to consider yet another taxonomy. It's provisions closely (and deliberately) parallel those associated with the trichotomy of decisions classes, but the focus here is on several basic classes of event alternatives:

> STATE-LEVEL: state-level event alternatives are to be distinguished in that they represent situations or occurrences that are qualitatively unique in terms of their fundamental structural or dynamic properties . . . i.e., state-level event alternatives are *different in kind.*
>
> THEMATIC: a thematic level event is to be viewed as a specific variant on some singular qualitative theme, such that thematic alternatives are best thought of as being *different in degree* rather than in kind.
>
> PARAMETRIC: parametric event alternatives differ from eachother mainly in terms of the particular magnitudinal or quantitative properties each exhibits.

As a quick and crude way of getting at the key practical distinctions between the three classes of event alternatives, we can take recourse to the popular vernacular. Specifically, state-level alternatives might best be represented by the proverbial Apples and Oranges. If so, then the derivative thematic alternatives would be the various varieties of apples (winesaps, etc.) or oranges (valencias, navels, etc.), and parametric alternatives might then be individual winesap apples or valencia oranges differentiated as to quantitative attributes such as relative size, sweetness, ripeness, etc. The key point here is that a transit from state-level through thematic to operational event alternatives is roughly equivalent to a shift in the focus of analytical attention from the more general to the more particular. And for its part, with respect to decision-making exercises, this shift in focus will underlie a corresponding reduction in the level of uncertainty with respect to the nature of the problem at hand.

The technician's hidden agenda can now be made explicit. For the way the trichotomies of classes of decision exercises and classes of event alternatives were constructed leads to the following conclusions:

- Strategic options are addressed against state-level event alternatives;
- Tactical options are formulated with respect to thematic event alternatives;
- Operational choices are defined for parametric level alternatives.

We'll return to consider these assertions in greater detail at several different points in the pages that follow. But again, taking recourse to an example might help put them in some immediate perspective.

And by way of an example, a quick survey of the quandary faced by those doing the early research into what subsequently came to be recongized as Legionaire's Disease might be particularly instructive. For initially, they were faced with a situation of ambiguity as to the basic nature or fundamental cause of the illnesses and deaths that were taking place. There were in fact at least two qualitatively disparate classes of causal agencies (state-event alternatives) initially thought to have some likelihood of being the true origin of the disease, Viral and Bacterial.

In that viruses and bacteria can be taken to represent qualitatively different orders of phenomena from a physician's perspective, then the assertion raised earlier would argue that each would demand a qualitatively-disparate order of treatment . . . i.e., a unique line of strategic response. For example, it may be that conventional medical wisdom or *doctrine* suggests that the preferred strategy for treating a virally-induced disease would be to concentrate all efforts on controlling the symptoms and abandoning any prospect of finding a cure in the short-run. In contrast, were a bacterial agent presumed to be at work, the preferred strategy may indeed be to concentrate all available energy and effort in the attempt to isolate a curative agent (i.e., developing an antibacterial formula that can kill the offending bacterium) rather than being content merely to treat symptoms.

A transit to the next level of analysis --where it is thematic event alternatives and hence tactical response options that are at issue-- will usually follow from a convergence on one or another of the state-level alternatives and hence a singular strategic choice. For the case at hand, we might presume that the medical researchers arrived at a concensus that Legionaire's Disease was bacterial in origin. This would then trigger acceptance of the corresponding strategic initiative which, as suggested just above, would direct the concerted search for a curative agent. This would imply that the locus of challenge is now fixed on the need to make a choice among thematic alternatives. For the case at hand, these would be the various families of bacteria to which the offending agent might belong . . . Staphylococcus; E-coli; Bacillus, etc.

And to make the desired association, it can be suggested that each of these several different families of bacteria --each of the thematic alternatives-- would pose the need for a unique order of tactical response. That is, because each of the subclasses of bacterial agents is characterized by a somewhat different chemical constituency, physiological structure and growth conditionals (aerobic vs. anaerobic, etc.), the chemistry, physics and attack profile of the antibacterial agencies that would be arrayed against them would also be somewhat different. Thus, for example, penicillin, tetracycline and sulfa-based formulations are not simple substitutes for eachother, but rather tend to be directed dominantly against different sorts of bacteria. Therefore, we might then think of treatment options orchestrated around different suborders of drugs as defining tactical choices . . . as representing remedial approaches that are better thought of as different in degree than as different in kind. For all could be perceived as variations on the general strategic platform arguing that bacterially-induced diseases are candidates for cure rather than containment, and that cure means killing the bug. Therefore, a tactical-level choice would be conditioned by the election of some particular thematic alternative, which would then allow for a transit to the point where it is parametric event alternatives and operational choices that are at the focus of attention.

For illustrative purposes, let's suppose that the medical researchers finally stuck upon some bacterial agent belonging to the cocci family as the most likely thematic alternative. In such a case, the preferred tactical choice would probably be a therapy centered on a penicillin-based drug. But before the decision exercise can come to a satisfactory conclusion, there must be an attempt to resolve parametric level uncertainty. This would imply an effort to pinpoint the specific cocci-type bacterium that is the exact cause of the disease. But because all members of the cocci family will be extremely similar in terms of basic structure and chemistry and behavior, etc., in order to distinguish which particular bacterium we are dealing with it may be necessary to take recourse to highly sensitive measurements designed to determine the proportion in which certain chemicals are present, or to determine the magnitude of certain physical features (e.g., the average diameter of the spherical bodies). That is, we've reached the point where discriminacy among alternatives depends on the way in which detailed quantitative matters resolve themselves.

Following the isolation of a singular bacterium as the culprit, there would then follow the requirement to make an operational decision choice. What is at issue here is not whether some family of antibacterial drug will be effective with respect to a coccus-type bacterium; such will have been resolved at the tactical level in terms of the decision to employ a penicillin-based therapy. As such, an operational choice would depend on answering for issues of the following type: Which particular brand of penicillin-derived drug has been demonstrated in the laboratory or in field trials to be relatively most efficient against the specific bacterium of interest? What sort of dosage should be employed, given a patient's size, weight and age, etc.? What duration of treatment --at what levels-- would be most appropriate for different levels of intensity of infection? That is, our choice as to a singular best operational alternative will --as with parametric choices on the event side-- tend to be informed mainly by conclusions as to quantitative matters.

By way of quick summary, the members of both the trichotomoies we've dealt with both can be distinguished in terms of the same basic criterion:

Criteria	Event Classes	Decision Classes
Different in KIND	State-level	Strategic
Different in DEGREE	Thematic	Tactical
Different in MAGNITUDE	Parametric	Operational

The corollary was that any state-event implies the need for the formulation of a unique strategic response option, while thematic events pose the requirement for tactical decision choices, etc.

But there is another and most critical consequence of the distinguishing criteria that we've employed here. For it is the natural vanity of the technician to view any organization not so much as a socio-cultural phenomenon (a collection of people, as it were) but rather as a collection of decision problems to be resolved. And as for decision problems, what is most interesting to the technician is the sorts of instruments required to allow for a rational resolution. Thus, underlying the taxonomies of event and decision classes is yet a third taxonomy, this setting out three basic orders of decision support technology.

And as suggested in the table below, each of these three families of technical support instruments can be taken to represent the singularly preferred source of technical discipline for one of the three different classes of decision exercises.

In this sense then, an alternate basis for distinguishing strategic, tactical and operational decision exercises is the nature of the technical support that is required. Particularly, in that a strategic choice must be taken from among a collection of qualitative disparate options, it would tend to follow that qualitative analysis initiatives of some kind would be the most appropriate basis for making such a choice. And as things now stand, judgement-driven

OPERATIONAL	Deterministic Algorithms . . . Instruments belong to this order of decision technology are usually based on some generic mathematical function which --when supplied with a set of qualitative arguments (parameters) pertaining to some specific situation-- can generally be relied upon to lead to a singular, ostensibly *optimal* solution to sufficiently well-bounded, well-behaved problems
TACTICAL	Probabilistic Decision Aids . . . Here would be included all the various tools and techniques that have been devised to help us make disciplined statistical inferences about the structural or dynamic properties of phenomena, process or systems having some simple stochastic potential
STRATEGIC	Judgemental/Subjective Protocols . . . Techniques designed to accommodate subjective or *soft* predicates, and so are available to help discipline decisions in cases where empirical/objective data is sparse. For the most part, these protocols will use simple logical or quasi-axiomatic mechanics to impose some degree of formal *structure* on sets of non-quantitative arguments

decision protocols are the obvious vehicles for conveying qualitative analysis methods into the management arena. At the other extreme, in that operational level decisions rest primarily on quantitative matters, such tend to become the natural target for resolution via some sort of mathematical maximization/minimization seeking technique (e.g., linear programming provisions or the other algorithmic methods that constitute the basic operations research repertoire). Resting mid-way between these two extremes, tactical decision exercises may usually be distinguished by their amenability to resolution via statistical decision-aids . . . such belonging to the order of instruments that can accomodate a higher level of complexity that deterministic algorithms, but which cannot be relied upon as a basis for resolving qualitative ambiguity.

We'll be returning to such matters at several later points, where a more detailed elaboration and defense can be offered. But with some key technical concepts now in mind (however precariously at this point), we can now go on to pose a technically-inspired ammendment to the conventional portrait of organizational management.

1.2 The Strategic Focus on Organizational Positioning

In the interests of eventually getting at a proper technical understanding of strategic management requirements, what can now be suggested is that the key function for which the higher-management authorities of any enterprise are dominantly responsible is organizational positioning, with strategic planning being just one of the avenues along with that function might be carried out. In the most rudimentary sense, the organizational positioning function is the process that attempts to effect an adequate degree of congruence between the properties of the organization and the properties of the context in which it is resident . . . the process by which an organization accomodates itself to the set of exogenous influences to which it is subject. More simply, the ambition here is to *position* the organization in such a way as to be best able to take advantage of whatever prospective opportunities that may emerge, and at the same time guard against projected perils.[2] The organizational positioning focus is then on factors outside the enterprise itself, and most particularly on the two primary aspects of context: Environmental and Competitive.

Though we'll shortly go into more detail, the environmental dimension of context would be comprised of the array of broad social, political, economic and technological conditions to which an organization is subject, while the competitive dimension would be concerned with the nature of the exchanges between an organization and any direct or indirect adversaries. We might then think of the magnitude of the challenge associated with the organizational positioning function as being determined primarily by the complexity of the environmental and/or competitive conditions of the context in which an organization is resident. And for its part, we might think of complexity of the environmental or competitive dimensions as having two basic components, structural intricacy and dynamic volatility.

As suggested in the following tableau, each of these attributes would be assessed differently depending on whether it is the enviromental or competitive aspects of context that are of immediate interest. Any increases in intricacy and/or volatility will then tend to translate into increasingly elaborate sets of environmental and/or competitive situations with which an organization might have to contend (with increases in elaborateness meaning a larger number of and/or greater disparity among the array of possibilities it includes).

But for our purposes here, the more telling test of the complexity of an organizational context is not simply the number/diversity of the situations that might be authored in an organizational context, but rather what might be referred to as the locus of contextual challenge. For this has to do with whether uncertainty --and hence risk-- will appear at the strategic or merely the tactical or operational level. Thus, one way of looking at the locus of contextual challenge would be to draw on the several different classes of event

	ENVIRONMENTAL	COMPETITIVE
Structural Intricacy	richness & diversity (heterogeneity) of the population of field properties	the range of actual or prospective adversaries with which an organization might be engaged
Dynamic Volatility	the potential for properties to undergo extensive and/or rapid change	the nature/intensity of the competitive relationships among the array of inter-dependent organizations

alternatives defined in the previous section:

STATE-LEVEL, where uncertainty/risk derives from the prospect of their being two or more qualitatively disparate environmental and/or competitive situations or threats with which an organization might be confronted during some period.

THEMATIC, where uncertainty and risk is associated with doubt as to the particular variation(s) on some singular state-level event/threat to which an organization might be subjected.

PARAMETRIC, where the seat of uncertainty/risk is focussed on ambiguity as to the detailed provisions --e.g., specific quantitative attributes-- that might be associated with some particular thematic event/threat to which an organization expects to be exposed.

What may then be said is that a requirement for organizational positioning committments to reflect strategic planning considerations does not arise unless an organization finds itself confronted by instances of state-level uncertainty. By the same token, an organization resident in a context holding only a potential for thematic level uncertainty/risk would be said to have no strategic planning requirements, but only tactical, etc.

In short, we're harking back again to assertions of the sort raised earlier . . . that state-level event alternatives are an occasion for a strategic decision choice, and so forth down the line. The reason for this is clear enough. For from a clinical perspective, the key difference between planning and decision-making is that the former entails operating in advance of the fact. That is, planning exercises are decision exercises that have been conducted prior to the appearance of the situations against which they are directed. Therefore, by way of a fairly obvious generalization, the greater the range and variety of situations that might arise in an organization's context, the more onerous the planning requirements and --by extension-- the greater the order of analytical challenge devolving on those higher-management authorities responsible for conducting the organizational positioning function. This same generalization can be expected to hold for both of the environmental and competitive dimensions of context.

1.3 Managerial Implications of Environmental Complexity

The environmental aspects of organizational context might be thought of as constituting a matrix of *field* properties in which an organization (or set of such) is embedded, e.g.:

- broad macroeconomic conditions and legislative constraints that affect all firms in some industry;
- prevailing public affective or sentimental predilections that serve to indirectly inform --proscribe or prescribe-- individual or collective organizational behavior;
- extensive constraints on natural or other resources, or general technological (state-of-the-art) limitations.
- collective threats, such as the universal peril from the deterioration of the ozone layer, acid rain, drug addiction, terrorism, etc.

All such factors gain their pragmatic import as considerations to be *internalized* in an organization's planning/positioning calculus. The basic managerial impact of environment may then be addressed on four subdimensions:

(a) The extent to which an organization is susceptible to environmental influences:

(b) The variety of exogenous factors present in an environment;

(c) The form in which exogenous proscriptions/prescriptions appear;

(d) The extent to which any set of environmental properties is subject to change or alteration (their volatility).

Taken together, the consequence of technical interest from the above is an idea of the number, diversity and stability of the exogenous factors an organization must *internalize* in its decision-making exercises.

As for (a) above, it's necessary to consider that not all organizations may be expected to be equally open to environmental influences. Indeed, we can conceive of organizations that are essentially autonomous, shielded to some considerable extent against the vaguaries of exogenous factors. This may occur either because the organization has made a determined effort to be as self-sufficient as possible (as, for example, with an autarchic economic enterprise or certain *closed* socio-economic systems such as the Amish), or because the organization is in fact able on its own accord to influence exogenous circumstances in its favor . . . i.e., able by dint of strength or will to pretty much author its own environment. An example of such would be an industrial enterprise which has the potential to effect the passage of legislation buffering it against losses that might follow from unfavorable macroeconomic conditions . . . e.g., the subsidies and price supports made available to agricultural concerns. But if we can conceive of organizations that are effectively impervious to outside factors, then we can also postulate the existence of organizations that are highly open and sensitive to exogenous influences. These we'll refer to as *dependent* entities, such that the first of the environmental subdimensions described a continuum bounded at one extreme by essential autonomy, and at the other by abject dependence.

The second and third of the subdimensions refer directly to the matter of the structural complexity of an environment. As for (b) above, we might also postulate a continuum of possibilities, this time bounded by extremes of homogeneity and heterogeneity. An essentially homogeneous environment would then be one whose properties display very little in the way of diversity, such that what's there can be easily apprehended given any tenure in the field. We might then think of a model of such an environment consisting of only a very few, perhaps highly intercorrelated (or reflexively associated) determinants. For example, a socio-cultural system comprised of individuals who are all of one ethnic, racial, ideological and political persuasion would imply an essentially homogeneous context for any firm that would plan to do business in such a community.

On the other hand, heterogeneity implies significant differentiation which, given the reference we just employed above, would imply the tendency for the individuals in a community to come from different racial or ethnic backgrounds and/or to adhere to disparate ideological and political agendas or value-systems . . . i.e., to be divided into a welter of different and perhaps not always congenial *special interest groups*. In this sense then, what might be suggested is that the broader the geographic reach of an organization and/or the more general its mission (the more people or places it can effect), the greater will be the heterogeneity of the environmental influences it might have to incorporate --i.e., internalize-- as elements of its decision calculus so far as positioning is concerned.

To some extent then, an organization's degree of exposure to environmental influences may be in part a consequence of an organization's own decisions. For example, the large-scale multiproduct/multinational enterprise has largely of its own volition courted heterogeneity as a consequence of the spread of product-market targets it has set itself. Or, from a somewhat different perspective, a firm devoting itself to the production of nuclear military weapons might reasonably expect to be more of a target for social intrusion than a department store. Similarly, a company attempting to do genetic engineering is more likely to be subject to particularistic governmental constraints than one manufacturing and marketing small appliances. Firms with a presence in the microcomputer industry are more likely to be affected by broad technological innovations than fast food chains or basic service providers. In other cases, the variety of environmental influences an organization must consider may be thought to be endemic to mission or location. For example, we can expect that the usual decision taken by the mayor of New York City will generally be subject to a greater variety of exogenous considerations than that taken by the mayor of an essentially isolated small town with a more or less homogeneous population. Even more broadly, industrial concerns operating in the confines of a totalitarian system given to centralized economic planning will generally have more exogenous constraints to contend with than those embedded in an essentially laissez-faire capitalist political economy.

In turning to (c) above, there are three different *forms* or guises that environmental directives or constraints can adopt:

> DEFINITIVE, which means that they take the form of discrete, fully-elaborated specifications (e.g., *Rules of Engagement* in the military, which prescribe exactly what action a commander is to take should some specific situation occur).
>
> DOCTRINAL, where prescriptions or proscriptions are in the nature of generic principles that always involve some level of ambiguity --and hence raise the demand for some degree of discretion-- when applied to specific instances (the principles of Seamanship, for example, as opposed to laws of navigation).
>
> PUTATIVE, essentially suggestive referents, whose implications both in general and specific demand much in the way of interpretation (e.g., Ethical or other informal *codes* of conduct).

In general, environmental complexity will increase with any increase in putative vs. doctrinal, or doctrinal vs. definitive, constraints. For such argue not just for the need to allocate more managerial time and wit to discretionary or interpretive tasks, but also for an increased likelihood of encountering instances of negative cross-impact or even mutually-exclusivity among the members of some set of exogenous prescriptions/proscriptions.

But of the several environmental subdimensions, it is the dynamic attribute --the potential for scope and rate of change-- that must be expected to be the generally most significant determinant of managerial challenge. For given sufficient time, an organization might be expected to learn to satisfactorily navigate its way through even the most intricate of structural situations . . . to gradually arrive at an adequate map of the disposition of heterogeneous properties across a field, or eventually acquire a decent pragmatic understanding of the prevailing interpretive nuances of putative constraints. But as in so many other areas, change is the adversary of comprehension. Therefore, the single most critical characteristic of organizational environments is the sort of dynamic towards which they tend.

And the single best way of trying to generalize about dynamic simplicity or complexity is to make use of some common ideal-type referents that speak to the matter of the breadth and pace of structural transformations:

PLACID: The set of environmental properties to which some organization(s) is expected to remain basically unchanged, or essentially stationary, into the foreseeable future.

EVOLUTIONARY: Environmental properties are subject to incrementalistic changes in a given direction (a more or less steady line of increase or decrease). In the short-run or during any interval then, changes would generally be thought to be restricted to perturbations . . . to relatively modest departures from the routine or status-quo that are best thought of as *thematic* events.

EQUIFINAL: Where there are two or more qualitatively distinct and pre-definable ways in which environmental properties might resolve themselves over some interval . . . i.e., two or more *state* level transformational possibilities to consider. Equifinality thus implies the potential for some number of concluding-states to be arrived at from any given set of starting-state conditions. The simplest instance of equifinality being a pendular dynamic involving the more or less regular interchange between just two different sets of conditions or states, with a modular dynamic posing a larger set of state-transformation candidates.

TURBULENT: Under this worst-case situation, environmental properties may transform themselves in many different ways, with not all of the possible future possibilities being capable of being defined in advance of the fact of their occurrence. That is, a turbulent environment holds the potential for properties to undergo rapid and extensive or transmutative alterations through time.

The practical implications of these four referents are perhaps most obvious in terms of the ascending level of technical challenge that each entails for the event-projection problem.

Of these four ideal-type referents, the implications associated with the first and fourth (the Placid and Turbulent cases) should be familiar. For they are of course the two boundary conditions for the widely-referenced taxonomy of field types developed by Emery and Trist, and have now become conceptual staples for modern organization theorists.[3] And interestingly, both these cases may generally be taken to exclude the requirement for the most usual type of predictive exercises, those based on the employment of some sort of data-driven, quantitative extrapolation technique. The invariability of properties associated with a turbulent environment would tend to make such exercises largely gratuitous (that is, the future will presumably be only trivially different from the past). On the other hand, the Turbulent case may make such exercises largely infeasible because of the extraordinary richness of transformational possibilities that --via a transmutational dynamic-- may have only the most tenuous correlation with any historical precedents (so depriving quantitative instruments of the sufficiency of information they need).

In contrast, an Evolutionary dynamic is an obvious target for any of the large collection of data-driven, quantitative projection instruments available in the management science repertoire. Two types are especially familiar:[4]

(a) The simple mathematical structures --based primarily on sets of first-order differential equations-- that underlie the projective mechanics of Forrester's Industrial Dynamics, and *world* models such as those authored by the Club of Rome;

(b) Statistical techniques such as those that underlie simple linear econometric extrapolation (and, much more rarely, complex non-linear or spectral analysis).

In general, the effectiveness of the above sorts of instruments depends on time-dependent variations being of a relatively modest or *smooth* order, and most especially on the degree of *variance* in the historical data base that provides the input arguments for such instruments.

Attempts to capture the possibilities inherent in a Equifinal dynamic demand an entirely different order of instruments. These will generally be much less familiar and have only a spotty history of real-world employment, so we shall have to elaborate on them in some detail in a later chapter. But just to give a quick idea of what is involved here, there are at least two classes of instruments that might possibly be employed: (a) Markov-type conventions that can be used to impose a structure over systems or processes that have some n-states they might assume, given that we have some basis for generating a set of state-transform functions; (b) Certain non-computational mathematical conventions that can capture basic characteristics of ill-behaved (e.g., non-asymptotic) systems.[5]

Were we then to summarize our arguments about environmental matters, the key point would be that the need for true strategic planning/positioning capabilities on the part of management would not really arise in any significant way until we consider the third and fourth of the referents. For it's only the Equifinal and Turbulent cases that hold out the likelihood of an organization routinely being confronted by state-level event alternatives (with, again, the difference being that the former suggests that all state-transformation possibilities will be subject to projection, while the latter case implies that at least some of these possibilities cannot be pre-defined, such that they would come as something of a strategic surprise should they actually occur). And for its part, the Evolutionary case would primarily pose the demand for tactical planning/positioning facilities, this because of the clustering of enviromental changes around perturbations qua *thematic* event possibilities. And finally, to the extent that the placid case might lead to anything at all in the way of changes, they are most likely to be merely *parametric* in significance, and hence occasion for operational (vs. tactical or strategic) address.

1.4 Managerial Consequences of Competitive Intensity

In contemplating the effects of competition on managerial requirements for business firms, consider the several ideal-type market structures shown in **Exhibit 1.1** (whose general implications would also extend rather neatly to the governmental and military sectors, as we'll see in later chapters).[6]
Just as with the array of environmental referents, the requirement for strategic capabilities does not really arise until we consider the third and fourth of the competitive referents. In contrast, even the highest-level authorities of precompetitive enterprises may be concerned primarily with what are mainly just operational matters.

1.4.1 The Operational Focus of Precompetitive Enterprise

One example of pre-competitive enterprise would be firms operating in approximately *purely* competitive markets. For such firms, the operational focus arises as a matter of default. For by definition, critical market parameters --and most especially price-- remain beyond the control of any individual enterprise. Rather, they arise from additive (collective) effects of a large number of producers operating independently of eachother . . . or are set by the actions of authorities that rest beyond the influence of any single organization. Moroever, not only does the organization lack the wherewithal to meaningfully determine its own price, but there will usually be no basis for product differentiation (given that tendencies towards pure competition, however weak these days, are restricted to primary industries growing or harvesting agricultural products, etc.).

Therefore, the only factors that may be said to be within the sphere of influence of the organization are those of stricly *local* significance. Thus, even higher-management authorities tend to be largely preoccupied with what might be thought of as essentially operational decisions aimed at effecting

EXHIBIT 1.1 :
Technical Effects of Transit from Less to more Challenging Economic Market Contexts

Market Referents	**Competitive Characteristics**	**Technical Consequence**
Precompetitive (pure competition or monopoly)	De facto or legislated dominance	Decisions at all levels of enterprise cluster around local Optimization and hence Deterministic decision/control methods
Constrained (Monopolistic or regulated)	Radical forms of competition are excluded because of nature of product and/or causal or imposed conventions	Higher- and lower-order decisions tend to become intelligible as aspects of Equilibrium Maintenance and hence targets for Probabilistic decision instrumentation
Extensive (weakly constrained oligopolistic)	There is an expansion of the forms of feasible competition to include radical vs. incremental initiatives	Organizational positioning decisions now tied to judgemental (notional) projections of possible competitor-authored initiatives and/or possible counter-actions to our own initiatives
Predatory (unconstrained)	There are now no constraints on the competitive initiatives that might be taken in terms of type or intensity	Organization must now be prepared to *reposition* itself in effective real-time, in light of emergent (vs. definite) perils and opportunities

local optimization. In fact, as a suggestion that may brook some argument on fine points, it can be suggested that there is a singular strategic objective -- indeed, imperative-- that can be taken as a *given* for all such firms, simply because there is no other alternative under which they might operate: Simple maximization of output over a series of short-runs! For not being able to make any meaningful determinations about likely price structures or aggregate demand, etc., would pretty much preclude attempts to maximize profits via the usual tactical initiatives (e.g., trying to arrive at a capital-labor ratio and scale-of-plant, etc., that will promise to minimize the long-run average costs).

But an even more compelling example of precompetitive enterprise is the firm enjoying monoplistic priviledges. For monopolistic enterprises in both their forms --legislated or de-facto-- gain their abstraction from exogenous factors not by default, but by design. For the legislative monopoly has in effect been granted a government-sanctioned guarantee of dominance within some region or sector, while de-facto monopoly means that a firm has obtained such on its own initiative. In either case, we can expect an effect similar to that ascribed to pure competition. That is, key decisions, such as those involving pricing, tend to be largely endogenously determined (e.g., demand may be assumed either essentially inelastic or -- more pertinently-- significantly conditioned by what the monopolist chooses to supply during an interval at non-prohibitive prices). Thus the key technical consequence of dominance is that certain critical parameters that would remain exogenous variables for non-monopolistic enterprises may be treated as endogenously-determined *constants* by the monopolist.

But there is an even greater gift to consider. For many monopolistic enterprises may be endowed with a *guaranteed* rate-of-return on investment or assets . . . some assured level of *affluence* as it were! The de facto monpolist obtains this guarantee by virtue of earned market dominance. For the legislated monopoly, it is a present from the chartering authority, defensible as a means of attracting investment by adjusting perceived risk-return ratios. Irrespective of how this gift is obtained, its practical import is to effectively insulate managements not merely against adverse vaguaries that might arise in the environment, but also against the consequences of their own errors or misjudgements. For by putting a *floor* under the extent to which rate of return can fall, it also tends to mitigate against any depreciation in stockholder equity, and hence against any material cause for investor action against management. Therefore, it is perhaps not too much of an oversimplification to suggest that the key strategic challenge for the higher managements of monopolitstic enterprises is not technical, but political . . . attempting to maintain some positive influence over those governmental officials who set values for *constants* like the guaranteed rate of return, or the officers of regulatory agencies whose good will, is much to be desired.

In terms of focal decision demands then, even the highest-level executives of the usual monopoly may be intimately engaged with largely *operational* matters, of which the following are standard examples:

1) Attempting to influence the schedule of demand (via a *peak-load* pricing scheme, for example) so as to effectively minimize the level of capital investment in production facilities --plant and equipment-- required to provide some aggregate level of service.

2) The regulation of logistical matters --e.g., manpower loadings; inventory control; negotiation of futures contracts for critical raw materials-- in order to support desired output or production/service schedules.

3) Maintaining compliance --at all levels of enterprise-- with the usually definitive (vs. doctrinal or putative) requirements that tend to be imposed by governmental, state and/or local regulatory authorities.

Were we then to try to generalize about the organizational positioning requirements associated with precompetitive enterprises, we would stress the central role played by operational level --vs. strategic or even tactical-- decision and control facilities.

Indeed, each of the three examples of operational level tasks given just above may be taken to represent a target for one or another of the three basic categories of operational management instruments, all of which are intelligible as sources of deterministic discipline, as shown in the table below.

	INPUTS	OUTPUTS
Mathematical/ Analytic Models	Situation-specific parametric arguments	Decisions meeting the criteria for local optimization
Simple Process Control Systems	Variance from desired/ tolerable standards	Computers/executes a most efficient correction
Decision Tables for Managerial	Discrete, predefined condition or event	Directs execution of one preferred response option

For example, task-1 is a classic case of the sort of management function that is appropriate target for one or another of the techniques inspired by optimization theory, such still constituting the major part of the modern operations research and engineering repertoires.

There is of course a rich and varied collection of such instruments, including most mathematical programming algorithms, computer-based numerical methods, finite-state systems engineering computational facilities, etc. What all have in common is the ability to accept certain inputs as decision predicates (arguments) about a situation with which a manager is faced and then generate an output --via a *directed* or analytic mapping-- that represents a singular best course of action. Such demand the existence of a generalized formula which, when supplied with a set of situation-specific or local parameters (qua numerical arguments), can be relied upon to deliver a deterministic conclusion. The most generally familiar example of such would be a linear programming construct. For when we specify an objective function and set of constraints, it has mechanics (usually simple matrix algebra facilities that specify certain operations over hyperplanes) that inform us as to a best feasible resolution.

For its part, task-2 can be taken to represent a function well-suited to support via deterministic process control technology in one of its guises (e.g., numerical control mechanisms). For what's basically called for there is an attempt to keep actual production rates as close as possible to some desired or target schedule, which is an objective comprehensible by control mechanisms of the following formulation:

$$b = f(a) \in \{a\} > t, \text{ where}$$

(a) defines a value for a process parameter that outside some predetermined range of tolerable values (t). Any non-zero value for (a) thus represents a specific variance, with the mapping operator **f** being a response function capable of directing an optimal correction in terms of some **b** for any variance that falls somewhere within the domain of the continuum **{a}**. To use a familiar example, if the process at hand is a lathe operation, then Mj may refer to the diameter of the finished product. Correction would thus raise or lower the *bit* in order to increase or decrease diameter. In any case, the authority of the response function may be taken to extend across the bounds of **{a}**. Therefore, should actual variance exceed the upper limit of **{a}**, an appropriate correction cannot be made via the directed- mapping response function **f**, but must rather be formulated elsewhere (usually by an authority sitting at the next higher level of enterprise or a superior control function).

Finally, task-3 --concerned with maintaining compliance with regulatory requirements-- might be considered a target for discipline via decision table technology. For decision tables are merely discrete versions of deterministic process control facilities, and provide a basis for higher-level managers to choreograph or pre-determine the decision behavior of their subordinates via directed mappings of the following sort:

$$\text{DECISION TABLE} = f([a] \times [b]),$$
$$\text{such that: } a \in [a] \rightarrow b \in [b].$$

That is, for any discrete input **a** ∈ [**a**], the function **f** will point to one and only one discrete output as some **b** ∈ [**b**]. As typically employed, the members of the set [**a**] will refer to various conditions (events, problem situations, etc.) expected to arise in some organizational unit, with [**b**] then housing the repertoire (range) of response options that some operational decision functionary is authorized to carry out. When working under a decision table discipline then, a decision functionary is expected to be alert for any of the conditions encoded in [**a**] and then to execute the singular appropriate element from among the set [**b**]. Should some condition occur that does not map directly to some member of [**a**], then the decision functionary will have to pass the problem on to some higher-order authority.

It's important to understand that the term *decision functionary* may here apply to either a machine or a man. In the case of the former, what is clear is that many computer systems ultimately reduce to one or more decision tables, where a machine is programmed to *recognize* only the limited set of conditions entailed in the set [**a**], and then programmed to execute the predetermined correlate from [**b**]. But many lower-order managers may also be operating under a decision table discipline, at least with respect to the functional (vs. human relations) aspects of their position. In such a case, the elements of [**a**] reflect the set of events to which a manager is expected or allowed to respond, while the *directed* response mappings reflect the dictates or preferences of his superiors in the organization. In short, operational management may often be reduced to an array of deterministic if:then conditionals, with little demand or latitude for discretion (e.g., the detailed *rules of engagement* under which line military officers will often operate).

1.4.2 Constrained Competition and the Tactical Planning Focus:

What was just said about precompetitive enterprises was not meant to suggest that there are no requirements for tactical planning. Most public utilites, for example, would be in for some embarrassement were they to allow the equation between generating capacity and actual demand to run too far out of balance for too long. Yet again, in cases where demand tends to be either inelastic and/or signficantly dependent upon supply, the tactical managerial challenge is not paramount.

In contrast, tactical concerns dominate the managerial requirements for organizations resident in markets characterized by constrained competition. For here, pricing and supply decisions, etc., must now be taken in light not only of the actual or prospective behaviors of direct competitors, but in recognition of the fact that demand is now in some measure within the sphere of influence of organizational authorities by virtue of price and promotional (advertising) elasticities, etc. What may then be posed as the key organizational positioning requirement associated with residency in a context characterized by constrained competition is equilibrium maintenance. What this implies is an accomodative capability whereby organizational properties can be varied or adjusted in response to changes in exogenous properties. For the usual commercial firm, what equilibrium-maintenance implies is the attempt to keep supply more or less continually well-balanced with demand. And this objective would argue for a prototypical sequence of tactical management initiatives that would include the folllowing:

1) Forecasting exercises aimed at the determination of some expectedly most likely level of demand for some product;

2) Logistical programming efforts to determine the level and mix of factors-of-production (capital, labor, financial resources and raw materials, etc.) required to generate a supply to meet projected demand;

3) The allocation of resources to the various aspects of the production/service process such that a given level of output is expected to be obtained most efficiently (in the short and long-run, via optimal scale-of-plant, etc.

4) The establishment of some sort of monitoring/feedback mechanism that will provide current information on actual vs. projected demand, and so suggest the need to advance or retard the rate of production or output.

Similar interpretations may apply in both the military and governmental sectors. For what equilibrium-maintenance means with respect to tactical military management is the attempt to provide (minimally) for a *balance of forces* with respect to some adversary's capabilities. And for many public enterprises or governmental agencies, the core tactical challenge is also addressable in terms of equilibrium-maintenance: The attempt to maintain an adequate balance between the legitimate demand for some social service and the level of supply that can be supported by available resources.[7]

In any case, what the four management initiatives just listed above suggest is that, for the most part, what equilibrium-maintenance requires in terms of decision support technology are the probabilistic decision-aids earlier suggested to be the dominant source of discipline for tactical decision exercises. And of the probabilistic decision aids that are currently available, those employed most frequently will be statistical instruments designed to support inferential decisions along one or another of the following lines:

Attempts to infer present and/or future possibilities as some calculable function of historical or precedented situations, or to generate longitudinal inductive inferences;

Attempts to infer properties to some population as a whole on the basis of information about the properties of some sample . . . to make cross-sectional inferences from the more particular to the more general.

To assist decision authorities in making disciplined longitudinal inferences, there is of course the extraordinarily diverse family of statistical forecasting tools based on time-series analysis initiatives, such covering the spectrum from simple linear extrapolation techniques (as with mainstream econometric methods) to some quite intricate techniques designed to do curve-fitting over complex non-linear or ill-behaved time series. And by way of the most obvious and familiar example of techniques to discipline cross-sectional inference generation, there are the statistical tools available to support market research exercises and help perform quality control, etc.

But there remains the issue of why organizational positioning in contexts characterized by constrained competition might be dominantly a matter of tactical rather than strategic planning. The answer follows from the fact that *constrained* competition implies the existence of certain limits as to the sorts of competitive initiatives that organizations can invoke. These limitations can arise from any of three sources:

- As a result of casual collusion among the members of some industry, such that there is in effect a gentleman's agreement to refrain from certain particularly threatening sorts of competitive initiatives;
- As a consequence of regulatory or legislative constraints that serve to proscribe certain means that organizations might otherwise use in the attempt to gain a competitive edge;
- As a result of natural economic considerations such as those that characterize monopolistic competition.

Of these three sources of constraints, the last is perhaps the most generally significant.

For in this case, the range of competitive initiatives that firms might undertake to any real effect is restricted by the fact that the products they are producing tend to be simple substitutes (as with beer and tobacco, for example). This limits opportunities for significant product differentiation. At the same time, opportunities for serious price competition are limited by the essentially simple (and relatively ancient) nature of the production and distribution processes involved, such that there is little real prospect for any one firm being able to effect a technological innovation that would allow its costs to drop significantly below those its competitors must charge. Thus, competitors are pretty much restricted to effecting merely incremental innovations in price and/or product quality. Indeed, by default, the axis of really aggressive competition in monopolistic competitive markets is in the attempt to devise advertising campaigns designed to convey the impression of (often in the absence of the fact of) product differentiation or innovation. In all other aspects, however, firms operating under constrained or monopolistic competition may consider themselves essentially immune from radical competitive threats, such that threats with which they will have to contend will majorally be intelligible as relatively simple and essentially predictable variations on long-familiar themes . . . merely *different in degree* from competitive thrusts encountered before.

As such, firms need be prepared to make only modest (different in degree) adjustments to their own pricing, production, etc., properties in order to either author or respond to such initiatives. Hence, in light of the earlier-noted technical convention, the basis for the assertion that organizational management under conditions of constrained competition will demand mainly tactical capabilities.

1.4.3 Arenas of Strategic-Level Competition

Threats of proper strategic significance will not appear then until we get to the third of the market referents, that allowing for extensive or weakly-constrained (oligopolistic) competition. Here will appear the basis for radical competitive thrusts. For the products in such a market will allow for real (vs. cosmetic) differentiation, and there should be opportunities for major breakthroughs in basic production technology (and hence some prospect of possibly radical adjustments in pricing structures). That is, firms are now required to consider the possibility of having to both author and respond to competitive initiatives that are different in kind --qualitatively disparate-- from anything being done now or having any historical precedent. For if there is a single managerial criterion that dominates here, it is the pursuit of monopoly profits via real (vs. merely cosmetic) innovation. Significant risk is endemic both for those who act and those who would wait.

There is thus a constant premium on exerting competitive surprise, and hence an equally constant premium on security . . . on depriving competitors of any *intelligence* that might allow them to impute ultimate intentions. Moreover, it is not merely the lack of useful information that is of concern now, but also the prospect of disinformation seeded by a competitor to deliberately mislead us as to his real intents and purposes. Here then, for the first time, we routinely encounter the demand for judgement vs. merely parameter or data-driven decisions. It's not merely the prospect of hard data being either sparse or perhaps of dubious merit that causes this. It's also that any attempt to project the set of competitive events to which a firm might be subject (as predicates for organizational positioning decisions) must now expand to include a perhaps quite wide range of *notional* or hypothetical possibilities . . . products of essentially speculative essays of the *if we were them, what would we do?* variety. In short, any transit from a market characterized by constrained competition to one allowing for extensive competition is a transit from the tactical to the strategic decision domain so far as the technician is concerned.

But while competitors operating in an extensively competitive market may do each other real harm, certain factors would intervene to put some limits on the damage that might be done, e.g.: Firms may be large enough to sacrifice a line of business; they may be wealthy enough to liquidite some assets to cover temporary operating deficits or weather a relative disadvantage; they may have diversification potential or perhaps a hard-core of dedicated consumers that puts a floor under which demand can fall; there may be danger of an anti-trust suit should a particular firm be too successful in cornering a market. For any of a variety of reasons then, truly antagonistic competitive initiatives are either infeasible or may carry with them a substantial threat for the firm attempting to invoke them (with Laker Airways perhaps a prime example of this latter).

But when we shift to consider contexts allowing for Predatory competition, the gloves are off entirely. For here, competitors perceive themselves as engaged in a constant or even zero-sum game, where one organization can advance (most expediently, if not exclusively) only at the direct expense of others. Thus, once we enter the predatory arena, it is not merely monopoly profits or ephemoral advantage that is at stake here, but possibly survival itself. This is true not merely of the military arena, but also of commercial, political, technological or atheletic enterprises as well. Whatever constraints may exist on the permissible forms of competition will have to have been imposed by some superior exogenous authority, for the competitors themselves can afford no scruples or generous stipulations of their own. Therefore, the range of competitive threats an organization might have to confront may now expand to include virtually any conceivable initiative. In the commercial arena then, to the prospect of product innovations or radical price changes that we considered part and parcel of extensive competition, we must now add the possibility of predatory pricing (designed to drive a competitor out of the market), pirating of key executives or professional personnel, attempts to corner the market on critical raw materials, industrial espionage or even sabotage . . . and of course the most urbane and modern form of predatory competition, the unfriendly take-over of acquisition (which may on occasion be followed by liquidation, which will then end the life of a business more surely and quickly than economic inefficiency).

Therefore, if a transit to extensive competition would force an organization's higher-management to take a step into the strategic domain, any tendency towards predatory competition would find them four-square in the middle of it. And as suggested earlier, the general technical corollary of any transit to the strategic decision domain would be a shift away from traditional probabilistic decision aids in favor of judgement-driven or subjective decision support protocols. We'll be devoting the major part of the final part of this volume to a detailed discussion of judgemental/subjective decision technology, so here we'll just very briefly mention the two basic classes techniques that are currently available.

The first class would contain the collection of what we'll refer to as ELICITIVE protocols, these being procedural schemes allowing for the generation and ordering of essentially speculative or *notional* event and/or response alternatives. Such are intended to inject some kind of formalism into the formulation and evaluation of problem-definitional (causal) or response alternatives that may have only the most tenuous rooting in precedent, and may even explicitly encourage the generation of hypothetical constructs that are perhaps deliberately abstracted from any empirical/historical referents. Among the members of the family of Elicitive protocols we'd number the Delphi technique, Synectics, the Nominal Group approach and any of a variety of *brainstorming* schemes.[8] What makes this appropriate is the just-mentioned need for managements of organizations engaged in extensive or predatory competition to contemplate the possibility of being confronted by situations substantially different than --or, more clinically, qualitatively disparate from-- anything encountered before . . . this a need for which statistical extrapolation or inference instruments cannot answer.[9]

The second class would be comprised of recently evolved decision STRUCTURING facilities, these being sophisticated based for bringing discipline to multiobjective/multicriteria decision exercises, e.g.: Interpretive Structured Programming, Analytic Hierarchy Processing or computer-based protocols such as ARIADNE. All have certain quasi-axiomatic mechanics that can help decision authorities generate rationalized preference orderings over goal-sets and related decision choices in cases where the ranking criteria will be at least partially (if not dominantly) subjective in nature.[10]

They thus represent the currently most sophisticated instruments available to bring discipline to multicriteria (multiobjective) decision exercises. Most begin by having the decision-maker (user) provide --as basic inputs-- an initiating array of goal and alternative courses of action, and some may also demand that he also enter an a-priori preference ordering as well. Following this, each decision structuring methodology will have certain facilities that can be used to help resolve *uncertainty* in the mind of some decision-maker as to where his best interests lie by doing the following:

a) Helping focus on a goal-structure that can be expected to represent a weighted *optimum at the margin* among a set of partially competitive or mutually-exclusive objectives;

b) Help rank alternative action-options as to expected effectiveness/risk with respect to some specific goal-set arrived at via (a) above.

Thus, both in terms of their potential resolution power and the order of complexity they can accomodate, modern decision structuring intruments represent a primary source of technical support for those enterprises that have elected or been forced to try to cope in the most perilous and demanding of competitive arenas . . . for enterprises whose organizational positioning committments must of necessity be strategic in nature.

1.5 Contextual Determinants of Strategic Sophistication

The discussions of the various levels of environmental and competitive complexity were intended to provide some sort of casual technical reinforcement for this familiar organization theory proposition: Any increase in the complexity of organizational context will argue for a more or less corresponding increase in the level of strategic sophistication required of higher-management.[11] We want now to be more precise about the technical consequences of contextual complexity. Hence, the typology below, and its focus on four generic contextual referents that are products of the various environmental and competitive ideal-types that were defined.

Environmental Ideal-Types	Competitive Ideal-Types	**Generic Contextual Referents**
Placid (Stationary)	Pre-Competitive	**State Determinacy**
Evolutionary (Perturbable)	Constrained Competition	**State Dominancy**
Equifinal (Modular)	Extensive Competition	**State Stochasticity**
Turbulent (Transmutative)	Predatory Competition	**State Indeterminacy**

These four generic contextual referents may be viewed as key intervals on a continuum of contextual complexity, with state-determinacy being the least daunting in terms of demands on higher managements, and state-indeterminacy designed to portray the worst of all possible worlds for those trying to carry out the organizational positioning function. For again, with respect to organizational positioning, the term *state* is basically just a code-word for talking about broad qualitative aspects of an organizational context as they might pertain during some period. We might then formulate a contextual *state* as follows:

$$Si = Ni + Mi,$$

where Si is a state defined over some unique set of environmental properties (Ni) and a specific competitive structure (Mi), such that Ni and Mi are themselves comprehensible as states.

For any Ni will be defined over some effectively unique collection of basic field properties (a particular conjunction of broad social, political, macroeconomic and technological conditions in which an organization is embedded), while any Mi might be used to summarize the current competitive status for an organization relative to its comeptitors in some field.

We might then consider some alternative contextual state, say Sj, such that one of the following conditions must hold:

if: $Si = Ni + Mi,$

then: $Sj = Nj + Mi$ . . . Sj is defined with respect to an environmental state that has some point(s) of fundamental difference from the enviromental state over which Si was defined

or: $Sj = Ni + Mj$ . . . Sj entails the same environmental state as Si, but is defined over a qualitatively unique competitive structure.

or: $Sj = Nj + Mj$ . . . Sj and Si are non-equivalent in terms of both environmental and competitive attributes.

As for the first of the above, the case where Si and Sj differ in terms of the environmental conditions they entail, the implication is that there is some very fundamental or qualitatively significant vs. merely superficial difference between Ni and Nj . . . some change in social, political, economic or technological, etc., properties that is such an order of import that it would be taken as an occasion to rethink the basic orientation for an organization.

By way of example of a fundamental social change, we might let Ni stand for the environment for the tobacco industry as of ten or fifteen years ago and Nj stand for the contemporary environment, with a major point of difference being the extradordinary shift in public sentiment against smoking. This difference is the major cause for these companies' aggressive attempts at both geographic and product diversification (efforts to penetrate foreign markets for cigarettes and the expansion into other lines of business). As an instance of a political initiative translating into a radical change in environment, we might consider the airline industry and take Ni and Nj to represent the environmental states before and after deregulation, with Nj containing vastly fewer competitive strictures than Ni. In fact, this example points to the prospect of interdependency between the environmental and competitive dimensions of organizational context. For deregulation may be interpreted as having forced the airline industry into a transit from constrained to extensive competition and so, for perhaps the first time, faced airline managements with the demand for true strategic sophistication. Another telling example of a politically-induced change in organizational environment is of course the enforced divestiture of AT&T. And again, this initiative not only affected AT&T, but also the competitive structure for the communications industry as a whole (in terms of the emergence of the regional spinoffs and revisions in the rules applicable to the contest among contenders for shares of the telecommunications market). Even the structure of the computer industry was effected, this via the emergence of AT&T as a major vendor of hardware and software.

By way of example of how broad changes in the economic aspect of environment might impact on organizations, we could consider the implications for the conduct of enterprise of the recent shift in philosophical orientation towards free-market concepts in China and, to a lesser extent, in the Soviet Union as a consequence of *perestroika*. An even more pointed example may be the alterations in patterns of ownership and management that have been forced on some countries as a consequence of lender dictates. In all the above cases, the essence of the difference between the prior environmental state (Ni) and the new (Nj) consists of macroeconomic incentives and initiatives that tend to favor privatization and decentralization over collectivism and bureacratization. Finally, as a classic case of a general technological advance forcing a basic change in organizational context, we might take the implication of the emergence of microprocessing technology on the computer industry, and particularly the dramatic shift in market environment this implied for traditional mainframe manufacturers.

To introduce now a particularly critical technical concept, each of the above mentioned instances of environmental change will now be taken to represent a state event. As an ammendement to the earlier appreciation of a state event alternative, we'll now use the term to denote any initiative or occurrence deemed capable of authoring a state-level change in organizational context. Throughout these pages, we'll be using the symbol E to refer to a state-event, such that we'd get this notation:

$$Ex \rightarrow (Ni \Rightarrow Nj),$$

which may be read as: The state-event Ex is deemed to be sufficient to effect (or to imply, as per the symbol $\rightarrow$) the transformation from environmental state Ni to some qualitatively disparate state, Nj, with => being the symbol we shall be using throughout to indicate a state-level transformation.

Much the same sort of considerations would hold were we to look at the competitive dimension of organizational context at a lower level of abstraction than that taken in the previous section. One way to do this is via a construct we'll refer to as the competitive matrix:

COMPETITIVE MATRIX: (X|Y)f = S([A] x [D])

Asset Categories	Competitive Subdimensions				
	D1	D2	D3	. . .	Dn
A1	s(1,1)	s(1,2)	s(1,3)	. . .	s(1,n)
A2	s(2,1)	s(2,2)	s(2,3)	. . .	s(2,n)
Am	s(m,1)	s(m,2)	s(m,3)	. . .	s(m,n)

A competitive matrix summarizes the competitive status for a subject organization (X) with respect to a specific adversary (Y) for some (f) representing a particular field of interest (e.g., a product-market sector).

For the rows of the competitive matrix (the A's) refer to whatever categories of assets or resources might be appropriate as arbiters of competitive advantage, usually the following:

A1: Skilled technical/professional personnel
A2: Plant/infrastructure
A3: Capital Equipment
A4: Factor supplies/materials
A5: Managerial sophistication
A6: Intangibles (reputation; employee morale, etc.)

The columns of the competitive matrix would then be used to array the several subdimensions on which competitive exchanges can take place given the field of interest, e.g.:

	COMMERCIAL	MILITARY	FOOTBALL
D1	Price	Land	Offense
D2	Product Quality	Sea	Defense
D3	Merchandizing	Air	Special Teams
D4	Advertising	Space	

Each of the s(i,j) entries in the body of the matrix would then be used to convey conclusions as to the the current competitive status of organization-X relative to organization-Y in terms of the i'th asset category (Ai) and the j'th subdimension of competition (Dj). As will be suggested in a later chapter, valuations for status assessments in a competitive matrix will most usually be qualitative or categorical (vs. quantitative) in nature, perhaps along the following lines:

s(i,j) = >> : significant advantage to X
<< : significant advantage to Y
> : marginal advantage to X
< : marginal advantage to Y
<> : parity between X and Y

Were then a competitive matrix to be formulated with respect to all organization-X's competitors in all the fields in which it maintains a presence, the result would be a model of X's current competitive state as some Mi.

And to parallel what we just did for environmmental matters, we might define a state-event as any initiative capable of effecting a change in the competitive state for organization-X or sufficient to force the displacement of Mi by some new competitive structure, Mj: Ex → (Mi => Mj). But given the competitive matrix, we can be more explicit. For the only initiatives that would be considered to represent proper *state* events would be those resulting in one of the following consequences:

a) Additions/deletions to the population of competitors [Y] that organization-X will confront in some field. For example, a new firm might decide to enter an industry, or a traditional competitor might elect to retire from some market via liquidation or divestiture.

b) Additions/deletions to subdimensions of competition [D], these a consequence of organization-X or any competitor(s) deciding to extend direct competition to some new subdimension (e.g., to include naval warfare as as aspect of the confrontation between two nations) or to retire from direct confrontation on some subdimension (as when some firm or set of such decide to back away from serious price competition with respect to some products or markets segment).

c) A change in the categorical (qualitative) valuation assigned any s(i,j) element of the competitive matrix.

Such changes may often derive from an organization's acquisition or loss of critical assets. For example, suppose that two football teams (X and Y) have traditionally been more or less on a par with respect to the quality of their offensive players. But were organization-X to somehow acquire the services of an exceptionally talented quarterback, the net effect might be to force a transformation from parity (<>) to a significant advantage for X vs. Y (or to >>) with respect to the personnel|offense conjunction. Or, as an alternative, the same transformation may be a consequence of organization-Y losing the services of one or more important players to injury. A second source of such changes may of course derive from organizational innovations, as for example with the potential for a major innovation to effect a radical change in competitive advantage so far as product differentiation is concerned.

In contrast, all the other competitor-authored initiatives that an organization might face would somehow be less sweeping in terms of the order of threat or significance they entail, and so be taken to represent not state-events, but rather one or another of the lower-order classes of events . . . Thematic or Parametric. To illustrate once again the flow of dependencies, we might work through a simple example. As an instance of state-level uncertainty/risk, we might consider the case of a nation facing an adversary that might launch an assault along any of three qualitatively disparate avenues . . . Commercial, Diplomatic or Military. In this sense, state-level uncertainty and risk may be said to arise as a consequence of ambiguity as to the particular *strategic* initiative that some competitor might array against us (or, with respect to environmental agencies, ambiguity as to what *policy* position might eventually be adopted). In contrast, uncertainty would pass to the thematic level following any fixity on one of the above qualitative options. To illustrate, suppose it had been determined that a military assault will be forthcoming, such that what now remains in doubt is the exact form in which the military attack will appear, e.g.: will it be an all-out attack, a limited surgical strike on a few isolated targets, an indirect assault (by proxy) using third-party troops? That is, thematic-level uncertainty and risk reflects ambiguity as to the particular *tactical* course of action a competitor or environmental agency will follow, etc. Finally, for the locus of contextual challenge to rest merely at the parametric level, there would have to have been a determination as to which thematic option will be employed by the adversary, such that what remains at issue are just matters such as timing and location . . . ambiguity as to the operational choice that the adversary will elect.

When we consider all the preceeding arguments in concert, the key pragmatic corollary might be stated as follows:

> The emergence of any state-event implies the need for an a strategic-level adjustment to prevailing organizational positioning committments, with thematic and parametric level events generally arguing for address at the tactical and operational initiatives, respectively.

And this, finally, gives us the basis we need for addressing the pragmatic implications of the four generic contextual referents that were shown in the typology with which we began this section.

For these referents are significant in terms of the level of analytical challenge they portend for carrying out the first of the analytical tasks associated with the organizational positioning function, event projection. This is directed at the attempt to anticipate the range of environmental/competitive *events* to which an organization might be subject during some future period (with the second of the organizational positioning tasks being aimed at trying to decide how such events should be accomodated if they occur . . . this a matter we'll deal with extensively in later chapters). For it is projected event possibilities against which an organization is to be *positioned.* It's thus both technically and practically useful to think of organizational positioning committments being given tangible expression in terms of a collection of strategic, tactical and operational plans, via the following associations:

Projected State Event	→	Strategic Plan
Projected Thematic Event	→	Tactical Plan
Projected Parametric Event	→	Operational Plan.

That is, strategic planning provisions tend to be arrayed against anticipated state-level event possibilities, with any strategic plan serving to encode higher-management's determinations as to how the organization in aggregate is to deal with that event should it occur. Thematic event possibilities will then inspire the formulation of a tactical plan, while parametric events would dictate the development of an operational plan.

As such, the essence of the strategic organizational positioning problem is focussed on the attempt to pre-define the array of state-level transformational possibilities that might be authored within some organizational context. The four generic contextual referents thus gain their significance in terms of the very different orders of challenge they entail with respect to this task, this because each entails a very different level of potential for state-level change:

STATE DETERMINACY, where there is effective certainty as to the contextual state that will prevail during some period, given that there can be identified one and only one Ni and Mi expected to have any real likelihood of occurence . . . this as a consequence of a tendency towards environmental placidity and a lack of serious, direct competition.

STATE DOMINANCY, where for any period or planning interval, there can be isolated a strongly-dominant, maximum-likelihood state, this via some Ni and Mi assigned a significantly higher probability of occurrence than any other options (but where the probability values remain below the level of effective certainty) . . . a situation most likely to arise from a tendency towards a neatly *evolutionary* environment and *constraints* that discourage radical competitive initiatives.

STATE STOCHASTICITY, where there are two or more environmental and/or competitive states expected to have some significant likelihood of occurrence during the period of interest, the set of which can be taken to substantially exhaust the repertoire of state-level possibilities that might arise . . . as per a tendency towards an environment having an equifinal potential and/or an arena allowing for *extensive* competition among the organizations resident there.

STATE INDETERMINACY, where the range of environmental and/or competitive states that might arise within some context is assumed to be so large as to include at least some possibilities that cannot be predefined, thus holding out the prospect of an organization being confronted by some entirely unanticipated opportunity or threat . . . via a tendency towards a turbulent (transmutative) environment or an arena where there are limits to the harm that adversaries might attempt to do to one another.

But our interest in these four contextual referents is not yet concluded. For as we'll try to show in the next chapter, each argues for a very different avenue of approach towards the pursuit of strategic *readiness*.

NOTES AND REFERENCES

---

1. This three-part taxonomy was introduced by R. N. Anthony in his *Planning and Control Systems: A Framework for Analysis* (Boston: Harvard University Graduate School of Business, 1965).

2. The organizational positioning function, as the focus of higher-management activities, derives from modern organization theory's preference for a *contingency* view of management. See, for example, Kast and Rosenzweig's *Contingency Views of Organization and Management* (Science Research Associates, 1973) or Chapter 7 of Osborn, Hunt and Jauch: *Organization Theory: An Integrated Approach* (John Wiley and Sons, 1980).

3. The Emery-Trist taxonomy was first formalized in their remarkable paper: "The Causal Texture of the Environment", *Human Relations* (18), 1965. For an extension of their ideal-types to managerial technology, see Chapter 4 of my *Systems: Analysis, Administration and Architecture* (Van Nostrand Reinhold, 1975).

4. For a discussion of the reach and limits of models of the Forrester type --the inspirator of the Club-of-Rome constructs-- see David Carhart's paper: "Global Models: Their Usefulness to Public Policy-Makers", in (Sutherland, ed.) *Management Handbook for Public Administrators* (Van Nostrand Reinhold, 1978). A good treatment of econometric techniques is still available from a reading of the papers in Hood and Koopman's *Studies in Econometric Methods* (Yale University Press, 1963). A comparison of these two techniques has been done by Manfred Sommer: "The Econometric Challenge to Systems Dynamics and Vice Versa", in *Technological Forecasting and Social Change* (25), 1984.

5. In Chapter 3 we'll suggest how Markov-type conventions can help organizations

cope with equifinality. The key is their capability for comprehending what are clinically referred to as Stochastic Finite-state Systems (which we abbreviate here as Stochastic State) . . . c.f., J. W. Carlyle's: "Stochastic Finite-State Systems Theory", in (Zadeh and Polak, eds.) *System Theory* (McGraw-Hill, 1969). For some idea of what non-computational mathematics might offer, see Michel and Miller's *Qualitative Analysis of Large-Scale Dynamical Systems* (Academic Press, 1977), or the appropriate sections in Buchanan's *Discrete and Dynamic Decision Analysis* (John Wiley & Sons, 1982). On the other hand, perhaps the finest discussion of the mechanics and implications of a *transmutative* dynamic was developed by Maruyama in his important paper, "The Second Cybernetics: Deviation-Amplifying Mutual Causal Processes", *American Scientist* (51), 1963. Or, for a more recent effort, see his "Morphogenetic Economics: Change-Amplification by Causal Loops", in *Technological Forecasting and Social Change* (29), 1986.

6. Ferguson's classic text, *Microeconomic Theory* (Irwin, 1966) is a fine source for a review of the traditional distinctions between market structures. There is, however, some current ambiguity as to how best to interpret Oligopoly, and our referent (extensive competition) departs somewhat from the old-line orthodox view, though it certainly runs close to the visions of Chamberlain or Robinson about contemporary economic market tendencies, with the Predatory case just taking competitive complexity one step further. But so does the view of contemporary markets recently provided by Baumol, et. al., depart from tradition; c.f.: *Contestable Markets and The Theory of Industrial Structure* (Harcourt Brace Ivanovich), 1982. In any case, for the management or decision scientist, what is significant about market contexts is the sorts of technical demands they pose; indeed, it's possible to perceive basic Operations Research as being an attempt to make operational the key managerial prescriptions posed by classical Microeconomic theory. In contrast, what is significant for the economist about market structures is the prescriptions they might yield about specific behaviors (pricing, etc.), not all of which will map well onto members of a taxonomy of decision challenges.

7. c.f., Sutherland, *Managing Social Service Systems* (Petrocelli Books, 1977).

8. For an excellent collection of articles on the Delphi-driven decision operations, see Linstone and Turoff (eds.) *The Delphi Method: Techniques and Applications* (Addison-Wesley, 1975). For an explanation of synectics, see W. J. J. Gordon's *Synectics* (Collier Books, 1961). A discussion of the Nominal Group approach is given by Van de Ven & Delbecq in "Nominal vs. Interacting Group Processes for Committee Decision Making Effectiveness", *Academy of Management Journal* (14; 1971). General comments about *brainstorming* are provided by Dennis Gouran in his *Discussion: The Process of Group Decision-Making* (Harper & Row, 1974) and by Walter C. Swap, et. al., eds., *Group Decision Making* (Sage Publications, 1984). For an interesting ancillary discussion, see T. J. Bouchard, "Whatever Happened to Brainstorming?", *Journal of Creative Behavior* (5; 1971).

9. Much of the contemporary planning literature is devoted to presenting approaches to Event Projection that are functional so long as contextual complexity is not too significant. The following citations might be used to get a quick appreciation of the more popular of these approaches: Ballard & Hall, "Theory and Practice of Integrated

Impact Assessment", *Technological Forecasting and Social Change* (25), 1984; de Filho, "Environmental Analysis for Strategic Planning", *Managerial Planning* (33, 23), 1985; Constance Bates, "Mapping the Environment: An Operational Environment Analysis Model", *Long Range Planning* (18), 1985; Bert Nanus, "QUEST: Quick Environmental Scanning Technique", *Long Range Planning* (15), 1982.

10. For an explanation of the basic of Interpretive Structured Programming, see the appropriate sections of John Warfield's *Societal Systems: Planning, Policy and Complexity* (Wiley, 1976). The main reference on Analytic Hierarchy theory and operations is Tom Saaty's *The Analytic Hierarchy Process* (McGraw-Hill, 1980). For a description of *Ariadne*, see A. P. Sage, et. al., "ARIADNE: A Knowledge-based Interactive System for Planning and Decision Support" in *IEEE Transactions on Systems, Man and Cybernetics* (14, 1; 1984). Or, for a generalized discussion, see Sage and Rajala's paper: "On the Role of Structure in Policy Analysis and Decision-Making", in *The Management Handbook for Public Administrators* (op. cit.).

11. For more on this, see J. R. Galbraith's "Environmental and Technological Determinants of Organizational Structure" in *Studies in Organizational Design* (Irwin, 1970); Child's "Organizational Structure, Environment and Performance: The Role of Strategic Choice", *Sociology* (6), 1972; or Reitmann's "Dimensions of Organizational Technology and Structure", *Human Relations* (30, 6), 1977.

CHAPTER 2

ALTERNATIVE APPROACHES TO STRATEGIC "READINESS"

The set of all the plans an organization has formulated constitutes a planning structure. As we now want to show, the integrity of any strategic management support system structure is to be adjudged as to the degree of readiness it provides an organization. For readiness reflects the extent to which an organization is prepared to deal --in an adequate and timely way-- with the stream of events, problems and situations that it might encounter. Our interest in this chapter is then focussed on the various ways in which organizations might elect to pursue readiness. More particularly, we'll be looking at the several fundamentally different approaches to strategic planning/positioning that are available to modern organizations, and considering the conditions under which each would become the preferred strategic management platform.

2.1 The Anatomy of a Strategic Planning Structure

We might summarize the key conclusion from the first chapter in terms of the following proposition:

> The more complex an organizational context, the greater the number and diversity of the state-events with which an organization might be confronted during some period.

Again, a state-event was defined as any initiative --authored either by the organization itself or some environmental or competitive agency-- deemed of sufficient significance to warrant a strategic-level adjustment to the prevailing set of organizational positioning committments. And as was also suggested earlier, organizational positioning committments become tangible in terms of a collection of standing strategic, tactical and operational plans to be arrayed, respectively, against projected state, thematic and parametric level events. As such, any state-event --actual or prospective-- may be taken as the occasion for the formulation of a new strategic plan that conveys higher-management's determination as to how the organization is to respond to the event, etc. It is this way that increases in contextual intricacy and volatility translate directly into the need for increasingly elaborate strategic planning sructures.

To give some concrete idea of the mechanics this involves, it may be well to take a quick look at an application area that apparently holds great fascination for business, government and military executives alike . . . professional football. At the very least, it is the most popular source of analogies for those wont to view competitive exchanges as admixtures of the romantic and the elemental. But for us here, it has the advantage of being a straight and simple path towards some pragmatic arguments that might remain elusive were we to try to approach them solely through the medium of abstract argumentation. In any case, as was noted at some point in the previous chapter, the several subdimensions on which football teams may engage in competitive exchanges were:

1) D1: Offense;
2) D2: Defense; and
3) D3: Special Teams.

And these, in turn, would lead us to allow for three fundamentally different sorts of strategic-level offensive initiatives (state-event alternatives, as it were), which then would dictate the formulation of three different categories of strategic-level defensive response options.

State-Event Alternatives	Strategic Response Options
E1: Run	R1: Defenses against the run
E2: Pass	R2: Passing defenses
E3: Kick	R3: Defenses against the kick

During any football game, the key task for the team currently on defense is to accurately predict the offensive team's strategic choice for the next play (run, pass or kick), such that the proper defensive set is in place. On the other hand, one factor that might dictate the election of a strategic option by the offensive team is some expectation as to the strategic choice that might be taken by the defense. For, generally speaking, the most dramatic gains by the offense will follow from a strategic error on the part of the defense . . . .e.g., setting up in anticipation of a kick but being confronted with a passing play.

Underlying any offensive strategic option will then be a collection of tactical options, e.g.:

E1 (Run) =	e1: off-tackle	E2 (Pass) =	e1: post
	e2: dive play		e2: shovel
	e3: reverse		e3: sideline
	e4: sweep		e4: screen, etc.

From the perspective of the defensive team against which they might be directed, each of the above would represent a thematic-level event alternative. As such, each of the three basic defensive strategic options would then entail a subset of variants qua tactical response alternatives:

R1 = r1 : Set up against a short-yardage play
r2 : Contain against a Sweep
r3 : Use a three vs. four down lineman, etc.

R2 = r1 : Blitz
r2 : Zone coverage
r3 : Prevent defense, etc.

Operational level choices might then deal with the precise assignments of manpower under one or another of the above tactical options. For example, an operational decision might involve the question of whether to use a linebacker, a defensive back or a safety to carry out a blitz.

But to look at strategic competition now from a broader perspective, we might consider that offensive and defensive choices a team makes during the course of any contest may be taken in light of what TV commentators refer to as the defensive *Game Plan*. That is, underlying the specific play-by-play strategic choices is some sort of more encompassing strategy that serves to set the approach to a game as a whole. At its simplest, these higher-level strategic choices might reduce to just two basic competitive orientations:

1) Strength against Strength
2) Strength against Weakness.

What in any particular confrontation (some specific football game) would likely determine the emphasis on one or another of these options would be the perception as to whether or not a competitor has any points of weakness that might be exploitable, and some idea of their relative significance in terms of the ultimate outcome of the context. And to recall a construct introduced towards the close of the first chapter, one approach to the formal encoding of such considerations is the Competitive Matrix. For any single game, its purpose would be to show how the assets for our organization (say Team X) stack up against those of some competitor (Team-Y) with respect to the several dimensions of competition, e.g.:

	Offense	Defense	Special Teams
A1: Player Personnel	s(1,1)	s(1,2)	s(1,3)
A2: Coaching	s(2,1)	s(2,2)	s(2,3)
A3: Intangibles	s(3,1)	s(3,2)	s(3,3)
...	...	...	...

But the Game Plan for any individual contest would be at least in part determined by decisions of a yet more fundamental and sweeping nature.

These decisions would relate to organizational positioning considerations not just with respect to a single game against a single opponent, but rather in regard to all the teams that will be faced during the course of an entire season, or perhaps a succession of such. These higher-level organizational positioning decisions would then be informed by a set of competitive matrices capturing the strengths and weaknesses of the team vis-a-vis the population of competitors in the league to which the team belongs. Such assessments should then serve as the basis for judgements as to where the particularly critical points of competitive leverage are to be found . . . offense vs. defense; coaching vs. player skills; the relative importance, in terms of both functional and market considerations, of having *stars* on the roster, etc. Higher-management's judgements will then translate into determinations as to which of the various asset/dimension conjunctions (e.g., player quality/offense; coaching skills/defense) should be given the highest priority for development. And these determinations, for their part, then gain concrete moment in terms of recruiting emphases or, more general still, the resource allocation schedule that is adopted.

It's in this way that the strategic decision options available to an organization in the short-run may become a consequence of strategic planning committments of long-run significance. This is perhaps merely a somewhat convoluted echo of the simple point that 'if it's not on hand, you can't use it'! But this brings us to a very troublesome point of both conceptual and pragmatic concern. For recall, once again, the general argument that the magnitude of the organizational positioning challenge derives from the number and/or diversity of the exogenously-authored events to which an organization might have to respond. It makes a great deal of difference, however, whether it is just large numbers of event possibilities or the degree of diversity among them that is the seat of complexity. Of the two, diversity may often be the more significant. The reason for this is fairly clear-cut: Diversity among event possibilities argues for diversity in terms of the planning provisions and assets required to deal with the events.

For example, if a football team were legitimately able to presume that its opponents were only going to run and never pass or kick, then the only plans it would need to formulate would be tactical in nature, those required to effect ground defenses appropriate to the several different categories of running plays (sweeps, dives, slants). And the only assets that would have to be acquired would be those necessary to invest the set of tactical reponse options . . . down linemen, linebackers, a defensive line coach, etc. Now, were it anticipated that an opponent might add some new variant to its repertoire of running offenses (say an end-around), this would then occasion the formulation of a new tactical plan, perhaps one designed to effect weak-side containment. But this new tactical response option may involve merely a reordering of existing player assets, such as altering the relative placement of linebackers and linemen to effect a spread. As such, additions to the repertoire of tactical response options will generally not pose the demand for the addition of any new category of asset, but merely a requirement for *more of the same* or perhaps even no additions at all to the organization's asset base . . . e.g., a given population of linemen and linebackers may be largely interchangeable among various tactical sets (and to some extent, linebackers and linemen may be perceived as effective substitutes).

On the other hand, once we pose the prospect of an opponent being able to effect two or more strategic options --to either run or pass or kick-- there is a corresponding requirement to add two new categories of strategic planning constructs, each demanding a unique category of assets. Particularly, in terms of asset requirements, the ability to counter passing plays would pose the need to acquire cornerbacks and linemen who are specially skilled at the pass rush, etc., while it is the kicking offense that gives rise to the need for various Special Teams tactical planning options (sets to block a kick or set up a return, etc.) and personnel (punt-return specialists). What occasions this requirement for the addition of fundamentally new classes of personnel is that, in all but the rarest instances, cornerbacks are not acceptable substitutes for linebackers or down linemen, nor is the usual offensive running back likely to be adept at the very specialized and perilous task of returning kicks. To generalize then, additions of some new state-event possibility implies the need to both formulate and invest a new strategic response option, which in turn poses the need for some effectively unique classes of organizational assets in terms of personnel skills, dedicated capital equipment, specialized supplies that could be turned to no other purpose, etc.

All the prerequisites are now in place to move towards a comprehension of the technical perspective on the substance of any strategic plan. In particular, any strategic plan (say some Rx, to follow our notational convention) would ideally take the form of a special type of multidimensional *model*, occasionally referred to in the military vernacular as a script. Any properly formulated script would entail specifications on at least the following dimensions for any strategic initiative:

WHO:	which of our organizational unit(s) are to serve as the conveyors of the initiative
does WHAT:	the specific actions comprising the initiative
to WHOM:	indicates the unit(s) of the adversary organization or environmental agency that are to be the targets of the actions
HOW:	indicates the sequence of actions
WITH:	specifies any asset/resource committments
WHEN:	indicates any temporal conditions for initiation, duration and conclusion
WHERE:	details any locational considerations
and WHY:	specifies the intended effect of the initiative or its strategic intent

As a natural complement, it would follow that any state-event possibility could also be formulated as a model defined over essentially the same set of dimensions as a script. Such would be referred to as a *scenario*. The difference between a script and scenario is that, in the latter, our organization is not the author of the actions but rather their target. That is, the locus of strategic initiative would now rest with a competitor organization or some exogenous agency.

Implicit in the concept of a script is that any strategic plan --defining an initiative to be taken by the organization in aggregate-- will entail certain tactical and operational derivatives. This, in effect, is the implication of the several *actions* of which any strategic initiative is comprised. For any action element specifies an aspect of the strategic plan that will fall to a particular organizational unit for execution. In this sense then, a single strategic plan may subsume a perhaps quite large number of tactical plans (or scripts), each specifying the way in which some middle-echelon unit of the organization proposes to carry out the responsibilities it has been assigned as an adjuct to the aggregate initiative. This same dependency would also apply to the matter of tactical and operational plans. For it's usually appropriate to think of a middle-echelon organizational unit as subsuming two or more lower-order or line level units (as, for example, a division of a corporation might be comprised of a collection of departments, or an army corps encompass two or more divisions, etc.). As such, any tactical plan may dictate the development of a multiplicity of derivative operational level scripts, with each operational plan indicating how a particular line-level unit intends to carry out any aspect of the tactical plan for which it is responsible.

Hence the general tendency for planning constructs to mirror the hierarchical configuration of organizations, i.e.:

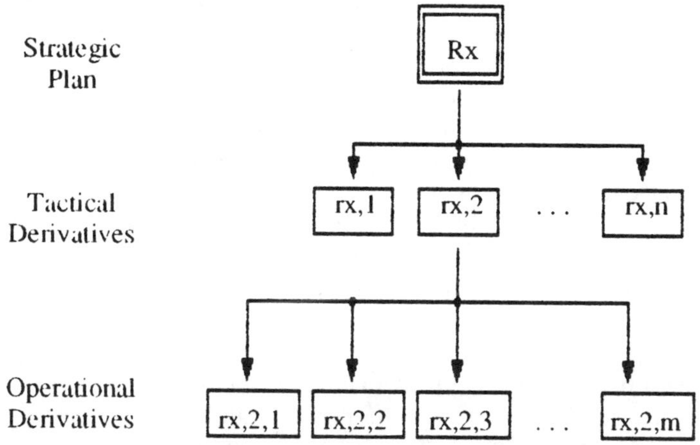

Hence also the tendency towards the essentially *geometric* increase in tactical and operational planning requirements that would follow from the generation of any new strategic plan.

However, when the technician talks about planning structures, it's usually a vector-based construct that he has in mind. That is, a strategic planning structure would be defined as follows:

$$(E1, E2 \ldots Em) \rightarrow [R]t = (R1, R2 \ldots Rm),$$

where the various E's are projected state-event alternatives and [R]t is the collectivity of the strategic response options (scripts) that are in place at some point in time (t). And this brings us back to the point where we began this section. For again, what will determine the elaborateness of any strategic planning structure --the number and diversity of the members in [R]t-- will be the number and diversity of the state-event possibilities or contextual influences to which it is exposed. But by way of a refinement to the appreciation of context under which we've been operating thus far, it's now useful to consider that, to a certain extent, the degree of contextual complexity to which an organization is subject may not be entirely a matter of exogenous determination. This is true, certainly, for any given context, as per our discussions of the different environmental and competitive ideal-types undertaken in the previous chapter.

But what's also true is that the set of contextual influences to which an organization is subject may also be conditioned by the number and diversity of the different contexts in which it seeks to maintain a presence . . . i.e., as a function of the degree of geographic and/or functional diversification. In some instances, the degree of diversification an organization exhibits may be dictated by matters largely outside its immediate control. For example, the range of adversarial and territorial situations with which a country's armed forces may find themselves concerned will ultimately be determined by what their political masters perceive to be within the reaches of the sphere of national interests. But in other cases, the contextual complexity with which an organization is confronted may, to a great extent, be a product of volitional decisions, and so of endogenous origin (self-inflicted, as it were). The most obvious example of this would be those large-scale, extensively-diversified firms that have emerged over the last two decades. Such may be exposed to an extraordinary profusion of both environmental and competitive state-event possibilities as a consequence of factors such as these:

a) They are most likely to be multinational (extensively geographically as well as functionally diversified), and so dependent to a considerable extent on the caprices of international trade, host nations' socio-political whims and perhaps at times hostage to grand geo-political ploys (as with those American firms that had a presence in Libya);

b) They may have some considerable portion of their income derived from programs that are either directly or indirectly within the province of governments, and so be subject to changes of fortune as a consequence of altered political preferences and priorities;

c) They will probably have a significant presence in *high-tech* or other essentially speculative ventures, and so be extraordinarily sensitive to technological changes which, in certain areas, have sprung up full-blown virtually overnight;

d) Most often they will be constructed primarily as abstract accounting artifices or as investment *portfolios* rather than vehicles for production. This is because extensive diversification implies that the various lines-of-business being pursued are so diverse from one another as to pretty much obviate any opportunities to realize economic *synergy* via sharing of assets or skills, etc. And because their rationale is primarily fiscal rather than functional, their prospects may be very sensitive to any alterations in macroeconomic policy provisions (interest rate structures, tax provisions, interpretations of anti-trust laws, etc.).

Indeed, the multinational conglomerrate, though widely touted by some as a prime example of business ingenuity, is a source of special concern to the technician.[1] For it may often be that the order of contextual challenge to which they have exposed themselves may be of such a magnitude as to demand a degree of strategic sophistication that cannot be obtained given the current state of-the-art. In fact, the more exotic of such enterprises may edge so perilously close to the outer limits of *manageability* as to be pretty much beyond even our farthest technical reach.

To see why this might be the case, consider the several different criteria used to adjudge the integrity of any strategic planning structure:

EXHAUSTIVENESS: To what extent does the set of state-event alternatives that have been defined answer for the full range of environmental and competitive situations to which the organization might be subject?

COMPLETENESS: Has there been a strategic plan or script defined for each of the state-event possibilities that has been defined? Has there then been developed an appropriate tactical and/or operational level plan for each of the action-elements entailed in the strategic script?

CONNECTEDNESS: Does each strategic plan have adequate provisions for the centralized coordination of --or for direct linkages among-- the various tactical level efforts it subsumes? Is the same true with respect to the operational units engaged in carrying out aspects of any tactical plan?

ROBUSTNESS: Does the planning structure contain procedural provisions that will allow the organization in aggregate or any unit to modify scripts as changes in exogenous circumstances dictate . . . in effective real-time, if necessary?

Finally, there is the most critical of the criteria for assessing the quality of any planning structure, this being the degree of strategic READINESS it promises. For readiness would encompass all four of the criteria just noted above, and then add this additional equivocation: To what extent have each of the strategic plans been *invested* with the assets/resources that would allow for their timely execution. It's this fifth criteria that is the crucial point of difference between being ready in concept and being ready in fact.

And now that the issue of readiness has finally been broached, we can move to consider the several different strategic planning/positioning approaches that contemporary organizations might follow in its pursuit.

2.2 Readiness Orientations and Strategic Management Modalities

When viewed as a technical criterion, *readiness* is intended to reflect the extent to which an organization is prepared to mount an effective response --in the short-run-- to any situations with which it is confronted. Our concern here is with strategic-level readiness, but the criterion could apply with equal authority to tactical or operational activities. But when it is strategic readiness that's of concern, the concept might be extended to refer to the basic orientation of an organization towards the world outside itself. And in this respect, there are four positioning postures that can be defined:

PROACTIVE: Attempting to force contextual situations to conform to an organization's own interests, or prevent the occurrence of any adverse state-events, either of which are avenues towards effective certainty;

CORRELATIVE: Gearing an organization to be able to effect a timely accomodation to the singularly most probable of projected contextual situations;

PREADAPTIVE: Preparing the organization to deal with the possible, or with some range of state-event alternatives taken to have some positive likelihood of occurrence;

REACTIVE: Standing ready to cope with the improbable via exception-handling facilities to be arrayed against any essentially unanticipated state-events that might occur.

It may be clear that the election of one or another of the above orientations would be dominantly determined by contextual considerations, as per this ammended version of the proposition with which we began this chapter:

> The more complex the context, the greater the number and diversity of the state-event possibilities with which an organization might be confronted during any period, and the greater the likelihood of being faced with a state-event it failed to anticipate.

But to be even more precise, it can be argued that each of the several generic contextual referents with which we closed the previous chapter --State determinacy, dominancy, stochasticity and indeterminacy-- would tend to recommend a different readiness orientation, and that each of the four orientations or positioning postured just defined would for its part tend to be best served by a very different approach to strategic planning/positioning. Hence the associations between contextual situations, strategic planning modalities and readiness orientations that are shown in **Exhibit 2.1.**

In the remaining pages of this chapter, we'll work through the rudiments of each of these four basic approaches to strategic management technology. But of the four, the two simplest --the Prescriptive/Goal-Driven and Sequential/Extrapolative platforms-- have pretty well monopolized the attention of both practitioners and academics. That is, the vast majority of the literature dealing with strategic management will in fact be focussed on one or another of these two approaches. And not unexpectedly, the vast majority of the technical instruments designed to support strategic planning will in fact have been designed to be used only in the confines of one or the other of these two simplest modalities. From the perspective of the serious technician, this continuing preoccupation with these two lower-order modalities is a matter of some concern. For there is much to suggest that more and more real-world organizations are now being forced to operate in contexts carrying a level of complexity that neither the Prescriptive nor Sequential approaches can accomodate. And here may be a prime cause for the apparent increase in instances of strategic-level error that punctuate our times.

Here also is the primary cause for the increasing interest in what might be gained by the transition to a proper contingency planning or adaptive management platform. But for the most part, discussions of these approaches have confined themselves almost exclusively to rhetorical rather than technical matters. As a result, there is very little in the way of suggestion as to just how an organization might go about actually effecting a preadaptive or reactive posture even if it were persuaded to do so. Thus, because of both their greater pertinence and their general unfamiliarity, our focus will be on the procedural and instrumental provisions required to implement a Contingency-based or Adaptive strategic management orientation. Indeed, we shall see in the three chapters in the second part of this volume to a very detailed discussion of these matters. But before turning to a consideration of these two higher-order strategic management modalities, it's well to take a quick look at the practical reach and limits of their two simpler predecessors.

2.3 Prescriptive/Goal-Driven Strategic Planning

Recall that state-determinacy was defined in the previous chapter to imply effective certainty as to the environmental and competitive states an organization can expect to face in the forseeable future. Recall also that there

EXHIBIT 2.1 :
Organizational Contexts, Readiness Orientations and Alternative Strategic Management Platforms

	Contextual Predicates	Readiness Orientation	Positioning Platforms
State Determinacy	Organizational Autonomy and Dominance Steady-State context (a placid environment and no direct competitors)	Proactive (certain)	Prescriptive (Goal-Driven Planning)
State Dominancy	Evolutionary environmental Constrained/Regulated competition	Correlative (probable)	Sequential/ Extrapolative (linear long-range planning)
State Stochasticity	Potential for equifinal environmental changes Extensive (weakly constrained) competition	Preadaptive (possible)	Contingency Planning
State Indeterminacy	Tendency towards a *turbulent* environment Prospect of predatory competitive threats	Reactive (improbable)	Adaptive Planning (for emergency and crisis management)

were really only two conditions under which such a situation might occur:

1) Residency in the simplest of all possible contextual contexts, the special case of state-determinacy we earlier referred to as a steady-state context. As suggested earlier, a tendency towards a steady-state condition would arise from a coupling of an essentially Placid environment (given its rooting in an essentially stationary-state dynamic) with the absence of any serious, direct competitors in a field (as with a legislated monopoly or the only barber shop in town).

2) The organization itself is both essentially dominant among some set of competitors --i.e., constitutes a de-facto monopoly-- and effectively autonomous with respect to environmental influences (or it may be that environmental constraints are naturally either absent or weak, as in the case of business firms operating in the confines of a basically laissez-faire economic system).

Either can allow legitimate recourse to the simplest of the strategic planning/positioning platforms, the Prescriptive modality.

For what the first of the above conditions implies is this: Any changes in state-level contextual properties that occur will expectedly be a consequence of initiatives taken by the organization itself, this because a steady-state context will ipso-facto preclude the prospect of their arising as a consequence of initiatives taken by outside agencies. And what the latter condition suggests is that, for lack of any effective sources of opposition, an organization can expect to have the future be pretty much what it wants it to be. In short, both of the above conditions pose the prospect of an organization being able to author its own context.

A prescriptive approach is thus appropriate whenever contextual causality may be said to rest with an organization itself. For typically, a prescriptive planning process is focussed on the postulation of some future state whose properties are determined largely as a product of higher-management's own aspirations or desires. This may be said to constitute a goal-state (or $S^{\wedge}$). As such, the general implications of any prescriptive planning construct can become intelligible in terms of the following simple expression:

$$Ax \rightarrow (Si)t \Rightarrow (S^{\wedge})t{+}n,$$

where Ax is some proactive strategic initiative intended to effect the transformation from an ostensibly less favorable current contextual state or (Si)t to the desired or goal-state prior to some period (t+n), this marking the planning horizon or the limits of the plannning interval. As the label suggests, any proactive initiative will have the aim of influencing exogenous conditions in such a way as to further the organization's interests, e.g.: A commercial enterprise may work to cause a favorable change in the tax code; a government may take steps aimed at displacing the political leadership in some foreign country with a more sympathetic set of functionaries, or undertake some effort intended to preempt the transfer of power to a less sympathetic political party.

It's thus important to note that, for the truly dominant or autonomous organization, strategic planning is more of a luxury than a necessity. That is, to the extent that such an organization does any strategic planning at all, it will be largely at its own volition rather than imposed as a context-related requirement. As such, the heart of the technical challenge associated with prescriptive planning is centered on the matter of the quality of the goal-set (and hence the desired contextual state conditions) that an organization's higher-management defines. And of all the technical challenges that might arise anywhere within the confines of strategic planning/positioning processes, the task of refining management-authored goal-sets is the task for which there is currently the greatest level of technical support. This support runs the gamut from relatively primitive deterministic Goal-Programming schemes (most of which are just simple computational variants on certain generic linear programming provisions) all the way to the most advanced multicriteria/multiobjective decision aids such as those decision *structuring* techniques mentioned in the previous chapter: Interpretive Structured Programming; Analytic Hierarchy Processing, etc.

The two reasons why there is so much in the way of technical support in the management science instrumental repertoire for prescriptive planning exercises is clear enough. First, instruments to support such exercises are generally the easiest for us to design and develop. For goal-driven planning exercises have the wonderful advantage of focussing on endogenous vs. exogenous factors . . . on managerial aspirations as opposed to the possible strategic intents and purposes of other organizations or agencies. The former are, by definition, subject to being resolved definitively, either as a matter of executive consensus or by fiat following from the predilections of the senior member of the managerial hierarchy. The technician's role in a prescriptive planning exercise may then be restricted largely to the selection and operation of tools designed to guide one or more higher-management authorities towards some more or less *deterministic* comprehension of where their organization's --or perhaps merely their own-- best interests lie. In signal contrast, when the locus of contextual causality is taken to rest outside an organization, there is always the prospect of having to contend with contextual state stochasticity or worse. And this is a prospect that few management scientists or operations researchers would wish upon themselves, not when they are allowed the luxury of confining their attentions to endogenous factors instead.

The second reason why we have so much in the way of instrumental support for prescriptive planning is mainly of cultural significance. Particularly, the prescriptive planning approach has the greatest intrinsic appeal for practicing executives, precisely because it gives center stage to their aspirations. Moreover, it is the planning/positioning approach most consistent with what still remains the most popular basis for organizational management, some sort of management-by-objectives scheme. For under such a scheme, it falls to higher management to articulate a set of high-level goals towards which the enterprise in aggregate will be oriented during the coming period, such constituting a strategic choice. These goals then serve as the referents for the assignment of objectives to all lower-order units of the enterprise. Each lower-order unit --qua Profit Center, or whatever convention may apply-- will be required to commit to a set of objectives that are in some way responsive to the goals established by superior units. Lower-order managers will thus have their performance adjudged by an after-the-fact (e.g., quarterly; year's end) audit of the extent to which they met the objectives assigned them. The distinction in terminology posed here is deliberate. For what we'll often find in practice is that the *goals* devised by an organization's highest-level managers will be rather more imprecise than the *objectives* that they will accept from their subordinates. The result will be something of an imbalance in accountability. For whereas objectives carry with them definite performance requirements for which a lower-level manager agrees to be responsible, aggregate organizational goals may be sufficiently vague so as to allow for a great deal of latitiude when it comes time to adjudge the quality of higher-management's performance.

The key weakness of the management-by-objectives approach has long been recognized. For should reality depart to any extent from the assumptive conditions under which goals and objectives were set, then either or both must ultimately prove to have been either suboptimal (less ambitious than they should have been) or infeasible (incapable of being obtained under the current conditions). Moreover, under the period-end performance audits characteristic of the traditional management-by-objectives scheme, this may not become apparent until after it's too late to do anything about it. But there is a question as to what we might do about it even if changes in conditions are recognized earlier. For the whole purpose of management-by-objectives is to establish some sort of *contract* between higher and lower-order management, such that the latter know what is expected of them over some extensive period of time. Any pragmatic value this scheme has is thus intimately tied to the constancy of goals, and hence objectives, once they are set. Start changing organizational goals and demanding reformulation of objectives every time there is a change in contextual conditions, and management-by-objectives becomes a managerial approach entirely empty of both technical and pragmatic significance. In short, one cannot inject a *dynamic* quality into a management-by-objectives scheme without destroying it.

Despite this criticism, management-by-objectives remains by far the most popular way for higher management to stamp its will on lower-order organizational units, and a Prescriptive/Goal-driven planning construct remains by far the most popular medium for higher management to formulate and articulate its will in the first place. For it gives concrete technical expression to the natural desire of executives to think that their visions, desires and preferences count for something. Unfortunately however, it may well be that such don't really count for very much unless the organization they are serving is in fact dominant and autonomous . . . or simply so affluent that the prospect of strategic errors is simply not all that daunting.

For again, when an organization is dominant in its field, the burden of strategic sophistication shifts almost entirely to competitors. It is we who may walk, and they who must run. That is, competitors are required to evaluate each possible move they might make in light of the possible counter-action that might be taken by the dominant enterprise. Moreover, being the dependent parties, competitor organizations have the added problem of having to spend considerable time, energy and wit trying to predict what competitive initiatives the dominant organization might effect, and more time, energy and wit trying to decide what to do about them should they indeed occur. In short, while the focus of executives heading non-dominant enterprises must always be outward, the executives of the dominant enterprise are allowed the luxury of introspection, spending their time and energy and wit worrying about just what it is that they want from the world. For to repeat an earlier point, dominance carries the gift of being able to make the future conform pretty much to their own aspirations.

Autonomy has pretty much the same implication. For again, the autonomous organization is in the happy position of being able to pretty much author its own context. As such, the natural tendency is to view the strategic planning/positioning function mainly as an exercise in self-fulfilling prophecy, aimed at charting a course along an assumedly unimpeded trajectory to the ends that higher-management has envisioned.

But if such are the blessings of organizational dominance and autonomy, the main implication of their reduction is also clear: Goals will become increasingly gratuitous as higher-management predicates! That is, for executives of non-dominant or non-autonomous enterprise, worrying about what they want is ultimately both less productive and less relevant than worrying about what others might want for us . . . or, even more generally, worrying about what we're likely to get whether we want it or not. As such, elaborate, goal-driven planning based structures do not always imply managerial sophistication. Rather, when employed by organizations that are in fact subject to the vaguaries of the world outside or not the unquestioned champions of their field, they may merely represent an executive vanity for which reality will exact a price.

And here's where the matter of an organizations *affluence* may come into prominant play. For what affluence implies is the happy prospect that even the most sweeping of judgemental or computational errors may not have entirely irrevocable consequences. And knowing that there are limits to the harm that might come to us from any strategic error, there may also be limits on the care we take in making strategic choices. It is thus no accident that the concept of *satisficing* came to displace optimality as the guiding criteria for executive practice. For it has the effect of transforming suboptimality from something to be avoided to something that should occasion no shame (a shift of perspective that has generally been embraced with great enthusiasm by practitioners, and applauded as a triumph of *realism* over academic idealism by many management scholars as well). In short, satisficing was a concept made for the high-rolling, rich 1950's and 1960's, where affluence was not merely a vestigial myth. And what for a long time passed for the uniquely American virtue of bold decisiveness is now being seen by some as something different . . . a carelessness born of the belief that there could be no quandary from which our dollars could not safely extricate us, and no price that any folly might exact that could not be paid. Perhaps here is the key to the complaint that, as a group, American executives are often wont to spend more wit and energy in attempting to recover gracefully from errors than in attempting to avoid them in the first place.

The consequence of any decrease in affluence is then obvious enough: Any decision errors we make will be increasingly expensive . . . increasingly difficult to recover from without incurring some possibly irretrievable and very real (as opposed to merely *opportunity*) losses. What this means in tangible terms is that strategic errors can now be expected to cost people jobs that will not be replaced in some other firm or in some other market sector. Inalertness or ill-judgement may cause the loss of competitive advantages that may never be recaptured. Indeed, there is cause for questioning whether America's transit to a service society is a consciously-considered volitional initiative taken in light of the laws of Comparative Advantage, or merely the inevitable and unintended consequence of a generation of basic manufacturing opportunities that have been squandered. Moreover, under conditions of scarcity, errors in one sector have almost immediately adverse consequences for other sectors, such that issues of the *guns or butter* variety become increasingly urgent and increasingly different to resolve by way of casual compromise. That is, the effects of errors concatenate, eroding a society's resilience to the point where it is increasingly less able to accomodate any future errors, etc. The ultimate prospect then is all too familiar: A socio-economic system that in aggregate becomes analogous to the classic portrait of a firm in decline . . . forced to liquidate its capital assets or let its productive infrastructure become obsolete in order to cover current operating deficits.

If decreases in affluence have the effect of making strategic errors increasingly serious in absolute terms, any decrease in either organizational dominance or autonomy must have the compounding effect of making strategic level errors more likely. For as we earlier tried to make explicit, such would act to directly (and perhaps dramatically) increase the complexity of the contexts in which American organizations are resident, which would in turn make a prescriptive/goal-driven approach to strategic planning (and the management-by-objectives schemes they underlie) increasingly inappropriate. And there is of course some evidence suggesting that affluence, dominance and autonomy may be little more than memories for an increasing number of American enterprises in general, and most especially for business firms.[2] For here, the effects of scarcity appear in terms of the general decline in capital-labor ratios in many industries, and the tendency, again, for capital investments to be used in increasing measure to support operating expenditures (or cover deficits in variable costs) rather than to retool plants or construct new production facilities. From an even broader perspective, it is well to consider that an emphasis on tertiary industry --happily taken by some as a proud sign that the U. S. is leading the way into the post-industrial era-- is also a characteristic of underdeveloped economies.

Symptoms of the strictures on autonomy are also well apparent at the level of the firm. e.g.: The increasing obtrusion of the judiciary, such that more and more corporate decisions are in effect actually made by, or constrained by, the courts; the determinacy of public sentiment is perhaps currently most evident in the matter of demands for divestiture of interests in South Africa. But most dramatic are the consequences of the reduction in opportunities for dominance, for this has the effect of forcing more and more American firms into increasingly demanding competitive arenas. We've already mentioned some examples of this in the section dealing with competitive intensity in the previous chapter. AT&T was one. For thanks in part to mandated divestiture, this firm was thrust in one fell swoop from the serenity and security of monopolistic privilege into the volatile, even predatory domain of *predatory* high-tech competition. Without question, the as yet somewhat disappointing performance of AT&T following its rude removal from the monopolistic nest is eloquent testimony to the escalation of raw managerial challenge such a shift entails. An equally dramatic transit was forced on the airline and banking industries following deregulation. The spate of bankruptcies, employee deprivations and looming dissolutions are again tangible evidence of the acceleration of managerial demands implied in a transit from restricted to all-out competition, and also evidence of many managements' inability to meet them quickly enough or fully enough. The new wave of mergers and acquisitions in the airline industry (which of course poses the prospect of a resounding defeat for the decentralization of market power that deregulation was supposed to promote) may perhaps best be understood as an attempt by airline managements to restore the industry to the days where competitive analysis was focused on issues such as whether to serve passengers real orange juice or Tang with their breakfasts . . . i.e., to effect a retrogression from *extensive* to monopolistic competition.

A similar story may be told of the American automobile industry. For until the Arab oil embargo, domestic US automobile producers obeyed a kind of unwritten law that competitive interchanges were to be restricted to merely *tactical* initiatives and counter-moves (minor alterations in prevailing price/quality parameters). But when the Japanese entered the market with products representing true *qualitative* differentiation --and with radical (vs. merely incremental) pricing structures-- the effect was to almost overnight force domestic managements to exercise *strategic* wits that had long been dormant. But because of the failure to take proper strategic initiatives a decade ago, the strategic choices now available may not be all that many. Hence what some perceive to be the relatively pedestrian nature of American strategic counteractions: lobbying for protectionist legislation; putting domestic labels on Japanese products; attempting to co-opt foreign competition through joint-ventures; forcing wage concessions from labor, etc.[3]

Thus, the tendency for both practice and technical support to cluster around prescriptive planning provisions is a matter of great concern. For it may mean that practitioners and technicians alike have invested the greatest amount of faith and technical attention in what is not merely the simplest of the several strategic planning/positioning platforms, but increasingly the least relevant irrelevant as well.

2.4 Sequential State and Cybernetic Managerial Provisions

With this second of the four strategic planning/positioning platforms, the focus begins to turn outward. For we are now concerned with organizations that are neither dominant and autonomous, such that their welfare will be determined in some measure as a function of how well they are able to accomodate themselves to exogenous properties. As such, the strategic management challenge now becomes dualistic, centered on the attempt to arrive at a reasoned compromise between often at least partially incompatible sets of predicates:

- higher-management's aspirations for the enterprise . . . their ideas as to what the organization should be striving to become over some interval.
- some idea of the array of environmental and competitive constraints that might emerge over the course of the planning interval.

As such, the strategic management challenge now is to try to strike a best resolution of the tension between the *ideal* and the *feasible*. Strategic management is thus no longer restricted simply to goal-formulation or decisions as to where an organization's best interests lie, but rather with decisions about the best that an organization can reasonably hope to do in light of the contextual conditions. Something of this sort is what most practitioners and academics alike have in mind when they talk about long-range planning.[4] The technical prerequisite to long-range planning is some sort of long-range forecasting facility aimed at getting some concept of the sorts of changes in contextual properties the organization is likely to see taking place. But as the *extrapolative* qualifier suggests, the changes that this second planning/positioning platform can comprehend must be of a relatively moderate, regular nature. Hence the assertion that the extrapolative modality is appropriate only for organizations resident in a context (or contexts) characterized by a tendency towards state-dominancy.

So far as the competitive dimension of context is concerned, state-dominancy was suggested to be a consequence of a tendency for organizations to engage in exchanges comprehensible as instances of constrained competition. In such a case, recall, the locus of confrontation tends to be more at the tactical than the strategic level, with radical competitive initiatives -- those calling for a strategic response-- being highly improbable. Changes of strategic significance are not ruled out. But, as a practical matter, they will tend to be taken more leisurely than precipitously, and be more predictable than capricious in nature, perhaps being built up to gradually along a natural *trend* line. This might allow legitimate access to some sort of a statistical forecasting technique, such that the point at which a state-level change could occur might be determined by extrapolating historical patterns or rates of change. For example, intelligence analysts may be looking at data pertinent to some nation's progress in military technology . . . the rapidity with which it progressed from the development of crude small arms towards machine or automatic weapons and from there to reasonably sophisticated mobile weapons platforms, etc. Given ancillary intelligence about educational emphases for scientists and engineers and the apparent priorities of items in the national research agenda, etc., a projection might then be attempted that would indicate a most probable time when the nation might accede to a nuclear weapons capability, and so constitute a qualitatively different order of threat than were it still only a conventional power. In much the same way, a commercial firm will typically give advance notice as to its intention to enter a new market (such representing a state-level change for the firms already operating there), if only to allow it to interest potential investors in providing the financial wherewithal for the expansion. Firms may also provide an early alert about prospective product innovations, this to deter potential customers from getting locked-in with other vendors, etc.

It is this tendency towards gradualistic, more or less predictable changes in competitve conditions that argues for the appropriateness of extrapolation as a basis for long-range forecasting . . . for assuming that future competitive states in a market or industry will be some calculable function of the past. And much the same thing would hold so far as the environmental dimension of context. For again, state-dominancy implies residency in an environment characterized by an evolutionary dynamic, such that changes in state-level properties will most often be comprehensible as the end results of a concatenation of incremental changes . . . e.g., the change in general public sentiment with respect to cigarette smoking. And in some cases, there may exist a normative model that would allow state-changes to become comprehensible in terms of a passage through a series of generalized *stages*. An example might be one of the taxonomies that attempts to capture the typical *stages* in the life-cycle of a new product . . . e.g., from initially sparse demand through accelerated demand through saturation following the emergence of competitors and from there back to sparsity again. Or there are the various theoretical models prescribing a series of protypical state-changes for conflict situations, most postulating a concatenative increase in tension that builds from an initial condition of mild resentment, goes through veiled animosity and may, if left unchecked, ultimate in unlimited warfare. Such models may serve as ready-made sub-scenarios for the generation of extrapolative constructs.

In sum then, what state-dominancy implies is the existence of a more or less regular evolutionary or concatenative dynamic, such that state-changes will occur both smoothly and along essentially predictable lines. And what this then implies is the opportunity for planners to converge on some set of significantly most-probable contextual properties for any future period . . . i.e., one pair of environmental and competitive *states* that are expected to prevail during each segment of the planning horizon. We would thus get a projection sequence appearing as a neatly linear progression of state-transformations:

$$P^{\wedge}(Si)t+1 \Rightarrow P^{\wedge}(Sj)t+2 \Rightarrow P^{\wedge}(Sk)t+3 \Rightarrow \ldots \Rightarrow P^{\wedge}(Sz)t+n.$$

In the above expression, the symbol $P^{\wedge}$ indicates a maximum-likelihood state alternative, with the projection interval running from the immediately next period (t+1) to some limiting or horizonal period (t+1). As such, the formulation suggests that state (Si) is anticipated to pertain during the first period or (t+1), with Si then expected to be transformed (or yield to) state Sj during the next period; Sj, will in its turn, then be expected to be succeeded by state Sk at the point of transition between periods t+2 and t+3, etc. Finally, the sequence of linear state-transformations is expected to conclude with state Sz expected to prevail during the horizonal period (t+n).

But to appreciate the implications of this sort of progression so far as strategic *readiness* requirements are concerned, it's best to move to a somewhat lower level of abstraction. For there was the earlier argument that the transition from one contextual state to another will follow from any change in environmental or competitive state-level properties. And for their part, such changes were earlier argued to result from the emergence of some state-event. For illustrative purposes, we might consider merely the environmental dimension, as per the following now familiar notation:

(Ni => Nj) → Si => Sj : a change in environmental states from Ni to Nj) is sufficient to trigger a change in contextual state from Si to Sj.

Ex → (Ni => Nj) :any state-event (Ex) is sufficient to trigger a change in environmental state.

Ex → Rx : any state-event is an occasion for a strategic-level adjustment to prevailing positioning committments, which as a practical matter means that any Ex dictates the formulation of a new strategic plan or some Rx.

In this sense then, what state-dominancy reduces to is the prospect of a linear sequence of state-events, which in turn poses the requirement for what we shall refer to as a sequential-state strategic planning structure. The general formulation for such a structure is as follows:

R1 | E1 => R2 | E2 => . . . => Rn | En,

which when disaggregated would involve a set of associations such as these:

Period t1 : E1 → (N0 => N1) → (R0 => R1)
t2 : E2 → (N1 => N2) → (R1 => R2)
etc.
tn : En → (Ny => Nz) → (Ry => Rz)

To provide a more concrete idea of what a sequential-state strategic planning structure might involve, **Exhibit 2.2** takes quick look at the strategic planning implications for tobacco companies that might follow from the progressive changes in social sentiment against smoking.

Thus, for any particular context --some specific geographic area or product-market sector-- a sequential-state strategic planning structure thus entails a sequence of pre-defined strategic response initiatives, each of which is designed to be brought into play following a particular prospective state-event. An organization having a presence in just one context (say a specialized firm) would then have only one sequence of strategic plans it needs to formulate, while a diversified enterprise might have several sequential-state structures it needs to define. In either case, the overall readiness-related ambition is thus to allow for longitudinal correlation between organizational

EXHIBIT 2.2 : Illustration of a sequential-State Strategic Planning Structure

	Environmental Consequences	Strategic Response Options
	N0 : indifference or even a romantic attitude towards cigarette smoking	
E1 : initial concerns expressed by public health officials as to a link between smoking and cancer	N1 : some initial public awareness of the threat from cigarette smoking	R1 : attempt to cast doubt on adverse research results; increase level of advertising
E2 : increase in data leads to shift from possibility to certainty as to hazards associated with smoking	N2 : some decrease in demand/emergence of collective antismoking movements	R2 : re-orient ads to suggest smoking as a behavior of healthy, active and attractive people; take some initial steps re: defensive diversification
E3 : first instance of restrictive legislation, i.e., the ban on TV advertising	N3 : acceleration of adverse public opinion & strength of collective opposition	R3 : implement new merchandizing emphases (more magazine ads and indirect promotion via sponsorship of athletic events; accelerate level of diversification
	etc.	
Em : significant legal restrictions on cigarette smoking; major penalties re: insurance rates, job prospects, etc.	Nm : completion of shift towards a significantly critical view of smoking; smokers now a belabored and increasingly insignificant sub-population	Rm : complete the retirement from the domestic cigarette market in favor of other product lines or international targets for tobacco products

posture and contextual conditions.[5] But during any period for any given context, given that there is only one state-event that has any significant likelihood of occurrence, the interests of readiness may be served by just a single strategic plan under which the organization will operate. And once that singular strategic plan has been formulated and invested, the main working focus of higher-management attention naturally shifts to how the organization is to adapt itself to thematic-level changes in contextual properties and/or respond to the various tactical threats that competitors might author within some specific context during some particular period.

This may have the important technical consequence of allowing intra-period organizational positioning to become subject to discipline via some sort of cybernetic managerial facilities. We need go into very little detail about these here, as such have been widely discussed for two decades and more.[6]

What distinguishes a cybernetic approach to organizational management is the focus on two basic control-oriented functions:

1) The prevention (or preemption) of deviations from some desired situation;

2) Rapid correction and/or quick dampening of any deviations that do occur.

Within the confines of the Sequential/Extrapolative platform, we might take the *desired situation* to be represented by the maximum-likelihood state for some period, which we'll designate as S*.

This S*, in its turn, will have been defined over what were determined to be the maximum-likelihood environmental and competitive substates the organization expects to encounter for period-t with respect to some particular domain. If the organization is neither geographically nor functionally diversified, then it will have a presence in only one domain. Otherwise, there would be defined some S* for each of the regions or product-market sectors in which it has a presence.

Any S* would then emerge at the conjunction of the statistically most probable enviromental (Ni) and competitive (Mi) substates drawn from among a population of possibilities arrayed as a matrix:

	P(M1)	P(M2)	...	P(Mn)
P(N1)	P'(S1,1)	P'(S1,2)	...	P'(S1,n)
P(N2)	P'(S2,1)	P'(S2,2)	...	P'(S2,n)
		etc.		
P(Nm)	P'(Sm,1)	P'(Sm,2)	...	P'(Sm,n)

where :

P'(Si,j) = P(Ni) x P(Mj)

Given this array, S* would become that particular S(i,j) having the highest conditional probability of occurence, or: S* = P^(Ni)t + P^(Mj)t.

But however its arrived at, S* will represent the particular contextal state the organization expects to occur, and hence that state it is prepared to deal with via the provisions of some singular strategic plan. That is, again, given that there is one and only one contextual state given any significant likelihood of occurrence for any domain over any interval, the organization need have defined and invested only one strategic plan in the interests of readiness. Hence the following formulation:

$$S^* \rightarrow R^* \supset [r1, r2 \ldots rm],$$

with R* being the strategic plan (and the set [r] its tactical derivatives) determined by higher-management authorities to be the best response posture with respect to the properties of S*.

It's thus in the organization's interests that S* persist throughout the period in question. For it's not really ready to deal with any other state. As a practical matter however, it may be suggested that the main concern is that S* not give way to some inferior or more threatening state. The central higher-management concern may then be said to be the preservation of the expected state or S*, for this is the prerequisite for the continuation of a satisfactory level of strategic readiness. And this is exactly the end that cybernetic facilities can support, as per **Exhibit 2.3**.

The first of such, the monitoring provision, would have organizational authorities remaining alert for anything that might signal the prospect of S* being displaced by some new state, or the likelihood of a transformation from S* to some Sk (via indications of the emergence of some Nj = Ni or Mj = Mi). Given such, the organization would be expected to undertake the formulation of a corrective initiative expected to have some chance of being able to prevent Sk from occurring. Should it be too late to prevent the emergence of Sk, then there would be an attempt to define a restorative initiative intended to effect the re-emergence of S* (or, at the least, act to reinstate as many of S*'s properties as possible). Some sort of feedback facilities would be put in place to allow empirical assessment of the effectiveness of any such initiatives (and perhaps suggest bases for their *modification* in order to increase their level of effectiveness). But should neither a corrective nor restorative initiative prove sufficient to avert the emergence of Sk, then it would be necessary to decide on some sort of modification to the organization's prevailing strategic posture, with the ambition being to realize the minimal modification consistent with the postulated or actual changes.

What's obvious is that this same set of cybernetic facilities might generally be applied with equal authority in the confines of the Prescriptive/Goal-Driven platform. It's just that instead of being aimed at minimization of departures from an expected state (S*), it would be some goal-state (S^) that is to be sustained. That is, a cybernetic protocol might be an adjunct to either a

EXHIBIT 2.3: Provisions of a Typical Cybernetic-Based Planning Exercise

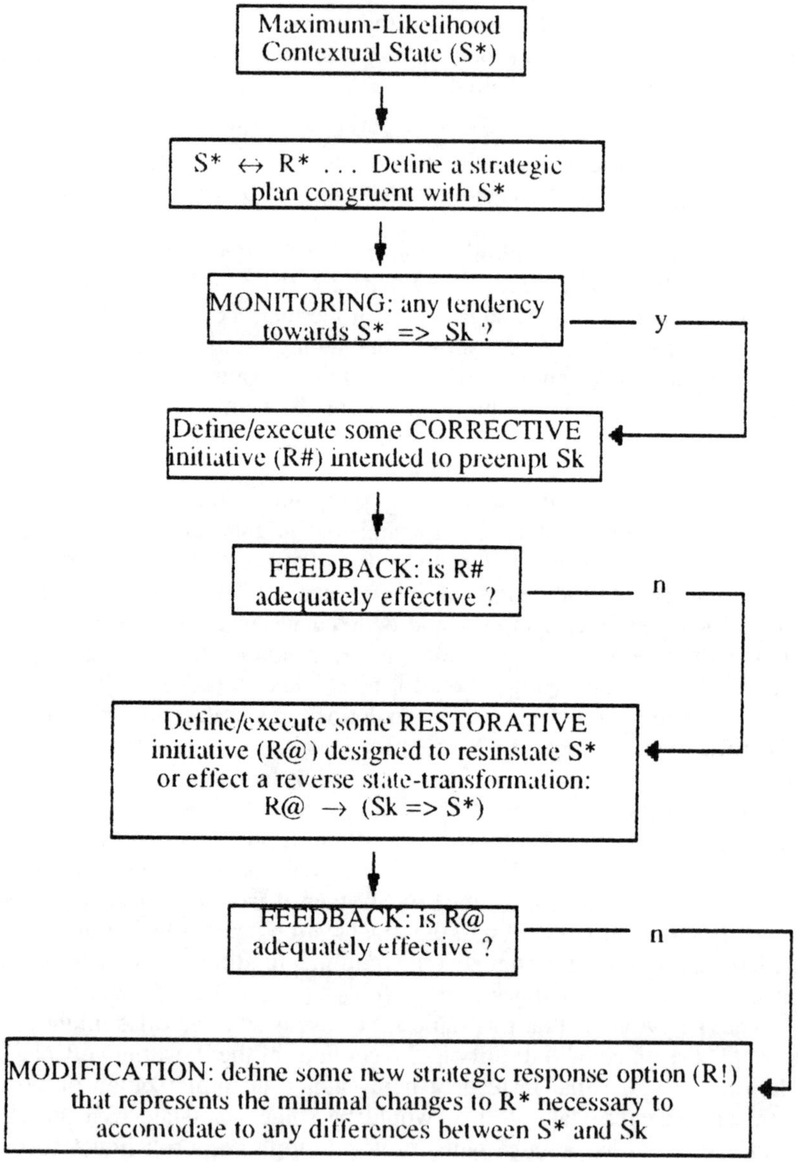

proactive or correlative approach to strategic readiness. But there would be an obvious point of difference in the orientation of cybernetic provisions for these two cases. For when employed as a complement to a Prescriptive platform, it is mainly the behavior of external exogenous factors or contextual agencies that is to be controlled, this in the attempt to discourage anything that might frustrate or defeat an organization's attempt to realize its desired goal-state. That is, the corrective and restorative provisions are more likely to be employed in prescriptive planning situations, simply because the organizations for which the prescriptive approach is appropriate are more likely to have the power to influence the status or behavior of contextual factors. In contrast, organizations operating under the Sequential/Extrapolative platform will be expectedly neither dominant nor autonomous, and so be very limited in terms of the leverage they can exert on exogenous agencies. In such cases, it is more likely to be organizational properties and not contextual properties that will be the objects of correction or modification.

The usual cybernetic-based managerial scheme is thus intelligible as an attempt to exert after-the-fact (reactive) control over contextual and/or organizational attributes in order to stay somewhere in the neighborhood of an acceptable *interface* condition . . . some target relational situation between the organization and elements of the world outside. And in most cases, what this desired interface condition will amount to is an *equilibrium* position of some kind (e.g., minimization of deviations between what consumers are demanding and what the organization is supplying; minimization of any imbalance between an organization's own competitive capabilities and those of some adversary by way of *balance of forces*). Thus, it's both possible and useful to view cybernetic technology as a vehicle for exercising *tactical* control, or carrying out the equilibrium maintenance aspects of organizational positioning. In fact, cybernetic technical and procedural facilities, by their very nature, are likely to be much more appropriate when applied at the tactical rather than the strategic level. For as has been explained elsewhere, cybernetic-based systems generally tend to become increasingly inefficient with increases in the complexty of the processes against which they are turned, or the contexts in which they're embedded.[7]

But then the same thing must be said of the Sequential-state strategic planning/positioning approach itself. For by their very nature, the extrapolative projections on which it rests cannot contemplate environmental or competitive possibilities that are substantially different from anything seen in the past. Therefore, both the Sequential-state and cybernetic schemes are likely to be of most service when the positioning challenge facing an organization is centered on the requirement to make a succession of leisurely and incremental (vs. precipitous and dramatic) adjustments. Both are then best employed by organizations resident in a context that pretty much excludes the possibility of radical, rapid contextual changes. Any tendency towards such would thus be taken as an occasion for higher-management to consider abandoning the extrapolative platform in favor of the first of the two more sophisticated strategic planning/position approaches.

2.5 A Brief on Contingency and Adaptive Strategic Management

The first place we'd want to look is at contingency-based strategic planning/positioning. Our exploration of this approach will here be very brief. For we shall be devoting the next chapter entirely to a detailed technical discussion of state-of-the-art contingency planning structures and practices. So here it is perhaps enough merely to try to mount a general defense of the assertion that a contingency approach is the most appropriate platform for coping with state-stochasticity, this the next step beyond state-dominancy in terms of contextual challenge. Again, what state-stochasticity implies is the prospect of there being two or more state-event possibilities that might arise within any period, this a consequence of either or both of the following:

- an organization being embedded in an environment tending towards an equifinal dynamic and so having a potential for modular (or revolutionary) vs. merely evolutionary change.
- an organization's being engaged in extensive vs. constrained competition, which implies having to be concerned about being confronted by competitor-authored threats of true *strategic* significance.

The classic example of an organizations operating in contexts likely to be visited by both of these sources of complexity are the firms constituting the high-fashion industry. For a key environmental factor is that very real but elusive matter of a collective consumer sense of what is or is not *in style*. In this sense, state-stochasticity extends to matters as diverse as what particular colors will be considered fashionable during the coming season, what skirt lengths will be considered chic and which dowdy, etc. Thus there is always the risk that a firm will elect to go with colors and configurations that will --seemingly spontaneously, as it were-- be condemned as unfashionable. To generalize then, environmental state-stochasticity --via an equifinal or revolutionary dynamic-- would reduce to the prospect of an organization being confronted by some multiplicity of state-transformation possibilities, or:

$$(Ni)t \Rightarrow P\,[Nj, Nk \ldots Nm]\,t+1,$$

where (Ni)t represents the set of basic environmental properties in force during the current period, with Nj, Nk, etc. being state-level alternatives assigned some probability of succeeding Ni during period t+1.

This tendency towards environmental state-stochasticity is then amplified on the competitive dimension. For here is a market that, as much as any, puts an extraordinary premium on *radical* initiatives . . . the development of designs that are deliberately dramatically different from those previously in favor and of such a basically *radical* nature so as to be unlikely to be duplicated by any other design house. Hence the natural emphasis on idiosyncratic inspiration --individual artistic license-- in pursuit of the innovative (which, in the hands of the less gifted, may mean merely an embrace of the outrageous). And what this translates into is the following:

$$(Mi)t \Rightarrow P\,[Mj, Mk \ldots Mn]\,t{+}1,$$

where (Mi)t is the prevailing competitive state with respect to some firm, and Mj, Mk, etc., are members of an array of possible successor states.

On the competitive dimension, state-stochasticity would stem not merely from the emphasis on innovation, but also from the opportunity for state-level changes in terms of basic structural attributes. For example, because the industry is one that allows for relatively free exit and entry (e.g., capital requirements are not overly onerous), the basic population of competitors is likely to be more fluid than stationary. Moreover, new classes (qualitatively disparate genre) of competitors may appear, an example being the specialty retailers --often organized as franchise operations-- that handle nothing but blue jeans, leather goods, etc.

The industry is also one that invites major changes in the dimensions on which firms might be engaged in direct competition, particularly as a consequence of the thrust towards vertical integration. For example, designers are increasingly moving into the production side (which means the extension of competition from product differentiation to price), while firms once content merely to manufacture designs created elsewhere are tending to equip themselves with an in-house design capability (which means that competition may now take place on both the price and product differentiation dimensions). This thrust towards vertical integration may also force firms into serious competition on yet a third dimension, advertising. For whereas marketing efforts may once have been confined to the individualized romancing of a few fashion magazine editors or department store buyers, there may now be a requirement to try to exert direct leverage on the mass market. And given the extraordinary importance of *image* as a consumer preference criterion, having the most engaging advertising campaign may be the surest route to the largest market share. And because new advertising campaigns can generally be brought on line more quickly than new products, the extension of competition to this dimension adds to the demand for alertness and responsiveness from higher-managements.

To sum up then, given any tendency towards contextual state-stochasticity, the interests of strategic readiness may best be served by an attempt to adopt a preadaptive orientation. For what this would involve is getting *ready*, in advance of the fact, for the state-event possibilities to which an organization considers itself potentially subject during some period. As such, the basic vehicle for effecting a preadaptive orientation would be a contingency planning construct of some kind, perhaps along the lines shown in **Exhibit 2.4**.

In light of earlier discussions of the pecularities of the strategic domain, there is the initial reliance on subjective (vs. simple statistical) projection technologies to support event-projection activities, and on judgement-driven *structuring* protocols to help discipline response-formulation efforts. These could then underlie a contingency planning construct of the following sort:

$$P[E]t \leftrightarrow U\hat{}[R]t.$$

The array P[E]t is the contingency event set, this taken to subsume some number of projected state-event alternatives, such that [E]t = (E1, E2 . . . Em). Each of the E's or contingency event referents is expected to have some positive probability of occurrence (via the operator P) during some period-t. The array U^[R]t is then a contingency planning set, the collection of strategic response options that the organization is prepared to execute --more or less immediately on demand-- during period-t: [R]t = (R1, R2 . . . Rm).

But as the tile of the exhibit suggests, the above represents a special type of contingency planning construct, a discrete-bipartite Model-based structure. The *bipartite* nature of the structure is indicated by the symbol $\leftrightarrow$, this dictating that there is a neat one-to-one correspondance (mapping) between a set of discrete event and response side referents. More specifically, the bipartite requirement is that any Ei $\in$ [E] will map directly to one and only one U^(Ri) $\in$ [R], with the U^ appendage indicating that Ri has been determined by higher-management authorities to be the maximal-utility *strategy* for dealing with Ei should it occur. Hence, with respect to the above construct, the implication is that E1 $\rightarrow$ R1, E2 $\rightarrow$ R2, etc. And it is a *model* base structure because of the earlier-noted convention directing that both state-event possibilities and strategic plans to be formulated as special types of discrete (integral) multidimensional models . . . as scenarios and scripts defined over specifications of the WHO, WHAT variety.

The condition under which a discrete-bipartite contingency planning structure can provide for strategic *readiness* is then clear-cut, this in terms of the criterion for a functional mapping:

> V = Ei $\in$ [E]t $\rightarrow$ Ri $\in$ [R]t . . . given that an actual event (V) maps directly to one of the state-event scenarios entered in [E]t, then the organization is in a position to mount a more or less immediate response via the appropriate strategic plan (script) in [R]t.

The aggregate probability of a functional mapping will depend on the extent to

EXHIBIT 2.4 : A Contingency Planning Construct as a Bipartite Model-Base Structure

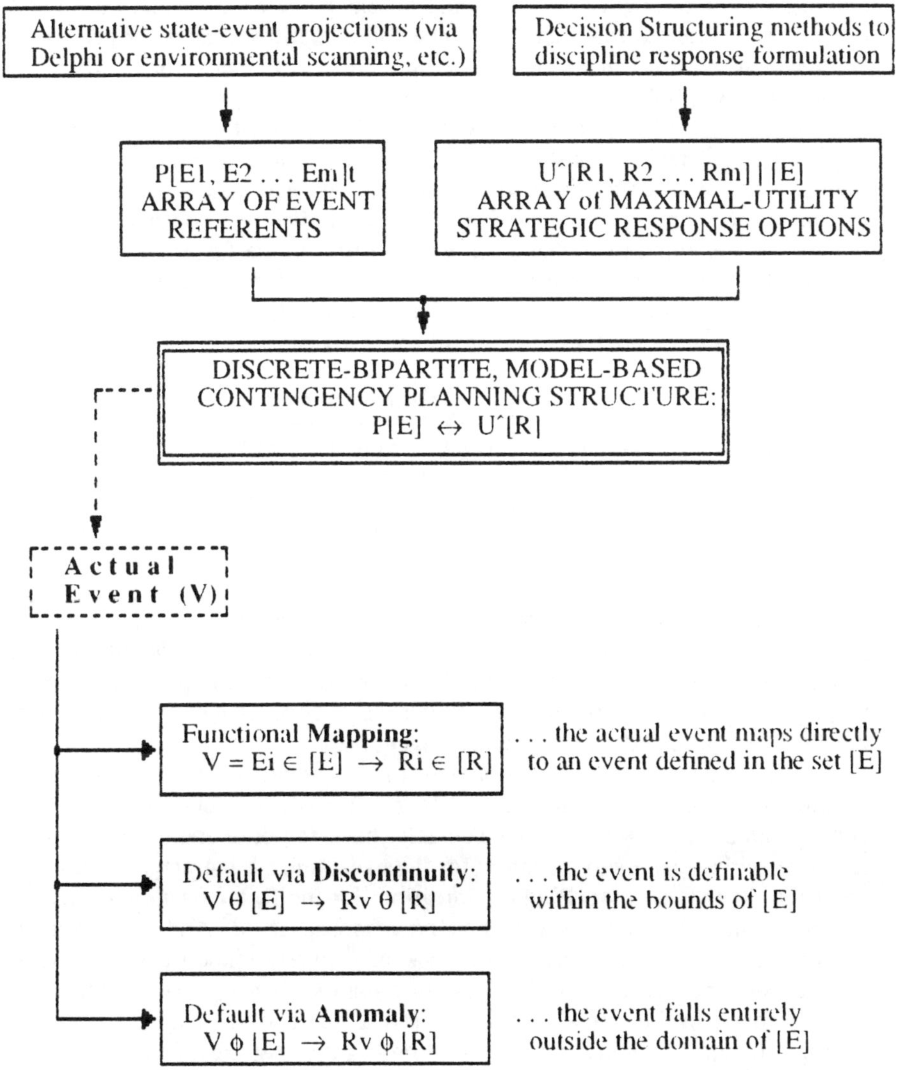

which the members of [E] can be presumed to *exhaust* the ostensible universe of state-events that might arise over the interval in question. To this extent then, it is critical to recall a key attribute of the two contextual predicates of state-stochasticity, an environment tending to exhibit equfinal characteristics and/or an arena of engagement allowing for extensive competition. For in both cases, it was asserted that there would be some legitimate basis for generating an adequate a-priori idea of the basic classes of state-events which an organization might be called upon to confront.

Though we'll have more to say about this later, the pragmatic or operative implication of state-stochasticity is that there are only a limited number of logically possible alternatives that might be authored in the confines of an organizational context. By way of example, simplified and contrived though it may be, this is much the situation in which a firm in the fashion industry may find itself. For in terms of the two previously-mentioned dimensions of interest --hemlines and colors-- we might consider just nine basic qualitative outcome categories as pretty much exhausting all alternatives:

	Color Preferences		
Hemlines	Bold	Muted	Dark
High	E1	E2	E3
Mid-length	E4	E5	E6
Low	E7	E8	E9

Given such an array, an organization might attempt to obtain maximal strategic readiness by positioning itself to meet any of these nine alternatives. What this would entail is the formulation and investment of nine different strategic response options, the practical consequence of which would be the development of nine different product inventories.

As ludicrous as such an approach may appear, it does allow us to reintroduce a key argument: That to be *ready* in fact rather than merely in concept, an organization must have actually have acquired and sequestered the assets/resources necessary to allow for the execution of a strategic plan in the short-run. This is a compelling qualification, for the lack of a *timely* strategic response may often be equivalent to no response at all. And in reasonably volatile or competitive contexts, the lack of a timely response is no less an instance of strategic error than is the formulation of a flawed or ineffective strategic plan. In this sense, simplistic as it is, the above example points to a common quandary facing those attempting to pursue strategic readiness via a traditional contingency planning approach: The need to decide whether it's preferable to face the prospect of losses by failing to be ready for some event that occurs, or losses that might arise from the fact of having invested in assets that remain idle because the contingency against which they are addressed does not occur.

In general, the analytical burden presented by this quandary will be a function of the degree of state-stochasticity inherent in some organizational context. For the greater number/diversity of the contingencies to which an organization might be subject, the greater the magnitude of the asset/resource committments required to *invest* any degree of readiness. As such, the only route to an entirely satisfactory degree of strategic readiness is for the universe of state-event possibilities to be limited enough --and the organization sufficiently affluent-- to fully invest a strategic response option dedicated to each and every contingency. The corollary is then that any scarcity of available assets/resources relative to the richness of contextual event alternatives will pose some limits on the level of strategic readiness an organization can afford, and hence raise the requirement for a compromise of some sort. And the most obvious route towards a reasonable compromise is to be selective in terms of those contingencies for which an organization elects to get ready and those which, however reluctantly, it elects to ignore. At least four different ordering criteria are available:

- Probability, this reflecting expectations as to the likelihood of occurrence of any contingency;
- Threat Potential, this an attempt to assess the magnitude of the damage (costs, losses) to the organization's welfare that might follow from any contingency should it occur; Utility, an assessment of the advantages to the organization that might accrue from any contingency;
- Expected Value, a weighted, composite of assessments as to probability, threat potential and/or utility for each contingency (with threat potential definable as negative utility).

Given the somewhat sweeping and elusive nature of contingencies qua state-events, the attempt to assign numerical values to the above criteria would not generally be a mark of great technical sophistication. Rather, for reasons that will be made clear in a later chapter, assessments in the strategic management domain are generally better taken with respect to qualitative valuations, perhaps simple categoricals of the sort introduced during the discussion of the competitive matrix, e.g.:

P(Ei) >> P(Ej) : Ei is deemed significantly more likely to occur than Ej;
P(Ei) > P(Ej) : Ei is taken to be marginally more probable than Ej;
P(Ei) <> P(Ej) : Ei and Ej are assumed to be more or less equally likely to occur (equiprobable).

If these three crudely defined categoricals are insufficiently precise to allow for a proper ordering, intermediate categoricals might then be added (e.g., an allowance for an event to be strongly or weakly more likely than another).

Irrespective of the particular criterion employed however, the objective of a selection exercise would be the same: The attempt to extract some subset of highest-priority contingencies for which the organization can *afford* to be ready. The result is an abbreviated contingency planning structure that allows only for partial strategic readiness:

$$[E^*] \leftrightarrow [R^*], \quad \text{where } [E^*] \subset [E].$$

That is, [E*] now represents only some proportion of the putative universe of state-event possibilities [E].

The most obvious basis for setting the membership of [E*] would be this:

> Let [E*] be defined so as to include the n-most probable threatening members of [E] for which a set of strategic contingency plans [R*] could be *invested* that would not violate aggregate resource constraints.

The maximum membership in [E*] would then be determined by looking at how far organizational assets/resources could be spread in order to be ready to effect --in the short-run-- a strategic response to any member of [E*].[8]

The quality of any abbreviated contingency planning structure might then best be evaluated in terms of the extent to which the planners can be said to have moved into the neighborhood of an ostensible *optimum at the margin* between strategic readiness and resource requirements. For given the way things have been set up, this should also be the neighborhood of minimally feasible strategic risk. This is because the extent to which an organization is at risk is a function of the proportion of the universe of contingencies for which it is not ready. Were it again probability of occurrence with which we were concerned, then a rough assessment of risk may be had as follows:

$$\text{Risk} = f([E^*] \div [E]),$$
$$\text{or: Risk} = \sum \{P([E] - [E^*])\}.$$

The former would allow for a qualitative valuation for risk, this in terms of some categorical assessment of the degree of correspondance between the universal set [E] and the reduced subset [E*] . . . e.g., Strategic risk might be said to be only marginal when [E*] can be said to account for a substantial proportion of the population of [E]. Were some sort of numerical scaling in effect (which might simply mean assigning quantitative values to categoricals), then the second formulation would allow for more precision. For what it suggests is that a measure of strategic risk may be had by taking the sum of the probabilities of occurrence associated with those contingencies that the organization has elected to omit from active consideration.

However it's computed, the pragmatic import of any measure of strategic risk is some indication of the likelihood of a discrete-bipartite contingency planning construct failing to provide for a functional mapping, and so failing to provide for strategic readiness, via the following:

> Should there emerge some real-world event (V) that fails to map directly to any of the members of the contingency event set, then it follows that an appropriate strategic response cannot be found among the members of the standing contingency planning set.

A failure of this sort may occur for either of two reasons. First and most fundamentally, it might be a consequence of planners generating a universal contingency set [E] that was insufficiently diverse in terms of the range of state-event possibilities it included (it was not, in fact, universal enough). On the other hand, a failed mapping may be a consequence of budgetary constraints or asset/resource strictures forcing an organization to operate under an abbreviated structure. For it may well be that the actual event was one that had been included in the originally formulated universal set [E], but ommitted from the active contingency subset [E*].

But from a broader perspective, both of the above routes to a failed mapping may be expected to become increasingly likely with any increase in contextual complexity. For again, increases in contextual complexity become of pragmatic concern in terms of the expansion in the number/diversity of the state-events that reality might allow. And such an expansion, in its turn, would mean an enlargement of the set of contingencies over which any given quantum of organizational assets/resources would have to be allocated, and hence an increase in the expected magnitude of any shortfall between the universe of events for which an organization would like to be ready, and the subset of events for which it can afford to be ready. That is, one common consequence of increases in contextual complexity would be the need to go with increasingly abbreviated contingency planning structures. Such would be defined over subsets that include an increasingly smaller proportion of the universe of projected possibilities, such that there is a decline in [E*]/[E] ratios and an associated increase in the level of strategic risk they portend. But a second and equally compelling consequence is this: The greater the range and variety of the environmental and/or competitive events that might arise naturally within some organizational context, the greater the likelihood that any ostensible *universe* of contingencies that planners might define will fail to include all potentialities (i.e., be increasingly *inexhaustive*).

As a distinctly critical practical matter then, it can be argued that organizations that are forced, or have elected, to operate in increasingly complex contexts might well consider abandoning a traditional contingency planning platform in favor of some other alternative.

Of such, the least dramatic exchange would be to move towards a more *dynamic* approach to contingency planning. The rationale for a transit to a dynamic strategic planning/positioning platform is this:

> Given any degree of contextual intricacy and volatility, the other factor that may be said to determine the likelihood of a traditional contingency planning structure failing to include some actual event is the length of the planning/projection horizon ($t1 \rightarrow tn$) . . . with the first term being the time at which a contingency planning construct is defined and the latter fixing the end-point of the period over which it is to apply.

Conventional technical wisdom would then suggest that any increase in contextual volatility --which we may take to mean increasingly *severe* state-stochasticity-- ought to be offset by a shortening of the interval between successive iterations of the contingency planning process. For this would foreshorten the planning/projection horizon. And this, in its turn, should reduce the likelihood of a default due to the failure of a contingency planning construct to reflect changes in the flow of real-world circumstances.

Hence the advantage that might be gained from adding a dynamic aspect to strategic planning/positioning activities. One avenue towards such is obvious: An organization might elect to make a move towards a dynamic approach simply by reducing the period of time allowed to elapse between the previous and the next planning cycle. But were we to carry this approach towards its logical conclusion, we'd come upon the much more interesting prospect of contingency planning constructs being subjected to essentially continuous modification. And the best practical expression of what this might entail would be procedures of the sort associated with Indicator/Warning-Alert technology as practiced in the modern military sector.[9] What this involves is a more or less constant stream of *intelligence* inputs that can be used to trigger changes in assessment about the currently most likely or critical threats, which would in turn be used as a basis for making changes in the organization's prevailing positioning posture. But Indicator/Warning-Alert provisions are not widely known outside certain niches in the military sector, and even there are not fully operational. Nevertheless, they hold such significant promise that we'll be using Chapter 4 to suggest how they might be both formalized and generalized, this to provide a basis for an Intelligence-Driven/Dynamic strategic management protocol that might be employed by commercial or governmental as well as military enterprises.

The second alternative to traditional contingency planning/positioning is of a more radical nature, both practically and technically. This would involve the shift to an adaptive planning/positioning platform of some sort. And from what's been said previously, such a shift would be occasioned were contextual complexity deemed to have passed beyond state stochasticity and begun to approach the worst-case situation, state-indeterminacy. For again, state-indeterminacy is a consequence of a context allowing for environmental changes of a transumutative order and/or for the range of competitor-authored initiatives to extend all the way to the Predatory. Hence the significant likelihood of realities consistently tending to depart from projections. As such, any tendency towards contextual state-indeterminacy would argue that higher management authorities should expect to be unable to predict the full range of threat or opportunities to which their organization might be subject. And this, in turn, poses the high likelihood of the organization being visited by a stream of situations that come as something of a strategic surprise . . . by events of such a novel or ill-precedented nature as to have been entirely unanticipated, or by events originally deemed so *improbable* that they were omitted from consideration as working contingencies.

Thus, what state-indeterminacy implies by way of a pragmatic managerial corollary is that --more by default than choice-- the need for a decrease in reliance on *preadaption* as a basis for pursuing strategic readiness, and a corresponding increase in reliance on a reactive orientation. Such a shift speaks to the obvious fact that one cannot be ready in advance for that which cannot be anticipated, but must rather consider having to deal with surprises on a more or less after-the-fact basis. This *more or less* qualifier is important. For reactive orientations may run the gamut from the very primitive to the very sophisticated. In its more primitive forms, a reactive posture would involve nothing more than a casual wait-and-see or essentially ad-hoc approach to management. But an ad-hoc approach would only be appropriate were the following assumptions to be legitimate: The events with which an organization will be confronted will be assumed to be both essentially random in terms of appearance and fundamentally unique in terms of their attributes.

But most real-world organizations will hopefully have some prior idea --vague or incomplete as it may be-- of the sorts of situations they will be called upon to face, such that *randomness* is neither a necessary nor clever assumption. As such, a higher-management opting for an ad-hoc orientation may often, and quite properly, be condemned as either incompetent or inappropriately arrogant. In its primitive guise then, reactive management has a well-deserved pejorative connotation.[10] On the other hand, when a reactive orientation is a consequence of an organization operating under an adaptive planning/positioning scheme, we may be approaching the extremes of managerial competence and sensibility. For the task for adaptive facilities would be intended to provide organizations with the wherewithal to realize --in practice rather than merely concept-- the virtues of alertness, quickness, resiliency and the capability for rapid learning/discovery..all virtues that extremely complex, volatile contexts would richly recommend. And this represents the highest point of challenge for both practitioners and management scientists alike, for what it reduces to is the following: The need for the rapid generation of effectively original solutions to a stream of essentially unprecedented problems. In the broadest sense then, the pragmatic appeal of an adaptive approach as an alternative to a contingency planning approach is to be found in the basic common-sense realization: When the richness of the events to which an organization might be subject is so great as to obviate any attempt to be *ready* in total for all possibilities, then the next best thing is to try to be as ready as possible in part for whatever might occur.

But from a more constrained perspective, an adaptive approach may be viewed as a natural complement to a contingency planning approach, with the former to be brought into play whenever the latter goes into default. Yet as was suggested in **Exhibit 2.4** there are two basic categories of default conditions that must be considered:

> DISCONTINUITY, where an actual event falls through the gaps that have been left among members of a contingency event set.
>
> ANOMALY, where the actual event is of a nature that would mark it as entirely alien to any of the situations the organization anticipated, such that it falls well outside the bounds of the contingency event set.

But while any organization that perceives itself as vulnerable to either of these sorts of default conditions would be advised to consider a shift to an adaptive platform, each of the above may be taken to argue for a fundamentally different approach to adaptive planning/positioning.

That is, it's necessary to consider defining at least two different varieties of adaptive technology. Both will be dicussed in detail in Chapter 5. But we can here give a very abbreviated summary of their rudimentary logic. The first of the adaptive varients we shall refer to as the Adaptive/Interpolative modality. The basic rationale for an *interpolative* treatment follows from the definition of a discontinuity as an actual event which, while it fails to map directly to any of the elements in the standing contingency set, is nevertheless capable of being defined somewhere within its boundaries, i.e.:

$$I \rightarrow V \notin [E], \quad \text{but } V\ \theta\ [E],$$

where the symbol θ means that V is includable within [E]. And what conventional technical wisdom would suggest as the preferred way to go about dealing with a discontinuity is this:

> Because V maps to no element in [E], there will be no direct mapping to any pre-defined response in [R]. But given that V is capable of being defined somewhere within the confines of [E], then an appropriate strategic response (Ra) may perhaps be defined as an eclectic initiative by drawing on elements belonging to two or more of the members included in [R].

Hence the prospect for an interpolative mapping solution along the following lines:

$$\text{if: } [E1, E2 < V < E3 \ \ldots \ Em]$$
$$\text{then: } [R1, R2 < Rv < R3 \ \ldots \ Rm].$$

Where we would look to define an Rv that bears a relationship to the members of [R] similar to that which V bears to the elements of [E], or in symbolic terms: Rv | [R] as V | [E]. Thus, for example, if V can be taken to fall somewhere in the interstices between E2 and E3, then we might look to script some Rv such that it is intelligible as belonging somewhere in the interval between R2 and R3.

The most significant point of technical distinction between the Adaptive/Interpolative modality and contingency planning platforms is that the former will be constructed around *categorical* event and strategic response referents . . . these as opposed to the realistic models (qua scenarios and scripts) employed by the latter. Categorical referents are best thought of as representing generic or ideal-type constructs defined at a relatively high level of abstraction. As will be shown later, the rationale for this exchange is that it considerably eases the burden associated with the generation of *interpolative* strategic decisions. For following such a conversion, we would be in a position to try to treat any actual event as a *special instance* of some generic referent, and view the strategic planning task as mainly a matter of *tailoring* some generic response referent to meet any situation-specific event properties. This should reduce the amount of original analytical work that would have to be done on a reactive or after-the-fact basis given the emergence of a discontinuity. As a practical matter, the Categorical/Interpolative approach is specifically designed to provide organizations with what amounts to a strategic emergency management capability.

The second variant, the Adaptive/Real-Time modality, extends our technical reach to its effective limits. This is because it is arrayed against the most demanding category of exceptional events, the anomaly. In that an anomaly is far more alien to any organizational expectations than a discontinuity, it follows that there will be an even greater emphasis on reactive or after-the-fact analytical activities. In fact, the anomaly becomes intelligible as the clinical definition of a crisis, such that this modality becomes the practical source of support for strategic crisis management activities. This modality is thus intended to carry the concept of a reactive readiness orientation to its logical conclusion. And once again, the technical key has to do with the level of abstraction at which referents are maintained. But this time, rather than being defined at a higher level of abstraction than those used in contingency planning applications, they will be defined at a lower level of abstraction. More particularly, as we'll show in Chapter 5, Adaptive/Real-Time strategic planning structures will be developed around primitives and templates, this in the interest of giving strategic management authorities a capability for a roll-your-own approach to both event-definition and response formulation.

Such, at any rate, is an overview of the several different strategic planning/positioning platforms under which modern organization may elect to operate, and some idea of the criteria under which each would be the generally preferred choice. Of these platforms, the two simplest --the Prescriptive/Goal-Driven and Sequential/ Extrapolative-- are of no further interest to us. For as noted earlier, not only have they been widely treated elsewhere, but they are increasingly irrelevant given the complexity of the contexts in which most organizations are resident these days. On the other hand, the four platforms deemed appropriate in light of today's contextual challenges --the traditional and dynamic contingency planning platforms and the two adaptive management varieties-- have not been dealt with very widely or well. Hence the focus for the next three chapters.

NOTES AND REFERENCES

1. For an explanation of why this is the case, see my paper: "A Quasi-Empirical Mapping of Optimal Scale of Enterprise"; *Management Science* (26) 1980.

2. When we think broadly about such matters, the aggregate implications of secular scarcity, subordination and dependency can be seen to punctuate virtually every aspect of national life. The effects of the first are apparent in terms of the intense and seemingly endless Congressional agonizing about issues of the *guns or butter* variety, all of which come to an amorphous conceptual focus in terms of the Federal budget deficit, but which also come to a head in pragmatic points that run the gamut from unrepaired pot-holes on national highways to the tearful reportage about holes in the social services *safety-net* that provide so much of the stuff of local TV news. The other side of the coin is genuine concern not merely about the efficiency of Pentagon allocations, but also about the basic effectiveness of these allocations (the star of the show being the passionate but perhaps ultimately pointless --if not perilous embrace-- of that technical chimera called *Star Wars*, interwoven with the unarguable fact of the shortfall in our ability to sustain conventional combat). And underlying all this are those incidents that sit at the pivot of the transition from military dominance to something less: The twin traumas of Vietnam and the abortive raid into Iran; the death of the Rapid Deployment Force from an overdose of bureaucratic inanity and inter-service adolescence; the massacre of the Marine peace-keeping force in Lebanon; our apparent impotence in the face of Terrorist initiatives; the emptiness of the threat of military counter-measures against the Soviet incursion into Afghanistan, the Cuban

presence in Angola or the Iranian and Iraqui adventures against shipping in the Hormuz Straights, etc. On the political dimension, especially in the international arena, there are the signals of the decline of the *pax Americana*. For whereas simple coercion --actual or promised-- was once sufficient to bring geo-political circumstances in line with our national interests, today we increasingly find ourselves reduced to flattery, apology, lamentation, dissemblance, indirection and petulance . . . all weapons that have no place in the political arsenal of the dominant. In terms of aggregate economic matters, the story of our times is plotted around the gradual transition from effective autarchy (i.e., economic autonomy or presumptive self-sufficiency) to dependency. The tale perhaps begins with the crippling Arab oil embargo of the mid-1970's, and continues to this day in terms of the escalating general Trade deficit, the dependency of our domestic capital position on inflow of foreign investment, and the admission (mainly in the form of as yet fruitless exhortations) that the welfare of the American economic sector depends to a significant extent on the willingness of European and other nations to move to stimulate their own economies. And beneath all this is the stochastic subplot, the spectre of looming default by third-world debtor nations, and the possible collapse of the core of the American financial system.

3. There is of course another strategy that some automobile manufacturers have taken that is of some real concern. Particularly, there is the popular move towards defensive diversification. But this is often simply a euphemism for the retreat from more challenging to more tractable, calmer waters where management can get out of harm's way as it were, e.g.: Building a presence in specialty chemicals or other producer markets where threats from competitors are not of great consequence; attempts to penetrate to third-world regions where political muscle can translate into de-facto monopoly; or attempts to secure sole-source US defense contracts, which usually amounts to the same thing. But this strategy of retreat is really not even original to the automobile firms; they are really merely following the lead taken earlier by Steel, textiles and other basic industries. But such may be merely symptoms of a deep-seated executive malaise that goes way beyond any particular industry. For too much of what is supposed to pass for Strategic thinking in American firms is directed not so much at meeting competitive threats, but in devising ways to escape them. But as we now know well enough, retreat provides only a respite, not a release. And today, more so than ever in our past, what both domestic and international realities seem to be telling American higher-management --in the governmental and military as well as the economic sector-- is what a grand master of the ring once told a prospective opponent: "*You can run, but you can't hide!*"

4. c.f., any of the following: George Steiner, *Top Management Planning* (Macmillan, 1969), or his: *Strategic Planning: What Every Manager Must Know* (Free Press, 1979); Ewing (ed.), *Long-Range Planning for Management* (Harper & Row, 1972); Denning (ed.), *Corporate Planning: Selected Concepts* (McGraw-Hill, 1971). There are of course also several journals where practitioner-oriented or quasi-academic articles of these subject routinely appear, e.g.: Long Range Planning, Strategic Management Journal, Interfaces, and Managerial Planning.

5. A more elegant expression the concept of *directive correlation* explored by Sommerhoff in his "The Abstract Characteristics of Living Systems", in Emery, ed.,

Systems Thinking (Penguin Books, 1969).

6. The most tireless and enthusiastic proponent of a Cybernetic orientation to management was of course Stafford Beer, c.f.: *Cybernetics and Management* (1959), *Decision and Control* (1966) or *The Brain of the Firm* (1972).

7. A discussion of why this occurs is given in my paper, "System Theoretic Limitations on the Cybernetic Paradigm", *Behavioral Science* (20; 3), 1975. But the essential limits of effectiveness of a cybernetic approach might also be approached from another direction. Particularly, from a strict technical perspective, the pursuit of correlation may be taken to be merely a special case of what we earlier referred to as the equilibrium-maintenance orientation for organizations having dominantly *tactical* vs. strategic positioning requirements. And indeed, the general technical consensus would likely be that cybernetic technology is more appropriate as a basis for controlling middle-management activities in the usual complex enterprise than for managing that enterprise in aggregate.

8. When operating under a traditional contingency planning approach, being ready for *any* event is the same thing as being ready for *all* the events in the contingency set, should they occur simultaneously. Hence the constant complaint about resource scarcity among organizations having critical, contingency-driven missions . . . e.g., the lament of the US Navy that it's expected to fight a *four ocean war with a two ocean fleet*. But each of the several more sophisticated planning/positioning approaches we'll be discussing in later chapters can be looked at as providing for some sort of avenue of escape from this classic contingency planning quandary.

9. Albert Clarkson has given a good survey of what Indicator/Warning-Alert technology is intended to accomplish in his *Towards Effective Strategic Analysis: New Applications of Information Technology* (Westview Press, 1981).

10. There is, however, one variation on a simple reactive orientation that might be considered as more ingenious than primitive. This is the mail-order house that does not actually produce an item until it has received a sufficient number of (often pre-paid) advance orders (hence the usual alert to allow six-to-eight weeks for delivery). This is perhaps the only really viable expression of an organization designed to evade (or at the least, soften) the tradeoff that finds return positively correlated with risk. Or, as an illustration of a class of enterprise that exhibits the virtues of reactive management, we might take an example in keeping with our earlier concern with the fashion industry. This would be what's known as a *knock-off* shop, such equipped to rapidly adjust production facilities to manufacture a stream of imitations of some original design once it has excited some significant degree of market interest.

PART II:

MODERN STRATEGIC PLANNING/POSITIONING PLATFORMS

CHAPTER 3

STRUCTURED STRATEGIC CONTINGENCY PLANNING

Though contingency planning is frequently mentioned as something that organizations ought to be doing more of, there has in fact been very little discussion of how they might best go about actually doing it in a properly disciplined way. This is not entirely surprising. For in terms of the technical provisions it might entail -- procedural and instrumental requirements-- it is a very demanding activity . . . especially when undertaken at the strategic level. Nevertheless, there are two different (but ultimately complementary) classes of structuring techniques that can bring some degree of formality to strategic contingency planning exercises:

1) Matrix-based (Markov type) structures
2) Simple stochastic network (tree) structures

For the most part however, use of these techniques has been restricted to the military sector (and not even there are they always properly employed). They do however have application for competitive contexts in general, not just the military. We'll thus use this chapter to go through a rather detailed examination of how organizations might make best practical use of these two structuring conventions, and what might they might provide in terms of strategic readiness.

3.1 Rudimentary Contingency Planning Concepts

As was suggested in the previous chapter, when an organization is resident in a context characterized by moderate state-stochasticity, it might attempt to answer for strategic readiness requirements by electing to operate under a bipartite, model-based contingency planning platform: [E] ↔ [R]. Again, both [E] and [R] can be expected to house referents that are comprensible as *models* . . . as scenarios and scripts, respectively. Given the *preadaptive* orientation of traditional contingency planning, the contingency event set [E] would be expected to contain the set of environmental and/or competitive state-level events to which an organization may be subject at some future period(s). The response-side set [R] will thus ideally contain a predefined and fully-invested strategic plan available for execution should any member of the contingency event set actually occur. In terms of its broad practical implications then, a contingency planning structure of this sort may be seen as a basis for bringing some degree of formal discipline to strategic analysis operations conducted over what is referred to as the SWOT quartet . . . the assessment of Strengths, Weaknesses, Oppportunities and Threats.

Much of modern management theory literature speaks to the advantages of a contingency approach to organizational management for enterprises resident in volatile environments.[1] But there is a signal scarcity of technical advice as to the sorts of facilities that organizations would have to have in place were they to opt for a contingency approach. Rather, almost all the procedural and instrumental initiatives developed by the mainstream decision and system sciences continue to be designed to support planning constructs centered on the two non-contingency based protocols mentioned in the previous chapter:

- Goal-driven processes, where the key predicates are the aspirations or visions of managerial authorities.[2]
- Sequential constructs based on linear (evolutionary) statistical projections of environmental properties.

Both the above will lead to singular (vs. stochastic) scenario-based planning structures. For as noted earlier, the typical strategic planning scheme used by real-world organizations will have environmental considerations entered in the form of a maximum-likelihood model defined over a single set of stationary exogenous conditions expected to be in force during some future period.[3] Frequently, this maximum-likelihood environmental referent will be taken to be a product of environmental scanning exercises centered on statistical forecasting techniques of some kind, perhaps amended by subjective judgements to account for determinants that the statistical mechanisms could not accomodate or merely to allow executive judgement to modify quantitative extrapolations (with the maximum-likelihood construct then being comprehensible as the Bayesian vs. simple statistically-dominant scenario . . . this a matter we shall be discussing in more detail in later chapters). Attention would then expectedly turn to the generation of a goal-set expressing higher-management's concept of where the organization's best interests appear to lie in light of the specific collection of opportunities and threats over which the maximum-likelihood model was defined. Finally, the action aspects of the typical singular-state strategic planning construct will emerge as a result of managerial consensus as to a set of initiatives (to be executed in concert or sequentially, as the case may be) expected to have the highest probability of effectively realizing the goals decided upon earlier.

But again, while such a planning approach has the advantage of being both simple in concept and minimally demanding in terms of the technical requirements it imposes (and has the added practical appeal of allowing managerial visions and aspirations the dominance that many executives might wish), it has the obvious disadvantage of not providing for organizational *readiness* should the environmental conditions postulated in the maximum-likelihood model fail in fact to materialize. And as is clear enough, the probability of such a failure must generally be expected to increase with any increase in the complexity and/or volatility of the context(s) in which an organization is resident. Hence the rationale for the recommendation that organizations operating in ill-behaved environments --or which must anticipate having to contend with particularly aggressive, ingenious competitors-- undertake the exchange from singular-state to stochastic-state planning platforms . . . this because the latter explicitly assumes the possibility of two or more fundamentally different sets of contextual conditions occurring, each arguing for a fundamentally different strategic response.

The key practical effect of the transition to a contingency approach to organizational management is then to get an organization *ready* to confront not merely one expectedly most-probable environmental state, but two or more state alternatives deemed to have some significant possibility of occurrence. This, in turn, would follow from the shift in the locus of initiative away from any organization itself and towards exogenous actors (as government agencies or competitor enterprises) as a consequence of any increase in environmental volatility and competitive intensity. In short, such increases have the net practical effect of making any local management's aspirations increasingly impotent as determinants of contextual realities, and goals increasingly gratuitous as planning predicates. Thus, as a critical complement of a transit to a contingency planning platform, managements are encouraged to worry a bit less about what they want and a bit more about what they might get . . . i.e., what others might want. And finally, as the locus of environmental determinacy moves away from the organization itself towards contextual agencies and competitors, there is this pragmatic corollary: Both common sense and conventional technical wisdom suggest that before strategic planners consider the pursuit of potential opportunities, they first attend to the matter of defining and meeting prospective threats.

In sum then, while contingency planning is frequently mentioned as something that organizations ought to be doing more of, there has in fact been very little discussion of how they might best go about actually doing it in a properly disciplined way. This is not entirely surprising. For in terms of the technical provisions it entails --apparent procedural and mechanical requirements-- it's a very demanding activity. Beyond this, it may be suggested that serious attempts to operate under a formal contingency planning approach have been largely restricted to certain segments of the modern military sectors of the major powers, and hence not widely discussed as yet in the mainstream management literature (and even in the military community, formal contingency planning exercises are most often confined to tactical rather than strategic-level issues). Our task here then is to offer some concrete suggestions as to what a formalistic strategic contingency planning protocol might actually look like.

As a first step, consider **Exhibit 3.1**, this indicating the four generic analytical operations that would underlie any formal contingency planning process. For the event-projection side of the process, the several operations would entail the following:

> REALIZATION: I $\rightarrow$ [E] . . . the attempt to work from a currently available information base (I) to an ideally *exhaustive* (universal) set of state-event possibilities defined as proper scenarios.[4] The information base (I) thus represents the set of planning predicates available at the beginning of the projection hozizon. As such, the realization operation is just a technical designation for the scenario generation process (which, as we'll later show, is a special sort of hypothesis-formulation).
>
> ORDERING: [E] $\rightarrow$ P[E] . . . leads to discrimination among the members of [E] in terms of some ordering criterion such as probability (or others we shall shortly note, such as threat-potential). That is, the ordering operation would then impose some sort of ranking --e.g., a likelihood density function-- over the various state-event possibilities.
>
> CONVERGENCE: P[E] $\rightarrow$ P[E*] $\subset$ [E] . . . if [E] is too large given organizational asset/resource capabilities, this operation will result in the extraction of some *affordable* subset of highest-priority (most likely and/or most threatening) contingencies via [E*]. The greater the number of possibilities encoded in the original set of possibilities [E], and the scarcer the organization's asset/resources, the greater must be the degree of reduction between [E] and some *affordable* subset [E*]. In terms of convergence outcomes, the most desirable contingency subset would be

EXHIBIT 3.1 : Formal Analytical Operations for Strategic Contingency Planning*

Analytical Operations	Event-Side	Response-Side
Realization	$\{I\} \rightarrow [E]$ the generation of an ostensibly exhaustive set of projected event possibilities	$Ei \in [E^*] \rightarrow [Ri]$ formulation of a set of alternative strategic response options for each of the contingencies
Ordering	$[E] \rightarrow P[E]$ to discriminate among the members of [E] as to probability of occurrence (P), or some other criterion	$[Ri] \rightarrow U[Ri]$ assigns each of the response options a utility (preference) valuation reflecting expectations as to its effectiveness/ efficiency re: Ei
Convergence	$P[E] \rightarrow [E^*] \subset [E]$ extraction of an affordable/ manageable subset of highest-priority events as active contingencies	$U[Ri] \rightarrow U\hat{}(Ri) \mid Ei$ isolation of the ostensibly maximal-utility response option (contingency plan) for Ei
Cross-Mapping	$[E^*] \leftrightarrow [R^*]$ ... where the set [R*] contains the maximal- utility strategic response option for each and every member of [E*], such that any $Ei \in [E^*] \rightarrow Ri \in [R^*]$	

* The same operation could also be employed at the Tactical level. It's just that the event-side domain of inquiry would be restricted to the realization,

one that contains the fewest number of alternatives entailing the lowest level of qualitative differentiation (diversity). Convergence outcomes would then become increasingly *unactionable* as [E*] expands to include more, increasingly qualitatively distinct possibilities . . . as there is an increase in *spread*. The response-side implications for the several operations are similar. Realization would have planners attempting to formulate the range [Ri] of alternative courses of strategic action (treatment or remedial modalities) for each of the event possibilities (all Ei [E*]) encoded in the active contingency set. In the ordering stage, there would be an attempt to discriminate among these options in terms of their ostensible utility, this reflecting expectations that some particular Ri will ultimately prove to be the most effective and efficient of the realized alternatives. The convergence operation would have planners isolate a singular response option as U^(Ri), this being the preferred basis for dealing with Ei if it should arise.

Finally, the cross-mapping operation would yield a working contingency planning construct, for the set [R*] encodes the singularly preferred strategic response plan for each of the active contingencies in the event-side set [E*].

With these basics in mind, we can now turn to the matter of the technical mechanics for the generation and use of properly disciplined or structured contingency planning constructs, particularly along the lines shown in **Exhibit 3.2**. The focus is mainly on the employement of two different families of structuring conventions, Matrix (and especially Markov-type) Network based provisions. In that the former are usually prerequisites for the latter, we'll deal first with the rudiments of a Markov-type provision for injecting formal structure into contingency planning constructs.

3.2 Matrix-Based Strategic Planning Structures

The first appearance of a Markov-type contruct could be a simple matrix like this:

	E1	E2	E3	. . .	Em
E1	p(1,1)	p(1,2)	p(1,3)	. . .	p(1,m)
E2	p(2,1)	p(2,2)	p(2,3)	. . .	p(2,m)
		etc.			
Em	p(m,1)	p(m,2)	p(m,3)	. . .	p(m,m)

EXHIBIT 3.2 : Structured Contingency Planning Procedures

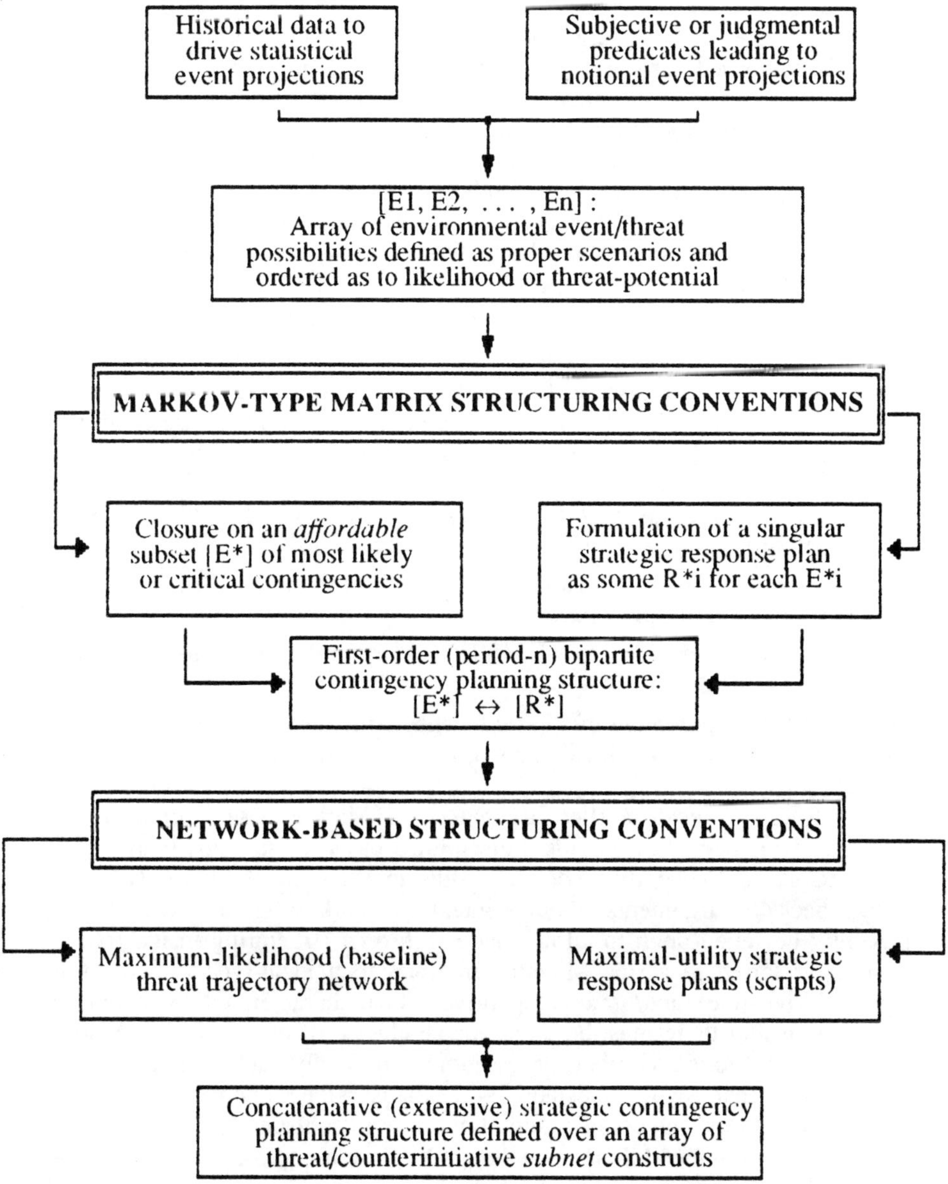

Here, E1, E2, etc. are members of some *universe* of state-event possibilities. And as in all Markov-based exercises, the main focus of our attention shifts to the body of the matrix, where the various p(i,j)'s may all be taken to represent state transformational probabilities. The usual Markov-based process will thus be aimed primarily (though not exclusively) at discriminating among contingencies as to their relative *likelihood* or probability of occurrence.[5]

But within the confines of strategic planning exercises, the most critical and restrictive of the conditions is the requirement that the array of state-event alternatives [E] have a legitimate chance of being in fact exhaustive. In simple symbolic terms, what this reduces to is the following:

$$P[E1 .or. E2 .or. \ldots Em] = 1.$$

In practice, planners can fudge this requirement by introducing some *dummy* state, this assigned a residual probability value (the likelihood that something other than the substantive Ei's might occur) which merely reduces the absolute probability values assigned the meaningful state-event alternatives.

Each of the rows of the matrix then lays out the state-transform possibilities available from some specific Ei:

p(i,i) = the probability that Ei will persist over the interval in question, to the exclusion of other states;

p(i,j) = the probability that Ei will give way to (be exchanged for) some other event, Ej ∈ [E].

The secondary requirement of a basic Markov structure is thus that the sum of the probabilities for any Row equal unity, such that: p(i,j) = 1.0 for all j (including j = i).

Therefore, to recall earlier arguments, a Markov-based protocol can generally be expected to provide a disciplined basis for strategic planning up to and including the condition defined as discrete state-stochasticity. Or, to tie things back to arguments about context, a Markov-based approach can generally be relied upon to allow adequate formal structuring in the face of what we referred to as the Modular environmental ideal-type (based on an equifinal dynamic) and/or a competitive arena characterized by extensive competition. For there must be a reasonable chance of planners being able to realize some limited number of essentially mutually-exclusive state-event alternatives that will substantially exhaust the competitive and/or environmental states an organization might have to confront.[6]

On the environmental dimension then, a Markov-based protocol ought to be able to reach to any situation where there is some reasonably neat equifinal dynamic at work, where planners can up-front define two or more qualitatively unique *states* into which a context might possibly resolve itself over some time frame . . . to the effective exclusion of all other possibilities. As a basis for capturing the substance of modular/equifinal movements, there is a class of social science literature --and even more obviously, the *macro* or Toynbeean school of historical analysis-- that tends to define environmental dynamics around certain basic *states* that may appear in some sort of transitional sequence. For example, one aspect of macroeconomic theory is devoted to the concept of *pendular* swings between boom and bust, inflation and deflation, recession and recovery. For its part, Marxian-inspired socio-economics is focussed on the prospect of a broad *dialectical* engine at work, fashioned around the several Hegelian states (thesis, antithesis and synthesis) and exchange dynamics. And there are some sociologists whose work is fixed on the possibility of sweeping transitions among various highly generalized state referents, e.g.: spiritual/transcendental vs. secularist/materialist vs. solipcistic/anarchic tendencies; theocratic vs. rationalistic or matriarchal vs. patriarchal axiological anchorings.[7]

But whatever the phenomena of interest, for a modular/equifinal environmental dynamic to be captured in a Markov construct, it is necessary first of all for planners to be able to define some finite set of *logically possible* (vs. merely probable) qualitative event alternatives, and secondly for the planners to have some basis --statistical, judgmental or whatever-- for assigning values to the transitional possibilities occupying the various cells of the matrix . . . the p(i,j)'s. Essentially the same would hold true were we to consider the competitive dimension. For again, the basic requirement would be that planners have some basis for predicting the range of strategic initiatives that competitors might possibly author, and then have some basis for posing the conditions under which one or another becomes more or less likely. A Markov-type matrix might then be formulated to support strategic analysis for any competitive situation up to and including what we defined in the first chapter as the *extensive* case.

Consider, for example, that strategic threats will generally be restricted to alterations in Pricing structure, Product Differentiation (innovation), Advertising/Merchandizing policy and perhaps what are referred to as *X-efficiencies* (these including matters that rest beyond the usual microeconomic sources of efficiency).[8] With the basic dimensions of competition bounded, market or competitive analysis exercises may quite often be able to isolate some limited set of *logically possible* competitor-authored event possibilities and formulate them in terms of some universal set [E]. Popular management literature (most often industry or sector-specific) offers much practical advice about what sorts of strategic initiatives might be taken on which dimension(s) under what conditions.[9] Some trade associations and agencies within the US Department of Commerce have recently been working with technological forecasting models in the attempt to define various avenues of approach that the Japanese might take in their pursuit of fifth-generation computer systems (and the more sophisticated of these forecasts may also offer a casual ranking of the approaches as to their relative likelihood of occurrence and eventual success). Studies such as these might lend themselves readily to incorporation into a planning structure reflecting US computer vendors' (perhaps acting as a consortium) determinations as to their own research and development priorities.

In any case, depending on the nature of the context at hand, a Markov-based protocol can be used to help structure either cross-sectional (intra-period) or longitudinal (inter-period) event projection and evaluation. We'll deal with the former first, as it provides a natural starting point for the latter.

3.2.1 Single-Period Strategic Threat Projection Structures

Here, a Markov-type matrix construct would be used to represent assessments (as to relative probability) for all State-transitional possibilities for Period-t. For example, a commercial enterprise may be trying to comprehend and evaluate the strategic initiatives that a competitor might possibly invoke for the coming selling season; foreign policy officials might be trying to realize/order potential shifts in socio-political sentiment that might occur in some country of interest; or an intelligence analyst could be charged with defining and ranking possible strategic military threats that might be mounted by an adversary within some interval. In such cases, each of the rows of the matrix would be interpreted as follows:

> Given that any Ei actually occurs (or is proposed to be the starting-state condition for some period), the several p(i,j) values would express the estimated likelihood that Ei will give way to some Ej within period t, with p(i,i) being the probability that Ei will continue to remain in force as *the* contextual state throughout the interval in question.

Expectations about the likelihood of any Ei emerging as the starting-state or *triggering* event for some Period-t would be given by a master distribution function like this:

$$P[E1, E2, E3, \ldots Em]t.$$

We may define at least four categories (or basic *morphologies*) the function might assume:

> STATE CERTAINTY: One member of [E] may essentially exhaust all likelihood, such that there is some Pmax (Ei) $\rightarrow$ 1.0.
>
> STRONG STATE DOMINANCE: There may be only one alternative deemed *significantly* likely to occur . . . only one (Ei) is assigned a

probability value exceeding some minimum threshold level (with the threshold level set to reflect planners' tolerance for uncertainty).

WEAK STATE DOMINANCE: There are two or more state-event alternatives that are considered significantly likely to occur, with one having a modest advantage over the other(s). This will generally mean that the maximum-likelihood event (or triggering state) will carry a probability value that is significantly less than unity: $Pmax(Ei) \ll 1$.

EQUIPOTENTIALITY: All members of [E] are deemed more or less equally likely (or unlikely) to occur: $P(E1) = P(E2) = \ldots = P(Em)$.

The first two situations showed allow planners the luxury of focussing their further efforts on just one row of the competitive matrix.

For illustrative purposes, let's assume that alternative E2 emerged as either an effectively deterministic or strongly-dominant choice, such that analytical attention now shifts to a *focal* row: p(2,1); p(2,2); . . . ; p(2,m). The several situations defined above would also apply here, but this time with respect to the transitional possibilities, p(E2 => Ej)t. That is, as we've done earlier, we'll take determinacy to mean the emergence of some $p(2,j) \rightarrow 1.0$, such that one transition E2 => Ej is assumed to be an overwhelmingly likely choice. A strongly-dominant transition is one which, alone among options, is seen to exceed some minimum likelihood level. A weakly-dominant choice would then reflect an incremental edge for some E2 => Ej, while equipotentiality would in effect mean essential *symmetry* or indiscriminacy.

Within the confines of a Markov-type strategic planning matrix, the *net* event projection situation would thus be defined over a set of simple conditional probability products:

$$P'(Ei \Rightarrow Ej) = P(Ei) \times p(i,j).$$

We could then generate an extended Markov structure, such as that shown below:

Trigger Event	State-Event Array E1	E2	E3	. . .	Em
P(E1)	P'(1,1)	P'(1,2)	P'(1,3)	. . .	P'(1,m)
P(E2)	P'(2,1)	P'(2,2)	P'(2,3)	. . .	P'(2,m)
			etc.		
P(Em)	P'(m,1)	P'(m,2)	P'(m,3)	. . .	P'(m,m)

where :

$\Sigma P(Ei) = 1$ for all i

$\Sigma p(i,j) = 1$ for all j

It provides us with a framework for considering the repertoire of state-level transformations available among the members of some set of event alternatives. And depending upon the resultant *morphology* of the distribution over the P' values, some implications for strategic *readiness* might become readily apparent.

For example, the simplest and best of all possible worlds from the strategic planning/positioning perspective would occur were there to emerge some P'(i,i)t $\rightarrow$ 1. For what this would imply is effective state certainty in an extended sense, where:

$$P(Ei) \rightarrow 1.0 \text{ .and. } P(i,j) \rightarrow 1.0.$$

That is, not only is Ei given extraordinarily (exhaustive) odds of being the actual starting-state event for some period t, but that same state-event is also assumed to be virtually certain to persist throughout that period. As a consequence, planners would need to define only one strategic response plan an organization need be *ready* to execute over the duration of period t. The worst-case situation would then occur under the condition where there is distributed *equipotentiality* . . . where all P'(i,j) are considered more or less equally likely to occur. Here, the interests of strategic *readiness* might well dictate the development of a strategic contingency plan for each and every transitional possibility defined above . . . i.e., for all elements of the universe [E] or: all Ei $\in$ [E] .and. all Ei => Ej. That is, there is no rational basis for *extracting* any reduced subset of highest-likelihood state-event possibilities, not at least without incurring a more or less proportional decrease in strategic *readiness* or commensurate increase in strategic risk . . . as per our discussions in a previous section.

Between these two extremes (extensive certainty and equipotentiality) would lie opportunities for generating a contingency event set that contains fewer members than the original realization (universal) set, for defining some [E*] $\subset$ [E]; each member of this contingency set --any E*i-- would then refer to some particularly *interesting* state transition, some (Ei => Ej). But to get to [E*], planners must either be prepared to eliminate from active consideration one or more members of [E] and/or one or more of the P(Ei => Ej) or intraperiod transitional possibilities. This could be done either by a simple threshold-based extraction operation, or a somewhat more sophisticated *marginal optimum* basis. The first would merely demand that all Ei => Ej elements in the extended Markov matrix be arrayed in terms of descending value for the P' index. Having eliminated extensive equipotentiality as a possibility, the result would be a more or less *asymmetrical* distribution, with membership in [E*] designed to:

- Incorporate all (Ei => Ej) alternatives whose conditional probability of occurrence (P') exceeds some minimal threshold level.

- Or, if there are some fixed asset/resource constraints within which planners are to work, then the above extraction might be performed until the set of highest-likelihood (Ei => Ej) possibilities entered into [E*] have exhausted the aggregate resource/asset base.

Note, however, that the asset/resource requirements (A) associated with any R*i | E*i would be defined as:

$$A(R^*i \mid E^*i) = A(Ri \mid Ei) + A(Rj \mid Ej),$$

or as the sum of the asset/resource bases demanded by the two state-event constituents of any transitional pair. Therefore, the aggregate resource/asset requirements {A*} needed to fully *invest* any contingency event set [E*] need consider any particular Ei only once (irrespective of the number of transitional possibilities in which it appears).

It is also worth noting here that response-side constraints may perhaps dictate the elimination of certain state-event alternatives, irrespective of how high a likelihood value they have been assigned. For to repeat arguments from the last chapter, the addition of any new strategic response alternative (qua Contingency Plan) to an organization's readiness repertoire is not so much significant in terms of incremental increases in resources/assets of some existing order, but in terms of its demand for at least some resource/asset categories essentially dedicated to itself . . . i.e., in terms of the unique *qualitative* requirements and/or initiatives it entails.

Therefore, we must consider the possibility of an organization being forced to ignore certain state-event possibilities because --even were they to occur-- nothing could be done about them, e.g.:

(a) their treatment would demand some resource/asset category that is for some reason inaccessible to the organization within the time frame of interest. For example, a business firm may be considering the prospect of a competitive enterprise coming on to the market with a dramatically innovative product. But if the firm in question lacks the capital or research facilities to effect a response on this dimension (and cannot retreat from the market), this is a contingency that it might as well exclude from its active contingency event set, though it may well remain a figment of managerial nightmares.

(b) an organization might be proscribed from taking certain sorts of strategic initiatives by virtue of policy constraints or exogenous prohibitions passed down by some superior agency. State-event alternatives which could be treated only by a proscribed initiative might as well be excluded from any [E*]. For example, if a military commander faces the prospect of being overrun by a vastly superior adversary force that could only be deterred by deploying a nuclear weapon --but if he is disallowed access to such-- then little is to be gained by devoting much analytical time or energy to this contingency.

In other cases, there may no pre-established resource/asset constraints to consider, or we may merely be interested in the effects of tightening or relaxing such constraints.

In such instances, planners might try to drive towards an [E*] that represents a most favorable *optimum at the margin* between strategic readiness (or risk) and resource/asset requirements. The procedure could be fairly straightforward. For when working with an extensive Markov structure, an indication of the extent to which an organization is going to be at strategic *risk* may be accessible as a simple residual:

$$K = (1.0 - \sum P'[E^*1, E^*2 \; \ldots \; E^*m]).$$

As such, the cost-benefit consequence of adding any Ei => Ej transitional possibility to [E*] --or deleting it-- would be available by looking at the incremental increase/decrease in net strategic risk relative to any associated increase/decrease in resource requirements. However, a usually more meaningful approach to *marginal* risk/return considerations may often result were planners to factor in the other extraction criterion, Threat Potential (H). Extraction operations would then be focussed on the following formulation, and priorities for inclusion in [E*] assigned accordingly:

$$P' \times H(Ei \Rightarrow Ej) \; / \; A(Ri \mid Ei + Rj \mid Ej).$$

Making marginal calculations of the above sort will almost always involve some considerable degree of analytical difficulty and imprecision. Yet there are obvious advantages in planners being as imaginative and active as possible in searching for any *common denominators* that might serve to cojoin the risk or readiness and resource sides of the equations. For example, in a typical commercial context, it may sometimes be possible to translate readiness into some general surrogate such as expected profit-impact or potential for return, Risk considerations may then perhaps be collapsed into prospective real and opportunity losses, and resource/asset requirements into investment or purchase costs . . . all of which may ultimately be made intelligible in terms of dollars. In contemplation of military confrontations, it's sometimes possible to treat readiness and risk in terms of the conservation or loss of certain combat resources or assets (e.g., troops; aircraft), or in terms of the extension vs. loss of control over territory as a function of level of commitment --and acceptable levels of expenditure-- of combat resources, etc. In such cases, a quasi-computational *optimum at the margin* would be determined in the classical manner: By looking for the neighborhood at which additional increments of resource/asset committments (or expenditures) begin to fail to yield a more than proportional increase in readiness or decrease in risk.

However, attempts to try to reduce what are fundamentally *qualitative* matters to simple quantitative surrogates is always a perilous expedient. And even more to the point, numerical computations will usually demand a level of projective precision that will seldom be met in real-world strategic planning exercises. Therefore, it may most often be necessary to employ some sort of simple *qualitative* basis for ranking state-event alternatives as to likelihood (or threat potential), or assessing their risk/readiness implications, e.g.:

Ei:Ej = >> implies a significant advantage for Ei vs. Ej
Ei:Ej = > implies a marginal advantage for Ei vs. Ej
Ei:Ej = <> implies rough equivalence between Ei and Ej
Ei:Ej = < implies marginal advantage for Ej relative to Ei
Ei:Ej = << implies significant advantage for Ej vs. Ei.

Some discipline, of course, might be brought to the choice of a relational category for some Ei vs. Ej comparison by using *Fuzzy* Set operations designed to help determine membership in qualitative classes.

3.2.2 Longitudinal Strategic Event Projection Structures:

When turning to the matter of using Markov-type conventions to support temporal vs. cross-sectional state-event projection, the basic requirements and procedures would both be simple variations on the themes established for the intraperiod case. Indeed, the matrix would be formulated in the same way:

	E1	E2	. . .	Em
E1	p(1,1)	p(1,2)	. . .	p(1,m)
E2	p(2,1)	p(2,2)	. . .	p(2,m)
		etc.		
Em	p(m,1)	p(m,2)	. . .	p(m,m)

where :

Σ P(Ei) = 1 for all i
Σ p(i,j) = 1 for all j

All that really differs is the way in which we now interpret the elements of the matrix. For when it is between-period state transitional possibilities in which we're interested, the various p(i,j)'s would have the following implication:

> The expected likelihood that, if event Ei is the state-event in force during some period-t, some event Ej will then be the state-event in force during Period-t+1, etc.

As such, the p(i,i) entries would now be used to display the expected likelihood of some singular state-event (Ei) persisting through both period-t and t+1.

This is perhaps also the point to note the way in which a longitudinal oriented Markov-type structure might apply to response-side operations . . . in either a reactive or proactive orientation. Again, the former differs from the latter in terms of the *locus of strategic initiative*. In the reactive case, the generation and evaluation of strategic alternatives is conditioned by the prior definition of the state-event to which they are to be turned, and hence with their expected utility as treatment or remedial options.

In contrast, proactive planning is concerned primarily with the generation and evaluation of strategic initiatives of the organization's own authoring, and their likelihood of being able to cause certain state-events to occur . . . particularly those state-events that would align most completely with the interests or ambitions of an organization's senior management. More simply, reactive strategic analysis operations are directed at trying to find the best way to deal with some problem or threat that has arisen, whereas proactive strategic analysis is concerned with the assessment of various action options in terms of their effectiveness/efficiency in achieving developmental goals.

And subject to certain limitations we have earlier mentioned (and will deal with again in the next chapter), strategic planners may turn to the class of modern Decision Structuring techniques to help move towards some ostensibly maximal utility strategic option for either the reactive or proactive case. For the matter of attempting to isolate an expectedly best problem-solving strategy is roughly technically equivalent to the task of trying to fix on a best proactive strategic initiative to take with respect to some predetermined end(s).

Therefore, planners could take recourse to a Markov-type convention to guide either type of strategic analysis exercise, as the ultimate effect of either a reactive or proactive initiative will become comprehensible in terms of a *state-event* imposed on some competitive or environmental agency(s). Thus, all that's required is a simple exchange of referents, e.g.:

Let: Ai = a strategic action (a proactive initiative or some Ri | Ei) an organization is considering taking;

[O] = a set intended to house a mention of all possible state-level consequences as *outcome* events.

Planners would then, as a first step, generate the following high-order probability density function:

$$Ai \rightarrow P[O1, O2 \ldots Om] \mid t1,$$

this serving to express the likelihood that some Oi will emerge as the first-order outcome consequence of Ai . . . the state-level consequence associated with period-t1. A longitudinal Markov-type matrix would then be generated over the above to yield:

	O1	O2	...	Om
O1	p(1,1)	p(1,2)	...	p(1,m)
O2	p(2,1)	p(2,2)	...	p(2,m)
		etc.		
Om	p(m,1)	p(m,2)	...	p(m,m)

where :

Σ P(Ei) = 1 for all i

Σ p(i,j) = 1 for all j

Each p(i,j) would thus reflect the likelihood that, if Ai $\rightarrow$ Oi is the first-order (initial period) outcome consequence, that some Oj will follow as the second-order (next period) consequence, etc. The p(i,i) possibilities would then be used to convey expectations about the first-order outcome state (Oi) persisting into the next period.

Thus, in so far as basic mechanics are concerned then, it does not matter whether we are concerned with state-events whose origin rests exogenous to the organization (the members of [E]), or with state-events that are the consequence of some strategic organizational initiative (the set [O]). For in either case, the most favorable of all possible temporal event-projection situations would then occur were there to be found one state-event alternative that is assumed certain to remain in force for the two periods . . . some Ei or Oi with p(i,i) $\rightarrow$ 1.0. In such an instance, planners will have postulated what amounts to a steady-state condition for t $\rightarrow$ t+1; this means the organization need invest just one strategic plan (some Ri) in order to be deemed *ready*.

But a Markov-based planning structure may also be extended to consider successively more remote intervals as well, such as the interval between Period t+1 and t+2, then between t+2 and t+3, etc. Of these extensive possibilities, the least challenging of planning outcomes would be the situation where planners isolate one and only one state-event alternative that is considered to be essentially *certain* to remain in force throughout all intervals of the strategic planning horizon:

$$\begin{gathered} P(Ei)\,|\,t \rightarrow 1.0 \\ \text{and: } P(Ei)\,|\,t{+}1 \rightarrow 1.0 \\ \text{etc.} \\ \text{and: } P(Ei)\,|\,tn \rightarrow 1.0. \end{gathered}$$

In such a case, planners would be required to define --and the organization required to *invest*-- just one Strategic Plan (some Li = f(Ri) | Ei) to apply throughout the foreseeable future. Thereafter, attention may quite properly shift to tactical and/or operational aspects of organizational positioning. Or, for the proactive planning case, the counterpart would be the postulation that there will be one and only one *long-run* state-level consequence that might follow from some strategic initiative the organization takes. This is roughly equivalent to assuming that there will be no strategic counter-reaction to the initiative. But such situations are really of very little interest to us. For they could only occur when the organization of interest is resident in an extremely simple context (one characterized by placidity and/or only very mild forms of interorganizational competition), or when the organization is either clearly *dominant* among any competitors or essentially *autonomous* with respect to any exogenous influences.

A somewhat more interesting situation would follow from the ability to identify one and only one significantly likely (e.g., effectively *certain* or strongly-dominant) transitional possibility for each and every between-interval case, such that there is some singular $p(Ei \rightarrow Ej) \rightarrow 1.0$ for all $(t \rightarrow t+1)$. The consequence of this would be to define a neatly linear state-event *trajectory*, $Ei(t) \rightarrow Ej(t+1)$, etc. And the practical consequence of this is to allow an organization legitimate recourse to a sequential-state platform . . . this the *preferred* basis for dealing with an evolutionary dynamic:

$$[L] = L(t) \rightarrow L(t+1) \rightarrow L(t+2) \rightarrow \ldots \rightarrow L(tn);$$

$$\text{where: } \begin{aligned} L(t) &= f(Ri \mid Ei) \\ L(t{=}1) &= f(Rj \mid Ej) \\ &\text{(etc.)} \\ L(tn) &= f(Rm \mid Em). \end{aligned}$$

That is, given that we are effectively *certain* about the specific state-event that will be in force during each interval of the planning horizon, the organization need be *ready* to implement only one strategic response option. A familiar commercial example would be the case where a firm is assuming that its experience with some new product line will follow a typical life-cycle, with the elements of a sequential-state structure perhaps something like that shown in **Exhibit 3.3**.

The proactive equivalent to a neat evolutionary dynamic would be the case where a strategic initiative taken at some point (t) is presumed to be sufficient to set off some singular sequence of outcome states as:

$$Ai(t) \rightarrow Oi \mid t+1 \Rightarrow Oj \mid t+2 \ldots \Rightarrow Om \mid tn.$$

Macroeconomic policy formulation provides perhaps the most generally familiar example of simple sequential state-transition sequences, of which the following is typical:

t: Ai = cut income tax rates
t+1: Oi = increase in demand for products
t+2: Oj = increase in capital investment by businesses resulting in increased supply, creation of new jobs, etc.
t+3: Ok = increased tax revenues/savings rates, etc.
tn: Om = self-sustaining upward economic spiral, with minimal inflation.

EXHIBIT 3.3 : Empirical Example of a Sequential-state Strategic Planning Structure for a Commercial Application

t :	The starting-state condition (Ei) will see an initially flat growth curve, which is expected to rise steeply after the first n-months. Prospect is for high monopoly profits.	A Plan (Lt) = f(Ri) may involve: Building a large product inventory; have ready an "Informational" advertising campaign; have a restricted network of dealers to exclude discounting; be alert to opportunities to acquire small competitors, etc.
t+1 :	Ei will give way to Ej, this the point where some competitors start to bring out look-alikes, at a significantly lower price.	L(t+1) = f(Rj | Ej) would now be invoked, involving: Reduction in rates of production; move from informational to critical comparative advertising; arrange for foreign licensing; file distractive legal suits to deter further entries.
t+2 :	The transition from Ej to some Ek would occur as there is a shift in direction of aggregate demand and/or relative share of market; promotional elasticities turn negative.	Under L(t+2) = f(Rk | Ek): Remaining inventory would be cleared through radical price reduction/rebates; the retreat from this product line or market niche would be completed.

At any rate, all situations other than a neat deterministic/singular transformational projection would demand recourse to a strategic contingency planning platform. For there would be two or more transitional possibilities that must be considered significantly likely to occur between any t and t+1. And following the Markov convention, a contingency state-event set --some [E*]-- might then be represented as:

	State Event Alternatives				
Periods	E1	E2	E3	. . .	Em
t1	P(1,1)	P(1,2)	**	. . .	P(1,m)
t2	**	P(2,2)	P(2,3)	. . .	P(2,m)
t3	P(3,1)	P(3,2)	**	. . .	**
			etc.		
tn	**	P(n,2)	**	. . .	P(n,m)

where: all P(i,j) > s, with s being a threshold value for P

Such a construct can be used to cojoin expectations about both within (intraperiod) and between-interval (longitudinal) state-event possibilities. Inclusion in the contingency event set is restricted only to *significantly* likely possibilities. Therefore, the symbol ** is used to represent instances where a contingency has been eliminated because its likelihood value fell below the likelihood threshold, or where P(i,j) < s.

The lower the degree of discrete state-stochasticity represented in a construct such as the above, the fewer will be the strategic contingency response plans that will have to be scripted and invested, and hence the greater the likelihood of the organization being able to approach strategic *readiness* in full measure. However, should the set of *active* contingencies determined above still be unaffordable or exceed aggregate resource/asset constraints, then planners are again back to the familiar crunch: Either they eliminate some members from the contingency set (perhaps by raising the probability threshold value that allows entry into the final contingency set), or they ask for a relaxation of certain constraints.

But in the tradition of Markovian operations, what happens at any future period (say t+1) is conditioned by what has occurred (or is expected to occur) for the previous period (t). Moreover, this sort of dependency would apply irrespective of whether it is event-projection or action-driven outcome consequences that we are seeking to concatenate. And as the reader may already know well enough, the usually preferred basis for expressing temporal conditionality --or longitudinal discrete state stochasticity-- is not to establish a series of Markov transitional matrices, but rather to shift to the other platform available to modern strategic contingency planners.

3.3 Simple Strategic Tree Structures

Were we to look for a way of displaying sequences of state-events or outcomes, a simple stochastic *tree* structure is usually sufficient. As shown in the figure below, the various P(Ei)'s arrayed for period one represent the relative likelihood of each of the state-event alternatives being the *triggering* or starting-state for Period-t1. In moving to period-t2, we begin to get the explosion of possibilities characteristic of a stochastic *tree* structure. The likelihood of any particular event emerging as the *state* for t2 will usually be different depending on which state-event was in force during t1.

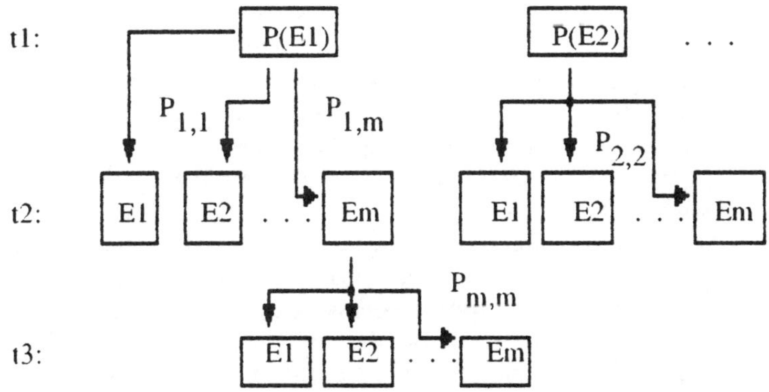

Thus for example, P(1,m) represents the conditional probability that if E1 occurs during period-t1, that Em will occur during period-t2. On the other hand, P(m,m) would represent the conditional probability of persistence for Em over the interval t1 and t2, which will likely be either greater or lesser than P(1,m), etc. In considering possibilities for period-t3, the probability assessments may be of two different sorts:

- They may again be simple one-stage Markov conditionals, under the traditional convention that next period transitions are essentially entirely dependent on current period events. In this sense then, P'(m,1) would suggest the likelihood that if Em occurred during Period-t2, E2 would be the *state* during Period-t3.
- They may be *concatenative* conditionals, such that P'(m,1) for period-t3 is a product of: P(E1) | t1 .and. P(Em) | t2 .and. P'(m,2).

In electing the latter, we abandon Markov-based conventions in favor of stochastic network conventions.

The key condition that would most likely cause strategic planners to opt for the latter is perhaps clear enough: There is the prospect that subsequent periods will entail state-event sets that are different from those that pertained at previous periods (that is, [E]t2 will have at least one member that was not included in [E]t1, or the reverse). That is, a stochastic network convention becomes the preferred protocol whenever planners have reason to suspect that they are dealing with a *transmutative* rather than equifinal dynamic. Therefore, planners must consider having to replicate the event definition, evaluation and extraction operations for each new period. Yet *within* any period, adequate discipline could usually be supplied via the basic Markov-type procedures described earlier, for any period need no longer be viewed as mutually-exclusive, but may rather appear in concert or as complements.

Working from the Markov-type base structure we just developed, it is possible to be relatively specific about what is involved in using stochastic network or *tree* structures to support strategic planning exercises. And while such structures might be employed in an extremely wide variety of practical situations, perhaps the classic illustration of their use is to support high-level competitive analysis as a prelude to a possible military engagement. **Exhibit 3.4** shows a typical framework for such exercises, with the key network-based facilities shown in bold.[10]

As per the exhibit, planning *predicates* are of two sorts: intelligence information pertaining to the expected capabilities and intents of adversary forces; and data about the resources and assets available to our own forces. Given such predicates, the first of the analytical tasks would be the undertaking of Net Assessment. This is focussed on the attempt to define the various points of relative strength and/or weakness between the two forces on the several dimensions pertinent to a large-scale (i.e. Theater-level) military confrontation. The confrontation might occur on any or all of four different *stages*: Land, Air, Sea and Space. For any one or all of these *stages*, a Net Assessment would be generated for each of the four critical aspects of Military engagements:

(a) Combat power;
(b) Positioning;
(c) Maneuverability/ mobility; and
(d) Sustainability.

To put all this in perspective, planners might employ a simple variation on the Competitive Matrix construct that we introduced in a previous chapter:

EXHIBIT 3.4 : Simple Tree Structure Imposed On a Set of Event/Threat Possibilities

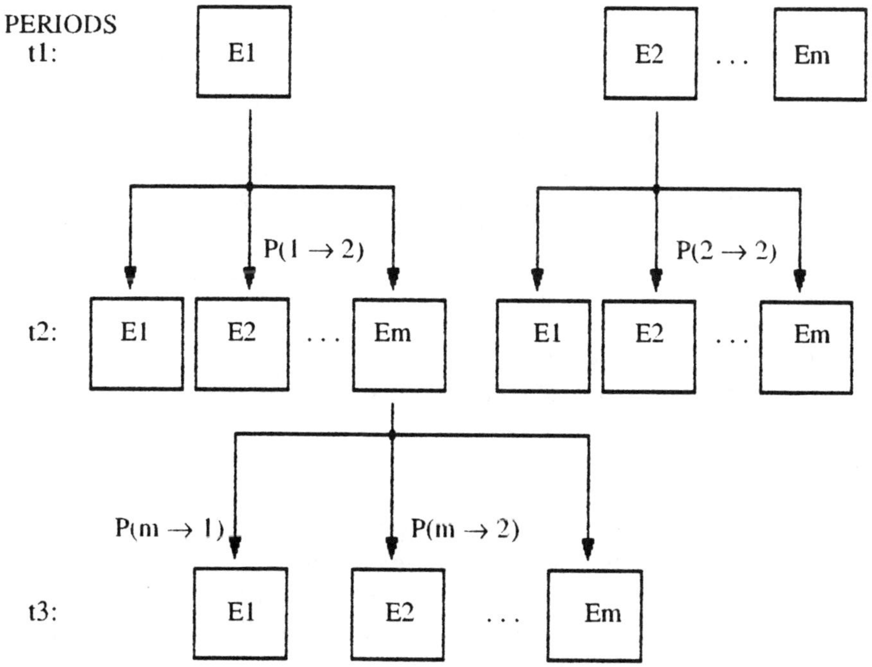

Where :

[E] is a set of event alternatives expected to exhaust the universe of possibilities for interval t1 → t3;

P(i → j) is the conditional probability that event Ei will occur and then be succeeded by event Ej.

	Combat Power	Positioning	Maneuver-ability	Sustain-ability
LAND	v(1,1)	v(1,2)	v(1,3)	v(1,4)
AIR	v(2,1)	v(2,2)	v(2,3)	v(2,4)
SEA		etc.		
SPACE	v(4,1)	v(4,2)	v(4,3)	v(4,4)

Here the rows of the matrix might be used to represent the asset categories (or, alternatively, confrontational *stages*), with the engagement aspects appearing as the columns. The cells of the matrix would then contain valuations --the v(i,j)'s-- that are *aggregate* assessments as to relative Own vs. Adversary force capabilities for the several columnar headings for each of the several row designations.

In all instances, **combat power** would refer to the size and/or quality of military assets of the two competing forces. Land-based assets would include the following:

1) Strength and training/readiness of ground troops or infantry units;
2) Number/capabilities of ground-support elements (armor and artillery);
3) any Special Force units, etc.

Assessment of capabilities as to air forces would include specifications as to:

1) Number/sophistication of tactical support aircraft;
2) Size/training level of airborne units;
3) Number/capabilities of airmobile assets (helicopters, etc.);
4) Long-range platforms such as missiles and bombers, etc.

Assessments of sea-based combat power would be directed at the relative number/sophistication of various Naval assets, e.g.:

1) nuclear-powered battle group configurations;
2) attack/hunter submarines;
3) ICBM carrying submarines;
4) missile cruisers, etc.

Assessment of space-based capabilities would consider the number of --and reliability of-- launch vehicles that are available, and also the number, precision (sensor sophistication) and robustness of both passive (communication and surveillance satellites) and active (tracking/targeting; anti-satellite) platforms that are available to own vs. adversary forces.

The second of the columnar headings, **positioning**, refers generally to the quality of the *deployment* opportunities available to own vs. adversary forces of the various sorts. For example, the quality of infantry positions is generally assessed over factors such as the availability of natural cover for troops and armor, good fields of fire for artillery units, proximity to lines of resupply, adequacy of potential avenues of advance or withdrawal, etc. For Air and Airmobile assets, Positioning is usually determined by the availability of defensible staging areas that are sufficiently close to the forward lines of engagement and well within range of key adversary targets, etc.

Quality of positioning for Naval forces is generally determined by the relative security of port facilities . . . their existence behind easily fortified *straights* that might deter attack in force from adversary surface units, or the absence of good cover for adversary submarine raiders; the absence of any choke-points that might be held by an adversary to prevent outward passage of own forces; security of main ports and key lines of transit from attack by adversary air units or close-in reconnaissance by satellites or other intelligence-collection assets, etc. Relative quality of Positioning for Space-based platforms would be determined over factors such as the availability of defensible/sufficiently remote launch-sites with generally favorable weather conditions, quick access to high-interest orbits or trajectories, access to safe waters for recovery of reusable units, a securable and sufficiently redundant network of communication and/or *dump* sites, etc.

As for **maneuverability** of land-based forces, this is in part determined by positional criteria (access to favorable avenues of assault and/or disengagement). But most critical is the relative level of investment in mobility-related facilities such as: Adequacy of rapid, versatile (all-terrain, etc.) troop transport equipment; mobile artillery platforms; size/readiness of rapid deployment (e.g., paratroop) units; existence of engineering facilities for construction of bridges, sophistication of cover/deception capabilities to help shield movements from early detection; familiarity with or training in on-the-run maintenance operations or real-time logistical support. Maneuverability of Air elements would refer to factors such as their ability to tolerate adverse weather conditions, the range of aircraft themselves, quality of navigational aids and networks, and degree of versatility of alternative attack platforms . . . e.g., cruise missiles to defeat local radar detection; *stealth* bombers to penetrate orthodox air defenses. The relative *mobility* of Naval forces is usually assessed relative to their capability for carrying out *blue water* or open-ocean transits, and the ability --via emission control or other masking technologies-- to conceal critical maneuvers from adversary intelligence-gathering assets. Finally, the maneuverability of space-based assets might be evaluated in terms of: The *portability* of launch-facilities for satellite, ballistic missile or long-range bombers; the ability to revise or redirect such vehicles once underway; their security from electronic interference or EW (electronic warfare) countermeasures, etc.

Finally, **sustainability** would be concerned with factors that may effect the duration over which effective military operations can be maintained, e.g.: The depth and quality of *ready* reserves; the rate at which expended resources -- troops, equipment, etc.-- can be replaced or expanded; the tolerance of home-front or civilian elements for losses or sacrifices; the ability to confine the confrontation to territory accessible to supply lines, and the defensibility of such.

Strategic (vs. tactical or operational) net assessment activities will take place at a relatively high level of aggregation. Therefore, the key questions to be resolved at the Net Assessment stage are those that might be thought pertinent to the development of a basic *game plan* for some prospective confrontation:

1) Where are the points of greatest vulnerability for own forces, as per any < or << valuations?

2) What are the opportunities to pit own-force strengths against adversary force weaknesses, via a >> or > value?

3) Where might we want to --or have to-- go strength-against-strength, such given by the <> entries?

Under modern strategic planning technology, planners might seek to answer for the first of the above questions by generating a simple network-based construct over potential perils.

3.4 Strategic Threat Projection Networks

Again, potential *threats* to own-force interests would be located primarily in any cell(s) of the Competitive Matrix where own forces are assumed to be at a marginal or significant disadvantage relative to an Adversary. For it is at these points where we find the key opportunities for an adversary to pit his strengths against our own weaknesses. Let us then define the set [C'] to contain all instances where v(i,j) = < or <<. A crude measure of the threat potential associated with any C'k ∈ [C'] might then be a product of:

1) the likelihood (L) of the own-force weakness (disadvantage) being apparent to adversary-force strategic planners;

2) the categorical seriousness of the threat (H) to own-force welfare/mission that might follow from some weakness, using categories something like these:

H1: may effect complete defeat of own-force assets and/or failure of Strategic mission;

H2: may require own-forces to settle for some suboptimal strategic outcome . . . e.g., a political compromise or stand-off vs. total military victory;

H3: may act to delay the achievement of own-force mission and/or make its achievement more expensive in terms of expenditures of resources, etc.

The net threat potential (H') for any C'i would thus be crudely available as H'(C'k) = L x H, with an aggregate threat ordering being H'[C'].

Planners may then initiate the development of a Threat-Projection network --qua simple *hierarchical, node/arc* structure-- by starting with any C'k (though a usual preference would be to work first from that condition carrying the highest H' value).

To quickly illustrate, let's assume that the expected locus of greatest threat to own-force interests (H' max, as it were) is located in Cell (1,1) of the Competitive Matrix, which now becomes C'1. Under the convention we've been using, this implies that an adversary has been assigned a significant advantage in terms of Combat Power for land-based forces or, to use our symbolic terms, v(1,1) = <<. At this point, planners would then seek to define --as proper scenarios-- the set of strategic threats an adversary might elect to mount with respect to C'1, e.g.:

T1,1: direct an assault-in-force against own-force positions with the intent of outright victory;

T1,2: undertake a major encirclement of own forces, designed to prevent resupply/reinforcement and their redeployment.

Alternatives such as the above would be collected within some set [T1,j] | C'1, with each T(1,j) assigned some probability (P) of emerging as the adversary's opening strategic *gambit* in the prospective confrontation, and hence as the starting-state threat that own forces will have to confront. That is, we now have an ordered set of threat possibilities for period-t1:

$$(t1) \rightarrow P[T1,1; T1,2; \ldots T1,m] \mid C'1.$$

Under the simple network convention we've been following, each of the various T(1,j) possibilities becomes a *node* defined at the highest (first) level of a hierarchical *tree*. As such, it is useful to now think of designating any specific threat as: T(t,k,j), where:

t = the period to which it applies or the level of the hierarchy at which it it appears;
k = the particular member of [C'] to which it applies (which ties it to a cell of the Competitive Matrix);
j = the within-cell designator.

Planners may now turn their attention to the next-level (period-t2) threat possibilities that might follow from each of the nodes defined for period-t1, thus moving to add another level of specification to the hierarchical *tree* structure that is being constructed. In the simplest instance of strategic threat projection (where there is one and only one cell where own forces are at a disadvantage), then second-period threat possibilities might also be confined within aspect C'1. For example, we can consider two possible follow-on threats that might derive from T(1,2) above:

T(2,1,1): encirclement of own forces will be maintained until own forces must surrender for lack of suppplies, with the adversary thus gaining victory with minimal casualties.

T(2,1,2): the adversary maintains a fractional force sufficient to keep own forces bottled-up, then moves his main body to attack critical rear-echelon targets which are now only lightly defended.

We would thus have generated a simple network *segment* that would be displayable as:

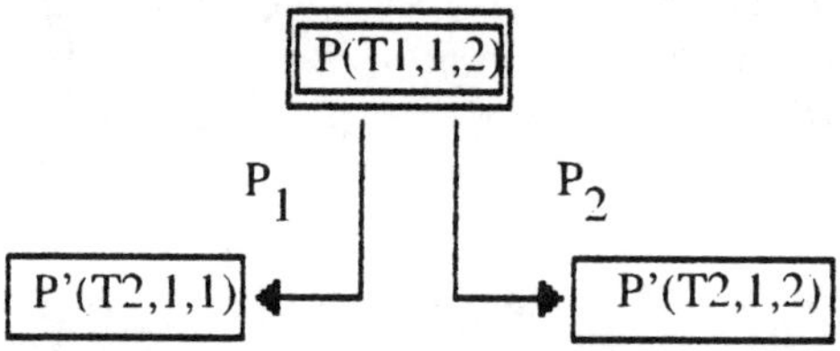

And once again, the P' values for the possible second-order nodes are conditionals, computed as: P'(T2,1,j) = P(T1,1,2) .and. P(T2,1,j). But to approach more *realistic* threat projection structures, we must consider cases where starting-state threat possibilities may emerge with respect to two or more C'k aspects . . . not merely the singular C'1 we have considered thus far. Such an expansion of the threat alternatives to be considered at the first-level of the hierarchy could occur because:

a) There are two or more cells within the Competitive Matrix where own forces are at a strategic disadvantage, with some uncertainty about the specific C'k $\in$ [C'] where the adversary will elect to make his opening strategic initiative. For example, let's assume that adversary forces have two points of significant advantage:

Cell (1,1), which again means superiority of ground forces;

Cell (3,3), which translates into superior range, etc., for naval elements.

In such a case, there may be ambiguity as to whether the initiating strategic threat to own forces will arise from infantry/armor assaults on front-line positions, or from sea-based attacks on coastal staging areas, attempts to close off sea-lanes carrying critical supplies, etc.

b) There is some likelihood that the adversary might elect to open the confrontation by simultaneously mounting strategic initiatives within two or more C'k aspects. Indeed, this is precisely the sort of situation that is envisioned by modern *Air-Land* battle management doctrine, where any major initiative is taken to involve the coordinated employment of both ground assets and air elements.[11]

In either of the above instances, the first-period or starting-state threat possibilities would expand to include more than one set of alternatives:

$$(t1) \rightarrow P[T1,j] \mid C'1 + P[T2,j] \mid C'2 \ \ldots \ + P[Tm,j] \mid C'm.$$

Were we then to decompose these into *nodes* for the first-level of the hierarchical *tree*, we'd get the following array:

$$\{[T(1,1,1 \ \ldots \ T(1,1,m)] + [T(1,2,1 \ \ldots \ (1,2,m)] + [\ldots T(1,k,m)]\}.$$

Moreover, each of these threat alternatives would be assigned some probability index, P'(T1,k,j) = P(C'k) x P(Tj) . . . the product of the likelihood of the pertinent C'k times the likelihood of the particular Tj within C'k.

Once again, each of the T(1,k,j) possibilities represents a stochastic *node* from which will radiate one or more *arcs* leading to possible period-t2 follow-on threats within the same or other C'k aspect(s). The result is a series of period-t1 → t2 transitional network *segments*. The remaining --3rd to n'th period-- levels of a stochastic-state *tree* structure would then be generated in much the same way. A fully-elaborated threat definition *tree* structure would then house all such threat-definition segments, with each individual strategic threat-event defined for some t serving as the nodal anchor for a potentially unique follow-on sequence of sub-nets for periods t+1, t+2, etc.

The result is a potential multitude of stochastic-state expansions such as that shown in **Exhibit 3.5**. So stochastic-state *tree* constructs can quickly grow to considerable size and complexity. But as a practical matter, it will usually be possible to extract one single *trajectory* --one linear sequence of node/arc transits-- that will be of dominant interest to strategic planners. This we shall refer to as the Baseline Threat Model, shown in the exhibit as the trajectory drawn in bold. It can be defined to meet either of two criteria:

- It may represent the maximum-likelihood sequence of strategic threats (qua *nodes*), and so be defined along that linear path which at all points follows the *arcs* that have been assigned the highest probabilities of occurrence. That is, a maximum-likelihood threat model entails those adversary-authored initiatives we are most likely to see.

- It may represent the path of imputed maximal-utility for the adversary force . . . i.e., that *trajectory* that is presumed to lead most directly to the defeat of own forces (perhaps qualified so as to assure such defeat at minimum expenditure of adversary force assets). Thus, from the perspective of own-force planners, the Baseline threat projection model

EXHIBIT 3.5 : Aspects of a Strategic Competitive Analysis Process (Military Application)

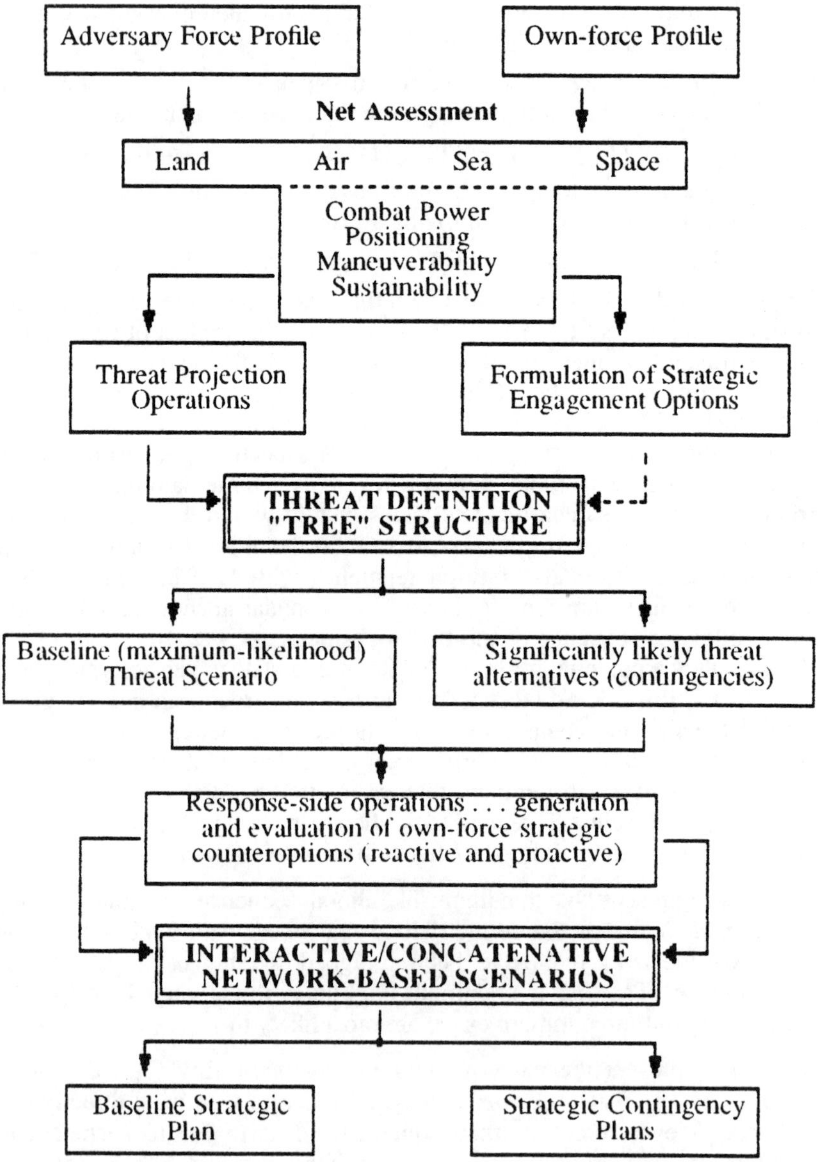

> would here appear as a *worst case* strategic scenario . . . that series of ultimately most threatening initiatives with which an adversary might confront us.

In many if not most cases, planners can expect the maximum-likelihood and maximal-peril Baseline threat trajectories to be roughly coincidental. But if they are not, then the latter should generally take precedence. For it is the threats highlighted in the maximal-peril Baseline projection model that own-force strategic planners will be most anxious to guard against . . . or, even better, avert altogether. As such, they become the prime targets for efforts at strategic *scripting* activities.

3.5 Interactive Strategic Event/Response Sub-Structures

To repeat an earlier point, the threat definition operations that we've just gone through were directed at those cells of the Competitive Matrix where (via Net Assessment) the adversary was assigned a marginal or significant advantage relative to own forces . . . i.e., points where there is a prospect of the adversary pitting its strength(s) against our weakness(es). And it's perhaps well to mention here what would obviously be a *trivial* Net Assessment outcome: the case where all entries in the Competitive Matrix point in a given direction of relationship. For in such a case, there is little in the way of *strategic* analysis or planning that needs to be done.

For example, all valuations may be either > or >>, such that own forces are presumed to be *dominant* over adversary forces on all dimensions of interest. Were this to occur, own-force planners may legitimately skip right to the consideration of the tactical aspects of a prospective confrontation. Such a situation is representative of the US assault on Grenada, or of the prospect of a US invasion of Nicaragua, were planners to a priori exclude the possibility of the Sandinistas receiving support from Cuba or the Soviet Union. It might be suggested that such a possibility could be excluded only by planners operating in a frenzy of optimism or crippled by the most extraordinary geo-political myopia. Yet recent history shows no lack of examples where this must have been the case, among them the misadventures of the French and US in Vietnam and the embroilment of the Soviets in Afghanistan. But as earlier noted, such may perhaps best be appreciated merely as special instances of the tendency of planners in general to short-circuit messy strategic issues in favor of more tractable tactical matters.

There are then at least two signals of *illigitimate* transit to the tactical decision domain, both familiar to us from earlier discussions:

a) Event-definition operations that result in insufficiently broad *universes* of state-event possibilities;

b) Evaluation operations that are informed too greatly by what planners or their line superiors want to have happen, and too little by objectively-anchored logical possibilities.

On the other hand, a *trivial* Net Assessment situation may also result from an imputed *disadvantage* for own forces on all competitive dimensions, with all valuations being < or <<. What this would suggest is that whatever *strategic* analysis is done had better be directed at the generation and consideration of non-military initiatives . . . e.g., at diplomatic initiatives that might have a chance of averting a direct military confrontation.

There are therefore only two *non-trivial* Net Assessment situations to consider. First, a prospective confrontation may be characterized either by equivalence on all competitive dimensions . . . i.e., all v(i,j) = <>. In such a case, both Own-force and adversary planners must by default confine their strategic planning to variations on *strength-against-strength*. The second non-trivial situation is both more interesting and probably the more likely, as it would involve some *mix* of competitive advantages and disadvantages. Were this to be the situation, then the crux of strategic analysis and planning thus shifts to this issue:

> To what extent might advantages on one competitive dimension at least partially compensate for disadvantages on some other dimension(s)?

Planners would then first focus the search for possible strategic *trade-offs* to either rows or columns, but must ultimately consider both.

For example, let's assume that own forces are taken to be at a significant disadvantage relative to adversary forces in terms of Combat Power/land-based assets, such that v(1,1) = <<. What common sense would then suggest is that an own-force *strategy* be built around initiatives that would reduce the likelihood of the outcome of the confrontation being *decided* in Cell (1,1) of the Competitive Matrix. Working row-wise, planners would be looking to devise situations where own-force advantages in other asset categories might be exploited, e.g.:

a) If v(1,1) = << .and. v(2,1) = > or >>, an own-force strategy might be scripted around the presumption of tactical air supremacy, with one obvious alternative being this:

- rely on air assaults to reduce the effective adversary land force through attrition and/or interdiction of supply lines, etc. The point here would be to try to weaken the adversary land forces to the point where they are inferior to own land-forces . . . i.e., to force a qualitative shift in the valuation for v(1,1) . . . from the original << to a > or >>. Were this to occur, the follow-on strategy then would be to force a direct confrontation in Cell (1,1). At the same time, strategic air superiority might be used to direct strikes against critical targets in the adversary's rear or home front, to weaken resolve or ability to reinforce the now-weakened Land elements, etc.

b) If v(3,1) = > or >>, the search for strategic options would be directed at ways in which own-force control of the seas might be used to offset the adversary's edge in land-based assets. For example, own naval forces might be used to attempt to distract adversary attention/resources, this by penetration exercises directed at port facilities or coastal cities and interdiction of sea-based supply lines, etc.

As for columnar strategic *trade-offs*, military science is repleat with pertinent doctrinal advises.

For example, let's again take v(1,1) = <<, such that an adversary force is allowed a significant *aggregate* advantage in Combat Power (D1) for land-based assets. We may then consider the implications of our own forces having an advantage on one or more of the remaining dimensions: D2 = Positioning; D3: Maneuverability; D4 = Sustainability:

	D1		D2	.or.	D3	.or.	D4
Land Forces	<<	.and.	> or>>		> or >>		> or >>

Were we to allow own forces an advantage in Positioning such that v(1,2) = > or >> and assume parity or equivalence for dimensions D3 and D4 such that v(1,3) and v(1,4) = <>, then an own-forces' strategy might be scripted around digging-in behind a strong fixed defensive front, and forcing the adversary to come to us if a confrontation is to be joined.

Even more rich are the various doctrinal and historical referents suggesting how a classic guerilla strategy, orchestrated around the deliberate cultivation of advantages in maneuverability --quickness, elusiveness and resiliency-- can be employed to gradually wear down a much superior but more ponderous adversary. Indeed, in the minds of many military historians, the victory by the Allies over Germany in World War II perhaps owed more to the ultimately superior *sustainability* of the former than to any other factor.[12]

What we have just gone through are some simple examples of the attempt to define and evaluate fundamental strategic engagement alternatives . . . focussed on the systematic evaluation of all qualitatively significant differences in valuations among the cells of the Competitive Matrix. Thus, any true strategic plan will involve the coordinated employment of two or more qualitatively disparate asset categories (e.g., Land and air forces acting in concert), and must also address --simultaneously and/or sequentially-- all of the columnar cases where there is qualitative non-equivalence. In contrast, *tactical* Net Assessment and engagement analysis exercises would be focussed on any differences that appear within cells, given some aggregate qualitative valuation, and so take place at a much lower level of aggregation. For example, a typical tactical analysis exercise within Cell (1,1) --Combat Power for land-based forces-- might look for any imbalance in an adversary's commitments to asset subcategories that might be exploited on the battlefield . . . e.g., too great a reliance on infantry vs. armor.

If there is any aspect to strategic analysis in the military arena --and from all indications, in the political and commercial sectors as well-- that might be considered *fun*, it is thinking up nasty things that we might do to an adversary. But the mark of wisdom among strategic planners is to reserve such pleasure until one has considered the nasty things some competitor might do to us. The threat projection operations we went through in the previous subsection serve just this purpose, and point us towards the suggestion that strategic planning exercises should look to contain or avoid potential perils before worrying about how to exploit potential opportunities.

Hence the primacy of the elements of the *Baseline* threat model --when defined under the maximal-peril criterion-- as strategic planning referents. For again, the Baseline threat model is constructed around those competitor-authored initiatives that are deemed most likely to serve the interests of the adversary force, which should usually be those initiatives most likely to disserve own-force interest. But implicit in the way the Baseline model was constructed was this qualification:

> Any transit through the Baseline threat definition model --from a threat at period t to the maximum-likelihood (or maximal-peril) threat for some period t+1-- depends on the adversary being able to successfully execute the strategic initiative that authored the period t threat.

Therefore, the focus for own-force strategic planning would be to follow the Baseline threat trajectory, looking for the earliest possible point(s) where we might devise a script for a strategic counteraction that could impede an adversary's progress along his assumedly maximal-utility trajectory. Reminiscent of the categories we used earlier to distinguish between different degrees of peril, there are at least the following categories of strategic initiatives we might consider in the attempt to counter some threat:

> Preemption, whereby we are able to take some action that in effect *seizes the strategic initiative* from the adversary force, and so has some likelihood of invalidating all subsequent elements of the Baseline threat trajectory.

> The partial or perhaps even complete *defeat* of a strategic initiative (threat). A severe enough defeat of a threat at some period-t may serve to

obviate any downstream adversary-authored initiatives anchored by the defeated threat (so perhaps setting up a condition where own-forces might attempt to seize the strategic initiative, as above).

Actions that have some likelihood of causing the adversary force to undertake a *diversion* --at one or more points-- from the Baseline path in favor of some lower-utility (and hence less threatening) trajectory.

Perhaps the least that can be done is to attempt to take actions that might *delay* the adversary force's movement along the Baseline trajectory, this in the hope that denial of a timely execution may either represent a form of defeat for the initiative in question, or perhaps buy own-forces time to gear up to better deal with some subsequent period threat(s).

The election of one or another of these strategic counterthreat postures would in practice be dependent upon how factors such as effectiveness, risk and cost are expected to resolve themselves.

But for our immediate purposes here, what is of interest are the network-based consequences of any prospective strategic counteraction. For when we consider the options just noted, the most modest of effects would be the need to enter some sort of revision into the Baseline threat trajectory, this to indicate at what point the adversary is forced off his maximal-utility path and caused to follow some other sequence defined within the fully-elaborated threat-definition *tree* structure from which the Baseline model was extracted. On the other hand, if planners are sufficiently confident about the prospect of some counteraction being able to shift the strategic initiative to own-forces, then it would be necessary to generate an entirely new sequence of node/arc segments, this time anchored by own-force initiatives that pose a threat to the adversary. That is, the strategic planning focus now shifts to the attempt to define what we might think of as a maximal-utility *scenario* constructed from the own-force perspective.

The basic mechanics for construction of interactive (or, more properly concatenative cross-impact) scenarios are similar to the Markov-type convention introduced earlier to help structure outcome consequences following from some proactive strategic initiative . . . only now we'd be using strategic countermeasures as the focus, and be generating network vs. matrix expansions. That is, suppose planners were to direct their attention to a specific adversary-authored threat possibility, some T(t,k,j). It would then be necessary for them to generate a set of alternative counterinitiatives, or [~T] | T(t,k,j). The issue would then be to attempt to get some idea of the relative merits of the alternatives defined within [~T] = ~T1 . . . ~Tm. An appropriate *structure* for considering such would be to lay out a longitudinal expansion model for each of the following starting-state conditions:

$$T(t,k,j) \text{ .and. } {\sim}Ti \in [{\sim}T] \quad \text{for all } i.$$

As such, the first task would be to define and rank the first-order possible outcome consequences from some ~Ti | T(t,k,j) interaction:

$$P[T(t+1,1,1)\ \ldots\ T(t+1,k,m)] \mid {\sim}Ti\ .$$

We might think of the members of the above set as representing possible adversary counteractions to our original own-force essay, ~T(t,k,j). Therefore, planners would move to assess the first-order *utility* of ~Ti over a simple expected value operation of the sort with which we are already familiar. Specifically, each of the members of the first-order consequence set defined above would be equipped with some sort of relative (scalar or categorical) Threat index which we shall again denote as H. The following computation would then give us the first- order utility estimate we require:

$$U({\sim}T) \mid t+1\ =\ (P \times H)\ \ \text{for all } T(t+1,k,j).$$

The value for U --and hence the attractiveness of any strategic countermeasure candidate-- would thus tend to be greater as the options left open to the adversary become increasingly less threatening, or as the more threatening options become successively less probable. Or, to tie things back to the general logic we've been using here, the pragmatic utility of any ~Ti is ultimately to be found in its ability to force the adversary away from the Baseline trajectory (his maximal-utility scenario), such that the net threat to own-forces for period-t+1 --given ~Ti-- is less than it would have been otherwise. And indeed, if the ~Ti in question were to be deemed sufficiently powerful to allow own-forces to seize the strategic initiative from the adversary, the effect might be to yield an essentially *empty* set of significantly threatening next-period adversary options.

Finally, were planners to make an estimate of the expenditure of resources/assets (A) that might be associated with ~Ti, a crude cost-effectiveness ranking would then be given by ~Ti $\rightarrow$ U | A(t+1). It should then be possible to generate a simple ordinal ranking over the set of strategic counterinitiative candidates, ~Ti, ~Tj . . . ~Tm, and then look for that alternative which has the maximal value for the ratio U | A(t+1).

But of course it is not merely the first-order consequences against which the utility of some strategic counterinitiative is to be assessed . . . except for the special case where planners expect that its only likely effect would be to force the adversary to undertake a radical shift from an offensive to defensive posture. In all other instances it is necessary to consider the 2nd and nth-period possibilities that might follow from some ~Ti executed at time t. And because the first-order (period t+1) consequences were defined as possible adversary counteractions to ~Ti, the natural next step is for planners to script possible own-force counterinitiative options for each of the alternative adversary countermoves or some particularly interesting subset of such.

That is, own-force planners would now have to define a new set of strategic countermeasure candidates [~T(t+1)] for each significant member of the set [T(t+1,k,j)]. And for each such candidate, an estimate of its relative utility -- vs. other alternatives for countering some T(t+1,k,j)-- would require planners to go through the sequence of operations we just went through to get a cost/effectiveness measure for ~Ti(t). Moreover, to get an estimate of the net (concatenative) consequences of ~Ti(t), we would then have to replicate all the above operations for all subsequent periodic transitions, from T2 → t3, etc. Thus, each strategic counterinitiative that own-forces might consider putting into implementation against some threat at any time (t) ultimately authors a unique *subtree*, such as that shown in **Exhibit 3.6**.

A properly disciplined assessment of the net attractiveness of any strategic counteraction ~Ti | T(t,j,k) thus demands that we resonate out (concatenate) its downstream consequences over some sort of reasonable projective interval. Planners would then be expected to elect that strategic counterinitiative --for any T(t,k,j) that yields the highest aggregate value for the ratio U/A computed for all t → tn. Or, more generally, planners might be tasked with developing a series of sub-nets expressing *interactive* expansion possibilities arising from the collision of prospective adversary initiatives and elected own-force counterinitiatives.

Interactive network scenarios would be the natural technical medium to help planners deal with the horns of the proverbial strategic analysis dilemma: Suppose an adversary does X to me; then should I do A, B or C to him? But if I do A, what then might my adversary do to me in return? However, there is one other point we might mention here (though we shall return to it at a later point with hopefully more authority). In most confrontations --military or whatever-- there will be more than one point at which we might seek to throw an adversary off his maximal-utility path. Indeed, this was made explicit in earlier discussions. Therefore, the exercises we just went through to attempt to isolate a best strategic countermeasure for some threat may provide a basis for planners to reach a decision about just which threats it is they most want to try to interdict.

That is, suppose that there are two different threats (some T1 and T2) which --if successfully countered-- would both lead to the same happy ultimate consequence for own-forces. For example, in the traditional Air-land battle scenario, an adversary could be put out of business not merely were we to defeat his ground maneuver units, but also were we to effect an assault (preemptive or otherwise) that would deprive him of the requisite Air force elements. Planners might then generate concatenative scenarios in order to identify the ostensibly *optimal* countermeasure for prospective threats. The interests of rationality would then generally be well served were they to compare countermeasures in terms of the level of cost and risk, etc., each entails, and then elect to attack that threat for which we have the safest and

EXHIBIT 3.6 : Threat definition Subnet Segments (with Baseline Threat trajectory shown in Bold)

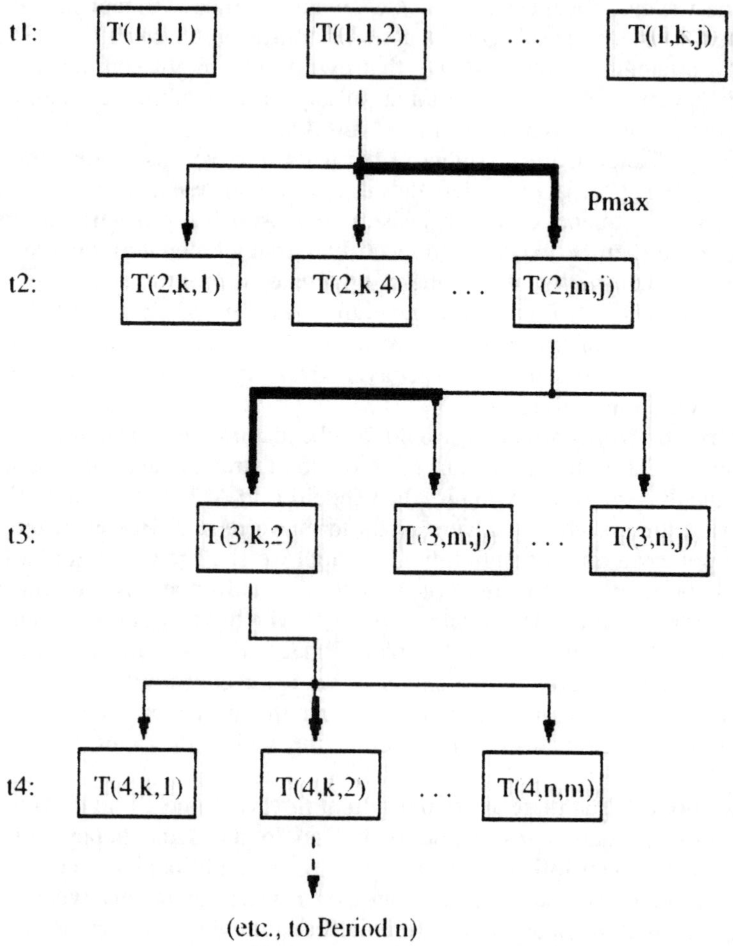

cheapest countermeasure. **Exhibits 3.7a** and **3.7b** indicate the basic structuring conventions that might be employed.

What's perhaps now clear is that the conclusion of a formally-disciplined planning exercise is a Baseline planning structure that details the own-force approach to some prospective confrontation. By following the procedures suggested here, this base planning structure would contain the following:

- a set of strategic scripts, each laying out an ostensibly best (as per the above evaluation criteria) countermeasure for all those perils defined in the baseline Threat Definition model that we cannot safely presume to be able to avoid (or merely wish to accept and deal with).
- it would also specify a *script* for an ostensibly most favorable proactive course of action (to be determined via a Markov-type analysis) to be imposed at any point in the confrontation where own-force planners have elected to try to seize the initiative from the adversary, and hence force him off the baseline Threat Definition trajectory.

Moreover, we might once again raise the practical distinction between levels of scripts. True *strategic* scripts would be recognizable in either of three different ways:

a) they pertain to a concerted action to be taken by more than one *kind* of unit . . . e.g., an initiative involving infantry divisions in company with an air wing; a large-scale infantry deployment against one adversary front coupled with a fleet-level Naval maneuver on aother front);

b) they orient own-forces in aggregate towards some qualitatively-unique option or posture, e.g.:

- assault in force with intent to secure total military victory as the strategic end;
- defense in force in order to frustrate/defeat a prospective adversary strategic initiative aimed at the expedient securing of new territory, the intent of which may be to increase the likelihood of a diplomatic vs. military resolution to some conflict, etc.

c) they involve an initiative that may be said to effect a qualitative change in the nature of the confrontation, e.g.:

- the decision to shift from employment of conventional to chemical or nuclear weapons, etc.
- a major escalation of the dimensions of competition, such as that which might follow from the decision to destroy an adversary's surveillance/reconnaissance satellites rather than continue to employ passive countermeasures (jamming or electronic interference).

EXHIBIT 3.7a : Subtree/Subnet Structure

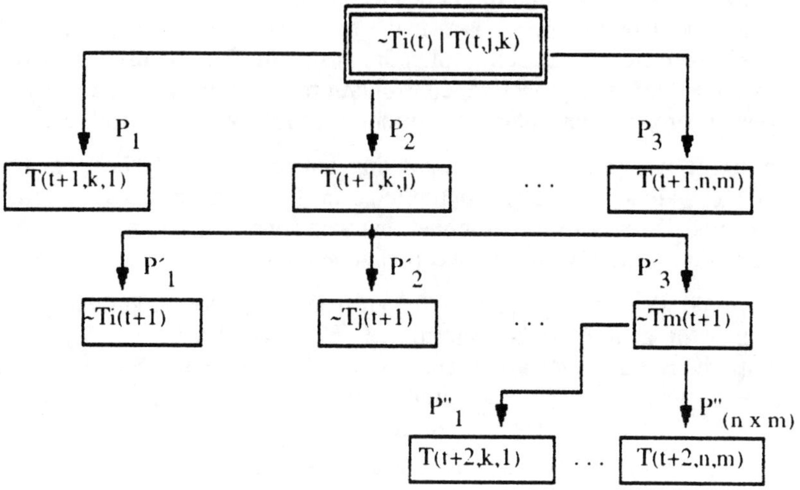

EXHIBIT 3.7b : Subtree/Subnet Definition

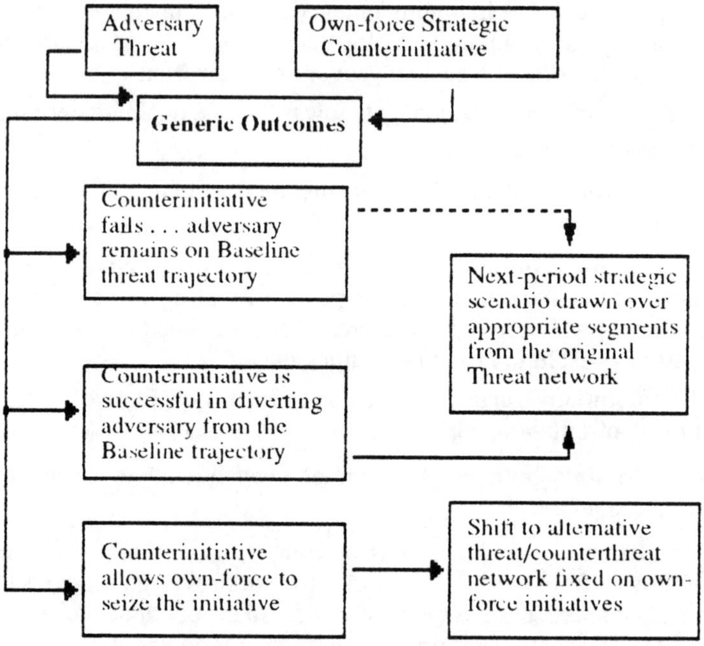

And given the hierarchical essence of modern planning protocols, any strategic *script* would then subsume a set of tactical reactive/proactive initiatives, each defining a *mission* for some lower-order *unit* to be taken on some given dimension (an action to be taken by an army corps or set of infantry divisions; a set of sorties to be flown by a fighter wing, etc.). Each tactical script would, in its turn, subsume a set of scripts directing actions to be taken by still lower-order units . . . e.g., specifying what tasks fall to a specific infantry division within a corps; the tasking for a fighter squadron. Indeed, the details of what any unit is to accomplish within an aggregate plan should be conveyed to them in the form of a proper *script*, along with a proper *scenario* that serves to collect all available intelligence about the capabilities and intents of the adversary unit(s) they are expected to confront.

In short, the ultimate end of all the operations laid out here is to make sure that the overall course of action to which we finally commit our own-force will represent the best that we can reasonably expect to do, given our capabilities vs. those of some adversary with respect to some given confrontation and/or *theater* of operations (the commercial equivalent of which is some basic product/market sector). Therefore, again, there would be a need to replicate the strategic planning process (generate a unique planning structure) for each unique adversary/theater combination with which the organization might be confonted.

But to add now the obvious qualification, both common sense and common technical wisdom will also dictate the requirement for some sort of Contingency Planning structure as a back-up to the Baseline plan, this to hedge against either of the following possibilities:

- cases where an adversary authors threats other than those defined on the Baseline trajectory;
- instances where a (proactive or counteractive) strategic initiative that we ourselves author results in an outcome other than that which was most desired or deemed most likely.

And the determination of how extensive or limited this contingency planning structure ought to be would follow from the spread (degree of stochasticity) of the various event-side probability distributions that were generated and the spread of outcome event possibilities (first and n-order consequences) associated with the response analysis/evaluation exercises.

By way of summary then, the two sorts of structured strategic planning/positioning protocols we've dealt with here have much to offer those who would try to impose some sort of discipline on Event (threat) Projection and Response generation activities. Moreover, the same set of structuring procedures would apply were it commercial or political (vs. military) adversaries with which we were engaged, or for that matter were it environmental (vs. competitive) events for which we were trying to be *ready*!

But some readers may be troubled by the intricacy these structuring protocols would demand of planners. The natural question to ask is if it's really worthwhile going to all the effort that the various operations entail? The answer that we would give is simple: It depends on how much the planner's organization might stand to lose if a strategic error is made. And in business or government no less than the military, even the most crude computations will probably suggest that there is enough to lose to warrant executives and their staffs investing the incremental analytical effort these formal structurng conventions demand.

Some practitioners, however, may seek to escape the demands of the sorts of network structuring conventions we've introduced here by raising a question about whether or not these contemporary strategic planning protocols are really sufficient to their needs. And in some cases, this question may be very well taken. For some organizations will find themselves operating in contexts that are sufficiently volatile to warrant a transition to a yet more powerful contingency planning platform, this a *dynamic* approach to strategic readiness we'll deal with in the next chapter.

NOTES AND REFERENCES

1. For more on the rationale for a contingency-based approach to management, see the following: Burns & Stalker, *Management of Innovation* (Tavistock, 1961); Hofer's article, "Towards a Contingency Theory of Business Strategy", *Academy of Management Journal* (18; 1975); Lawrence and Lorsch's book, *Organizations and Environment* (Harvard University Press, 1967), or Miller & Friesen, "Strategy-Making and Environment", *Strategic Management Journal* (4; 1983).

2. As an indication of the extent to which the goal-driven approach monopolizes not only popular but also academic attention, one of the most popular and widely-referenced of management authors, Russell Ackoff, has written that "Planning consists in conceiving a desired future and the practical means of achieving it" (*Concept of Corporate Planning*; Wiley, 1970). But as we've suggested in this volume, this can only be taken to be an adequate description of planning requirements only for those those corporations that are effectively dominant in their fields and/or autonomous, and so essentially immune from exogenous threats. In all other cases, following Ackoff's advice as to what planning entails would very likely put organizational authorities in peril of being visited by a steady stream of unpleasant strategic surprises.

3. For more on singular-scenario or essentially linear-sequential strategic planning practice, see: Fry & Killing's, *Strategic Analysis and Action* (Prentice-Hall Canada, 1986); Green & Jones, "Strategic Management Step-by-Step", *Long Range Planning* (15, 3; 1982); B. E. Gup's book, *Guide to Strategic Planning* (McGraw-Hill, 1980); or Naylor's paper, "Strategic Planning and Forecasting", *Journal of Forecasting* (2; 1983).

4. For ideas on generating scenarios, see Michael Godet's, *Scenarios and Strategic Management* (Butterworths, 1987); Hirschhorn's paper, "Scenario Writing: A Developmental Approach", *Journal of the American Planning Association* ((46, 2); 1980); or McNulty's "Scenario Development for Planning", *Futures* (9; 1977).

5. An excellent discussion of Markov operations is in Massey, et. al., in their: *Stochastic Models of Buying Behavior* (Cambridge: MIT Press, 1970). Indeed, interest in the employment of Markov processes seems to have peaked during the early 1970's, at least so far as non-engineering applications are concerned. Note also that Markov structures could be fitted over either strategic, tactical or operational event possibilities without any major modification (and indeed, most of the actual uses to which Markov analysis has been put are better thought of involving operational or tactical than strategic choices) . . . c.f., Rowland & Sovereign, "Markov-Chain Analysis of Internal Manpower Supply" , *Industrial Relations* (9,1), 1968.

6. There are of course other methods for trying to display concatenative dynamics. Of such, perhaps the most widely employed is the *influence diagram*, c.f.: John Diffenbach, "Influence Diagrams for Complex Strategic Issues", in *Strategic Management Journal* (3), 1982). There are, however, no formal manipulation mechanics underlying this or any of the more popular graphic display media designed for direct use by managers. Somewhat more sophisticated approaches to representing simple state-transform dynamics (which could easily be extended to a graphic format) are certain of the computer-based modeling grammars now under development. For a description of a typical approach, see Arthur M. Geoffrion's *An Introduction to Structured Modeling* (Western Management Science Institute, UCLA: Working Paper No. 338, June 1986).

7. For more on the generation and use of generic referents, see Part II of my *Societal Systems: Methodology, Modeling and Management* (New York: North Holland, 1978).

8. Discussions of the concept of X-efficiencies appeared in the Summer 1980 issue of the *Journal of Post-Keynesian Economics*, e.g.: Roger Franz, "On the Existence of X-efficiency", or my paper: "Corporate Autonomy and X-inefficiency".

9. Of such books, those by Michael Porter are of enormous appeal to practitioners; c.f. his *Competitive Advantage* (Free Press, 1985). But while easy to read and engaging for executives that have no good disposition towards serious academic argument or technical dissertation, such works may often encourage strategic planners to be preoccupied with searching for opportunities they can exploit by virtue of apparent competitive advantages (some of which may be more a matter of wishful thinking than fact) their firm enjoys over others. But while such an emphasis would be entirely appropriate for effectively dominant enterprises (being really just a natural extension to popular goal-driven planning practice), the better part of valor for organizations operating in highly competitive contexts --or significantly vulnerable to environmental

vaguaries-- is to worry about dealing with what others might do to us before undertaking the more entertaining task of speculating about what we might do to others. Hence, again, the reason why the Structured contingency planning protocol discussed in this chapter is *threat-driven.*

10. Operations over tree structures and other simple network-based constructs are simple expressions of basic graph theory conventions, c.f.: Harary, et. al., *Structural Models: An Introduction to the Theory of Directed Graphs* (Wiley, 1965). Or for a more recent discussion of their decision implications, see the appropriate sections in Andrew Sage, *Methodology for Large-Scale Systems* (McGraw-Hill, 1977); or Sage and Rajala's paper: "On the Role of Structure in Policy Analysis and Decision-making (in *Management Handbook for Public Administrators*: Van Nostrand Reinhold, 1978).

11. For example of combined-force concepts, see a document developed by the BDM Corporation under a grant from DARPA (the Defense Advanced Research Projects Agency): *The Airland Battle Management Program*: Corps Operations and Scenario Description, October 31, 1985. This is representative of what popularly passes in the contemporary defense community as a Planning scenario, and also shares with virtually all of its counterparts this vital aspect: The NATO forces always win.

12. To generalize from this point, there is one very critical caution that might be directed not merely at those doing military planning, but also at corporate planners. For as a consequence of trends noted in the very first chapter of this book --the increasing quality of foreign competitors, coupled with (indeed, in part a cause of) decreasing general American affluence-- we are running into more and more situations where strategic planning must be done in anticipation of possible tactical-level disadvantages. That is, both US commercial firms and military elements may for the first time be called upon to confront adversaries who are relatively richer in assets. Doing high-quality, disciplined strategic planning, oriented towards realistic net assessments rather than comforting fictions, now takes greater urgency than even before. For if you're not as rich or strong as the other guy, about the only way to avoid defeat is be smarter (or of course luckier, though so much of what is taken at first to be the spawn of luck may in retrospect better be seen to be the consequence of wit).

CHAPTER 4

INTELLIGENCE-DRIVEN, DYNAMIC STRATEGIC PLANNING/POSITIONING

The welfare of organizations operating in highly competitive, volatile contexts is intimately tied to their ability to accurately forecast the threats to which they might be subjected. Given sufficient notice, they might then move to avert or preempt a threat or, lacking that, position themselves in such a way as to be able to best weather it. But as things now stand, there is no general agreement what a properly dynamic planning/positioning platform might look like. But one particularly promising avenue of approach would be to adopt procedures of the sort that the professional intelligence community has evolved to support command/control systems in the modern military sector, especially those grouped under the general heading of Indicator/Warning-Alert (IWA) operations. In this chapter we want to suggest how certain of these procedures might be both formalized and generalized so that they might be applied by commercial and governmental as well as military enterprises.

4.1 Characteristics of Modern Command/Control Systems

As was suggested in an earlier chapter, the most popular of approaches to organizational management is still some sort of management-by-objectives (MBO) scheme. This, in turn, will be given tangible expression in terms of either a simple bifocal model-base structure of the type underlying a goal-driven/developmental or sequential-state/cybernetic management system configuration. But no management-by-objectives scheme can be made dynamic --i.e., have its objectives modified or adjusted with any frequency--without sacrificing the appearance of consistency that lends it its essential pragmatic appeal. This weakness has served as the basic point of departure for all those arguing the case for some sort of alternative to the MBO approach. That alternative posed most often in the popular management literature is centered on the suggestion that enterprises adopt more of an *entrepreneurial* elan. Naturally enough, advocates of this approach generally tend to view traditional management-by-objectives schemes as the essence of bland corporate bureacracy, and chastise its practitioners for being too wedded to the familiar and the precedented . . . too much given to setting pedestrian objectives that always leave their organization a step or two short of the leading edge of technological innovation in their fields of endeavor.

Consider, for example, this prologue to a recent article in that flagship of popular management patronage, the Harvard Business Review:

> An X ray of the entrepreneurial organization reveals these dynamic characteristics: encouragement of individuals' imagination, flexibility and a willingness to accept risks.[1]

Yet as with most other work pleading the entrepreneurial case, the discussion is notable more for its rhetorical richness than for the intricacy of its reasoning. For in this article, as in most all mainstream management theory essays on entrepreneurialism, what *flexibility* ultimately translates into is merely another route towards risk-minimization. Particularly, under the guise of greater flexibility, managers are urged to adopt a carefully staged commitment of resources (via some sort of generalized rent-vs-buy logic) in various product-market sectors, such that their exposure is consistently limited should things not work out as hoped. That is, the demand for greater flexibility more often than not becomes transmogrified into a kind of backhanded apology for defensive diversification. And while this sounds clever in concept, it may often prove to be utterly inane in practice. For if such advice were to be carried to its logical conclusion, the net effect would be to spawn a class of commercial dilettantes, each trying a little of this and a little of that, but never investing fully enough to stand against competitors who are not tentative about their degree of commitment. For given the dictate that *return follows risk*, there are few games we can look to win by consistently hedging our bets!

For those organizations that would abandon the security of static management-by-objectives for an entrepreneurial posture then, the advice that's needed is not so rhetorical, but rather some idea of the kind of process by which enterprises might come to appreciate the terms of the trade-off between risk and return such that we know that degree of resource commitment (and so risk exposure) required for a significant vs. trivial presence in any product-market areas. Unless this question can be answered properly, there's always the possibility that what is supposed to pass for a studied embrace of the tentative is in fact merely executive timidity.

Our concern here is then to suggest a possible practical detour around this trap. Particularly, the pages remaining in this chapter will concern themselves with how --and why-- organizations might constitute themselves as what are referred to as command/control or C3/I systems, with the three C's being Command, Control and Communications and the I standing for Intelligence.[2] The concept of organizations operating as command/control systems arose in the military sector, and so entails certain assumptions about the sorts of enterprises for which it is appropriate:

- the organization should be geographically dispersed, and possibly functionally diversified as well;
- the organization will have a *critical* mission, such that the consequences of default (via either decision error or untoward delay) may have serious survival implications;
- the organization will have to contend with one or more ingenious, aggressive competitors that might author an extremely wide range of highly threatening initiatives.

And while these conditions apply most obviously in the military sector, they may also be readily extended to encompass many modern commercial firms operating in particularly challenging markets and governmental agencies having emergency management missions, etc.

The key structural properties that might serve to distinguish a command/control system are summarized in **Exhibit 4.1**. It will take the form of a dispersed hierarchy, with the several levels of the command/control system mirroring the three classical levels of management. Thus, as a general rule, the Central Headquarters will house those individuals (higher management functionaries) who have been allocated strategic decision responsibilities, or whose concern is the welfare of the organization as a whole. It's then convenient (and usually legitimate as well) to think of middle-echelon managers as having tactical authority within some geographic area (region) or over some division of an enterprise (e.g., a manufacturing

EXHIBIT 4.1 : Command/Control System Architecture

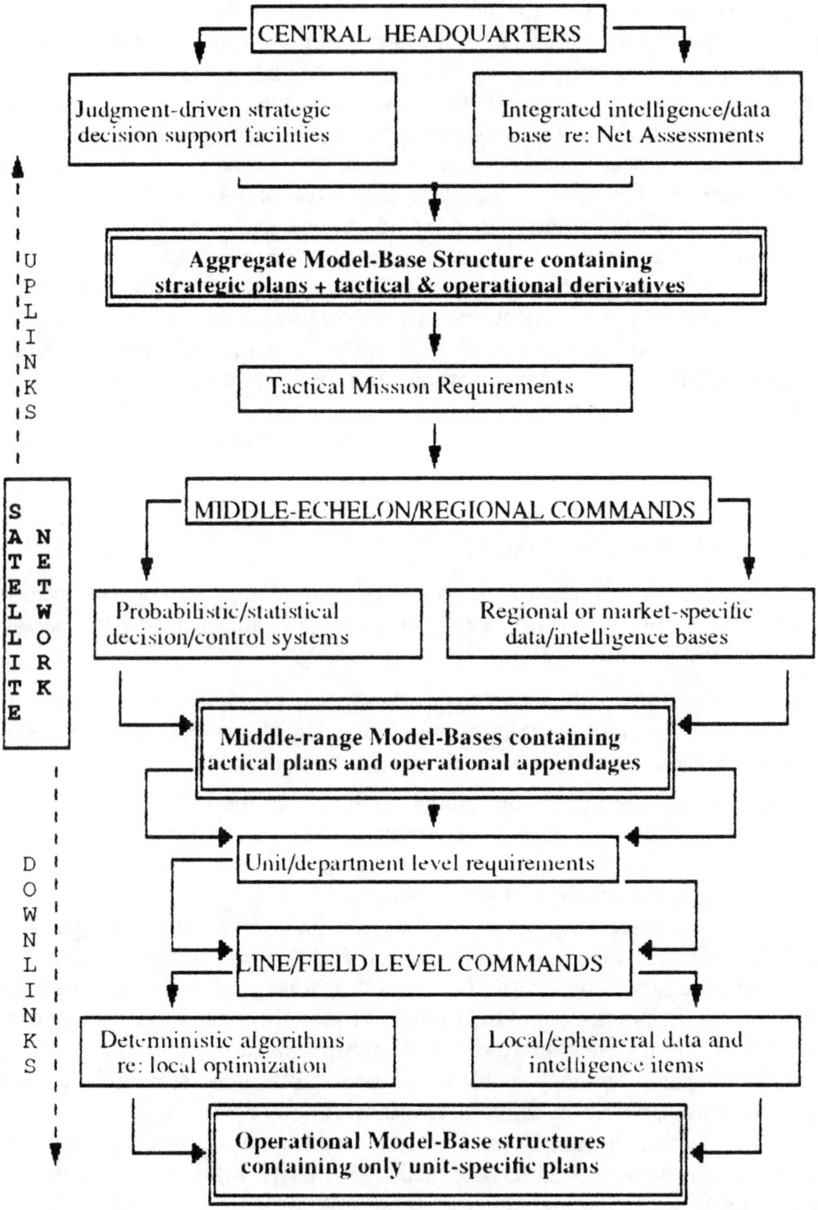

plant, product line or market sector). In contrast, line-level functionaries (e.g., the head of a functional department in a firm; the commander of an infantry division or naval battle group) are usually charged with operations-level decision responsibilities. Field commands thus tend to be most remote from the central headquarters in terms of distance, and assigned well-bounded *local* domains of interest or spheres of influence.

There will then be a communication network in place (e.g., the satellite based, wide-area network shown in the exhibit) that can link all organizational units with all others. Downlinks are used by central headquarters functionaries to convey tactical mission requirements and constraints to regional command centers, or to charge them with those aspects of some strategic plan(s) they are responsible for carrying out. Regional commanders then use the command downlinks to make their field-level subordinates aware of those operational-level aspects of some tactical plan(s) for which their unit is responsible or for passing along any constraints, perhaps in the form of a decision table or *rules of engagement*. The communications aspects of a command/control system are intended to allow for more or less *real-time* exchanges of the following sorts:

- for higher-order units to disseminate standing orders to lower-order units (e.g., for central headquarters to inform regional authorities of their tactical responsibilities following from some strategic commitment; for regional authorities to communicate operational requirements to field units deriving from some tactical choice), or provide lower-order units with advice as to how to respond to some non-routine event.
- for lower-order units to inform a superior or higher-echelon unit about conditions/events occurring within their purview;
- for lower-order units (regional offices and/or field units) to be able to talk freely among themselves without having to channel peer-level communications through a higher-order node.

Such linkages --and particularly the first two-- are of course the pragmatic essence of command/control. For to the extent that they are intact and of sufficient capacity, the effect is to allow lower-order functionaries to give their superiors a running commentary or blow-by-blow description of what's taking place at some remote site, and for the superiors to then provide a steady flow of advice (or dictates, as the case may be) about what actions the subordinate should be taking. From the higher-order commander's perspective then, the *real-time* communication aspects of command/control systems are the next best thing to actually being where the action is.

Superimposed on the dispersed organizational structure will be a distributed model-base structure, this encoding the entire array of planning commitments at which an organization has arrived.

Typically, a command/control system will organize its model-base as a *centrifugal* construct. Under a centrifugal scheme, the Central Headquarters will maintain the master or aggregate model base, this housing the organization's strategic plans plus a copy of all tactical and operations-level appendages. The middle-echelon or regional command centers will maintain at their site those Tactical plans for which they are directly responsible, as well as a copy of the operations-level plans drafted by the various line or field units they subsume. The line-level units will then have at hand only those operational plans specific to their local responsibilities.

A centrifugal model-base is recommended for command/control systems for several reasons. First, it answers for security interests in highly competitive contexts, as it is a concrete expression of the *need to know* criterion. Secondly, it is generally economical; indeed, one of the primary reasons for the allocation of smaller computer systems to lower-echelon units follows from the fact of a successive reduction in the size of the model-base they must maintain on-site. It's also a generally efficient approach. For each element of the organization's command structure will have on-site only those information system facilities pertinent to the array of events/problems with which it is routinely expected to be confronted and so charged with being able to resolve locally in *stand-alone* mode.

As a practical matter, most working command/control systems tend to operate under a contingency planning approach to readiness, this resulting in an overall organizational planning structure like that shown in **Exhibit 4.2**. But again, the basic rationale for any organization to constitute itself as a command/control system would be to increase its potential for coping successfully in particularly volatile competitive contexts. This would suggest that organizations operating as command/control systems would want to make a modification to the sort of contingency planning protocol we described in the previous chapter, one that would lead to a more *dynamic* approach to strategic planning/positioning. And the specific modification that we have in mind is the obvious one:

> Increases in contextual volatility should argue for a corresponding decrease in the length of the planning/projection horizon ($t1 \rightarrow tn$), with the first term again representing the point in time at which a contingency planning construct is defined and the latter fixing the end-point of the period over which it is to apply.

That is, conventional technical wisdom suggests that volatility be countered by shortening the interval between successive iterations of the contingency planning process. But were we to carry this reduction to its logical conclusion, we'd come upon the much more interesting prospect of contingency planning constructs being subjected to essentially continuous modification.

EXHIBIT 4.2 : Distributed Contingency Planning Structure

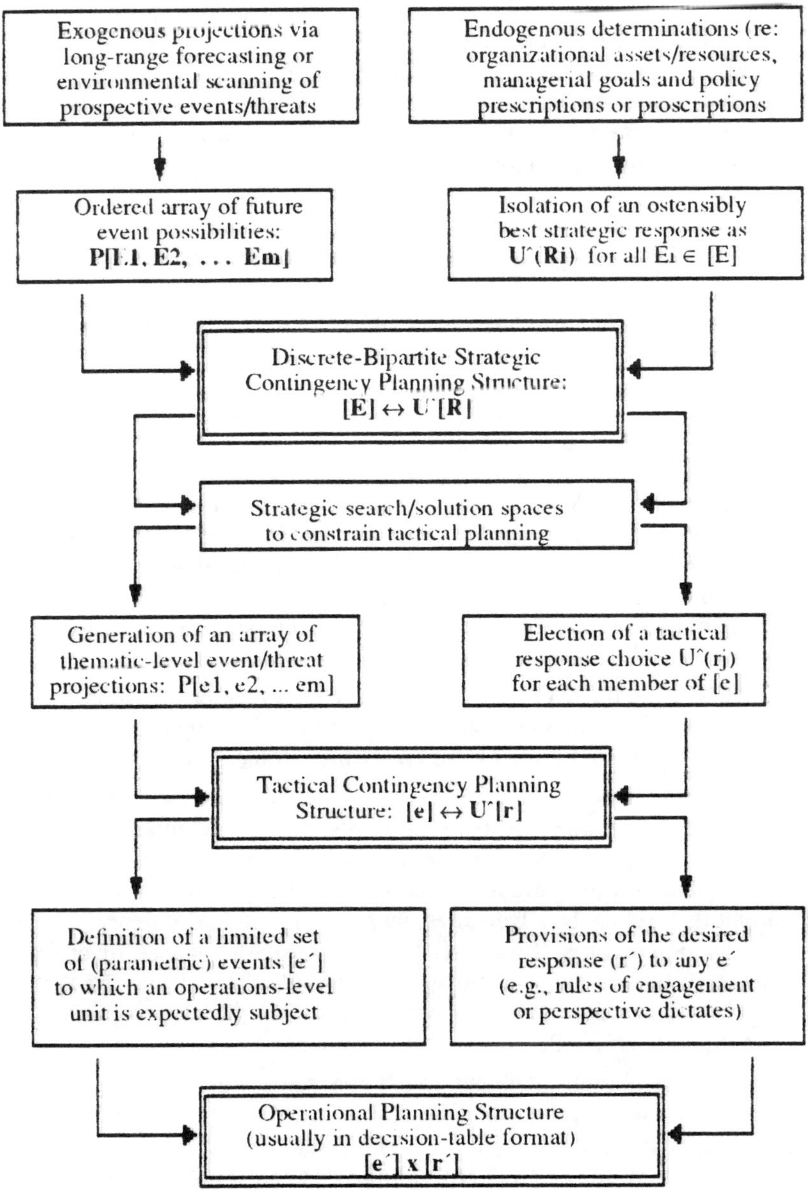

And the best practical expression of what this might entail is known in the military community as Indicator/Warning Alert procedures, where strategic planning structures and positioning commitments are expected to be responsive to a more or less continuous stream of *intelligence* inputs.[3] It's these I/WA procedures that add the Intelligence (I) aspect to C3/I systems. And when properly formalized and generalized, certain of these provisions might be seen to be the most direct path for organizations to add a dynamic quality to their strategic management practice.

4.2 Strategic Indicator/Warning-Alert Facilities

Most modern nations will have some sort of Indicator/Warning-Alert (IWA) facilities in place to warn them of any situations that might pose a potential threat to their national security. Or, lacking that, IWA facilities would be expected to alert them to some actual vs. prospective threat (to provide early recognition of actions already taken). As a secondary function, nations may also deploy IWA facilities to scan not merely for actual or prospective threats, but also for any perhaps fleeting windows of opportunity that might be exploited if they can move quickly enough. But for organizations faced with aggressive and ingenious competitors, it is *threats* rather than opporunities that are of paramount concern.

Because threats may be of two basically different sorts, IWA activities may have two very different orientations:

> ORIENTATION X|Y . . . where an organization-X would have its IWA facilities looking for signs of any direct threats that might be directed against it by a declared competitor, some entity-Y.
>
> ORIENTATION Yi|Yj . . . where X would have its IWA facilities focussed on the interface between two second-party entities (Yi and Yj) where there is thought to exist some potential for an incidental threat . . . i.e., a situation that might extend to imperil X. For example, Yi and Yj might themselves be adversaries, with X committed (by treaty or perhaps merely pragmatic self-interest) to come to the assistance of one of the parties in the event of a threat from the other. Or it may be that X is dependent on a commodity whose flow might be interrupted as a consequence of conflict between Yi and Yj.[4]

In that both orientations demand much the same thing in terms of IWA technology, we can simplify things by dealing with just the first or X|Y case.

But talking about IWA *technology* is somewhat deceptive. For even at their most sophisticated in the modern military sector, IWA activities have a strongly casual character about them, with much dependent upon the proclivities of the particular individuals involved. And this is perhaps as things should be. For given that intelligence-driven (vs. simple data-driven) decision processes are so inordinately dependent upon interpretive sensibilities, attempts to subject them to any sort of rote algorithmic discipline might very well prove unfortunate. This would then suggest that those seeking to bring a common order to IWA operations content themselves with posing support facilities in the form of non-mandatory structuring conventions.

For structural aids are intended to provide a framework to help organize and guide reasoning about matters that will not lend themselves well to any sort of computational artifices. As such, IWA *structures* would be designed to help regularize analytical efforts without trying to fix methodological matters too rigidly (and, as an aside, to allow for computers to perform much of the clerical work that would otherwise devolve on the IWA analysts themselves). Of the sorts of structures that might serve these ends, five will be elaborated and defended here as particularly promising:

The Confrontational Tableau
The Contingency Tableau
The Competitive Matrix
The Contingency Transformation Matrix
The Indicator Tableau.

When viewed in concert, these five structures might be seen to provide a basis for *top-down* analysis directed at the two key requirements of IWA-based planning/positioning exercises, Threat-Projection and Threat-Assessment.

4.3 Structures to Support Dynamic Threat-Projection

The first of the structures is intended to help establish the basic bounds of inquiry for IWA exercises. This is the Confrontational Tableau shown below:

	Dimensions				
Categories	D1	D2	D3	. . .	Dn
C1	{N}1,1	{N}1,2	{N}1,3	. . .	{N}1,n
C2	{N}2,1	{N}2,2	{N}2,3	. . .	{N}2,n
			etc.		
Cm	{N}m,1	{N}m,2	{N}m,3	. . .	{N}m,n

As a rule, the row entries (C's) would be defined so as to represent ideal-type intervals on a continuum of relational states that might pertain between any two nations or geo-political entities . . . any X and Y. A typical collection of relational categories might be comprised of the following:

[C] = C1: extensive (unlimited) aggression
C2: limited (constrained) conflict
C3: subversion (covert/deniable aggression)
C4: harassment (indirect aggression)
C5: conciliation (disengagement).

The columnar entries (D's) would then identify the dimensions on which two entities might engage in a confrontation. The dimensions actually used would of course depend on the particular context of competition, e.g.:

Business Firms:	*Nation-States*:
D1: Price	D1: Military
D2: Product quality	D2: Commercial
D3: Merchandizing	D3: Diplomatic
D4: Advertising	D4: Ideological

That is, were X and Y business firms, competitive exchanges might be centered around price, product differentiation, etc. And on any of the dimensions, the intensity of exchanges might run the gamut from no-holds-barred *predatory* competition (an interpretation of a C1 relationship between economic rivals) all the way to some sort of collusive or C5-type protocol where the firms agree to refrain from direct competition.

But when it is nations or geo-political entities with which we're concerned, we'd have to consider the possibility of confrontations choreographed around military, commmercial and diplomatic as well as ideological exchanges. Hence a Confrontational Tableau such as that shown, in abbreviated form, in **Exhibit 4.3**, with the focus of practical attention fixed on the cell-level entries or N(i,j,k)'s, each of which would be used to define some generic confrontational initiative. Any generic confrontational referent would be used to give a rough idea of what a Ci-type action might look like were it undertaken on the j'th dimension. In this sense, the collection of N(i,j,k)'s entered into a Confrontational Tableau might be said to constitute IWA analyst's comprehension of the basic strategic alternatives open to the adversaries of interest. But in practice, it would be expected that the community of IWA analysts would have been at work defining generic confrontational alternatives as a more or less continuous background exercise.

As such, IWA analysts working on any specific X|Y confrontation would not have to start building a Confrontational Tableau from scratch, but might rather look to borrow much from alternatives that have been defined by their predecessors. It might thus reasonably be hoped that by drawing upon the collective wisdom of the field, and then supplementing with alternatives of

EXHIBIT 4.3 : A Sample Confrontational Tableau

Relational Categories	DIMENSIONS OF CONFRONTATION: D1: Military	D2: Commercial	D3: Diplomatic	D4: Ideological
C1: Extensive Aggression	N(1,1,1): Area weapons (chemical or nuclear) used without dis-crimination	N(1,2,1): interdiction of critical materials; N(1,2,2): expropriation of assets	N(1,3,1): breaking of diplomatic relations; N(1,3,2): attempted assasinations	N(1,4,1): attempts to incite civil war or foment rebellion
C2: Limited Agression	N(2,1,1): selective surgical strikes; N(2,1,2): sponsoring terrorist incidents	N(2,2,1): boycotts; N(2,2,2): limited embargos; N(2,2,3): industrial sabotage	N(2,3,1): recall of ambassador; N(2,3,2): agitation for UN sanctions/ condemnation	N(2,4,1): "black" propoganda; N(2,4,2): excitation of defections
C3: Subversion	N(3,1,1): supplying arms to insurgents; N(3,1,2): infiltration of agents	N(3,2,1): abettment of strikes or aiding attempts at disruption of production	N(3,3,1): support of a government in exile and/or internal opposition	N(3,4,1): incitation of racial/inter-class tensions
C4: Harassment	N(4,1,1): initiation of incidents at borders; N(4,1,2): Fly-overs or other forms or close re-connaissance	N(4,2,1): attempting to get financial institutions to recall loans; N(4,2,2): "dumping" of products	N(4,3,1): attempts to weaken third-party support (via coercion of allies or manipulating international agencies)	N(4,4,1): using "dirty" journalistic tactics . . . planting functional reports, etc.
C5: Disenga-gement	N(5,1,1): withdrawal of forward units; N(5,1,2): lowering of readiness levels (stand downs)	N(5,2,1): easing trade barriers; N(5,2,2): moves toward economic linkage	N(5,3,1): moves to restore normal diplomatic relations	N(5,4,1): cultural exchanges; N(5,4,2): restraining adversarial rhetoric

their own original authoring, that IWA analysts might be expected to generate an array of generic confrontational initiatives --some set [N] = all N(i,j,k)-- that would stand a reasonable chance of answering for a majority of the *logically possible* strategic options from which adversaries might elect.

As a look at the examples shown in the exhibit might make clear, the sample Confrontational Tableau has been constructed such that any transit away from the far Northwest corner --to the right and/or downward-- is tantamount to a relaxation of the threat-potential in the relationship between X and Y. A de-escalation of tension would then follow ipso-facto from any shift from a higher to a lower-order relational category, say from extensive aggression (C1) to limited aggression (C2), etc. Equally compelling but somewhat less definite is the effect of a rightward shift among the dimensions . . . e.g., from the military (D1) to the commercial (D2), from the commercial to the diplomatic (D3), from the diplomatic to the ideological (D4). For all things considered, it would generally be preferable to have two nations engaged in a war of words or wages than weapons.

In contrast, any shift leftward and/or upward would then imply some degree of threat escalation. For those N(i,j,k)'s having the lowest i and j index values (which would again cause them to appear in closer proximity to the Northwest corner) will generally be taken to carry the highest peril not just for the organization towards which they are directed, but perhaps also for the organization that has elected to author them. Thus, as a natural side-effect of the way in which a Confrontational Tableau is laid out, there will be what amounts to a ready-made ranking of the various strategic options as to their relative threat-potential.

What would come next in a typical IWA exercise would be a shift in the level of analysis from the general to the more specific. For analysts would turn away from their concern with generic referents towards a consideration of the range of *tactical* alternatives that might be employed to give real practical moment to any of the strategic options or N(i,j,k) entries. It's these tactical alternatives that constitute *contingencies*, per se. For again, the generic confrontational initiatives are high-order referents, deliberately abstracted from any situation-specific conditionals. As such, any generic confrontational initiative is best seen as a supra-referent capable of subsuming a number of lower-order or reality-based event referents, i.e.:

$$\text{any } N(i,j,k) \rightarrow \{E\} \supset (E1, E2 \ldots Em).$$

In IWA based contingency planning/positioning processes, the G's serve as the contingencies.

For the G-level referents would be used to tailor the generic confrontational initiatives to the conditions specific to a particular X:Y interface and time interval. Thus, any contingency (Em) would postulate some variation on the basic theme posed by the anchoring generic referent. Were we then to take any N(i,j,k) as answering for the general substance or *strategic* import of a prospective competitive initiative, then any properly-defined contingency referent --qua *scenario* model-- should provide situation-specific specifications the following aspects (Sj's):

S1(WHAT): details the set of operational actions underlying a working (tactical) variant on some N(i,j,k)

S2(HOW): indicates the sequence (order) in which these operational actions are to be executed.

S3(WHO): which unit(s) of which entitity (X or Y) will be expected to actually convey the initiative;

S4(WHOM): the other entity's unit(s) or assets that are the likely targets of the various actions;

S5(WHEN): details any temporal conditionals that might apply as to initiation, duration and conclusion;

S6(WHERE): provides locational/geographic details or otherwise bounds the scope of the initiative;

We'd thus get the following format for any of the event/threat possibilities included in an IWA-based planning exercise:

$$Em \in \{E\} \supset N(i,j,k) = Vm(S1) + Vm(S2) + \ldots \; Vm(S6),$$

where Vm(Sj) indicates the specific attributes associated with contingency Em for the j'th aspect. At this point then, we might take the basic unit of analysis of an IWA exercise to be a contingency E(i,j,k,m) where:

i: the i'th Relational Category (C)
j: the j'th Dimension (D)
k: the k'th generic initiative within some set {N}i,j
m: the m'th member of the array {E}.

The set of all so-defined event/threat possibilities would then constitute the Master Contingency Set: [E*] = all E(i,j,k,m)'s.

But to simplify notation, we may refer to any E(i,j,k,m) by a single index while still reflecting the ordering logic of a Confrontational Tableau. This, recall, had lower (i,j) values pointing to generic initiatives of increasingly higher threat-potential (those closer to the far Northeast corner where we locate the worst-case relational situation). Therefore, we might want to let E(1,1,1,1) = E1 ∈ [E*], E(1,1,1,2) = E2 ∈ [E*], etc., to the point where we'd close the set with some Gz that is the last variant on the last of the N(i,j,k)'s.

Once these notational translations have been done, we'd have the basis for yet another IWA structure, this the Contingency Tableau:

Contingency Referents	Aspects				
	S1	S2	S3	...	Sm
E1	V(1,1)	V(1,2)	V(1,3)	...	V(1,m)
E2	V(2,1)	V(2,2)	V(2,3)	...	V(2,m)
			etc.		
Ez	V(z,1)	V(z,2)	V(z,3)	...	V(z,m)

The cell entries or V(m,s)'s would thus convey the specifications for the s'th aspect of the m'th contingency . . . e.g., V(3,1) would indicate the WHO provisions for E2.

Any two contingencies --say E1 and E2-- must then be different in terms of the provisions they entail on at least one aspect . . . this the miminal condition for uniqueness. Maximal disparity between any E1 and E2 would then occur were they to have essentially *empty* intersects (have no specifications in common) for all six aspects, such that:

$$(E1 \cap E2) = 0 \quad \text{for all } V(Sj),\ j = 1 - 6.$$

In all other cases, there would be similarities (non-empty intersects) as well as differences between contingencies, with any differences accessible as:

$$V@(Sj)E1{:}E2 \ = \ V(E1 \cup E2) - (E1 \cup E2) \quad \text{for any/all } Sj.$$

This will have practical importance for a later point. But for now its the matter of threat-assessment that concerns us.

4.4 Structures to Formalize Strategic Threat-Assessment

For not all the threat-projection possibilities included in a master contingency set [E*] --irrespective of the threat potential they carry-- will be of genuine interest in real-world IWA exercises. Rather, of equal and often even greater significance, is the likelihood that some particular threat might materialize. And with this matter we'd transit to the threat assessment stage of an IWA exercise. For the pressing objective of threat-assessment activities would be to help fix an organization's attention on those contingencies that are both most threatening and most probable. It's these for which an organization would wish to be most *ready* . . . these against which it would want to martial the majority of wit and resources. But in many cases, the most expedient way to get to the above is to first work to eliminate *uninteresting* contingencies . . . those that pose only trivial threat potential and/or are highly unlikely to materialize.

Indeed, IWA analysts may want to recognize and reject uninteresting contingencies even before getting to this point. That is, they might look to try to eliminate --right at the outset-- certain generic confrontational initiatives that are for some reason considered *implausible* in a particular X|Y conjunction. For this would have the effect of obviating the need to define any contingencies or G-level referents associated with any N(i,j,k)'s that have been determined to be unworthy of any further consideration. But whether at the generic or the contingency level, it's always important to try to recognize and then eliminate any alternatives that --given the parties to a confrontation or the time period of interest-- are expected to have only an insignificant likelihood of occurrence. For even in generously funded and well-staffed military intelligence applications, there will almost always be more alternatives to consider than can be adequately treated. It will then usually be necessary to take some steps that will allow IWA efforts and assets to be focussed on some limited number of most probable confrontational possibilities. And once again we might use a Competitive Matrix to initiate the Net Assessment aspects of strategic competitive analysis:

	Dimensions of Competition			
Assets	D1	D2	...	Dm
A1	q(1,1)	q(1,2)	...	q(1,m)
A2	q(2,1)	q(2,2)	...	q(2,m)
		etc.		
A1	q(1,1)	q(1,2)	...	q(1,m)
Net	Q1	Q2	...	Qm

where q or Q =

>> : significant advantage to X
<< : significant advantage to Y
> : marginal advantage to X
< : marginal advantage to Y
<> : parity between X and Y

From the above, IWA analysts should be able to neatly capture and display the points of relative strength and weakness between X and a competitor Y.

For the columnar entries (D's) would once again be the four dimensions on which nations might confront eachother (Military, Commercial, etc.) while the rows would again refer to categories of competitive assets:

A1: Human resources
A2: Plant/infrastructure
A3: Capital equipment
A4: Factors (supplies, materials)
A5: Intangibles (reputation; morale), etc.

Each of the cells in the body of the Competitive Matrix would house a q(a,j) entry, this being an assessment of the competitive status between X and Y for the a'th asset category on the j'th dimension. The Q(j) entries in the last row --the *net* assessments-- would then emerge as some sort of composite product of the pertinent q(a,j) predicates. To the right of the matrix is displayed an array of *qualitative* or categorical values that might be taken on by the q(a,j) or Q(j) elements. One might of course propose to use some sort of mathematical or statistical algorithm to do scaling. But because most IWA inferences will have to be made in the absence of a sufficiency of *hard* data, being too enamoured of the precision offered by quantative scaling techniques is more often a signal of an intelligence analyst's inexperience than his sophistication.

But however they're arrived at, the Q(j) conclusions or net-assessment valuations would be used by IWA analysts to make reasoned assertions about those locations in a Confrontational Tableau where real-world competitive initiatives are most likely to be clustered. In working with net-assessment or Q(j) valuations, there are no hard and fast procedural rules to be followed. But IWA analysts would generally be expected to first direct their attention to any comparative extremes or instances where some Q(j) = either >> or <<. Such are of particular interest because they set up the classic condition whereby one party might be expected to be extremely likely to essay its strength against the other's weakness. By the same token, what might be suggested with perhaps even greater authority would be the improbability that an organization having a significant disadvantage on some dimension would elect to either prosecute a confrontation or respond to an initiative on that dimension. Rather, it would be most likely to try to move things to some dimension where it has an advantage or, lacking that, where there is effective parity.

We might of course come upon some essentially trivial situations where one party has a significant advantage on all the dimensions of confrontation . . . e.g., where Q(j) = >> for all j. In such a case, there would normally be little likelihood of the disadvantaged party undertaking anything except an essentially conciliatory initiative. All really interesting cases will then have some admixture of valuations. For example, we might suppose that analysts had arrived at the following assessments:

Q(1) = >>: X significantly stronger militarily than Y
Q(2) = < : Y has an edge in commercial power/prerogatives
Q(3) = < : Y has a diplomatic advantage (re: alliances, etc.)
Q(4) = <>: X and Y equal in ability to wage ideological conflict.

Given such, the odds are that if a confrontation is to be joined, analysts would have some basis for making probabilistic inferences about the respective initiatives qua opening gambits that X and Y might take.

For one thing, given that it is at significant disadvantage with respect to X on the military dimension, Y is unlikely to open a confrontation by undertaking any initiative that would be defined within Cell (1,1) or even Cell (2,1) . . . any sort of attack-in-force. Rather, if Y were to elect to take any sort of military initiative, it would be more likely to be of a covert or indirect nature and so be a contingency definable somewhere within the reaches of

Cell C(3,1) or Cell (4,1). Indeed, the most plausible initiating action from Y might be choreographed around a contingency qua *commercial* thrust designed to provide some limited advantage for Y without overly provoking X. Or as another likely starting point for Y, it might attempt some sort of Diplomatic initiative intended to discourage X from playing its strong suit . . . to preempt or delay a military assault by X.

For given the net-assessment outcomes just postulated and the general tendency for adversaries to lead with their strength, a military initiative from X will be highly probable. Indeed, if X were sufficiently motivated and/or sufficiently indifferent to possible diplomatic consequences (the most telling of which would be the prospect of some militarily powerful third-party nation coming to Y's defense), it might even decide to undertake an assault-in-force that is intended to result in the total and immediate capitulation of Ya, or perhaps even its destruction . . . i.e., to take an action that would be defined somewhere within Cell (1,1) of the tableau shown as Exhibit 4.3. Lesser provocation or greater concern for diplomatic sanctions or world opinion might cause X to be more temperate. It might perhaps content itself with a variant on initiative N(2,1,1) or a limited strike against selected targets, perhaps by way of a warning or preemptive move. Were X yet even more sensitive to possibly adverse commercial or diplomatic consequences, it might forego even the above option for a covert (and hence potentially deniable) initiative of the sort available in Cell (3,1), etc.

What we've been concerned with thus far is of course a *prospective* confrontation . . . one where X and Y are potential rather than actual adversaries. But where X and Y have already been engaged for some time in a confrontation, then IWA analysts might have some empirical basis for attempting to isolate probable from essentially implausible initiatives. As a first and most basic step, analysts would look to fix the current relational state between X and Y.

The most obvious way to do this is to locate the place in a Confrontational Tableau where the last exchange between X and Y took place. This would be done by trying to map the particular action that X just took against Y --or Y directed against X, as the case may be-- onto one of the predefined generic referents or N(i,j,k)'s. The (i,j) indices would then point to the cell where X and Y are now engaged, which would then be denoted as Cell(i,j)t. The next obvious step would then be to try to get some idea of the direction of any changes in the relationship between X and Y. This we'd do by identifying the cells where yet earlier initiatives would be placed, e.g.: Cell(i,j)t-1, Cell(i,j)t-2. A trend might then become apparent in either of two ways:

- if the successive (i) and/or (j) indices are increasing in value, X and Y would be escalating the level of conflict;

- if successive (i) and/or (j) indices are decreasing in value, this would signal that X and Y are taking steps to relax the level of tension;
- X and Y may also confine their competitive actions within some single cell of the table, such that (i,j)t = (i,j)t-1 = (i,j)t-2, etc.

Some indication of the *rate* at which a X|Y confrontation is escalating or diminishing in intensity would then be available by examining the intervals of time that elapsed between successive changes.

This sort of information is useful because it may provide analysts with some basis for making reasoned assessments of where things might be going in the future . . . what contingencies are most likely to appear at (t+1) and so on. For there is much evidence --both empirical and normative (this in terms of theoretical models of conflict escalation and reduction)-- suggesting that confrontational situations tend to be subjected to a kind of natural *ratchet* effect, where the level of adversarial intensity or enmity tends to get cranked-up or reduced in stages or increments.[5] In short, the generally most plausible of conflict-escalation or reduction scenarios would tend to be built around cases where the preceeding and succeeding confrontational initiatives are less rather than more disparate (or, alternatively, more rather than less proximate in the confines of a Confrontational Tableau).

For their part, the q(a,j) level entries in a Competitive Matrix have two functions. First, they serve as the predicates for any net-assessment or Q(j) level valuation. Working from the former to the latter may sometimes be quick and clean, most so when all of the q(a,j)'s have been assigned the same value. For example, were q(a,j) = >> for all a, there may be little doubt that the valuation for Q(j) would also be >>.

Mixed cases would be more analytically demanding, with instances of considerable ambiguity generally leading to a presumption of parity or a <> assignment. But in their second and more interesting role, the q(a,j) entries are the obvious sources of inspiration for both generating and evaluating the competitive alternatives that might be undertaken on some given dimension (or, more broadly still, within some singular cell of a Confrontational Tableau). And because the information leading to q(a,j) level assessments would have been collected at a quite low level of aggregation, they should be a primary source of inspiration for the detailed provisions or aspect-level specifications of contigencies. Just to quickly indicate the level of analysis at which IWA analysts may now be working, let's assume that the following q-level assessments were generated for the military (D1) dimension:

q(1,1) = >>: X significantly superior in number/quality of armed forces personnel (troops; commanders, etc.)

q(1,2) = < : Y maginally superior in weapons manufacturing facilities and other infrastructure, etc.

q(1,3) = <<: Y has a significant advantage in combat hardware . . . number/quality of planes, tanks, etc.

q(1,4) = <>: X and Y roughly equal in terms of factor bases (inventories of combat supplies, etc.)

q(1,5) = >>: X is assigned a significant advantage in terms of morale, motivation, willingess to sacrifice, etc.

As was suggested earlier, q(a,j) level information is mainly of use in considering options that might arise *within* a single cell of a Confrontational Tableau. Therefore, for illustrative purposes, suppose it was the prospect of all-out war between X and Y that was being considered, such that attention would be focussed on Cell (1,1).

And within this cell, the q(a,1) valuations shown above might lead IWA analysts to propositional positions such as these:

a) Given Y's significant superiority in combat technology (hardware) and disadvantage in manpower and morale, it would be most likely to opt for a military posture centered mainly on remote/mechanical platforms (e.g., bomber aircraft).

b) Given its edge in manpower and morale, X may be served by hit-and-run, guerilla-type tactics so that Y could not make good use of its high-tech hardware. Stressed here would be constancy of movement and dispersion of forces (this to avoid giving enemy remote platforms any concentrated targets), etc.

Such, in any case, is the sort of essentially speculative analytical stuff from which the contingency-level referents in an exercise might be spun.

By way of summary then, the pragmatic import of all Competitive Matrix related activities --q(a,j) and Q(j) level-- is to provide IWA analysts with a basis for imposing a probability function (P) over the master contingency set, or for generating the ordered array P[E*]. And from here --if any constraints on resources or other considerations recommend it-- analysts might then move to generate a more constricted contingency set as follows:

$$P[E] \subset [E^*], \quad \text{where } P > h \quad \text{for all } Ei \in [E].$$

That is, [E] is a subset of [E*] containing only those contingencies that have been assigned probability indices that exceed a minimum threshold value (h). The set [E] is thus used to isolate what IWA analysts feel to be the collection of *most interesting* contingencies. And were we operating under a traditional contingency planning protocol, the projection-related activities might end with the generation of P[E] as a *vector*. But in IWA exercises, the appropriate contingency construct is a Contingency Transformation Matrix:

	E1	E2	E3	...	Ez
E1	P"(1,1)	p(1,2)	p(1,3)	...	p(1,z)
E2	p(2,1)	P"(2,2)	p(2,3)	...	p(2,z)
E3	p(3,1)	p(3,2)	P"(3,3)	...	p(3,z)
			etc.		
Ez	p(z,1)	p(z,2)	p(z,3)	...	P"(z,z)

Implicit here is that any Contingency Transformation Matrix is not only defined for some specific X|Y pair, but also intended to pertain only over some definite projection interval (to $\rightarrow$ tn). Both the row and columnar entries are the various members of the [E], such that the above structure might be viewed as a Markov-type construct.[6] For the cells of the matrix are comprised of two different sorts of probability indices:

- Any P"(i = j) --or, alternatively, P"(Ei)-- would reflect the likelihood that the Gi heading a row will occur and then dominate (to the effective exclusion of all other possibilities) throughout the planning interval.
- In contrast, the various p(i,j)'s are conditional probabilities, such expressing the likelihood that should the Ei heading a row actually occur, it will subsequently be displaced by some alternative Ej.

It is the latter that are generally of greatest interest in IWA contexts, dealing as they do with state-transformation or *dynamic* possibilities.

In working with a Contingency Transformation Matrix, we might get to any row of the construct in either of three ways. One way, as is clear from the above points, is that we might get to some Ei via a state-transform or p(i,j) operation. Another route to a given row of the matrix would be available whenever the confrontation between some X and Y is an ongoing one. For in such a case, the focal row would be that headed by the particular Ei that represented the last (most recent) of the competitive exchanges between the parties. But if we are approaching an X|Y confrontation for the first time, or if we are working with prospective possibilities, the first step that IWA analysts would take would be to impose a different sort of ordering over the contingencies in [E]: P[E] => P'[E].

The difference between the two ordering schemes is this: The original ordering --the P[E] obtained in the previous phase-- was concerned merely with the likelihood that any Ei will occur at all, without any concern as to sequence or causality, etc. In contrast, the P'[E] ordering is used to express the likelihood that one of the contingencies in [E] will emerge as the starting-state or opening gambit in a possible X|Y confrontation. Analysts would then try to fix on a maximum-likelihood alternative --some P'max(Ei) $\in$ [E]-- as the contingency they feel has the highest probability of proving to be the action that will be the true *triggering* competitive initiative.

Thus, along either of the three lines just noted, IWA analysts would be led to a focal row of the Contingency Transformation Matrix. And once at this focal row, the interpretation of its constituents is fairly straightforward. To illustrate, let's suppose that we got to the row headed by contingency E2, such consisting of the following:

$$E2 : \quad [\, p(2,1); P''(2,2); p(2,3); \; \ldots \; p(2,z) \,].$$

This assumes that E2 is currently in force or postulated as the triggering initiative for a confrontation, with the p(2,j)'s representing conditional probabilities such that:

$$p(2,j) = P'(E2)t \times P(E2) \Rightarrow (Ej)t+1,$$

where P'(E2) is the probability that E2 will be the contingency pertinent at time (t). Note that in the instance of an ongoing confrontation, the value for P'(E2) might approach unity --and hence certainty-- if it has been determined that E2 was in fact the substance of the last exchange. But in any case, the expression p(2,1) thus poses the likelihood that E2 will be succeeded by E1, with E1 representing either a follow-on thrust by the party authoring E2 or a counter-move from the other party. The same interpretation would hold for p(2,3), etc. to p(2,z). On the other hand, P"(2,2) would pose the probability that E2 will not only be the opening (or next) move but also the closing move in some stage of a confrontation, i.e.:

$$P''(2,2) = P'(E2) \times P(\sim Ej),$$

where P(~Ej) is the probability that there will be no other contingency following E2, or the probablility of not (~) any Ej.

It's perhaps clear that IWA analysts using a Contingency Transformation Matrix might reasonably expect to be able to map out a concatenative sequence (string) of the thrusts and parries that two adversaries might direct at one another over some interval. Thus the Contingency Transformation Matrix is the key structure for dynamic contingency planning/positioning practice. But it is not the last of the IWA structures to be built.

4.5 Definition and Use of Indicators

For each of the elements in the Contingency Transformation Matrix would now become the target for the definition of one or more indicators, so yielding the IWA Indicator Tableau:

	E1	E2	E3	...	Ez
E1	I(1)	I(1,2)	I(1,3)	...	I(1,z)
E2	I(2,1)	I(2)	I(2,3)	...	I(2,z)
			etc.		
Ez	I(z,1)	I(z,2)	I(z,3)	...	I(z)

The row and column entries are the same as for the Contingency Transformation Matrix. But in the cells are indicators used to specify any conditions that might alert IWA analysts that some contingency has occurred or warn of its impending prospect. As such, the two different classes of indicators present in the tableau thus have the following implications:

I(i)'s: Indicators that pertain to either the fact or the likelihood of the emergence of some singular contingency, such that evidence of any I(i) provisions would serve to increase the probability that contingency Ei either has already occurred or is in the process of taking place.

I(i,j)'s: Indicators pertinent to a dynamic possibility (state transformation), such that evidence of I(i,j) is taken to increase the likelihood of Ei => Ej, and hence a shift in the locus of confrontation between X and Y; or, the emergence of I(i,j) would have the effect of making some contingency Ej relatively more probable than Ei.

Any of the P"(i = j) entries in the Contingency Transformation Matrix --such arguing for the occurrence and persistence of a singular contingency-- would then be constructed around the emergence of the appropriate I(i) indicators and the absence of any I(i,j) indicators, or I(i) and ~I(i,j) $\rightarrow$ P"(Ei).

I(i) indicators are thus defined so as to suggest what evidence we ought to be looking for --and where and when we are most likely to find it-- that would serve as a signal that Gi has taken place, is taking place or will take place. By way of a quick illustration, suppose that Ei had been defined as a variant on generic referent N(1,2,1) in the Confrontational Tableau shown in Exhibit 4.4. Ei would then postulate the possibility that X would act to interdict the flow of some critical material(s) to Y. Among the factors that I(i) might direct us to be looking for as *indicative* of this contingency might be the following:

- attempts by X --directly or through third-party agents-- to corner the market in the commodity(s) of interest;
- maritime companies are threatened with the loss of X's business should they transport cargo for Y;
- X's encouragement of longshoreman's or other organized labor groups to refrain from handling certain cargos bound for Y;

As an example of a dynamic possibility or Ei => Ej transformation, we might consider defining some Ej alternative around the prospect of X electing to use military force vs. merely economic measures to deny critical materials to Y.

If so, then I(i,j) type indicators might then direct attention to the following for *clues* as to X's willingness or intent with respect to Ej:

- any redeployment of naval forces towards the vicinity of any choke-points along the main routes of supply (sea lanes) between Y and supplier ports;
- any preparations (e.g., special training/staging of commando units, construction of sinkable obstructions) that would put X in a position to attempt an outright blockade of Y's home ports;
- evidence of any intent towards the evacuation of X's political leaders and their families towards an area more remote from the border with Y; etc.
- signs that X is attempting to infiltrate demolition gear and/or sabotage teams into the port areas of Y's suppliers, this as a prelude to destroying cargos at source; etc.

Note that one implication of the examples we've used here is that indicator-related information may often not be accessible in the absence of some special efforts on the part of collectors.

That is, given the constant premium on security in competitive contexts, indicators will frequently dictate the collection of information qua *intelligence*, this being information that others may not want us to have. As such, it may often be that the information to meet indicator-directed requirements cannot be relied upon to arise naturally, but must be deliberately provoked. For example, military adversaries often *tweak* each others' defensive systems, as when an aircraft is flown towards the territory of another in order to see what sort of radar systems the adversary will employ (i.e., provide some basis for an assessment of the quality of the adversary's defensive assets). Tweaking is thus the intelligence community's counterpart to the empirical experiments of the laboratory scientist. But even *provoked* data ought to be examined in light of these possibilities: Is the information real or is it disinformation that has been *seeded* by an adversary to mislead us? Is what we saw when we *tweaked* an adversary what we'd see if we were attacking for real?, etc. (this a matter we shall discuss in a later chapter).

But to return again to the IWA Indicator Tableau, there is this display-related feature to consider: Assuming that we had indeed followed the earlier-noted translation convention that would assign the most threatening contingencies the lowest index values, then the transformational possibilities should all fall rather neatly into two partitions. Particularly, to the left of the major diagonal we'd encounter those indicators which would signal transformations that would be comprehensible as instances of threat-escalation. That is, all I(i,j)'s where $i < j$ should lead to Ei => Ej shifts portending a heightening of tension/conflict between X and Y. To the right of the major diagonal would then be found all those I(i,j)'s with i > j, each of which should signal some Ei => Ej transformation that implies a relaxation of tension or threat-reduction.

The relative magnitude of the threat-escalation or threat-reduction consequences expected to follow from transformation would of course depend on an assessment of the degree of difference or qualitative disparity between Ei and Ej. Three basic orders of changes might then be considered:

1) Ei and Ej may be variations on the same generic N(i,j,k) referent (included in the same cell of the Confrontational Tableau). The transition from one to the other would then be of least strategic significance.

2) Ei and Ej may be defined at the same categorical level in a confrontational tableau (e.g., both might be expressions of C1: extensive aggression) but on different dimensions. The significance of any Ei => Ej transition would then be determined by the degree of difference between the dimensions. For example, if E1 were an ideological (D4) action and Ej a contingency of military (D1) implication, then the putative impact of the Ei => Ej transition would be greater than were Ej to be an initiative of diplomatic (D3) tenor.

3) Ei and Ej may indeed represent contingencies implying different levels of competitive intensity. The putative impact of any Gi => Gj transformation would then be dependent upon the difference between the relational categories (Ci vs. Cj) to which the two contingencies belong, with (C1 - C5) being the instance of maximal disparity.

But as an encouraging practical matter, work done at previous stages should provide IWA analysts with the wherewithal to define both types of indicators with which we're concerned.

The most obvious source of inspiration would be the provisions entered into an earlier-contructed IWA structure, the Contingency Tableau. For these, recall, set out the specific aspect-related provisions or V(Sj) specifications that would allow us to uniquely identify any contingency, i.e.:

Ei = Vi(S1): what? + Vi(S2): how? . . . + Vi(S6): where?

An Indicator array I(Ei) would then direct the search for evidence of any tendency towards this particular collection of conditions. And as a rule, the greater the body of evidence suggesting the emergence of these conditions, the greater would be the expected likelihood that Ei has or is about to occur.

Any indicator set covering a dynamic or state-transform possibility --some I(Ei => Ej)-- should then be able to call upon the entries in the Contingency Tableau to do the following:

if: $Ei = Vi(S1) + Vi(s2) + \ldots Vi(S6)$,
and: $Ej = Vj(S1) + Vj(S2) + \ldots Vj(S6)$,
and: $Ek = Vk(S1) + Vk(S2) + \ldots Vk(S6)$;

then: $V@(i|j) = (Vi = Vj)$ for any S1 - S6,
and: $V@(i|k) = (Vi = Vk)$ for any S1 - S6.

Thus, an I(i,j) indicator set would be aimed at collecting any evidence of the emergence of properties consistent with Ej but inconsistent with Ei (that is, any $Vi \neq Vj$). The strength of such evidence would then be used to help set the value for p(i,j). By the same token, the indicator set I(i,k) would direct the search for evidence of any properties consistent with Ek but inconsistent with Ei. Increasing evidence of such would then act to increase the expectation of the transition Ei => Ek. More refinement of expectations might then be had by considering the status of I(i,j) vs. I(i,k). If the body of evidence pertinent to the former is richer and more persuasive than that related to the latter, then the usual consequence would be for analysts to consider the transition Ei => Ej rather more probable than the possibility that Ei will be followed by Ek.[9]

But there is also a second important source of suggestions for the definition of indicators, this the Competitive Matrix. For either of the following might serve as signals that some transformation is about to occur:

1) $I(i,j) \rightarrow \Delta q(a,j)$, which contemplates the possibility that either of the parties to a confontation (X or Y) either acquires or loses certain resources (personnel, capital, etc.) at a level that would dictate a qualitative change in the assessment of the status of X vs. Y for the a'th asset category on the j'th dimension of competition.

2) $I(i,j) \rightarrow \Delta Q(j)$: changes in one or more q(a,j) level values are high enough to dictate a change in a net-assessment valuation.

Changes like the above may arise as a consequence of actual competitive exchanges . . . e.g., one of the parties might have its asset/resource base seriously eroded as a consequence of a defeat in a military engagement. Or they may be volitional in origin, as with a deliberate decision by one of the parties to reallocate resources (say Y elects to put more assets into military as opposed to commercial forms of competition with X). Or they might result from any of a variety of ancillary factors (one of the parties acquires or loses a major ally; one party is forced to divert some resources to another confrontation; changes in domestic socio-political sentiment dictate a forced change in the strategic orientation of one of the parties).[8]

Some sense of the relative impact of events of the above types might be had by considering the magnitude of the postulated changes in the q(a,j)'s or Q(j)'s. For such can run from the dramatic (say a radical shift in relative advantage from >> to <<) to the relatively minor, as from a shift from <> (parity) to a marginal advantage for X (>) or Y (<). But in general, alterations in a q(a,j) element would usually be expected to author Ei => Ej transformations of relatively modest (tactical) nature of the sort suggested in (i) above . . . to shifts confined within a single cell (or perhaps closely neighboring cells) of a Confrontational Tableau. In contrast, any Q(j) level change might very well author an Ei => Ej transformation signaling a major (strategic) shift from one dimension to another as in (ii) above or even a type (iii) transition that would move the level of competitive intensity to an entirely different level.

With the generation of an Indicator Tableau, we'd have come to the last of the IWA structures to be built. It's time then to move from the matter of their construction to a brief discussion of their employment.

4.6 Dynamic Modification of Strategic Planning Structures

Again, each IWA indicator will pose certain information requirements by way of *clues* to the potential behavior of the parties to a confrontation. Charged with actually collecting indicator-related information would then be an organization's own or some free-lance intelligence acquisition facilities: Field agents (HUMINT providers); surveillance-reconnaissance platforms (ELINT sensors); electronic listening devices (COMINT interceptors), etc. Any information or intelligence item that is actually collected would usually be referred to as an observable. Whatever *observables* are collected would then be pumped into a stream of inputs flowing back to the organization's cadre of analysts and managerial functionaries. We might then denote any observable as some Ot, with t a time designator used to date-stamp the input (or, as a common alternative, to tag it as the t'th observation on some matter of interest). And given the nature of the various IWA structures, the appearance of any intelligence input (Ot) would kick off a chain-reaction that could conceivably work its way back up through those structures along the lines shown in **Exhibit 4.4**.

The first task following the appearance of an intelligence input (Ot) is the attempt to map it to one of the standing indicators that have been defined. And given the earlier-noted orientations for IWA indicators, any observable would generally pertain to one of the following:

1) $Ot \rightarrow$ I(Ei) . . . Evidence of aspects associated with the assumedly in-force contingency, with Ei representing either the most-recently executed initiative in a series of competitive exchanges or that action having the greatest likelihood of triggering a prospective confrontation.

2) $Ot \rightarrow$ I(i,j) . . . Any information that might signal the prospect of an impending transition from Ei to some Ej, with the latter having some

EXHIBIT 4.4 : Impacts of Intelligence Inputs in an Indicator/Warning-Alert System

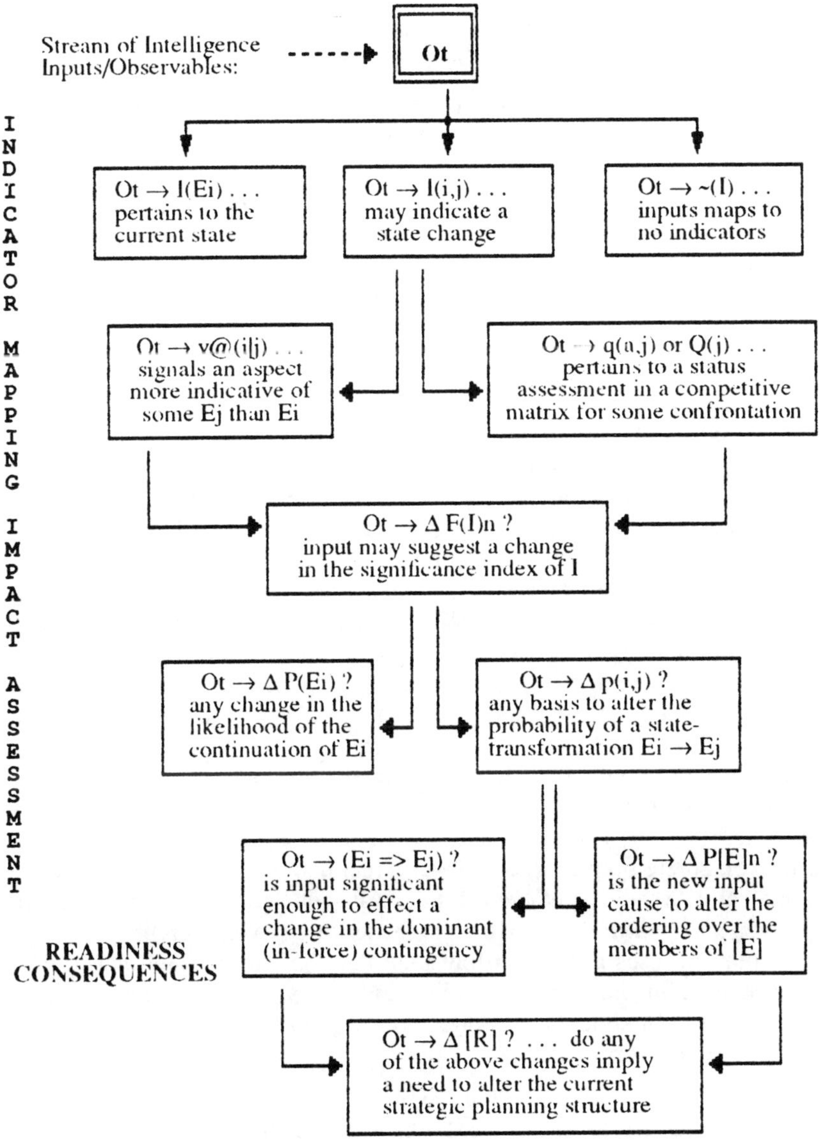

possibility of ultimately proving to be the competitive initiative that will be put into execution. From what's been said earlier, the two sorts of information most likely to be of interest here would be:

- indications of any aspect-attributes(s) that have been determined to be a point of difference between Ei and some Ej.
- indications of a change in the status of X vs. Y with respect to some asset category or dimension of competition.

Both the Ei and the Ei => Ej alternatives would of course be extracts from an up-to-date Contingency Transformation Matrix, with analyst's attention fixed mainly on the row headed Ei. Were we say to let P*(Ei)n = E2, then a focal row might be this:

$$E2: \quad [\, p(2,1);\ P''(E2);\ p(2,3);\ p(2,4);\ \ldots\ p(2,z)\,].$$

where the p(2,j) entries refer to the expected likelihood of the various transformational (dynamic) possibilities and P"(E2) represents the likelihood that E2 will persist.

We also hold out the possibility that an observable may map to none of the indicators that have been defined, this via the provision shown as $Ot \rightarrow \sim(I)$. This could occur because (hopefully) not all of the intelligence inputs analysts receive and consider will have been specifically tasked . . . i.e, collected in response to some indicator-derived requirement. That is, an IWA system also remains open to --and in fact may actually encourage-- the submission of *unsolicited* inputs, such that collection assets (agents, etc.) are expected to forward all observations that they feel might possibly be of interest. It is this feature which appends a *learning* capability. For when an intelligence input fails to map onto any of the standing indicators, it may very well imply that some situation is emerging that was not anticipated. Unsolicited or untargeted intelligence inputs would then have a critical contribution to make to the ambition of maintaining some degree of congruence between the various IWA structures and perhaps constantly altering realities. For they could point out the need to elaborate on the existing IWA structures . . . for analysts to define a new indicator, a new contingency that was not heretofore considered or perhaps even some entirely new strategic (generic) N-level referent.

But for our purposes here, we'll presume that the current intelligence item does indeed map to one of the standing indicators. As such, the next step would be to see if *Ot* should occasion any change in the significance index or for an indicator, this formulated as:

$$F(I)n = c(a),$$

where *a* is an assessment of the level of activity with respect to the matters towards which the indicator points us and *c* a confidence index and *n* indicates that it's the prevailing valuation. A change in the significance index for an indicator might then result from a decrease or increase in either of its components. To illustrate, suppose that the indicator of interest was one mentioned earlier as pertinent to the prospect of X acting to interdict (by force) a flow of materials to Y:

> Redeployments of certain of X's naval forces towards the vicinity of any choke-points along the main routes of supply (sea lanes) between Y and supplier ports.

We might seek to get a measure of *a* for this indicator by looking at the intensity or sweep of the redeployments, e.g.: How many ships of what sizes and capacities are involved? Are they just transiting in the neighborhood of channels or are they sitting in-force directly on stations?

A value for *c* (the confidence index) might then reflect IWA analysts' judgements about the quality of any *Ot* in consideration of: a) The historical reliability and precision of the author or source of an intelligence input: b) The nature of the observable (is it a product of a direct measurement on a real variable or an essentially subjective conclusion drawn with respect to some surrogative or indirect factors?); c) The extent to which *Ot* is consistent with inputs generated from other sources at other times, etc. But a confidence valuation might also be made in light of even more fundamental issues, e.g.:

- Is *Ot* even a valid intelligence item or is it a fabrication of some field agent or perhaps seeded as disinformation?
- What degree of reliance ought we place in the value of *a*? Does it perhaps overstate actual redeployment efforts?
- Is the activity that's being reported really *indicative* of X's intent to interdict material flows to Y or might it perhaps imply something else (e.g., X's redeployment may be a defensive move against a perceived threat to itself from some other source, not an offensive move against Y)?

In general, our confidence with respect to the first two issues would be greater the greater the credibility of the author of the triggering intelligence input (*Ot*), were *Ot* to be the n'th rather than just the first observation reporting such activity, were the current observation to be replicated by some other source, etc. As for the third issue, what would tend to increase confidence would be the emergence of any *corroborating* evidence (say the interception of a communication that might expressly state the purpose of the redeployments is to choke-off supplies to Y). In contrast, were there doubts about any of the above, c would be used to deflate a significance index by reducing the net effect of any activity-level assessment.

Any input *Ot* might of course add nothing new to either the quantity or quality of intelligence pertinent to an indicator and so would cause no change in the significance index. But should analysts elect to change a significance index, the next step would be to consider if this change might then trigger any of the several higher-order changes shown in the exhibit. Of these, the generally least impactful will be the case where the impact of a new intelligence item is restricted to causing an increase in the value of the probability index assigned the assumedly in-force or maximum-likelihood contingency, or where *Ot* → P(Ei). Such would follow were *Ot* to provide some additional evidence that might alert analysts that Ei is either in the process of being executed (i.e., that one of the parties to a confrontation is apparently getting ready to mount it) or has already in fact taken place. Suppose for example that Ei was taken to be this earlier-mentioned scenario: X will undertake commercial actions to interdict the flow of materials to Y.

To illustrate, recall one of the examples of indicator-related information that might tend to support this projection:

> attempt by X, directly or through third-party agents, to corner the market in the commodity(s) of interest.

Were *Ot* to provide concrete evidence that X's activities in this respect were intensifying (say copies of buy-up contracts or indications of transfers of more funds to more agents), then analysts would likely want to act to increase the absolute value of the probability for this contingency so that it moves closer to unity, or P(Ei) → 1. And if the approach is close enough, IWA analysts may choose to view Ei as an effectively certain rather than merely maximum-likelihood alternative.

But given the orientation of IWA exercises, the more significant consequences of an observable would be an increase in the probability of some state-transformation alternative, or the case where *Ot* → ↑p(i,j). For again, the effect of this would be to warn us about what might prove to be the next competitive exchange in some X|Y confrontation. And if we recall the properties of a Contingency Transformation Matrix, any change in any p(i,j) must be taken as an occasion to rework the entire set of dynamic probability valuations in the focal row of the Contingency Transformation Matrix. To illustrate, we might pose the following row elements:

Ei : [P"(i); p(i,a); p(i,b); . . . p(i,j)].

Unless there is a specific reason for doing otherwise, common technical convention (via Markov-type logic) would dictate that P"(i) + Σp(i,j) = 1. Therefore, any intelligence item that would serve to increase the likelihood of any one of the transformation possibilities must cause a corresponding reduction in the likelihood index assigned one or all of the other possibilities. And in all cases, any increase in a p(i,j) value must lower P"(Ei), this because P"(Ei) = 1 – Σp(i,j).

But within the confines of an IWA exercise, the only cases where changes in p(i,j) values would be of immediate pragmatic import is when they somehow reverberate to cause a change in either the ordering or membership of a Contingency Transformation Matrix. To suggest what an observable-driven *reordering* might entail, suppose that the following represented the ordering over a focal row of a Contingency Transformation Matrix prior to the emergence of intelligence input *Ot*:

$$t\text{-}1: \quad p(i,a) > p(i,b); \quad p(i,b) > p(i,c); \quad p(i,c) \; = \; P''(i),$$

such that the transformation from Ei => Ea is deemed most likely and the transformation Ei => Ec (and the continued dominance of Ei) least likely. Any *Ot* might of course merely have the effect of altering probability indices without impacting on their ranking. On the other hand, suppose that following *Ot* there was the following ordering:

$$t: \quad p(i,c) > p(i,a); \quad p(i,a) > p(i,b); \quad p(i,b) > P''(Ii)$$

What's different is that the prospect of Ei being succeeded by Ec is now considered more likely than the Ei => Ea transition that was deemed dominant in the original (t-1) ordering.

As for the matter of changes in membership, three different possibilities must be considered:

1) $Ot \rightarrow p(i,j)t > h$: *Ot* might force an increase in the value of p(i,j) such that it now exceeds some minimum threshold level (h) established to distinguish *significantly* likely alternatives, whereas it had previously carried so low a probability as to be considered only a distant also-ran.

2) $Ot \rightarrow p(i,j)t < h$: *Ot* might have the result of forcing the value for p(i,j) below the significance threshold, such that the transition Ei => Ej is no longer considered to be a really serious possibility.

3) $Ot \rightarrow p(Ei => Ej) \approx 1$: *Ot* might increase the likelihood associated with some Ei => Ej transformation such that analysts would now want to assume that Ej will (or perhaps already has) become the new in-force or expectedly maximum-likelihood contingency. This would in turn then force a shift in the focal row, such that attention would now move from the old Ei-driven possibilities to the following:

$$Ej: \quad [\, P''(Ej); \;\; p(j,i); \;\; p(j,k); \;\; \ldots \;\; p(j,z) \,].$$

And, as a final assertion, what may already be well apparent is why changes of the above sort are of such moment:

> Any alterations in the ordering and/or membership with respect to a Contingency Transformation Matrix should be taken as a possible cause to effect a change in an organization's *readiness* posture.

For as new information causes us to either dismiss old contingencies as now somewhat improbable or advance new ones as increasingly likely to occur --or to alter our conception of how alternatives ought to be ranked-- there should be a corresponding adjustment in the way in which an organization would position itself to be ostensibly most ready to meet the currently most probable and/or threatening contingencies . . . i.e., a sympathetic change in the sorts of assets and resources it seeks to acquire and how it chooses to deploy them.[9]

But while intelligence-driven provisions of the sort discussed in this chapter can indeed allow for more dynamic strategic planning/positioning, the level of dynamism they provide is not nearly so great as that which can be expected to follow from adoption of either of the two adaptive strategic management approaches that we'll be discussing in the next chapter.

NOTES AND REFERENCES

1. This quote is taken from the *blurb* to Stevenson and Gumpert's article, "The Heart of Entrepreneurship", *Harvard Business Review* (March-April, 1985), pg. 85.

2. The usual source for practitioner-oriented articles on command/control systems (usually under the notation C2 or C3/I) is the journal *Signal.* For a set of extended, MORE technically-DETAILED arguments on the subject, see the special winter (1986) issue of the *IEEE Transactions on Systems, Man and Cybernetics.* There have also recently appeared some books collecting articles on command/control topics, c.f.: Jon L. Boyes and Stephen J. Andriole, *Principles of Command and Control* (AFCEA International Press, 1987) and Andriole and Heilmeier, *High Technology Initiatives in C3/I* (AFCEA International Press, 1986).

3. For a thorough and eminently readable overview on modern Indicator/Warning-Alert precepts, see Albert Clarkson's *Towards Effective Strategic Analysis: New Applications of Information Technology* (Boulder: Westview Press, 1981). However, as the recent spate of intelligence-related failures suggest, actual practice may not always align well with normative provisions. For some very disturbing, concrete testimony that this is indeed the case, see Peter M. Dunn and Bruce W. Watson, eds., *American Intervention in Greanda: The Implications of Operation Urgent Fury* (Westview Press, 1985).

4. Organizations may often maintain IWA facilities pertitnent to both types of orientations. For example, a business firm would certainly want to have a set of X|Ya focuses covering its relationship with each of its direct competitors. But were it a multinational firm or otherwise dependent on matters as they might resolve themselves in the international arena, it would also have set of Yi|Yj focuses aimed at: a). Informing it of changes in the relationship between countries that might effect its commercial interests (e.g., if Yi and Yj are edging towards a serious confrontation, a company may have to decide which of the parties it will continue to serve); or b).

Assessing any changes in the relationship between a sitting government (Yi) and one or more opposition groups (Yj's) within some foreign country that might rebound to effect the corporation's welfare (for example, were an unsympathetic opposition party appear to be heading towards an electyion victory or coup, the might pose the prospect company assets being destroyed or seized).

5. An indication of how this thesis might be applied is given by T. G. Belden in his "Indications, Warning and Crisis Operations", *International Studies Quarterly* (21, 1), 1977. A more or less technical appreciation of the analytical challenges involved in working in areas having an escalative threat potential is an aspect of the newly emergent studies into what's commonly referred to as *Logical Incremental Determinism.*

6. In general, IWA analysts would usually be prevented from considering a Contingency Transformation Matrix as a proper Markov construct because they cannot presume to have defined set of contingencies that would fully exhausted all possibilities that might arise over some planning horizon. But even were we able to assume that the set [E] is complete, there may be no basis for proposing any definite sequence in which the various contingencies (viewed as states) would be executed . . . e.g., we may not be able to presume that E2 will always follow E1, etc. As a practical matter then, it may be that we would want to actually display a Contingency Transformation Matrix as a simple network or stochastic *tree* structure. But when applied to any reasonably volatile context, even a *tree* structure can get terribly intricate unless the projection interval is kep constrained. But then no IWA structure --the Contingency Transformation Matrix included-- is intended as a facility to support long-range planning . . . this a luxury that only organizations resident in essentially simple contexts can afford.

7. It should be noted that, for the most part, probability assessments resulting from indicator-related intelligence inputs will be arrived at via a special type of Bayesian inference mechanics to be discussed in considerable detail in the last chapter of this volume (as will a somewhat more technically precise appreciation of the kinds of methodological initiatives that indicator-driven analysis operations might entail). But the point is that indicator valuation is usually going to be an exercise in putative evidential assessment, much along the lines of the approaches presented by Detlof von Winterfeldt and Ward Edwards in their recent book, *Decision Analysis and Behavioral Research* (Cambridge University Press, 1986).

8. For a very generalized example of an approach to socio-political or socio-economic event projection, see Theodore Raphael's paper, "Integrative Complexity Theory and Forecasting International Crises", *Journal of Conflict Resolution* (26), 1982. More specific to the political dimension is the study by Stephen Andriole and Gerald Hopple, *An Essessment of Political Instability Research Methodologies* (Marshall, Va: International Information Systems), September 1982, or their: *Revolution and Political Instability: Applied Research Methods* (Frances Pinter & St. Martins) 1984. See also Hunter's interesting book: *Political/Military Applications of Bayesian Analysis: Some Methodological Issues* (Boulder, Co: Westview Press), 1983

9. It should be noted that all this depends to some extent on technical advances being made along another line: the evolution of conceptual and technical provisions to support dynamic resource allocation at the strategic level. Certain approaches have

already received some speculative attention, though little in the way of technical elaboration. One is a distinctly *dynamic* basis for deploying military assets against projective threat situations. A good illustration of this approach are the U.S. Liberty ships --loaded with enough equipment and supplies to support a division size US Force for some limited period of combat-- that are routinely positioned around the world in proximity to high-likelihood trouble spots.

A second approach, attempted mainly by commercial enterprises, is to invoke some sort of liquidity-preserving scheme, i.e., to delay irrevocable resource committments until the latest possible point, on the understanding that in a volatile context, more current intelligence generally means better decision premises. In practice, this means attempting to schedule investments in such a way as to first procure those items that are the most liquid or least situation-specific. As perhaps the most dramatic example of the violation of this common sense criterion, we might consider those electric utilities that decided on nuclear technology as the basis for expanding their capacity. All too often, among the first of investments were nuclear-specific items . . . construction of cooling towers; procurement of reactors, etc. When circumstances subsequently tended to discourage the employment of nuclear technology, the result was the need to write-down extraordinary losses, for the items could not be used to support any other endeavor. In contrast, had they geared initial investments towards the least specialized items --all the plumbing and other facilities of a power plant that are independent of the steam generation technology-- losses would have been considerably lower.

As third line of approach is perhaps best expressed by the concept known as Flexible Manufacturing Systems (FMS) technology. What's involved here is the attempt to design production facilities around generic facilities . . . e.g., machines that can be quickly reconfigured to perform a number of different operations. Such provide a basis for *dynamic* positioning in that as changes in demand dictate changes in product characteristics, there may be no necessity to undertake a major re-tooling or invest in a totally new class of production equipment.

Finally, there is the concept of dynamic *thresholding*, this particularly pertinent to governmental service agencies or other client-centered organizations. In its simplest variation, it involves treating as *variables* two factors that are, under contemporary social service management practice, most often treaated as constants: Eligibility Criteria and Level-of-Service. Moreover, it would establish a dynamic linkage between both of these factors and the key independewnt variable, Level-of-Demand for services. For a more detailed explanation of what dynamic thresholding involves, see the first several chapters in my *Managing Social Service Systems* (Petrocelli Books, 1977).

CHAPTER 5

APPROACHES TO

ADAPTIVE STRATEGIC MANAGEMENT

As we now advance to consider adaptive strategic planning/positioning, we'll be looking at strategic management technologies that might be said to sit at the frontier of our contemporary capabilities. For here the focus is on facilities that promise to help organizations cope in contexts edging towards the worst-case condition we've identified, state-indeterminacy. For what this holds out is the prospect of organizations being more or less routinely confronted by events/threats that were essentially unanticipated. And this, in its turn, argues for the wisdom of such organizations relying less on --or perhaps abandoning altogether-- attempts to operate under a preadaptive approach to readiness via either the structured or dyanmic (intelligence-driven) contingency planning technologies discussed in the two previous chapters. Rather, they would be urged to consider moving towards one of two adaptive strategic management platforms:

> *The INTERPOLATIVE, intended to serve organizations that can predefine the broad classes of event/threats to which they might be subject, but not the more detailed particulars of the situations that will arise.*
>
> *The REAL-TIME, most appropriate for organizations that must be prepared to do much of their strategic decision making on an after-the-fact basis because of the high likelihood of their being visited by a stream of essentially novel or unanticipated exogenous events.*

Both of the above platforms provide the technical wherewithal to adopt an essentially reactive orientation to organization readiness. It's just that the former cannot accomodate as high a degree of contextual volatility and complexity as the latter.

5.1 Strategic Contingency Planning Quandaries

As suggested, adaptive strategic planning/positioning technologies are intended to serve as either complements to or substitutes for either the structured or dynamic contingency planning platforms we discussed in the two previous chapters. Both these approaches, recall, rested on planning constructs intelligible as Discrete-Bipartite model-base structures. Therefore, our need here is to be as explicit as possible about the conditions under which discrete-bipartite contingency planning technology may fail to provide an organization with an adequate level of strategic readiness. As a first step towards this end, consider the implications of the three basic analytical operations we first looked at in Chapter 3 for carrying out the event and response side aspects of a discrete-bipartite contingency planning structure:

Analytical Operations	EVENT-SIDE	RESPONSE-SIDE
Realization	{I} → [E] Definition of an ostensibly universal array of future event possibilities/scenarios given some available information base {I}	E*i → [R] Scripting of an array of strategic response alternatives for each member of the active contingency set [E*]
Ordering	[E] → O[E] Imposes a ranking over the alternatives as to likelihood of occurrence and/or threat-potential, etc.	[R] → U[R1 . . . Rm] | E*i Imputes an expected utility valuation to each of the alternative courses of action defined within [R] for each contingency E*i
Convergence	O[E] → [E*] Extraction of an *affordable* subset of most significant contingencies for which to be *ready*	U[R] → U^(Ri) | E*i Selection of a best (maximal-utility) strategic contingency plan for handling each event possibility in the subset [E*]

Contingency Structure : [E*] x [R*], where [R*] = U^(Ri) for all E*i ∈ [E*]

As may be clear, there are ample opportunities for strategic planners to be faced by frustration or even defeat with respect to all three of the above operations. And as may also be clear, the villain will be the by now familiar one . . . contextual intricacy and volatility.

For again, increases in contextual complexity argue for a corresponding increase in the number and diversity of event potentialities that would have to be defined within any universal set, [E]. But recall that one of the key analytical side-effects of transits into the strategic decision domain is *sparsity* of empirical event-projection predicates. This is because we approach contextual complexity either through the offices of future environmental states that are unlikely to be well correlated with historical themes, or via a competitive arena where the emphasis is on strategic surprise (novelty) and security. Either must be expected to lead to an information base {I} that is deficient in terms of hard data or intelligence . . . especially when electing or being forced to operate over an extensive planning *horizon*. Strategic planners must then routinely be expected to be deprived of a sufficiency of empirical/objective grounds on which to base realization operations. This, in turn, may lead to the generation of a contingency set that is itself too *sparse*, or which captures too little diversity in terms of the richness of the environmental and competitive state-event possibilities it contains. The obvious consequence of the above is to put an organization in peril of being confronted by some real-world event that it failed to anticipate.

Or, from yet another direction, we might echo the earlier argument that increases in contextual complexity may have the general effect of making the emergence of the *improbable* increasingly probable. In either case, the coupling of contextual complexity with sparsity of objective projection predicates leads to the worst-case condition we originally defined in the very first chapter of our book, the prospect of an organization having to try to conduct strategic planning/positioning exercises in the face of state-indeterminacy.

This, in turn, leads to the expectation that now matter how elaborate a contingency structure we might try to define, there will always remain the expectation that it will fail to exhaust all true possibilities. Hence, given any tendency towards contextual state-indeterminacy, strategic management authorities must despair of the feasibility of getting ready in advance (via a preadaptive orientation) for all the situations that will arise. Rather, the interests of strategic readiness are better served by cultivating the virtues of reactive management: Alertness, quickness, versatility and resilience.[1]

But we've also suggested another avenue along which an organization might be led towards a requirement for reactive strategic management capabilities. This avenue would lead to an troublesome condition that we'll refer to as *dispersion*, which is a consequence of the following:

- Realization operations will have resulted in an event/threat projection (contingency) set that entails too much diversity . . . i.e., contains too large a number of qualitatively disparate possibilities;
- Ordering operations have resulted in a ranking or preference distribution that is too symmetrical at too high a level of significance, such that there are too many contingencies assumed to carry a substantial likelihood of occurrence or threat potential.

Such would put an organization in danger of not being able to arrive at a satisfactory resolution to this tradeoff:

> Constantly expand and elaborate on the event possibilities defined within any contingency set or suffer the increased likelihood of failing to include some event that will actually occur.

And the failure to arrive at a satisfactory resolution of this tradeoff is equivalent to failing to arrive at a satisfactory outcome to a strategic contingency planning exercise.

For under an essentially *symmetrical* ordering all event possibilities are considered more or less equiprobable. Therefore, there will be no way to extract any reduced subset of event-possibilities --to structure any [E*] $\subset$ [E]-- without incurring an essentially proportional increase in the likelihood of having an actual state-event fail to map to an element of [E*]. Simply, if all elements of [E] are deemed essentially equally likely to occur (or, alternatively, more or less equally potent in terms of the *threat* they pose, etc.), then any contingency planning structure that does not extend to all elements of [E] will effect a reduction only at the price of an increase in the probability of some actual state-event failing to map onto any element of [E*]. There may then be no entirely satisfactory way of resolving the tradeoff between *affordability* and readiness . . . no contingency set that is a well-taken compromise between the strategic response options we can actually *invest* with an appropriate set of resources/assets and the richness of the contextual event alternatives to which we might be subjected over some interval.

Hence the ways in which an organization operating under a contingency planning structure may become vulnerable to a strategic default via the emergence of some unplanned-for event. And if we were to recall our initial discussion of default conditions in Chapter 2, there were two different forms in which such might appear, a discontinuity or an anomaly. And as shown in **Exhibit 5.1**, each serves as an occasion for taking recourse to one of the two orders of adaptive strategic management technology with which we shall be concerned in this chapter, the Interpolative and the Real-Time (each rests on a fundamentally different order of model-base technology).

Both discontinuities and anomalies are comprehensible as instances of unplanned-for or *exceptional* events. Any *exceptional* event will thus imply a

EXHIBIT 5.1 : Default Conditions for Traditional Contingency Planning Structures

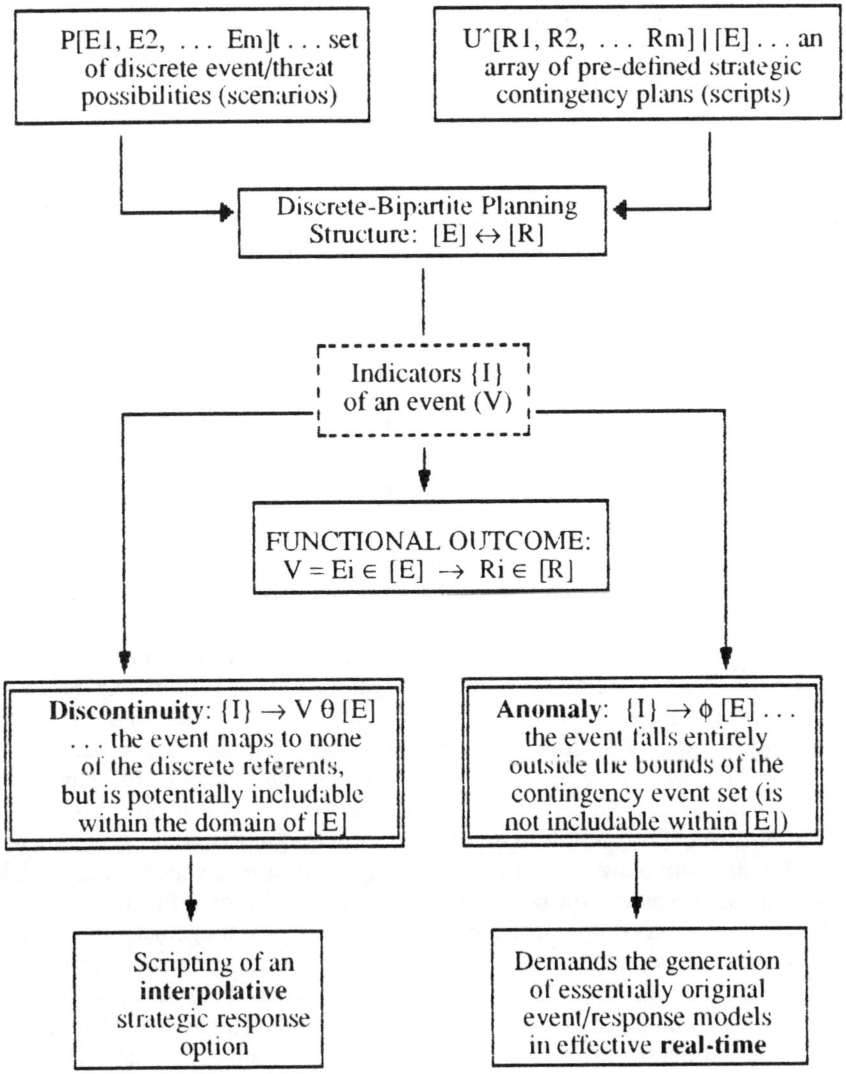

threat (or perhaps an opportunity) that was either not foreseen at all, or deemed so improbable as to have been dismissed from any active consideration. A discontinuity is the less formidable of the two default conditions. For to repeat some key arguments, a discontinuity results when an organization is confronted by an event that fails to map directly onto any of the members of a contingency set, but is nevertheless intelligible as being *includable* (via the symbol θ) somewhere within the boundaries of the set:

$$V \notin [E^*] \text{ but } V \, \theta \, [E^*].$$

There will then be no direct mapping to any of the standing strategic contingency plans defined in [R*]. But, and this is the critical point, if V is includable somewhere within the confines of [E*], then an appropriate strategic response (Rv) may be capable of being defined somewhere within the confines of [R*]. Hence again this rudimentary rationale for an interpolative approach to strategic scripting:

$$Rv : [R] \text{ as } V : [E],$$

which suggests the attempt to define Rv such that it bears a relationship (:) to the members of [R*] that is similar to the relationship that V bears to the members of [E*], e.g.:

$$[E1 < E2 < \mathbf{V} < E3 \ldots] \rightarrow [R1 < R2 < \mathbf{Rv} < R3 \ldots].$$

That is, if V falls somewhere in the interstices between E2 and E3, then it might follow that we could look to script Rv around provisions intelligible as belonging somewhere in the interval between R2 and R3 (or, alternatively, as an eclectic amalgam of provisions belonging to R2 and R3).

In this sense, a discontinuity may be said to constitute an emergency, this because it poses a situation for which an organization is not immediately ready but for which it might expect to be ready in the relatively short-run. When an organization expects to encounter *discontinuities* only rather infrequently, it might be enough simply to provide for an interpolative programming capability as a complement to a traditional discrete contingency planning platform. In such a case, the Interpolative programming facilities (constructed around a strategic planning construct taking the form of a Categorical model-base structure) would then be expected to provide the organization with the technical wherewithal for a disciplined Emergency Management capability. On the other hand, where discontinuities are expected to occur with some frequency, then an organization had best gear itself up to provide for interpolative solutions on a routine basis. This would mean using a Categorical model-base structure as a substitute for the more familiar discrete-bipartite contingency planning construct.

If a discontinuity is the clinical version of an emergency, then an anomaly may generally be taken to signal a crisis for an organization. For if an event is qualitatively different from anything we thought might occur, then there is every reason to suspect that an adequate strategic response would have to be formulated around initiatives that have not even been conceived of as yet. That is, the counter to an anomaly generally cannot be arrived at by interpolation or by generating a script around an eclectic amalgamation of provisions drawn from two or more members of the existing contingency planning set. And to add to the problem posed by an anomaly, there is the likelihood that any strategic response option we do formulate will demand at least some resources/assets that are not currently available in the organization's repertoire. Hence, the Real-Time platform may be viewed as a Crisis Management protocol.

This takes us to the pragmatic core of the technical requirements associated with adaptive strategic management.[2] For given either category of exceptional event --a discontinuity or anomaly-- there may be a high premium on *timeliness*. For in the real-world, opportunities may often be fleeting, ephemoral; the window opens for a moment and is then perhaps quickly closed by some agile competitor or environmental agency. Thus, a strategic advantage not quickly seized may be a strategic advantage irretrievably lost. As for perils or threats, the demand for quickness is perhaps even more obvious. For such have a natural way of amplifying themselves, becoming ever more dangerous the longer they are left unattended. And as a peril or threat grows in magnitude or urgency, the effect may often be to close off certain of the more economical, safer or more expedient strategic counter-options that would have been available to us at an earlier point. If then we were to ourselves about the managerial challenge an *exceptional* event implies, we might get the following:

> The need for the rapid generation of an essentially original solution to an unanticipated problem.

In short, when reality presents a situation that fails to align with any of the expectations encoded in a contingency planning structure, then decision-makers must be prepared to perform the event-definition and response formulation functions in a reactive or after-the-fact mode. That is, if an organization is not already (projectively or pre-adaptively) ready for some situation, then it must get ready as quickly as possible.

Such is the basic mission that the two adaptive strategic management modalities are intended to serve. But given that each is predicated on a very different order of model-base technology --the Categorical vs. Template-driven, both of which involve certain key points of departure from discrete-bipartite planning conventions-- each will approach the development of an adaptive organizational management capability along very different lines, as summarized in the following table:

Alternative Model-Base Technologies	Orientation to Organizational Readiness	Distinguishing Technical Characteristics
Discrete-Bipartite	Preadaption to a limited but effectively exhaustive (and affordable) array of probable events or threats	Employs integral (realistic, fully-elaborated) scripts & scenarios & allows for directed cross-mapping of event to response referents
Categorical (to support the Interpolative platform)	Used when all that can be projected are the broad *classes* of events that might occur, these used to define ideal-type intervals on a continuum of logical possible situations	Use of generic referents defined at a higher level of abstraction; actual events defined as *special cases* of ideal-type referents and scripting involves *tailoring* generic plans to situation-specific parameters
Template-Driven (re: Real-Time management)	Appropriate when an organization anticipates being visited by a stream of improbable events or unprecedented threats (qua anomalies)	Event and response referents are reductive (maintained at a low level of abstraction) to facilitate *reactive* scenario-generation and response formulation

By way of a quick preview, any organization (or any of its individual units, e.g.: command/control subsystems) might consider a shift from a discrete-bipartite to a Categorical model base structure. This would effect an exchange of the integral models used by the former (fully-elaborated scenarios and scripts) for generic event and response referents. As a consequence of such an exchange, any actual event might appear as merely a *special case* of one or another of the generic event referents. And to the extent that an event can be so treated, the response-formulation requirement may reduce to the attempt to *tailor* a generic script to accomodate certain situation-specific properties of the event. Both, as will shortly be explained, are examples of interpolative programming. In any case, this technology is most appropriate for organizations in aggregate or any constituent units that can predefine certain basic *classes* of opportunities or threats by which they might be visited, such that what remains in doubt are matters that are more superficial than fundamental.

In contrast, Template-driven model base structures would be intended to support organization/units that expect to be routinely confronted by events qua anomalies . . . by situations that consistently come as something of a grand surprise. This approach is then reserved for organizations/units that must operate towards the practical limits of projective uncertainty, and which then must consider carrying the shift from preadaptive to adaptive management towards its practical limits. What this then implies is a capability for the rapid generation of essentially original solutions to a stream of unanticipated, ill-precedented or effectively novel problems. Hence the emphasis on real-time event-definition and response formulation, the technical key to which is a radical reduction in the level of abstraction at which planning-related referents are maintained . . . i.e., the exchange of integral models (scripts and scenarios) for more *primitive* model base components.

It now remains to suggest some of the technical initiatives that might allow organizations to move towards the development of a practical adaptive strategic management capability. The first targets for discussion will be the general logic of the Interpolative planning/positioning and the Categorical model-base structures on which it depends.

5.2 Interpolative Strategic Planning/Positioning Provisions

In particular, any organization that expects to be visited by discontinuities would be urged to equip itself with a capability for *interpolative* strategic planning/positioning. For the provisions of the adaptive/interpolative approach is expected to be most useful for organizations that cannot legitimately expect to be able to define in detail (as fully-elaborated *scenario* models) all the events that might be authored in the confines of some context . . . or which cannot hope to afford to fully invest a contingency plan for all the event possibilities that can be identified. But there is a very important pragmatic qualification that must be met for an organization to make proper use of interpolative facilities:

> The organizations for which this modality is most appropriate must have some basis for being able to anticipate the basic *classes* of environmental or competitive situations with which they might be confronted, such that what is in doubt is mainly where or when such might occur, or the precise (situation-specific) form in which they will appear.

This pretty much describes the condition under which emergency-service enterprises are forced to operate, e.g.: Fire and Police departments; Rescue squads, paramedic units or disaster relief organizations such as the Red Cross; certain military units, most particularly those charged with essentially reactive missions such as the Rapid Deployment Force; governmental agencies responsible for responding to floods, environmental hazards (toxic chemical leaks, oil spills) or carrying out functions such as Air Traffic Control, immigration control or the interdiction of illegal drugs or other contraband. But many commercial enterprises may also find themselves operating under not too dissimilar conditions, especially those resident in markets characterized by extensive competition. For again, what this implied was that while the repertoire of competitor-authored strategic threats to which a firm might be subject is fairly broad, there is nevertheless only a limited number of qualitatively-distinct possibilities --basic classes of threats-- to consider.

As such, while there may be many occasions where actual events will have at least some perhaps novel aspects, they should not come as a total strategic surprise to an organization operating under an adaptive/interpolative protocol. For as shown in **Exhibit 5.2**, the first of its provisions calls for the exchange of integral, realistic scenarios and scripts for generic event and response referents . . . this acting to raise the level of abstraction at which the elements of a model base structure are maintained. Given such an exchange, an organization should then be in a position to treat a significant proportion of the actual events with which it's confronted as *special cases* of one or another of the generic referents that have been established. The corollary should then be strategic response options whose formulation is mainly a matter of *tailoring* some generic strategic initiative to meet any special or situation-specific properties of the event at hand.

We want now to deal in some detail with this and the other key provisions of the adaptive/interpolative modality. But it should be kept in mind that what we're looking at here is a next-generation strategic management technology, such that our focus is more on conceptual rather than mechanical matters.

5.2.1 Qualitative Continuua and Categorical Referents

The key to interpolative mappings is this: The situations against which strategic readiness is to be addressed must be intelligible as entries arrayed along some proper qualitative continuum. In the confines of traditional quantitative analysis, a continuum is the product of a *continuous* variable, or one that can assume an effectively infinite number of values within some definite bounds. In contrast, a *qualitative* continuum would emerge whenever we are able to generate an array (*string*) of categorical or ideal-type referents that bear some sort of meaningful sequential relationship to one another.[3] For our purposes here, we are particularly interested in three different configurations of categorical continuua:

1) The DICHOTOMY, representable as some {Sa; Sz}. This is the simplest of categorical continuua, being a *bounded* but otherwise empty event-side structure. It would thus be reserved for those cases where we either cannot --or

EXHIBIT 5.2 : Categorical Model-Base Provisions

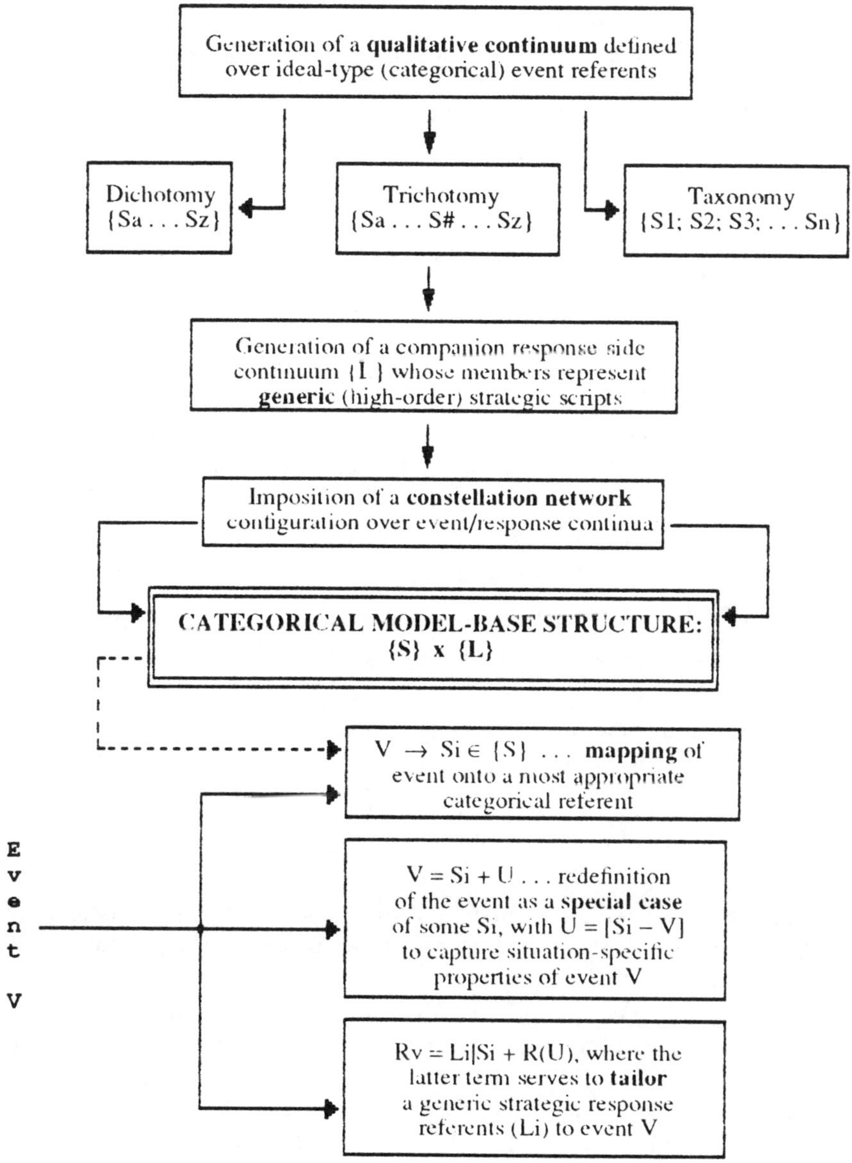

choose not to-- pre-define anything other than *limiting* state event alternatives to serve as the end-points of a continuum. To represent a proper dichotomy, Sa and Sz should be as disparate as possible in terms of the properties they entail. We use dichotomies then when --due either to sparsity of information, or the natural complexity of an organizational context-- we must work initially with an unelaborated event-side structure. The ordering function for a dichotomy would thus have the following partitions:

$$P\{Sa < .\mathbf{Si}. < Sz\} = 1.0 - [\, P(Sa) + P(Sz) \,].$$

The first term speaks to the likelihood of some actual state (Si) emerging that is definable somewhere within the region bounded by Sa and Sz, and so is used to capture the residual probability or the degree of continuous state stochasticity. Planners would take recourse to a dichotomy via the following language: *We don't know exactly what will happen. But what we do know is that it can either be Sa, Sz or something in between.* This might follow from a situation where there are so many *unknowns* that it would be either infeasible or impractical to define an *exhaustive* set of possibilites. An example might be the attempt to comprehend the ultimate consequence of the Iran-Contra scandal for long-range US:Soviet relations. Among the stochastic elements that would have to be considered are at least the following:

- will the Reagan administration be effectively convicted or absolved of either criminal culpability or ineptitude?
- if acquitted, will the administration take this as license to escalate the ideological confrontation with the Soviets? Will the Soviets then respond in kind?
- or if the administration is popularly convicted, will power over foreign policy then pass to Congress?
- if so, will Congress prove more conciliatory to the Soviet Union than Reagan? Will investment priorities shift away from preparing for external threats?
- if so, will Soviet authorities then view this as an occasion to become more aggressive, or will they seize upon it as an opportunity to attempt some sort of reconciliation?

So myriad are the event possibilities that might be generated here, that the better part of wisdom is perhaps to forego the temptation to spend time and energy trying to define a collection of discrete scenarios and instead be content to define merely a best and worst case construct (Sa and Sz, respectively).

Or from yet another perspective, we might employ Sa and Sz to represent the categorical end-points for some highly intricate continuum of situations for which an organization is expected (as per its mission) to be able to mount a different category of response. For example, a local Fire Department might be charged with the responsibility for handling a simple trash fire in a vacant lot (Sa), a major conflagration in a commercial highrise structure (Sz), or any of an extraordinary variety of situations that might arise between these two extremes (a kitchen fire in a private residence, etc.).

2) The TRICHOTOMY, displayable as {Sa; S#; Sz}, where S# is a referent whose properties would place it roughly midway between the boundary referents, Sa and Sz. The trichotomy is the natural way to express a dialectical event-side structure, where we would have: Sa = Thesis, S# = Synthesis and Sz = Antithesis. The ordering over a trichotomy would require assessments of relative likelihood for five different partitions:

$$P(Sa) + P(S\#) + P(Sz) + P\{Sa < .Si. < S\#\} + P\{S\# < .Si. < Sz\}.$$

The latter two partitions are indefinite intervals, in that there is any number of discrete state-events --more detailed qualitative situations-- that might be defined within their ranges. For example, we might consider a continuum of three ideal-type Political states:

{Sa: Autocracy < . . . < S#: Democracy . . . < Sz: Anarchy}.

From a dialectical perspective, Autocracy and Anarchy might be thought to represent polar opposite states, and Democracy a more or less stable synthesis of autocratic and anarchic properties. The indefinite intervals < . . . < might then be used to house any number of impure or transitional political states.

3) The TAXONOMY, representable as {S1; S2; S3; . . . Sn}, where each of the definite entries (Si's) may be taken to represent an ideal-type interval on a graduated array of qualitatively disparate state alternatives. What the term *graduated* implies is that there is some natural or logical linkage --via some complex common denominator, as it were-- among all the intervals. As such, referent S1 would imply the *least* of something and Sn the *most* of that something, etc. For example, microeconomic theory provides us with a taxonomy of ideal-type market structures (e.g., monopoly, monopolistic competition, contentious oligopoly) that may be taken to imply increasing intensity of competitive threats. Similarly, in considering military conflicts, we might use a taxonomy defined over increasingly serious forms of confrontation: Indirect harassment; constrained assault; unlimited warfare.

Given any continuum of categorical referents, the question then arises as to a response-side structure that will best answer for the interests of strategic readiness. Consider, for example, the alternatives available to us when working with an event-side trichotomy:

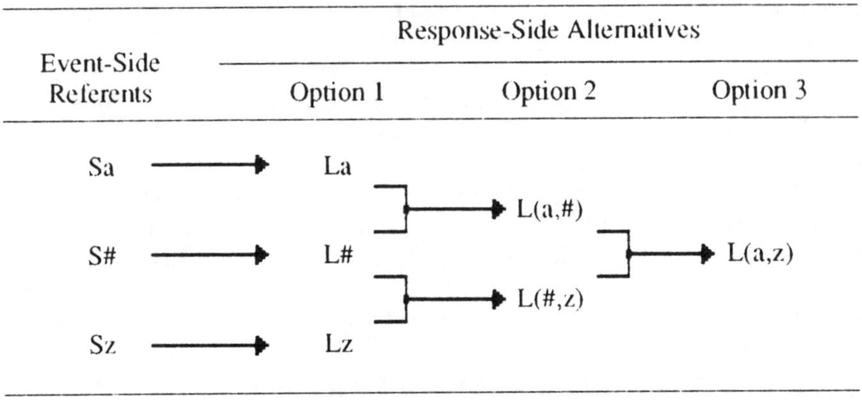

In the above, we use the term *L* to designate a generic strategic response referent, the implication being that any L may be taken to represent some general class of strategic response initiative. That is, any L will be capable of subsuming (as a supraset) some number of operational or situation-specific strategic response options, such that $L \supset [R1, R2 \ldots Rm]$.[4] This corresponds directly to the implication that any generic event-side referent (any Si) is considered to subsume some array of lower-order (discrete; realistic) state-event alternatives, such that we get: $Si \supset \{E1, E2 \ldots Em\}$.

We'll have more to say about this shortly. But for our purposes here it's enough to suggest that, as a general rule, the greater the degree of qualitative diversity among the categorical referents in any qualitative continuum, the more elaborate must be the array of generic response-side referents to allow for any prospective degree of strategic readiness. Thus, the election of a particular response-side configuration would be dictated by expectations about what we can refer to as the effective reach of any generic planning referent along the event-side continuum.

That is, the *reach* of any generic strategic response referent is to be assessed with respect to the breadth of different working strategic response options that might be authored under its auspices. Or more specifically, we might take *reach* to be an indication of the extent to which a generic strategic referent would be capable of containing some definite Rj for each and every realistic state-event alternative that might arise anywhere within the segment of the event-side continuum at which it is directed, or in notational terms:

$$\text{REACH: } Lx \rightarrow Rj \; \theta \; Lx \text{ for all } Ei \; \theta \; Sx$$

$$\text{REACH: } L(x,y) \rightarrow Rj \; \theta \; L(x,y) \text{ for all } Ei \; \theta \; \{Sx \ldots Sy\}.$$

As such, the circumstance under which we would elect the simplest of the options shown above (Option 3) would be this:

> The expectation that there is some singular generic strategic referent, $L^*(a,z)$, from which we can adequately reach to all situations that might arise anywhere within the bounds of the entire continuum, or: $L^*(a,z) \supset Ri$ for all $Ei\ \theta\ \{Sa \ldots Sz\}$.

But for us to be able to defend such an expectation, it must be that the degree of qualitative disparity between the two *limiting* state-events (Sa and Sz) is not terribly substantial.

The second of the options, L(a,#) + L(#,z), would thus be employed where there is somewhat greater qualitative disparity among the several categorical referents in a trichotomy, such that we do not expect to be able to define a single generic response-side referent that can reach across the entire continuum. We thus define L(a,#) so that it sits in the interval between Sa and S#, and so would serve as the basis for the generation of strategic response options for any event that might be definable anywhere on the left-hand side of the continuum, with L(#,z) doing the same for the right-hand segment. Finally, the most elaborate of the response-side arrays (Option 1) would contain a generic strategic response referent dedicated to each of the three members of the event-side continuum and so establish a one-to-one mapping. This option is appropriate when there is a degree of qualitative disparity among the event-side referents.

We could also postulate the situation where we wished to generate an even more elaborate mapping base, perhaps as follows:

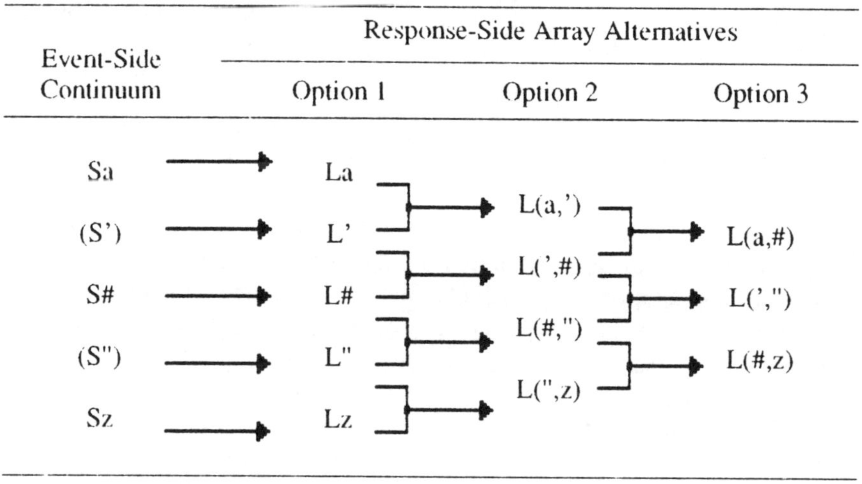

The key feature of the above is that we have introduced two new event-side referents, the categoricals S' and S", the effect of which is to transform what was originally a simple trichotomy into a five-partition continuum or taxonomy. We might want to do this when the three original referents (Sa, S# and Sz) entailed a very high degree of qualitative disparity such that the gaps that were left between them (the indefinite intervals, as it were) were too large for any single generic strategic platform to span with any promise of efficiency. Thus, the referents S' and S" would contract stretch of *empty* ground between the original members of the trichotomy. S' would thus be defined (perhaps as some sort of logical *median*) to effectively split the difference between Sa and S#, while S" does the same for S# and Sz. The result would be yet another set of response-side array alternatives, more or less elaborate as *reach* related considerations might dictate.

5.2.2 Model-Base Structures as Constellation Networks

The above discussions suggest that the categorical referents belonging to qualitative continua all serve to subsume some population (class) of event possibilities that share one or more critical qualitative properties. For example, let's look again at the continuum of Political referents we used:

{Sa: Autocracy < S#: Democracy < Sz: Anarchy}.

Each of the above entails a sub-continuum of lower-order alternatives, or Si = {E1 . . . Em}. To illustrate, consider the following variations on the Democratic theme:

- There's the typical Latin American democracy where the results of an election may be unlikely to reflect the popular will; such may then edge rather close to de facto Autocracy;
- At the other extreme would sit the ideal of pure Participatory democracy, where government procedes by a series of initiatives and referenda whose authorship rests solely with the populace . . . a scheme some see as bordering on Anarchy.
- And an intermediate state, there is Representative democracy, where the public will and purpose is filtered through a layer of elected officials who may or may not properly interpret or act on constituents' interests.

Now, once we consider that the generic referents we are working with represent general cases that in turn subsume an array of special (less abstract) referents, we have the opportunity to construct a model-base that will become intelligible as a special type of associative network, a constellation configuration.[5] For such will have three properties that can be extended to apply to the design of model-bases for management information systems:

1) The nodes in an constellation network can represent prototypes (genotypes), around which will radiate some collection of empirically-

significant phenomena taken to constitute a family. The prototype thus serves to anchor a cluster of variations on its central theme.

2) Each of the empirically-significant phenomena (qua *phenotypes*) in a particular cluster may be different in terms of the degree to which it expresses the properties of the anchoring prototype.

3) This degree of difference is capable of being displayed in terms of the Euclidean distance at which the phenomena is placed relative to the prototype . . . i.e., the length of the arc connecting the phenomenon to the central node. Moreover, an indication of the degree of difference between any two prototypes could also be expressed in terms of the length of the arc connecting them (with the directional orientation of the arcs also used to reflect relative similarities).

In any case, there are certain mechanical steps required to carry us from simple qualitative continua towards a proper constellation network.

Particularly, an attempt must be made to get a fairly precise comprehension of the degree of diversity among the categorical referents entailed in any qualitative continuum. We might then first attempt to isolate all points of fundamental qualitative *similarity* among any categorical or ideal-type referents (each of which will be accessible to us as some unique string of qualitative or state-level specifications).[6] We'd then attempt to capture the qualitative attributes shared by the categorical referents through operations such as these:

$$[S{*}a,\#] = ([Sa] \cap [S\#]);$$
$$[S{*}\#,z] = ([S\#] \cap [Sz]);$$

As a check for consistency we might also extract the similarities separately for $[S{*}a,z]$ as $([Sa] \cap [Sz])$. We might then collect all similarities into a master set that would indicate all qualitative level properties shared by all three categorical referents: $[S{*}] = ([S{*}a,\#] + [S{*}\#,z] + [S{*}a,z]\}$.

We would follow this with an attempt to isolate all fundamental qualitative *differences* among the categorical referents, and collect these in a set $[S\hat{}]$ that will serve to collect the following symmetric differences:

$$[S\hat{}a,\#] = ([Sa] \cup [S\#]) - ([Sa] \cap [S\#);$$
$$[S\hat{}\#,z] = ([S\#] \cup [Sz]) - ([S\#] \cap [Sz]).$$

If we want to assume commutativity, then we could define the master difference set as $[S\hat{}] = [S] - ([S\hat{}a,\#] + [S\hat{}\#,z])$. The importance of such operations is to give us some basis for assessing the event-side elasticity associated with any categorical continuum. An estimate of event-side elasticity should be available to us through certain qualitative comparisons (such being crude counterparts to ratio-based operations in the quantitative analysis domain) over the results generated above. Particularly, an idea of the qualitative similarity between categoricals could be given by:

[S*a,#] | ([Sa] + [S#]),
[S*#,z] | ([S#] + [Sz]),
[S*a,z] | ([Sa] + [Sz]).

We'd get an even better look at *elasticity* were we to go on to generate the difference-oriented complements to the above, e.g.:

[S^a,#] | ([Sa] + [S#]) or [S^a,#] | [S*a,#], etc.

In any case, given some rough indication of elasticity, we'd then be in a position to attempt the generation of a model-base qua associative network structure, as per **Exhibit 5.3**.

For there are key points of correspondence between the three aspects of a typical associative network and what's available to us as a consequence of the operations we've done. First, the concept of a *prototype* as employed in Associative Network theory is not materially different than the use of categorical ideal-types (Sa, S#, Sz and S' or S") as the central referents for a qualitative continuum. Secondly, as with a prototpye, each categorical referent would then serve to anchor a family of more specific event possibilities, such that [Ei] $\subset$ {Si}. Finally, the determination of the length of the *arcs* that would serve to position the various categorical ideal-types relative to one another would be determined by computations of the sorts made above, e.g.: d(Sa <--> S#) = f[S^a,#] | [S*a,#]. In practice, the values assigned the operator **d** might be categorical, e.g.:

d = 0: Sx and Sy are qualitatively equivalent;
d = 1: Sx and Sy are closely qualitatively related;
d = 2: Sx and Sy are moderately disparate;
d = 3: Sx and Sy entail substantial qualitative difference;
d = 4: Sx and Sy approach being polar opposites;
~d: Sx and Sy are *synthetic* constructs defined to have no commonalities and so have no connecting arc.

To extend the points of correspondence even further, there are three additional points worth noting:

- difference/similarity assessment operations could be used to position the various members of any event set [Ei] $\subset$ {S} relative to another, say some Ei|Ej. For operations of the sort suggested earlier should provide some basis for determining a relative arc distance d(Ei <--> Ej), and a residual value for each of the following: d(Ei <--> Si) and d(Ej <--> Si). We might also get an idea of the point at which we would want to position any Ei θ {Si} relative to nodes other than Si.

EXHIBIT 5.3 : Categorical Event Model-Base Structure arrayed as a Constellation Network

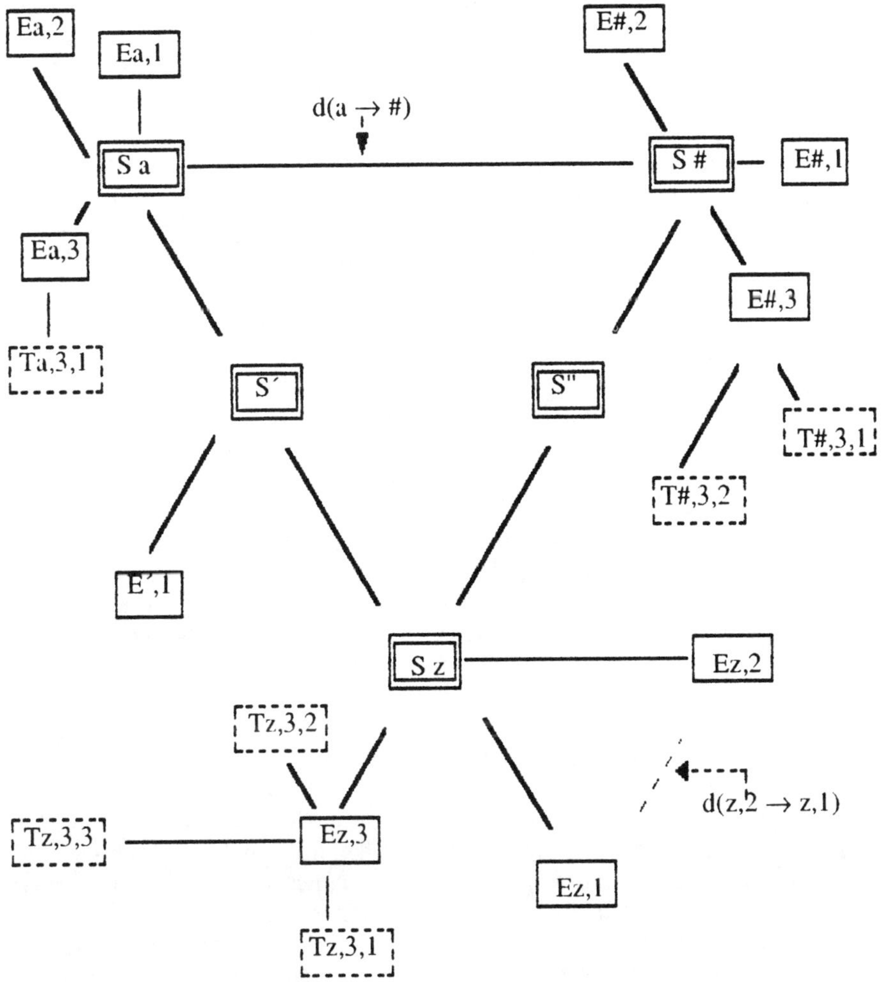

NOTE: $d(i \rightarrow j)$ is a measure of the vector distance between any two elements of a Constellation Network, which in turn is a reflection of the degree of difference in the properties over which the referents are defined (perhaps assessed via procedures of the sort discussed in chapter 7).

- a word should also be said about *intermediate* referents . . . such represented by some Ei that is more or less midway between two critical nodes, such that it could be interpreted as an aspect of either prototype belonging to two or more clusters). This of course was the case with the two fill-in referents we earlier employed, S' and S". For example, consider again the political state, Participatory Democracy. As was suggested, this could represent an intermediate node positioned essentially equidistant between the Democratic (S#) and Anarchic (Sz) ideal-types.
- were we interested in generating a hierarchical event-side structure, then the natural next step would be to move from the state to the thematic level. We'd thus let each Ei θ {Si} now represent an anchoring sub-node, around which would be arrayed a collection of thematic alternatives [T] ⊂ Ei representing still lower-order variations on any categorical, Si.

Exactly the same set of difference-assessment and positioning procedures could of course be employed to convert any array of response-side referents --defined as components of a Categorical model-base structure-- into an associative network construct.

It's merely that the nodes or prototypes would now be the various generic response options or Li's, with the collection of operational scripts each subsumes (some set [Ri,j] ⊂ Li) becoming the phenotypes radiating around the node. And once again, the length of the connecting arcs --the distance at which any Ri,j is placed from the node-- would reflect the magnitude of the correlation between the properties of Li and that variant, with the directional orientation of the arcs once more serving to reflect which script from any one cluster is more or less closely related to a script from some other cluster, or to indicate the strength of the disparity/similarity between generic options, etc. And if we wished to carry things to a still greater level of detail (or, alternatively, lower level of abstraction), we might then consider each Rj ∈ [R] ⊂ L to serve as a node around which will cluster some array of tactical response options, [r].

In such a way, we'd arrive at the Categorical model-base structure that was shown in Exhibit 5.3 as F'({S} x {L}), with the implication that both {S} and {L} may have been transformed into associative networks. The further implication is then that for any actual state-event that can be defined somewhere within the bounds of {S}, the continuous/categorical mapping function (F') will be used to point to an appropriate interpolative response option definable somewhere within the bounds of {L}. As such, when both event and response-side model base structures have been transformed into constellation constructs, we would have the wherewithal for testing the degree of *connectedness* between the scripting provisions in the latter and the scenario elements of the former . . . for systematically assessing the extent to which there is a response-side element that reaches to every event/threat possibility.

But all this may perhaps be somewhat abstract as yet. It may then be useful here to try to give a bit more concrete indication of the circumstances in which categorical model-base structures and interpolative programming technology might be employed to some practical advantage.

5.2.3 A Brief on Pragmatic Prospects

Given in a Categorical Model Base structure ($\{S\} \times \{L\}$), perhaps arrayed as a constellation network, $\{S\}$ will contain two or more referents comprehensible as *prototypes* including some number of subcategorical referents: $\{E1 \ldots Em\} \subset Si$. Any $Ei \in \{E\} \subset Si$ will have certain qualitative properties that mark it more as a member of the cluster anchored by Si than by any other categorical referent (qua prototype). Again also, the implication that any generic response-side referent will be capable of subsuming some indefinite number of operational response options pertinent to the event side referent(s) against which it is addressed, as per the following notation:

$$Si \rightarrow Li \supset [R];$$
$$Ri \in [R] \quad \text{for any } Ei \in \{E1 \ \ldots \ Em\} \subset \{Si\}.$$

A more concrete comprehension of what this might involve might best be approached by working through a simple example of how a typical emergency service organization --a Fire Department-- might actually employ a Categorical model base structure. For illustrative purposes, we'll consider the following trichotomy of ideal-type or generic event referents:

$$\{S1 \ \ldots \ S2 \ \ldots \ S3\}$$

where S1: Single-Alarm Fires (single dwellings)
S2: Multiple-Alarm Fires
S3: Complex Conflagrations (e.g., fires involving civil disturbances or other special hazards)

To focus things even further, consider the following subcategories of Multiple Alarm fires subsumable by S2:

E2,1: Large-scale *horizontal* fires, as when fire breaks out in an area of compacted inner-city dwellings, or when a broad-front brush fire threatens an entire neighborhood.

E2,2: Intensely-focused, vertical fires in high-rise structures . . . office buildings, hotels, hospitals, etc.

E2,3: Fires where there is a secondary peril, as with the prospect of a toxic chemical release or explosion, etc.

The formulation of a companion response-side structure would then involve defining a generic referent as some L2 | S2, where L2 would specify all those response initiatives applying more or less equally to all E2,j's:

- procedures for determining which fire-fighting assets from which different companies would be called upon as a function of proximity, availability, access to special equipment and skills, etc.
- procedures/techniques for determining a best routing for moving allocated assets from their home bases to the site of the fire, and for getting the assistance of police and other exogenous agencies in clearing the routes.
- a general protocol for establishing lines of command --for allocating authority and responsibility-- when multiple fire companies are involved.
- an indication of doctrinally-preferred initiatives for securing major fire areas against civilian incursions and for re-routing local traffic flows, etc.

With L2 so defined, then any lower-order response plan would be scripted over the provisions of L2 plus any initiatives specific to the particular event towards which it is turned. Therefore, given the several event subcategories defined just above, we might define (R-level) scripts as follows:

E2,1 → R1 = L2 +	1) a scheme for setting a perimeter defense against the spread of wide-area fires; and 2) advice on the use of airborne fire-fighting equiptment for large-area coverage.
E2,2 → R2 = L2 +	1) directives for using special equipment for handling conflagrations in tower structures (e.g., power ladders and chutes); and 2) doctrinal advice for containing vertical or *updraft* fires from bottom-up vs. top-down; from inside vs. outside, etc.
E2,3 → R3 = L2 +	1) provisions for *wide-area* evacuation given the type chemical involved and projected *spread* geometry, etc.

As for putting such structures to work, the first step would be use currently available indicators (I) about some actual/prospective event (V) in the attempt to map it to a most pertinent generic referent (prototype):

$$I(V) \rightarrow \{S1 \textbf{ or } S2 \textbf{ or } \ldots Sn\}.$$

Assuming that V is indeed deemed to be a special case of some Si, then the second task would be to try to map it somewhere onto the range of lower-order scenario referents subsumed by Si:

$$V \rightarrow \{Ei,1 \textbf{ or } Ei,2 \textbf{ or } \ldots Ei,n\}.$$

For illustrative purposes, let's assume that V is best thought of as a variant on Ei,2. A working event definition would then be constructed as follows:

$$V = Si + Ei{,}2 + [U],$$

such that V entails all the general properties pertinent to the prototype (Si), plus whatever lower-order properties have been included in scenario Ei,2, with [U] then containing a set of situation-specific parametric properties that serve to uniquely distinguish V from any other variant on (Si + E2,i). For example, were Ei,2 to represent a fire in a high-rise structure, the set [U] might specify the specific origin of the fire, the number of stories in the building, point-in-time occupancy patterns, currently accessible escape routes, etc. In such a case, a response to V could be scripted as:

$$V = Si + Ei{,}2 + [U] \rightarrow Rv = Li + Ri{,}2 + R[U],$$

with those response provisions that need to be formulated on a reactive basis (after-the-fact) restricted to the set of situation-specific parametric properties that V does not share with the subcategorical referent Ei,2 : $[U] = V - (Ei{,}2)$.

A more complicated case would arise were V to fall into an interstice between two subcategorical referents. For example, we might get a mapping like this: $\{E2 < .V. < E3\} \subset Si$. This would suggest the need for an interpolative initiative within the confines of a categorical model base structure. Again, this would involve the attempt to formulate an eclectic response over elements contained in some pre-defined R2 and R3 options, depending on what properties V shares with E2 and E3, or:

$$Rv = R2 \cap E2) + R3 \cap E3) + R[U].$$

That is, Rv is scripted over some set of R2 provisions given the nature of the intersect between V and E2, over R3 provisions given the properties in the intersect between V and E3, and some unique response provisions R[U] given those properties that V shares with neither E2 or E3.

More demanding is the case where an event falls into an indefinite interval between two categorical referents, or $\{S\# < .V. < Sz\}$. In such a case, the route to an interpolative solution may be made more expedient via the features of an associative network. For were we to attempt to map V onto such a structure, we'd get something like this:

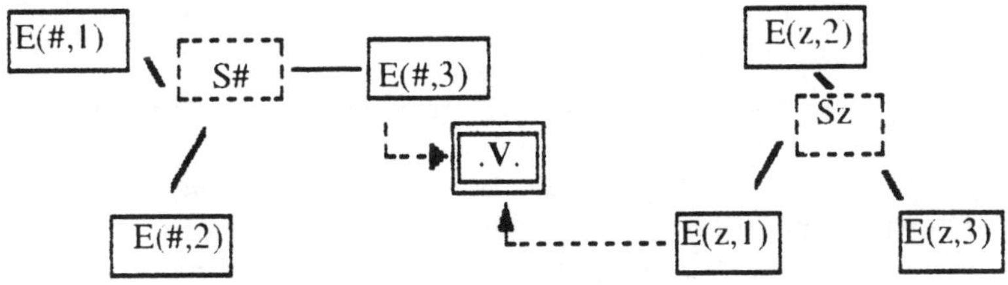

That is, **V** would be superimposed on the existing network structure so as to reflect the two standing event subclasses -- one belonging to the S# cluster and the other to the Sz cluster-- to which it is ostensibly most closely related. As shown above, the precise positioning suggests that **V** is relatively more closely related to E(z,1) than E(#,3). This in turn would imply that similarity/difference assessments would have determined that **V** is better thought of as an eccentric (outlier) member of the family of events anchored by Sz than as an aspect of S#, such that $d(Ea \rightarrow E\#,3) < d(Ea \rightarrow Ez,1)$. In such a case, we'd then look to generate a tailored response option as:

$$Rv = R\#,3 = f(\mathbf{V} \cap E\#,3) + Rz,1 = f(\mathbf{V} \cap Ez,1) + R[U].$$

Thus the only *original* scripting requirements --those that would delay our ability to immediately execute a response-- would then be directed at those properties of **V** that have no counterparts in either E(#,3) or E(z,1).

Finally, if **V** (qua discontinuity) is representative of some order of events we failed to provide for in our original continuum-building exercise, we might wish to use **V** or [U] as a basis to formulate a new categorical referent to anchor a cluster of event alternatives resident somewhere in the interstice we originally left between S# and Sz; this, in turn, would then inspire the formulation of a new response-side component. Hence the prospect of equipping Categorical model base structures with a *learning* capability.

But again, the pragmatic appeal of Categorical model base structures (and hence that of the adaptive-interpolative approach to strategic management they underlie) will depend primarily on the extent to which the actual events to which an organization will be subject will tend to fall neatly within one or another of the clusters anchored by some prototype . . . i.e., be intelligible as special cases of some limited set of generic situations qua categorical ideal-types. The facilities talked about in this section would then become increasingly inappropriate were the stream of contextual events to become increasingly *random* in nature . . . i.e., were more and more of them were to be definable only at some remote distance from any of the proptotypes (be essentially *extraneous* to any of the categorical ideal-types or clusters).

In such a case, it might be better for an organization to look to a still more exotic platform on which to base its strategic management activities, the adaptive/real-time modality.

5.3 Adaptive/Real-Time Strategic Management Logic

For this modality would use facilities designed to bring discipline to the situation where an organization expects --as a more or less routine matter-- to be confronted by a stream of events whose properties are likely to depart in significant ways from any pre-defined referents we might have been able to generate . . . discrete or categorical. As such, we're now concerned with provisions for handling exceptions in the form of *anomalies* or, even more broadly, with facilities that can promise to provide organizations with a strategic crisis-management capability. And to paraphrase an earlier point, the key challenge this would entail can be summarized as follows:

> When a real-world event falls outside the bounds of any of the event possibilities with which we are already prepared to deal, then an appropriate strategic response must be developed pretty much from scratch . . . with the premium often on rapidity as well as rectitude.

Hence, again, the emphasis on procedural and instrumental facilities that can help support the timely formulation of effectively *original* solutions to a stream of essentially novel, anomalous or otherwise unanticipated events.

As such, the technical focus now shifts to a type of model-base structure that would assist an organization in doing real-time event-definition and response formulation. For the prospect of an organization being visited by a stream of anamalous events would pose adaptive (vs. preadaptive) readiness requirements of the highest possible order. And by way of a critical technical propostion, there is this:

> The key to the development of facilities to support real-time activities is a reduction in the level of abstraction at which event and response referents are defined . . . i.e., the exchange of integral or fully-elaborated scenarios and scripts for some sort of more fundamental referent (e.g., primitives and templates).

Before going into a discussion of the technical implications of this proposition, it's well to take a quick look at the most familiar of the practical applications of primitives and templates.

5.3.1 Using Primitives and Templates as Referents

This is, of course, their employment by the modern police artist. He works with primitives that represent certain features of the human visage . . . e.g., different hair styles (straight, curly, afro), eye shapes (oval, sunken, almond), facial configurations (slavic, rounded, pointed), jaw types (lantern, cleft, undershot), etc. He will most usually also have a set of super-impositional primitives at his disposal, covering items such as varieties of eyeglasses (granny glasses, half-glasses, certain designer frames), styles of beards (Van Dyke, muttonchop), hat styles (porkpie, berets), etc. His basic reference set might then be structured something like this:

[Fi,j], where: Fi = the basic Feature of interest, e.g.:

i = 1: **Hair** : j = 1: curly; j = 2: straight;
i = 2: **Eyebrows** : j = 1: bushy; j = 2: arched, etc.

That is, the basic referent is some primitive F(i,j), which represents the j'th graded variation on some Feature-i. More elaborate referent sets would then be distinguished by: (a) A larger number of different features (Fi's) the artist is able to isolate and work with inidividually . . . can he, for example, work with cheekbones independent of general facial configuration; and (b) A greater number of graded variations (j's) within any feature subset . . . how many variations are there on any feature?

In terms of basic procedures, the police artist sits with a witness (or sometimes a collection of such) and attempts to transform their observations into a composite portrait of a suspect. In a sense then, he is attempting to construct a high-order or integral model (some Mi) by extracting a particular primitive (j) from each of the pertinent Feature subsets, or:

$$Mi = o(F1,j + F2,j + F3j + \ldots Fn,j),$$

where **o** is an ordering operator that determines which variation is to be extracted for each feature and how they are to be cojoined (or superimposed). As a rule, a proper model will require the witness to agree to some variation for each and every facial feature; that is, there must be a choice as to some particular j for each Feature-i. Where multiple witnesses are involved, and there is a conflict among their recollections, then there may be two or more models developed (say Mi and Mj), or perhaps an eclectic model (Mk) that represents a fusion of attributes drawn from Mi and Mj.

A template would then be a mid-range model defined around a collection of primitives that tend to be encountered in concert. For the police artist, templates might be developed to account for naturally occurring correlations (e.g., certain eye configurations often tend to appear in conjunction with a specific cheekbone structure) or to capture certain aesthetic proclivities . . . some styles of beards tend to be more congruent with certain facial configurations than others; certain social subgroups tend to favor certain hairstyles and types of eyeglasses; people with different head shapes or hairstyles tend generally to favor one style of hat over another.

The pragmatic significance of primitive/template based reference sets comes clear when we consider the alternative, the traditional Mug Book as a collection of integral models qua photographs (which may take to represent a *discrete* model base). The main problem with such is that a perpetrator who has not been previously (and locally) booked will have no entry in the mug book, so witnesses cannot effect a proper mapping from their observations to a mug book referent. In such a case, unless the agency has a Police Artist equipped with a primitive/template set, it will lack any *model* to help direct a search for actual suspects. Therefore, a primitives/template model base structure can be used to avert a default that would arise were only a discrete model-base structure available to a law enforcememt agency.

But the police artist and his primitive/template may also be posed as a complement to the Mug Book. For there are two other problems with the latter. First, a Mug Book may contain many thousands of entries . . . far too many for a witness to work his way through photograph by photograph. Therefore, Mug Books tend to be ordered into volumes defined around different classes of crimes (e.g., arson; child molestation; armed robbery). But suppose an armed robber suddenly decided to diversify into arson? A witness to the latter crime --given access only to the Arson volume(s) of the Mug Book-- would then again be deprived of the wherewithal to make a proper mapping. Were he then asked to work through all the other volumes, it will be a toss up whether it's his patience or his eyes that go first. Yet it's possible to have the police artist --as a routine background exercise-- go through the photographs in the collection of Mug Book volumes to assign a *key* that ties back a criminal's most distinguishing features to the members of his primitive/template array (e.g., an individual may have a lantern jaw and a penchant for wearing aviator glasses). The police artist is thus generating an alternate ordering over the elements of the Mug Book, and so opening up an alternate (indexed) search avenue via keys.

To make use of such a facility, an eyewitness would first be taken through the steps leading to a composite model emphasizing those features he remembers most clearly. Next, he would go to the volume of the Mug Book that pertains to the class of crime that took place. But instead of working through randomly, his search would be directed --via the keyed index-- to those photographs that most closely share the properties of the composite portrait that he just caused to be drawn. If no hit is made, the search would be successively expanded to include less well-correlated photographs within a specific volume. And should there still be no hit, then the composite portrait characteristics might then be used to direct the search to a few most highly correlated photographs from volumes dealing with classes of crime other than that which was witnessed. If no match is found, the multi-volume search could then be expanded to include second-tier subjects, etc. At some point, further search through the set of photographs might be abandoned in favor of using the composite sketch itself. The use of primitive/template referents as a prelude to the search through a Mug Book should then generally allow for more rapid closure on a singular mapping should it in fact exist.

Secondly, geographic diversification can also present a problem for the Mug Book. For criminals are certainly capable of mobility, and their profession might indeed recommend a change of venue from time to time. The mobile criminal might then be in Mug Books elswehere, but not in any community to which he's moved; witnesses will look for him in vain. It would then often be desirable to be able to extend the search for a mapping to remote locations. And while there is of course some precedent for wire transfer of photographs among different law enforcement agencies, the prospect of transferring entire volumes is obviously not very attractive. However, were two or more agencies to be employing the same set of primitive/template referents (or if a translation table existed), then a remote search might be made more feasible by a simple extension of the procedures just described for a local search. Particularly, the host agency would broadcast the set of primitive/template codes for the composite portrait that was just made to other agencies. These would then be asked to go through the indexes to their volume for the class of crime of concern, and to remit a wire-copy or bit-map of any photographs extracted from that volume whose *keys* align well with the codes transmitted.

The police artist is then a practical expression of the rudimentary logic for adaptive model-building. For from a quite limited set of lower-order referents, he can generate a virtually infinite array of composite portraits. Moreover, he may be considered to be doing model-building in effective real-time . . . in response to a running stream of prompts from witnesses. We want now to see how the police artist analogy may be extended to the problem of moving towards real-time command/control.

5.3.2 Characteristics of Template-Based Structures

Exhibit 5.4 summarizes our suggestions in this respect, and we'll now work briefly through each of its provisions. The first of these calls for the generation of what are referred to as extensive referents and involves the definition of pairs of event scenarios (Ea and Ez) and response scripts (Ra and Rz) that are intended to serve as *limiting* referents. The model-base generation focus thus shifts away from the attempt to project all possible environmental and/or competitive events to which an organization might be subject, which we've already agreed is not likely to be successful anyway when organizations are resident in significantly complex or volatile contexts. Rather, the initial analytical emphasis is now directed at trying to comprehend merely the extremes over which real-world events/threats might wander, as per the following rationale:

> To the extent that Ea and Ez indeed mark the extremes of the situations an organization might have to face during some period, then any actual event that occurs should be capable of being defined somewhere within the domain they bound.

The clinical challenge here is thus to make sure that Ea and Ez are indeed as different as possible. But as with the qualitative difference computations associated with the generation of categorical referents, this is a task that will require an order of technical facilities that will not be introduced until the final chapter of this volume. But here we can at least give a rough idea of the basic procedural steps that would be involved.

Particularly, we might employ a Delphi-type process or one of the other elicitive schemes such that that Ea and Ez would be intelligible as subjectively-predicated referents --*notional* or perhaps even deliberately fictional-- constructions. The pragmatic aim would be to have Ea defined so as to represent the best --the most benign or favorable-- of all possible worlds, with Ez then used to to portray a worst-case (most threatening) scenario. We may then elect to fill in the gaps left by defining an array of interval constructs to constitute the set [E#]. In the simplest case, [E#] might have merely one member, this being a dialectical or synthetic *median* portraying a situation roughly mid-way between Ea (as thesis) and Ez (as antithesis). Another option would be available had there been generated a set of discrete event referents as an aspect of a traditional contingency planning process, [E1, E2 . . . Em]. Given such, we might then look to identify that pair of referents (some Ei and Ej) that are maximally disparate and then take these to serve as the event extrema if the degree of diversity they entail is deemed sufficient. One or more of the remaining members of [E] would then be entered into [E#] to serve as intermediary or bridging referents.

A similar approach would be used to develop the response-side construct {Ra . . . [R#] . . . Rz}, whose rationale would then be this:

> Given that Ra and Rz proscribe the range of response options open to an organization, then any initiative the organization might mount should entail scripting provisions that would place it somewhere on the continuum bounded by the two response-side extrema.

In many cases, the substance of Ra and Rz may be taken to derive directly from work done previously on the event side.

For if Ra is to be set against Ea and Rz against Ez as maximally different scenarios, then Ra and Rz should represent maximally disparate Scripting alternatives in terms of the sorts of assets they require, the action-initiatives they entail, etc. But where we wish to conduct response-side activities independently, then we might replicate the analytical procedures we just went through for the event side. For example, a Delphi exercise might be aimed at defining Ra so as to represent a script constructed around the cheapest or most abundant assets/resources available to the organization (or at least those already on hand) and that action-initiative that represents the least demanding or safest (in terms of the sorts of counteractions it might provoke) of all options. Its polar opposite (Rz) might then be a script choreographed around

EXHIBIT 5.4 : Primitive/Template Model-Base Provisions

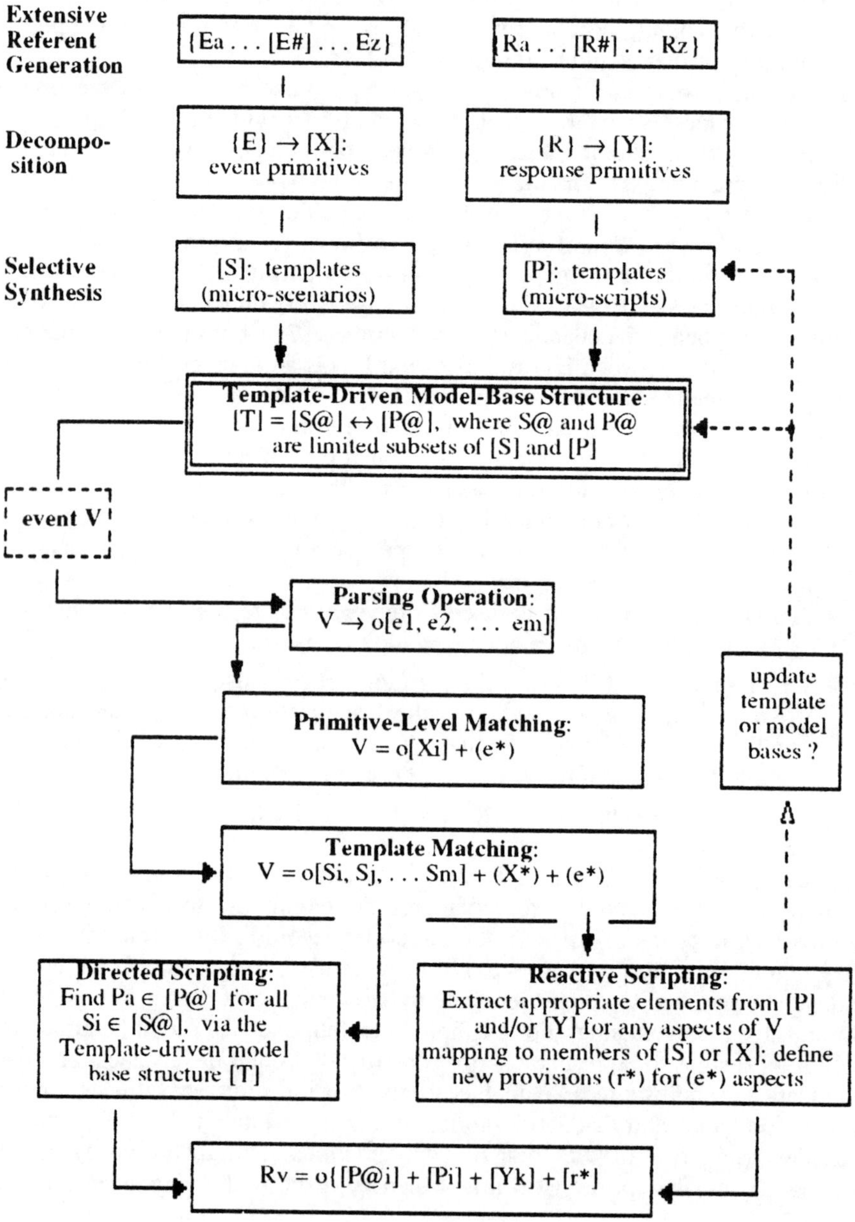

committments of the most expensive or scarcest of the assets/resources that might be available to the organization and the conceivably most perilous of action-initiatives we might possibly invoke. Or again, where there already exists some discrete-bipartite contingency planning construct ([E] x [R]), we'd try to extract the maximally disparate pair of standing contingency plans to serve as Ra and Rz. And then perhaps define some mediating referents to include in a set [R#].

But whatever the origin of the referents just defined, the next step is to undertake a Decomposition operation aimed at their reduction (disaggregation) to sets of event and response *primitives* . . . the collections [X] and [Y] respectively.[7] The decomposition exercises might best be undertaken over the several dimensions that apply to the definition of proper scenarios and scripts, or items such as WHO, WHAT, WHEN, HOW and WHY, etc. These dimensions might then be used to define *subsets* within which to house arrays of primitives, perhaps along the following lines:

EVENT-SIDE ARRAY: [X] = all [Xi,j], where:

[X1,j] = all *whos*, such that any X1(j) would indicate a specific adversary unit or exogenous agencies;

[X2,j] = all *whats*, with any X2(j) indicating some specific competitive threat or environmental event, etc.

This would be done for all members of {E}, for all dimensions, with any redundancies then removed. The result would then be a one-time-mention array of basic scenario-generation elements.

The same set of decomposition initiatives might then be used to work with scripting provisions, e.g.:

RESPONSE-SIDE ARRAY: [Y] = all [Yi,j], where:

[Y1,j] = all *whos*, with any Y1(j) designating some unit(s) from our own Organization;

[Y2,j] = all *whats*, with each Y2(j) designating a reactive or proactive Strategic initiative that our organization might author, etc.

The set [Y] would then be a one-time-mention array of all basic strategic planning (scripting) provisions.

Thus the sets [X] and [Y] should contain all the elements that would allow us to reconstitute any member of {E} and {R} merely by imposing some unique ordering (O) over the appropriate subset of primitives. i.e.:

$$\text{any } Ei\ \theta\ \{E\} = O[Xi,j] \subset [X]$$
$$\text{any } Rj\ \theta\ \{R\} = O[Yi,j] \subset [Y],$$

where the symbol θ again means *definable within*. Therefore, by extension, we should then be able to similarly generate a model for any event that might arise anywhere within the bounds of {E} or any strategic response option intelligible as falling somewhere within the confines of {R} . . . and do so on a *roll your own* basis as circumstances might dictate.

But consider now the operation designated as Selective Synthesis. It is this operation that generates event and response side *templates*. As in the example of the police artist, a template results from the conjunction of two or more primitives to form an intermediate level referent . . . one existing at some level of abstraction between the primitive and an integral model, i.e.:

$$Si = o\,(xi + xj \;\ldots\; xn) \subset [X];$$
$$Pj = o\,(ya + yb \;\ldots\; ym) \subset [Y].$$

Event-side templates --constituents of the set [S]-- are thus used to pre-configure or string together certain basic properties that naturally tend to hang together in the real-world, and which may emerge as components of several or perhaps many different scenarios (fully-elaborated models of actual events).

The practical purpose of using templates is clear enough. For example, to the extent that certain aspects of any actual event (some V) can be seen to map to one or more members of the template set [S], this saves us from having to generate an entire scenario by working only at the primitive level of analysis. The same thing would be true on the response side, for the route to a fully-elaborated response is generally shorter and less arduous when there are some aspects that can be handled by drawing on already pre-configured templates (qua standing micro-scripts available in [P]) than to have to generate the whole script from scratch . . . to work at the Y-level. Thus, templates become the *boilerplate* for adaptive management processes.

Templates may be defined at different levels of elaborateness (or aggregation) and be inspired either by empirical or subjective predicates. In the case of the former, we would look to define templates by examining the relative frequency with which two or more primitives tended to appear together as aspects of the historical events to which an organization (or some surrogates) were subjected . . . i.e., by looking for any significant correlations between WHOS, WHATS and WHENS, etc., authored by environmental agencies or competitors. But templates may also be trans-empirical or even counter-empirical in origin, in which case they are products of reasoning or logical inference rather than observations or statistical computation. Response side templates could also be formulated around conjunctions of asset, action and/or organizational specifications that have either empirical or notional/logical merit. As a general rule, we would want to maintain more elaborate (more highly integrated) response-side templates for what are deemed to be the more critical or frequently-employed of the scripting initiatives we contemplate having to execute.

The next step in the sequence would be to consider possible cross-mappings between event and response side templates. Here we would look for any response-side template that would appear --on the basis of experience or judgement-- to be particularly well-suited to some event-side template. The set of all such cross-mappings would then be encoded in the Template Driven Model-Base Structure, or:

$$[T] = ([S@] \times [P@]).$$

The arrays [S@] and [P@] include some subset of the event and response templates encoded in [S] and [P] respectively. Priority for membership in [S@] would expectedly be given to those event aspects (qua micro-scenarios) we expect to encounter most frequently and/or which are deemed most threatening, with the membership in [P@] then determined accordingly. Any Ti ∈ [T] will thus serve to link (via a bipartite graph) some event-side template with a singular response-side template, and so becomes comprehensible as a low-order Contingency Planning structure expressing collective consensus or doctrinal wisdom about what micro-script is best set against what micro-scenario. A templated model-base structure might start life as a relatively sparsely populated construct. But as time goes on, the templated model-base structure may gradually become increasingly rich in content. For we would use it as a slate for reality and experience to write upon . . . as a repository for wisdom gleaned from the stream of actual events the organization has encountered and the response initiatives it has mounted against them as per the *dynamic elaboration* provision shown in the previous exhibit. Such thus becomes the seat of disciplined learning/discovery within the confines of the adaptive/real-time modality.

The pragmatic import of the construct [T] would then reflect this line of argument: Again, in particularly volatile and complex contexts, organizations must face the prospect that each event/threat may be somewhat unique when viewed in aggregate or looked at as an integral phenomenon. However, when examined at a lower level of abstraction --i.e., at the template level of analysis-- the uniqueness of events/threats may not extend to all their attributes. That is, not all aspects of all events will be effectively novel, unprecedented or unanticipated. Therefore, we hold out the prospect that even the most anomalous or outlandish occurrence may have at least some of its properties map more or less directly to one or more of the micro-scenarios that have been encoded in the template array [S]. At the very least, this would then mean that we would not have to define the event/threat entirely from scratch, but would be able to make use of certain already-defined model components. Even more pleasing is the possibility that one or more of the event-side template referents will be included in the subset [S@], as these would already have been assigned a response-side correlate as some Pb ∈ [P@] via one or another of the mappings provisions (some Ti) included in [T]. Should this be the case, then there are at least some aspect(s) of the response-formulation or scripting task that need not be decided on a strictly *reactive* basis.

Overall then, the primary purpose of the template-related facilities shown in the previous exhibit is to help minimize the amount of analytical work that must be done in *real-time* following the emergence of some exceptional event (or, if there is no traditional contingency planning structure already in place, of any event that might arise). Or more broadly, the rationale for the conversion to a template-centered model-base structure is this:

> If the richness of the events to which an organization might be subject is so great as to obviate any attempt to be *ready* in total for all possibilities, then the next best thing is to try to be as ready as possible *in part* for whatever might occur. It's this latter ambition that the template based facilities are designed to serve.

Why this might be the case can be seen from a quick look at the procedural provisions associated with a template driven model- base structure. These would be initiated upon the appearance of indicators (field observations, intelligence inputs, etc.) suggesting the emergence of some event (V).

There would then follow a Parsing operation that would reduce the indicated event to a string of low-order constituents a simple transformation process: V => o[e1, e2 . . . en]. Again, the operator (o) would capture the ordering or relational properties of the event, while the various e's would apply to basic scenario aspects of the who?, what? variety. Next then would come the first of two basic matching activities:

$$V[e] \rightarrow [X] \;\; => \;\; V = o\,[xi, xj \;\ldots\; xn] \subset [X] \; + \; (e^*).$$

This expresses the attempt to find an adequate match (or mapping) between any of the e's over which V is defined and the array of primitives encoded in the set [X].[8] Any such matches then result in the exchange of the original e's for the equivalent x's. The collection (e*) would then be used to house all attributes of V for which there is no adequate match within [X].

The second of the matching operations would then attempt to find a match between any of the substrings of specifications over which V is now defined and any event-side templates included in the set [S], i.e.:

$$ok\,(xi, xj \;\ldots\;) \rightarrow [S] \;\; => \;\; V = o\,([Si, Sj \;\ldots\;] + (x^*) + (e^*)).$$

where **ok** defines a particular condition of connection between two or more primitives (which in the simplest case may be merely the co-appearance of primitive-level properties, but which in more sophisticated applications may impose some specific mathematical or logical relationship . . . e.g.: dictate a strongly positive correlation or a particular causality in terms of direction and magnitude of influence). In any case, following this operation, the actual event V is now redefined to include any template-level components (Si's) that might have been found to apply, with the collection (x*) then being used to house any of the primitives belonging to V that are not includable in any template, and (e*) still collecting those properties of V that have no match to any of the currently available primitives.

Once an event has been reconstituted in this way, attention would turn to response-side matters. And what's clear is that the best-case situation we might encounter is this:

$$V = o\,(Si, Sj\ \ldots\ Sm) \subset [S@] \;\rightarrow\; Rx = T(Pi, Pj\ \ldots\ Pm) \subset [P@].$$
$$\text{where: } [T] \;\rightarrow\; (Pi \mid Si, Pj \mid Sj, \text{etc.})$$

For what this expression suggests is that some actual event V is either empirically well-precedented or entirely anticipated (reflects some projected possibility), such that its salient aspects are virtually all ones that map more or less directly to event-side templates (micro-scenarios) encoded in the set [S@], i.e., the collections (x*) and (e*) are effectively *empty*. And again, because every Si ∈ [S@] will have been pre-assigned a response-side correlate via the mapping provisions of the templated model-base structure [T], the implication is then that a response (some Rx | V) would then be comprised of the appropriate subset of micro-scripts extracted from the set [P@] via the mapping logic entailed in [T]. We are here then as close as we can possibly get to the kind of automatically-directed solutions available from traditional contingency planning platforms. Or, from yet another perspective, this situation represents that which effectively minimizes *reactive* demands.

All other situations --instances where certain aspects of an actual event fail to map to elements of [S@]--would then imply some level of *reactive* response-side requirements as per the following situational provisions:

1) $U^\wedge(Pa \in [P])$ for any $Si \notin [S@]$;
2) $U^\wedge(P^*)$ for any $Si \in [S] \rightarrow \sim Pa \in [P]$
3) $U^\wedge(yk \in [Y])$ for any $x^* \notin Si$;
4) $U^\wedge(r^*)$ for any $e^* \notin [X]$.

The first of the above requirements suggests that we might look within the set of standing response-side templates [P] for an acceptable correlate to any properties of V that map to some event-side template that, while not in [S@], is present in the supraset [S]. If no appropriate micro-script is found in [P], then we may elect --as per (2) above-- to define some new P* to array against the Si in question. We may then further elect to incorporate this new P* into the set [P@] and its event-side predicate Si into [S@], thereby adding some new element to the templated model-base structure: $T^* \in [T] = (Si \leftrightarrow P^*)$. Should this Si appear again, we would then have the wherewithal for a directed (vs. reactive) solution.

The remaining two response-side requirements then pose the demand for efforts at the primitive level. Under provision (3) above, the search would be directed over the set of standing response-side primitives [Y] for a possible correlate as U^(yk) for any x* (which, again, is a primitive that was not included in any of the template-level components over which V was redefined). We might even choose to cojoin two or more of the x*'s belonging to V to constitute a new event-side template: o[x*] = S*. This might then be incorporated into either [S] or [S@]. In the latter case, we would combine two or more of the yk's to form some new response-side template or micro-scenario, or let P* = o[yk] ⊂ [Y] | S*. All the above serve to enrich the system's template-based facilities.

It's then through the provisions of (4) above that we might approach the situation that would maximize the analytical challenge that must be met in effective real-time. For again, the e*'s are attributes that have no match even within the system's standing array of event-side primitives, [X]. They thus represent properties entirely alien to both experience and expectation. We might then define the absolute worst-case situation around the emergence of an event that is of such an extraordinarily novel nature that virtually all of its properties are anomalous, or where V = o[e*] ⊂ [X]. The problem here is that any e* will likely demand an entirely original response-side primitive --some r* ∉ [Y]-- which might imply a scripting provision the organization cannot currently meet (e.g., demand some asset that is not on-hand). Happily, this worst-case situation is also the least likely to occur. But even if it should arise, an organization that has adaptive/real-time facilities in place should be in a much better position to cope than an enterprise that has not anticipated any need at all for a reactive management capability.[9]

By way now of a final alert, all of the adaptive strategic planning/positioning provisions that have been introduced in this chapter are inordinately dependent upon the quality of the arguments with which they are supplied. Being merely structuring conventions, they themselves entail neither wit nor discretion. Rather, they're merely passive frames-of-analysis within which to contain and organize the products of strategic decision authorities' judgement and subjective sensibilities. Yet as we shall try to make clear in the next chapter, once we begin to talk about the quality of arguments that might serve as predicates to any strategic exercises, we run up against the spectre of a critical *shortfall* in contemporary decision support technology. And unless this shortfall can be resolved, it's not only the ability to make good practical use of the two rather sophisticated adapitve planning/positioning modalities we've dealt with in this chapter that's in doubt, but the capability to do disciplined strategic management in any form at all.

NOTES AND REFERENCES

1. For a general discussion of reactive management concepts and technology, see my paper: "The Case for Reactive Management Systems: Elements of a Real-Time Decision Technology", in *IEEE Transactions on Systems, Man and Cybernetics* (Jan./Feb., 1984).

2. An informative treatise on the socio-cultural aspects of adaptive strategic management is available from Eric Trist's article "Developing an Adaptive Planning Capability in Public Enterprise and Government Agencies", in the *Management Handbook for Public Administrators* (Van Nostrand Reinhold, 1978).

3. One might look to certain AI-based knowledge engineering conventions to help define categorical referents, as per arguments in J. F. Sowa's *Conceptual Structures* (Addison-Wesley).

4. Interestingly, this subsumation concept corresponds rather well with a distinction that J. K. Friend raised over a decade ago between policy-making and decision-making. For in a fine paper, "The Dynamics of Policy Change" (in *Long Range Planning*, vol. 10; February 1977), he notes that " . . . *a policy is essentially a stance which, once articulated, constributes to the context within which a succession of future decisions will be made.*" The proposition that any generic strategic planning referent will serve to anchor some collectivity of lower-order (less abstract) or actionable scripts corresponds rather well with Friend's distinction between policy referents and decisions.

5. In practice, associative network structures are designed to express constructs that result from the superimposition of factors drawn from different populations. Thus, most working associative networks are in fact *data* base structures predicated on clusters of properties rather than records, as suggested by Miyamoto, et. al. in their "Directed Graph Representations of Associative Structures: A Systematic Approach", in *IEEE Transactions on Systems, Man and Cybernetics* (16, 1; 1986). They may also reflect neural-network theory speculations about the mechanics of associative inference and associative memory as a human cognitive characteristics, c.f.: Fukushima, "A Model of Associative Memory in the Brain" in *Kybernetik* (12, 1973), or T. Kohonen's volume on *Associative Memory* (Springer-Verlag, 1978). In contrast, a Constellation network is a *model* base network where generic prototypes represent planets, discrete event and response alternatives could be moons and arcs comprehensible as difference vectors.

6. The isolation of similarities and differences among some set of categorical constructs may be thought of as an exercise in qualitative substration, and so perhaps susceptible to formal discipline via fuzzy-set techniques for determining membership in or exclusion from qualitative sets. For more on the mechanics of such operations, see E. Backer's *Cluster Analysis by Optimal Decomposition of Induced Fuzzy Sets* (Delft University, 1978). But in the final chapter of this volume, we'll be introducing some

technical bases for the systematic recognition and extraction of qualitative vs. quantitative differences.

7. These are operations for which there is some technical precedent. First, there are certain Formal system science conventions that might apply, c.f.: Himmelbau (ed.) *Decomposition of Large-Scale Systems* (American-Elsevier, 1983). These are also techniques to help determine membership in *fuzzy* sets, e.g., E. Blacker, *Cluster Analysis by Optimal Decomposition of Induced Fuzzy Sets* (Delft University, 1978). Finally, some knowledge-engineering initiatives, especially those used by expert system designers, might be used to some advantage. For more on such, see J. Sowa's fine book, *Conceptual Structures* (Addison-Wesley, 1984).

8. Clearly, at least some of the basic matching/matching tasks that have to be conducted within a primitive/template structure could be computer-aided via modern pattern recognition technology. See, for example, Tou and Gonzales' volume on *Pattern Recognition Principles* (Addison-Wesley, 1977).

9. For some ideas about the critical practical constribution of Template-driven model base technology within modern Command/Control systems, see my article: "Enhancing the Role of Microcomputers in Command/Control Systems" in (Andriole, ed.) *Microcomputer Decision Support Systems*, op. cit.

PART III:

ADDRESSING THE SHORTFALL IN STRATEGIC DECISION TECHNOLOGY

CHAPTER 6

STRATEGIC ANALYSIS CAPABILITIES AND CONFOUNDATIONS

Up to this point we've taken a rather sanguine perspective on strategic management and decision-making. Particularly, we've pretty much assumed that there will be a neat, effectively linear progression through the various requirements posed by the several strategic planning/positioning platforms. But what we now want to do is introduce the prospect of confoundations that can either frustrate or perhaps even defeat attempts to rationally resolve strategic issues in the real-world. And once we bring these confoundations to light, there immediately follows a recognition of the points at which contemporary management science procedures and instruments can no longer be relied upon to guide us towards rational strategic decision choices. That is, we run up against the prospect of a serious "shortfall" in strategic analysis and decision technology, and hence in strategic management practice as well.

6.1 Decision Analysis Functions and Methodological Protocols

We've now identified two different occasions for strategic decision exercises. The first or *projective* occasion would find strategic decision exercises being used to set the contents of a planning/positioning structure. The result of such exercises would be the specification of an ostensibly best strategic response option for each of the projected event possibilities for which an organization desires to be ready (which may appear as integral models in a contingency planning construct or as generic or template-based referents when it is an adaptive structure that's being built). The second occasion for a strategic default, such again being triggered by the emergence of an event for which there is no entirely appropriate, pre- defined standing strategic response option (integral, categorical or template-based), such at least some --if not all-- of the provisions of an appropriate response will have to be determined on a *reactive* basis.

The distinction between the two orientations is merely that projective decisions are carried out in advance-of-the-fact or on an anticipatory basis, whereas in their reactive guise they are best thought of as problem-solving processes. But in either case, the convention for distinguishing strategic (vs. tactical or operational) decision exercises would still hold, i.e.: True strategic decision exercises will be defined so as to involve the need to generate and elect from among alternatives that represent *qualitatively* disparate options. Moreover, as was the case with projective decisions, reactive strategic decision exercises will also demand that choices be arrived at on two different dimensions:

(1) **DIAGNOSTIC**: the attempt to work from a currently available information base (observables, current intelligence, symptoms, etc.) to a singular causal/explanatory model of the event that has or is taking place . . . the requirement to fix on a maximum-likelihood problem definition.

(2) **REMEDIAL**: given the above, the attempt to converge on an ostensibly best (maximal-utility) strategic response option or strategic solution scheme.

In this respect, the difference between the projective and the reactive or strategic problem-solving orientations is that whereas the former is directed towards the definition of sets of event possibilities qua *contingencies*, the focus of the latter is on comprehending and containing just a single *actual* event.

Consider then **Exhibit 6.1**, this summarizing the implications of the four generic analytical operations through which a decision-making exercise might pass en-route to the conclusions called for in (1) and (2) above. Both the notation and the basic vocabulary of concepts will be familiar from work done

EXHIBIT 6.1 : Generic Analytical Operations for Reactive Strategic Decision (problem-solving) Exercises

	Event/Problem Definition Sequence	Response Formulation Sequence
Indeterminacy	**(I) → ~[E]**	**Ei → ~[R]**
1. **Realization** (hypothesis formulation)	~[E] → [E] -generates an array possible event/problem definitions (as causal or explanatory models)	P^(Ei) → [R] -results in an array of alternative response (remedial) options given some problem definition
2. **Ordering** (initial ranking)	[E] → P[E] → [E*] -assigns a probability value to each member of [E] reflecting the expectation of its proving to be the best (true) definition of the problem; may extract some subset [E*] of most interesting candidates	[R] → U[R] → [R*] -assigns a utility index to each member of [R] that reflects the expectation it will prove to be the best (optimal) response option; these indices may be used to isolate a subset [R*] of most promising options for more detailed attention
3. **Assessment** (hypothesis testing)	P[E*] → P´[E*] -acquisition of new evidence (derived from empirical efforts) to enhance the information base and so lead to more precise/reliable bases for discriminacy (via the P´ operators)	U[R*] → U´[R*] -subjection of options in [R*] to some sort of field trials designed to provide more concrete evidence on which to base valuations of relative effectiveness and efficiency (re: cost/benefit estimates, etc.)
4. **Selection** (decision choices)	P´[E*] → P^(Ei) ∈ [E*] -fixes on a singular, ostensibly maximum-likelihood problem definition model	U´[R*] → U^(Rj) ∈ [R*] -election of a singular, ostensibly maximal-utility approach for dealing with the problem at hand

Singularity: P^(Ei) and U^(Rj)

previously. Particularly, the use of the symbol E for event/problem definitional candidates suggests that it is once again state-level (vs. thematic or parametric) alternatives with which we are concerned, such that the response-side candidates or R's are strategic (vs. tactical or operational) options. And some idea of what the analytical operations might imply is available from the discussion in the last chapter about the analytical activities underlying the generation of a strategic contingency planning structure (with the realization and ordering operations being applied in a projective orientation). But to elaborate here on how they might apply in problem-solving exercises, we'll assume a starting point under the worst-case condition or indeterminacy, the common notational expression for which is:

$$(I) \rightarrow \sim[E] \quad \text{or} \quad Ei \rightarrow \sim[R],$$

where (I) is the currently available indicator (information) base and the symbol ~ is meant to express a not condition. As such, the expression (I) → ~[E] implies that we are operating under a condition of maximal ignorance. That is, we'll assume that [E] is essentially *empty* of any significantly likely alternatives . . . i.e., we currently have no really plausible causal explanations for what's going on. In a similar sense, the expression Ei → ~[R] would suggest that, while we have arrived at an event/problem definition, we have as yet no concrete ideas about what might constitute an appropriate response.

Assuming indeterminacy as a starting-state condition, then it would fall to realization operations to generate some concrete possibilities to fill up the *empty* sets. For when undertaken in the confines of a problem-solving exercise, realization activities are more or less equivalent to the hypothesis-generation phase that would initiate a formal scientific (academic) research exercise. Thus, for the problem-definition sequence, realizations activities would result in an array of alternative causal/explanatory constructs (models), each of which postulates a somewhat different set of structural and dynamic properties for the phenomenon, process or event of interest. Response-side realizations operations would then result in an array of alternative remedial or treatment options, each expressing a unique solution scheme or line of attack against what emerged from the problem-definition sequence as the maximum-likelihood causal/explanatory alternative.

An ordering operation might then be used to impose an initial ranking over the various problem-definitional and/or response alternatives that were realized. These rankings would reflect decision analysts' assumptions about which of the alternatives options are more promising than which others. Hence the implications of the transitions from the initially unordered realization arrays [E] and [R], to their ranked counterparts P[E] and U[R], where P and U represent probability and utility operators, respectively. When the number of alternatives is relatively large (and/or time and analytical resource constraints particularly severe), the conclusions arrived at during the ordering operation will be used to determine which of the alternatives is to be given what level of more detailed attention --in which order-- during the Assessment stage of a decision-making exercise. And in certain instances, the ordering function may result in the elimination of certain alternatives from any further consideration. One or more of the problem-definitional candidates that were realized might, for example, be excluded because of their practical implausibility. Some response candidates might then be discarded because of their apparent infeasibility (e.g., they violate some encompassing policy constraints as to means that can be employed or pose demands for skills, assets or levels of resources that cannot reasonably be met). Hence the reductive transformations shown as [E] $\rightarrow$ [E*] and [R] $\rightarrow$ [R*]. For the subset [E*] will be used to extract some limited number of causal/explanatory candidates deemed most likely to eventually prove to best capture the true properties of the problem at hand, with the subset [R*] then used to extract those members of [R] thought to have the best chance of being the ultimately most effective/efficient of the remedial candidates.

The *tentative* nature of the probability and utility functions arrived at during the ordering function may derive from their being based on evidence that is either somewhat dated, or that may have originally been collected with respect to subjects and/or under conditions that do not precisely match those of current interest (such that it's to be treated as *secondary* evidence). Or orderings may owe at least some of their substance to subjective or judgemental (vs. objective or empirically supported) arguments. Therefore, the main thrust of the Assessment phase of decision exercises is the acquisition of new information that will be of more recent origin or of more objective authority than that which was originally available.

These additions to the information base will hopefully translate into more precise and reliable (empirically validated) probability or utility valuations, as per the transformations shown in the exhibit as P $\rightarrow$ P´[E*] and U $\rightarrow$ U´[R*]. The implication is that, being based on a richer, more timely and/or tangible set of predicates, the P´ and U´ operators will hopefully provide decision authorities with the wherewithal for an essentially rational Selection of a singular most likely problem-definition and most promising response option . . . these the requirements for a satisfactory (actionable) conclusion to a problem-solving exercise.

Consider now the properties of the three orthodox methodological protocols that are available for disciplining scientific problem-solving exercises, as per **Exhibit 6.2**. As may be obvious, the procedural and instrumental properties of the Positivist protocol marks it as especially appropriate as bases for carrying out the analytical aspects of operational decision exercises, while the two variants on Inductive methodology --the Objectivist and Subjectivist

EXHIBIT 6.2 : Analttical Operations as Supported Under the Several Orthodox Methodological Platforms

Analytical Operation	*Inductive-Driven Bayesian Platforms*		
	Positivist	**Objectivist**	**Subjectivist**
Realization	Generation of exhaustive sets of possibilities via analytic methods (e.g., design-based event projection	Alternatives appear as hypotheses that are generalizations from historical facts (qua prior observations)	Allows a role for personalistic analytical frames of reference to constrain sets of alternatives
Ordering	[not applicable, as all options are deemed equally a-priori probable or preferable]	Often incidental to realization operations; based on cardinal probability (frequency-based) and utility distributions	Usually ordinal, based in part on subjective indices (degree of belief) and personalistic/ cognitive utility operators
Assessment	Fully-elaborated investigation of all alternatives under all contextual conditions in controlled/ contained laboratory settings	Additional data via more recent observations on a parameter to effect convergence via Dynamic Programming or other successive approximation methods	Acquisition of empirical data (via orthodox sampling-theory based experimental methods) to allow for empirical a-posteriori valuations
Selection	Isolation of the directly demonstrable, optimal option qua effectively deterministic decision choice	Election of what is determined to be the first-order Bayesian dominant causal and/or remedical choices maximal utility response options	Directs acceptance of the second-order Bayesian dominant choice (dominated by a-posteriori or *hard* predicates

protocols-- are alternatives for disciplining tactical decision activities (with the Objectivist position presented here in its Bayesian guise allowing for limited a-posteriori learning).

Each entails an effectively unique set of procedural and instrumental provisions for passing through the several generic decision analysis operations just discussed. Each of the protocols will then lead to Selection situations that will vary in terms of the level of confidence in the ultimate rectitude of any decision commitments that are made. But for reasons we'll try to make clear, the technical authority of these three orthodox protocols does not reach very far --if indeed, at all-- into the strategic decision domain.

6.1.1 Strictures on Positivist Decision Technology

In particular, the provisions of the Positivist protocol can allow for convergence on effectively *optimal* resolutions. That is, for the problem-definition sequence, Positivist-inspired procedures should lead to the isolation of a singular, maximum-likelihood alternative as $P\hat{}(Ei) \in [E]$ with the value for $P\hat{}$ approaching unity. This would imply effective certainty that the choice taken represents the only *true* expression of the structural/dynamic realities of the event, process or phenomenon of interest. On the response side, the Positivist protocol should lead to the recognition of an essentially *optimal* course of remedial action or solution scheme. In terms of its technical correlates then, decision exercises conducted under the Positivist protocol would expectedly make significant --if not exclusive-- use of instruments drawn from the class of deterministic techniques (e.g., linear programming, finite-state systems engineering techniques or other mathematical/analytical optimization seeking methods).

Yet while ostensibly optimal choices or deterministic resolutions might always be desired, legitimate access to Positivist initiatives would be restricted to instances where:

1) It can be reasonably assumed (or demonstrated analytically) that realization operations will have generated an essentially *exhaustive* set of problem-definitional or response options.

2) The alternatives that have been realized are few enough in number, and of such a nature, to allow for the following key conditions for Positivist-inspired assessment:

- all of their properties must be accessible to direct (unmediated) observation and exact measurement;
- they must be containable within a controlled experimental setting, with all attributes susceptible to experimental manipulation;

- within experimental settings, there must be the ability to introduce or satisfactorily simulate all the contextual conditions that might be met in the real-world.

It is then an informal canon of the working decision scientist that Positivist methodological initiatives and deterministic instruments ought to be reserved for instances where the explanatory (causal) and response alternatives of interest are inherently simple in terms of both their structural and dynamic properties . . . both well-bounded and well-behaved, as it were.

Indeed, the classic example of the target for positivist-inspired attack is an engineered artifice or mechanism. For it should be possible to have realization operations disciplined by some sort of finite-state system engineering technique that can be relied upon to recognize all structural/behavioral states (qua *design-based* events) the mechanism might be capable of evoking. Or for social-science subjects, we might take the positivist platform to be inspired in some measure by Phenomenological preferences, one aspect of which would look to get some comprehension of the behaviors of which a subject is capable by long periods of direct but essentially unobtrusive observation (as popularized, for example, by some of those that have undertaken long-term studies of animal or social groups by attempting to become more or less transparant as an observer). In any case, the key characteristic of Positivist assessment activities is that all the alternatives that have been realized will be subjected to the same set of elaborate, usually in-vitro experimental procedures in the interest of generating as rich as possible a set of objective bases for assessment . . . e.g., an attempt might be made to get a definite fix on the robustness of a mechanical artifice by examining its performance under extremes of temperature, humidity, power loadings or all other relevant environmental variables). As a practical matter then, Positivist-inspired assessment operations may sometimes appear to be centered around what amounts to *rote* trial-and-error initiatives, such intended to strike upon the indisputable truth of some matter --i.e., a deterministic resolution-- if only by dint of brute force.

6.1.2 The Reach and Limits of Probabilistic Decision Protocols

This leaves the Objectivist and Subjectivist protocols as platforms for dealing with decision issues characterized by some degree of uncertainty or, more broadly, for disciplining the pursuit of rational resolutions qua rational *probabilistic* choices. In general, recourse to a probabilistic (vs. deterministic) resolution is dictated whenever the nature of the subject at hand is such as to violate one or more of the criteria for a Positivist approach noted just above. Thus, those electing to operate under either the Objectivist or Subjectivist approaches must be prepared to go somewhat beyond the hard facts of a matter (beyond that which has been, or can be, directly observed, tangibly demonstrated or experienced at first-hand). These two protocols are thus appropriate for conducting decision exercises where a selection must be made from among a set of problem-definitional and/or response options whose properties will not admit to directly controlled manipulation in all their particulars under all possible contextual conditions.

In terms of their basic technical characteristics, both the Objectivist and Subjectivist protocols are intelligible as conveyances for statistical decision discipline. This is the accepted basis for the pursuit of rationality for probabilistic decision exercises. More clinically, it provides the operational basis for decision aids intended to guide us towards the generation of disciplined ampliative inductive inferences along any of these three lines:

LONGITUDINAL: the generation of a set of future possibilities that are variations on historical themes or precedented events (the most obvious managerial example of which is *forecasting* via some statistical extrapolation/projection technique).

CROSS-SECTIONAL: the effect of arguing from the more particular to the more general, or the imputation of properties to a population as a whole on the basis of attributes or behaviors observed in some sample (as, for example, with ANOVA-based market research exercises).

ANALOGIC: using secondary evidence --observations made with respect to some other subject, information collected by other agencies or experiences undergone by others-- to impute properties to some new situation (perhaps via recourse to factor-analysis, exploratory data analysis or other statistical techniques to help draw parallels or recognize and measure the degree of contextual correlation).

From the broadest possible technical perspective then, because they both are essentially just expressions of ampliative inductive inference, both the Objectivist and Subjectivist protocols are subject to the same sorts of practical strictures on their resolution power.

Particularly, the quality (precision and reliability) of any conclusions arrived at via ampliative inductive inference will be highly sensitive to any strictures on the richness, regularity and relevance of the empirical data base from which they are derived. For given the nature of statistical algorithms -- Bayesian or otherwise-- any sparsity of empirical data will imply a reduction in the level of confidence that can be placed in any conclusions. And any irregularities --instances of *variance*-- in the data used to drive such inferences will dampen the degree of discriminacy statistical instruments can provide. For example, in statistical forecasting exercises, the effect of any variance in a time series is to increase the dispersion of extrapolative possibilities and so decrease the value of the probability assigned even the maximum-likelihood estimator.

A similar stricture applies in the case of cross-sectional inference exercises, where variance or inconsistency appears in the form of any heterogeneity of properties in the sample population. Therefore, the greater the degree of diversity among the properties associated with some sample, the lower would be the confidence associated with any attempt to attribute some singular set of descriptive/predictive properties to the larger population (e.g., the greater the spread of the consumer preferences indicated during a market research exercise, the greater the statistical risk of a decision to invest any one of the product alternatives. And finally, *relevance* is the ultimate arbiter of the integrity of any analogic inferences (this concerned with the degree of consistency between the conditions under which any secondary evidence was generated and the conditions under which it is to be employed).

It's thus that while both the Objectivist and Subjectivist protocols can indeed support attempts to reach beyond that which has been or can be directly observed and demonstrated, neither can take us very far beyond them! For while the Subjectivist protocol is less dependent upon the richness and reliability of empirical data for the Realization and Ordering operations than is the Objectivist, it is nonetheless highly sensitive to there being a sufficiency of high-quality, relevant observational data during the assessment stage, else it cannot (any more than can the Objectivist scheme) guarantee the rationality of any decision choices during the selection phase. But to see why this might be the case, it's well to deal with each of the two inductive decision platforms in a bit more detail.

6.1.2.1 Objectivist Preferences and Pragmatic Restrictions

As was suggested in Exhibit 6.2, the first point of contention between the Objectivist and Subjectivist positions revolves around what are deemed to be legitimate predicates for informing longitudinal, cross-sectional or analogic inductive inferences. Specifically, proponents of the Objectivist position and its various operational variants generally recognize the legitimacy of only one class of probability operators, those of frequentist nature.

In this sense, they are very much the inheritors of the classical Fisherian statistical *significance testing* approach, as frequency-based probability estimates will always derive from observations taken within the confines of a properly controlled experimental design of some sort.[1] As a natural corollary, decision theoretical constructs defined by those of Objectivist persuasion are choreographed around the presumption of decision-makers operating under a continuous, cardinal utility function, even if such may not be fully explicated in the course of any decision exercise. From the mathematical perspective, such utility functions have the advantage of being indistinguishable in form from frequentist-inspired, continuous probability density functions (and indeed, in actual practice, it is sometimes very difficult to isolate probability from utility elements). Moreover, there is also the convention (implicit in many formulations) that the valuations of cardinal utility operators will ideally derive from the same sort of formal experimental initiatives as are used to set probability values or, lacking that, be based on historical observations that have been passed through some sort of statistical inference filtering (e.g., the assessment of payoffs from a proposed business venture might be predicated on past experiences in the market sector of interest).

The prototypical Objectivist formulation was of course the neo-Bernoullian scheme authored by von Neumann and Morgenstern, and subsequently elaborated and amended by Marschak and various others of the American school that would come to include many popular economic theorists.[2] Although often defended as a strictly *normative* construct (and therefore taken to be effectively immune to any criticism on pragmatic grounds), there are others who would question whether this was indeed their only or even primary purpose. For a systematic assessment of the elaborate set of axiomatic provisions they established would suggest that what they ultimately had in mind was to provide a protocol for operationalizing the key tenets of classical microeconomic theory, which were (prior to the emergence of the equivocations associated with Welfare economics, etc.) popularly taken to be the only feasible criteria of executive rationality. Or from an even broader perspective, the von Neumann-Morgenstern thesis in particular, and Objectivist procedural schemes in general, might be appreciated as attempts to provide a set of decision theoretical correlates for the canons of logical positivist epistemology, these still popularly thought to set the only legitimate criteria for rational scientific behavior.

But it is also important to note that is is possible to allow for a somewhat constrained Bayesian orientation during the assessment stage of the Objectivist protocol. In their Bayesian guise, Objectivist assessment-related activities will be directed at the acquisition of data of more recent origin than that which was used to inform the original ordering. But the key point is that this new data will be of exactly the same type (and collected in the same way) as the data driving the original ordering operation. The classic practical expression of this is Dynamic Programming.[3]

A widely used technique for resolving quantitative uncertainty, it's appropriate whenever the addition of more current data to a standing information base promises to increase the precision and reliability of estimates of the value that might be taken on by some variable of interest. It involves undertaking a series of iterative experimental efforts aimed at effecting convergence via successive-approximation, with a-priori arguments being the results of observations that have been taken during previous iterations and the a-posteriori valuation reflecting the presence of any newly-acquired data. Some variation on Bayes formula is then used to cojoin a-priori and a-posteriori predicates so that relatively more recent observations have relatively more impact on the concluding assessment of a variable's value. Conclusions arrived at via dynamic programming thus represent first-order Bayesian decision choices, this because both prior and posterior probability/utility assessments are informed by observations taken in the same way over the same set of factors, the maximum-likelihood and/or maximal-utility alternatives represent decision choices arrived at via first-order Bayesian mechanics. That is, in first-order Bayesian schemes, the distinction between a-priori and a-posteriori decision predicates is then merely that the latter are products of observations taken at a later point in time than the former.

Mainly because of its conceptual and computational simplicity, the Objectivist protocol tends to be the dominant theoretical presence in the management science curricula of modern schools of business and public administration, this despite some obvious concerns about its practical integrity. The most basic of such is obvious: The sorts of computations called for to support the elaborate probability and expected utility (risk) assessments presume that decision authorities can indeed generate a significantly rich and reliable objective data set to drive them. Moreover, the actionability of any such estimates will be extraordinarily sensitive to the consistency characteristics of the data (which, in turn, will reflect the natural stability of the phenomenon or process to which the data refers, etc.). As such, the various Objectivist-based algorithmic systems become increasingly irrelevant (or even impotent) should circumstances of any sort conspire to restrict the acquisition of hard data on which to predicate quantitative probability or utility computations.

Another source of concern is the Objectivists' fondness for couching their arguments with reference to games of chance. One key technical consequence of this preoccupation is that Objectivist-inspired decision schemes, in their stricter forms, may often have no assessment-related activities that are prescribed . . . first-order Bayesian or otherwise. For an axiomatic game-based orientation will ultimately tend to lead to a paradigmatic preference for having decision issues resolved essentially a-priori, i.e.: on the basis of information that is already known to the decision-maker in terms of historical facts and/or whatever algorithmic (mathematical or statistical) manipulations to which that historical data might have been subjected. In this sense, though realization constructs may be a product of inductive inference, the provisions for determining decision choices might perhaps better be thought of as products of strict axiomatic (deductive) inference, this because the basis for a rational probabilistic decision choice is given, once decision authorities have determined which particular decision rule they wish to employ.

But the pragmatic problem with this orientation is that it appears that the sorts of games that Objectivists tend to employ to illustrate their propositional preferences often appear to have been chosen more for their axiomatic expediency than for their relevance to real-world economic behavior under uncertainty and risk.[4] For example, the games that are used as referents are almost always those where the odds of winning (or losing) are fixed and knowable a-priori; that is, they are in effect *deterministic* as a consequence of assumedly stationary rules. This is a luxury that many real-world decision-makers will be denied, if only by virtue of their being resident in economic contexts (markets) that allow for the rules of the game --the conditions of competitive confrontation-- to change through time, and for competitors to execute initiatives that may have no historical precedent and which then cannot, under the frequentist probability convention, be assigned any positive probability of occurrence as a prospective threat. In short, the Objectivist thesis may be taken to be of pragmatic merit as an analogy only in situations where there can legitimately be presumed to be no significant likelihood of competitive innovations.

Secondly, in Objectivist-inspired decision schemes, the conditions for determining victory vs. defeat are also a-priori fixed, unambiguous and definitely recognizable (indeed, the most popular of referents are simple Bernoulli-type processes or constant-sum games). But things are not so cut and dried in the real-world. For example, there is the long-running controversy as to whether success in economic ventures is to be adjudged in terms of short-run performance (say quarterly increases in stock prices or earnings, etc.) or in terms of long-run integrity which may often only be gained at the expense of short-run performance. More generally, there is the controversy as to whether the ultimate test of executive success is local optimization with respect to an individual firm, or whether the rectitude of decisions are to be adjudged in terms of the impact on the general socio-economic welfare.

Thirdly, game-based axiomatic provisions and the analogies they drive tend to presume a game being played over the long-run, involving a large number of successive iterations (indeed, a sufficiently large number of iterations for mathematical expectations operators to reach a stable asymptote). This of course begs the issue as to when a game is actually over.[5] For many commercial confrontations --along with struggles in war and love-- hold out the prospect of the first move being the last, which is equivalent to a gambler betting all he has on the first role of the dice. Such situations can still be accommodated within the confines of game-based analogies, but only tenuously (usually demanding the imposition of a set of reality-crippling assumptive constraints).

Fourth, there is this critical technical stricture following from Objectivist schemes' rooting in game-based analogies: Such schemes are restricted to the comprehension of decision exercises where all the alternatives considered --in terms of problem possibilities and/or response options-- are intelligible as variations on some singular qualitative theme . . . i.e., different merely *in degree* rather than in kind. For example, all the outcome possibilities permissible in the sorts of games that Objectivists use as referents can be reduced to a neatly compressed Pay-Off matrix, with one outcome consequence distinguished from any others simply in terms of the different magnitude of the value taken on by some parameteric decision criterion such as risk-return, maximal minimum loss or some composite index such as expected value.

To again take recourse to common proverbial distinctions, this suggests that Objective-based schemes cannot accommodate situations where decision choices represent the proverbial apples and oranges, or where there is no common quantitative denominator, capable of assuming any value on a definite continuum, to which alternatives can be reduced. Rather, they are relevant only to those cases where the choice is among apples or oranges, with a selection to be determined on the basis of simple parametric properties (size, sweetness or ripeness, etc.).

6.1.2.2 Subjectivist Stipulations and Strictures

But then, to a somewhat lesser extent, the same thing may also be said to be true of the Subjectivist protocol, particularly in terms of the first of the points at which it departs from Objectivist preferences shown in Exhibit 6.2: the allowance for subjective predicates to inform ordering operations. The rationale for the Subjectivists' position here has perhaps been best summarized by the recently crowned Nobel laureate for economics, Maurice Allais:

> The fundamental error of the entire American school is its indirect and unconscious neglect of the dispersion of psychological values.[6]

In short, strict Subjectivists are offended by the Objectivists' neglect of psychological or cognitive determinants of risk and utility. That is, mainstream Objectivist constructs are condemned mainly because of their neglect of a class of qualifier variables that others feel are essential to the formulation of any proper decision theory.

In mainstream Subjectivist formulations then, subjective predicates reflecting decision-maker's personalistic *degrees of belief* are allowed to modify (inflate or deflate) objectively-determined probability or utility indices.[7] From the working decision scientist's perspective, this aspect of the Subjectivist position has the advantage of allowing decision-theoretical formulations to better reflect the conditions under which real-world decision-makers (vs. their academic research counterparts) are so often required to labor. For example, subjective predicates can inform realization operations whenever there exist two or more alternative analytical frames-of-reference that might be employed, with the election of any one of these (perhaps even tacitly) having the effect of introducing some a-prioristic constraints (idiosyncratic, academic, ideological, etc.) on the search spaces within which problem-definitional models or response options are to be generated.[8] This is in some contrast to the Objectivist preference for realization constructs or hypotheses derived from historical facts or empirical data. As for Ordering operations, the Subjectivist approach takes the entirely laudatory step of allowing for partially-judgemental, ordinal likelihood and preference (utility) functions vs. the cardinal and empirically-predicated operators demanded by strict Objectivists. Hence, the Bayesian approach allows for subjective predicates to qualify or *conditionalize* algorithmically-generated estimators (as, for example, when it is felt that a forecast generated by some statistical extrapolation technique had best be modified to account for a prospective change in policy or market conditions).

Yet when examined solely with respect to its implications for realization and ordering operations (or for a-priori operations, as it were), Subjectivist constructs maintain an extraordinarily high degree of correspondence to both the axiomatic and algorithmic preferences of the Objectivists. Most notable is the Subjectivist penchant for using the same sort of game-based or gambling analogies that preoccupied the Objectivists. Therefore, it is mainly with the respect to assessment and selection operations that the provisions peculiar to the Subjectivist protocol become of interest to working decision scientists. For Subjectivist-based assessment activities will always involve a *learning* aspect. Moreover, the approach to learning will be reflective not merely of simple Bayesian computational mechanics (as with the first-order provisions sometimes encountered in Objectivist-inspired schemes), but off Bayesian epistemology, per se. One noted epistemologist has painted this portrait of what a Bayesian *learning* approach entails:

> The picture is a kinematic one: a Bayesian agent moves along in time having at each moment a coherent set of degrees of belief; at discrete intervals he learns new facts and each time he learns a new fact, e, he revises his degree of belief by conditionalizing on e. The discovery that e is the case has confirmed those hypotheses whose probability after the discovery is higher than their probability before.[9]

Thus, it is that an hypothesis may be deemed to be confirmed when the posterior probability, conditioned by new evidence, is greater than the original or a-priori probability via whatever conditionalizing algorithm is employed.

Were we now to transport these provisions from the epistemological to the decision domain, we would have the basis for second-order Bayesian decision choices. For in the confines of second-order Bayesian decision processes, subjectively-influenced (usually ordinal) likelihood and utility preferences represent a-priori decision predicates. It then falls to the assessment stage of Subjectivist-inspired decision exercises to acquire additional information in the form of a-posteriori data. This a-posteriori data will always be essentially *hard* in origin, ideally generated via some sort of well-controlled, formalistic empirical experimental design. In the normal course of events, a-posteriori data will then be used to effect a gradual exchange of objective predicates for any *soft* predicates that were used to inform the original ordering function. As such, in the typical second-order Bayesian decision exercise, assessment initiatives are aimed at the displacement of subjective operators -- psychological or cognitive probability/utility preferences-- by empirically-predicated valuations.

But, there must be a fairly high degree of correspondance between the predicates used to inform a-priori likelihood or preference valuations and the evidence to be acquired during the assessment phase. Thus, assessment-related activities will expectedly be turned towards the acquisition of empirical information pertinent to exactly the same set of factors (determinants, coefficients, parameters, etc.) that underlay a-priori valuations.

As such, the Subjectivist approach to decision theory may suffer from somewhat the same identity crisis as does the Bayesian epistemology on which it rests. For just as with the Objectivist position, the ultimate arbiter of rationality is that which is empirically validated. And this, in turn, may often lead to the technical irony whereby a-prioristic predicates may ultimately have only negligible impact on the final formulation.[10] Yet the alternative might be a cause for equal concern. For were there no empirically-grounded Assessment operation to intervene between ordering and selection (as is the case with the casual, catch-as-catch *brainstorming* schemes currently so popular among practicing executives), then the effect would be to allow personalistic preferences a greater role in determining decision courses than even die-hard Subjectivist's would wish.

In all then, the Subjectivist protocol is not dramatically different from the Objectivist in terms of the range of decision issues it can formally resolve, if only by virtue of both being rooted in inductive inference initiatives. Therefore, from the perspective of the working decision scientist, the complaint with formalistic Subjectivist-inspired decision schemes, and the Bayesian mechanics on which they rest, is that they do not in fact depart far enough from Objectivist predilections to allow them to reach far enough into the domain of complex decision issues.

That is, Subjectivists have perhaps not been bold enough in asserting their independence from empirical predicates and numerical methods. As a result, true strategic decision issues --given their *qualitative* predication-- entail certain confoundations that none of the trree orthodox methodological protocols can help resolve.

6.2 Uniquely Strategic Analytical Confoundations

Consider, particularly, the two analytical requirements we have in previous chapters consistently associated with strategic management, either of which can put strategic analysis beyond the reach of either of either Positivist or Inductive techniques:

1) The need for the formulation of hypotheses (realization of problem definitional and/or response alternatives) that are trans-empirical or even *notional* in inspiration . . . this because strategic decision-makers consistently face the prospect of being confronted by essentially novel problems that will call for essentially novel response options.

2) This in turn suggests not just that ordering operations will be strongly subjective in origin, but also anticipates there being some limits on the ability of orthodox empirical assessment-related initiatives to provide a sufficiently rich set of *hard* data to allow for any significant degree of objective discriminacy.

Thus, in contrast to the Positivist platform's preoccupation with the directly observable or demonstrable and the Inductive platform's insistence on hypotheses that are well-anchored in the factual, realization constructs appropriate to the strategic decision domain may be only very weakly correlated with any empirical or historical predicates.

Such constructs will generally fall into one of the following three broad categories:

IDIOSYNCRATIC: Alternatives that will appear to have arisen essentially ab-intra. Such may be posed by their authors as being *intuitively obvious* in appeal, either because no formalistic defense has been attempted or because they are rooted in highly personal recollectives or perspectives).

PARADIGMATIC: Propositions arrived at via formal argument (usually some variant on deductive inference) but which are ultimately dependent upon certain premises --some of which may be transparent or tacit-- which either have not been, or cannot be, subjected to proper validation.

AXIOLOGICAL: Value-based positions that are products of informal reasoning and defended mainly via rhetorical argument designed to convey some moral authority or affective appeal.

It's the tendency for strategic exercises to be dominated by such constructs that makes them so vulnerable to confoundation. For a confoundation is anything that would have the effect of delaying, or even defeating, the convergence on the condition shown below as *conjunctive singularity*:

	Causal	Remedial	Conjunctive
Closure	I → ~[E]	Ei → ~[R]	~[E] and ~[R]
Dispersion	I → P[E]	Ei → U[R]	P[E] and U[R]
Singularity	I → P^(Ei)	Ei → U^(Rj)	P^(Ei) and U^(Rj)

More particularly, closure and dispersion are best thought of as second-order confoundations. For their respective effect is to introduce an order of indeterminacy or stochasticity into strategic decision exercises above and beyond that which would derive from the natural complexity of the event/problem itself.

For closure would indicate that realization alternatives are too limited in terms of the real-world possibilities they reflect, either because it is in the interests of managerial authorities to so limit them, or because of the narrowness of the knowledge or skill bases that are brought to bear on some decision or problem-solving exercise . . . the failure of local analysts or decision authorities to reach beyond themselves. Thus, closure results in realization sets that have too little diversity because of too little diversity of perspective among the parties to a strategic decision or problem-solving exercise (perhaps as a reflection of the general tendency for senior executives to surround themselves with advisors or staff members who *think like they do* or who *share the same values*).[11] Therefore, a common source of Causal Closure would be strictures that derive either from an unwillingness to study an issue in the aim of resolving it and/or a reluctance to accept some high-quality causal hypothesis as valid. An excellent case in point is the matter of Acid Rain. For clearly, the consensus of serious scientific evidence is that it is caused by the heavy stream of pollutants emitted by certain electrical utilities and manufacturing plants located, for the most part, in the midwestern United States. However, some senior political authorities prefer to think of acid rain as being a phenomenon whose cause is indeterminate. For this allows them a temporary escape from the potentially politically perilous requirement to impose restrictions --and new investment demands-- on this influential segment of the industrial community.

For its part. Remedial Closure can arise in either of two ways. First, it can occur when the absence of expectedly effective response alternative(s) owes less to the nature of the phenomenon at hand than to certain potentially addressable contextual constraints. For example, it is often suggested that the absence of any effective strategy for combating the national increase in serious crime is not so much due to the irremediable nature of the process itself, but rather to constraints that tend to exclude the really high-utility options from the feasible solution space, e.g.: insufficient economic resources to fight poverty and ignorance; legal rulings that restrict the initiatives open to law enforcement agencies; budgetary/manpower constraints imposed on police, the courts and the penal system; socio-cultural sympathies seen as frustrating attempts to impose timely, sufficient penalties, etc. As a second instance, an essentially *empty* set of strategic options may arise from the fact that we are trying to work with a set of objectives that does not admit to any feasible solution. Perhaps the best example of this are the notoriously futile efforts of those trying to deal with the problem of international hostage-taking along the following lines:

- obtain the safe release of the hostages already taken;
- discourage any attempt at hostage-taking in the future.

For these two objectives are in certain critical ways competitive (and the case has been made that they are in fact even mutually-exclusive). If so, then closure results from the fact that there can be defined no single strategic option that has much chance of answering adequately for both.

Finally, as for Conjunctive Closure, we'd be looking for classes of phenomena or entire domains of inquiry that are being neglected because of essentially ancillary concerns. For example, there is some natural reluctance among professional researchers to undertake certain sorts of studies that have racial or sexual implications . . . e.g.: prevailing social sentiment would argue vehemently against any attempt to study the possibility that genetic factors may be a cause of the relatively poor performance of blacks on standardized tests. That is, such a hypothesis tends to be excluded not because it is logically infeasible, but because it is axiologically unpopular.

But as a practical matter, Dispersion is the generally more frequently encountered source of confoundations in the strategic decision domain, and hence the primary target of concern here. For it points to the situation where the emergence of a multiplicity of causal and/or remedial candidates (and hence stochasticity) is owing at least in part to a-priori dissensus among the parties to a strategic decision process . . . to a deep-seated divergence of opinion or judgement. And this, in turn, would be a reflection of the tenacity with which the parties involved in some strategic decision exercise hold to the various Professional, ideological, affective, bureuacratic, academic (disciplinary) or idiosyncratic agendas that they bring with them. Hence we have a spread of causal and/or remedial hypotheses that is a reflection of an underlying dispersion of judgement or opinion, and hence the likelihood of a recriminatory rather than merely competitive ordering over the candidates.

This is particularly to be feared. For when causal and/or remedial hypotheses are *recriminatory*, each of the candidate alternatives attempts to make its case not merely by stressing its own advantages (as with the former instance), but also by positing defects for all its competitors . . . and often by using these defects to make dire prophecies about the dysfunctional consequences that would follow were any of its competitors to be selected! Recriminatory confrontation is also likely to be particularly acrimonious and persistent, for apologists for a position are never so fierce as when it is matters of personal or professional judgement or opinion that are at stake.

In any case, examples of Causal Dispersion are common enough. For here we'd be concerned with the case where --given a set of Indicators-- the parties to some strategic analysis/decision exercise advance two or more contentious hypotheses as to what actually took place. When viewed as a product of second-order confoundations, causal stochasticity would derive from dissensus as to the proper perspective to take on some situation. That is, the emergence of two or more alternative event definitions has less to do with scarcity of information than with the presence of two or more competitive interpretive positions vying for dominance, each arguing for a different conclusion from the same set of facts. As an example, consider the case of the hijacking of TWA Flight 847 in Lebanon. For from the same set of facts, there emerged two distinctly contradictory event definitions:

(a) The seizure of the plane was an act undertaken by Shiite patriots in retaliation for provocations allegedly committed against their community by Israel (the presumed agent of US interests in the Middle-East), and hence is to be seen as a means of calling the attention of the United States to the need for some redress.

(b) The hijacking was merely another instance of essentially random violence committed by terrorists serving only the interests of anarchy, Iranian-inspired theocratic aggression or the Communists' intent of destabilizing the west.

The quandary here is that unless there is some consensus as to the event that actually took place, there can be no consensus as to any strategic option. For if (a) above defines the true event, then an appropriate strategic response would have to be orchestrated around perhaps very fundamental changes in US foreign policy in the middle-east (e.g., a move towards injecting greater balance between Arab and Israeli interests). But if (b) is the true explanation for the event, then an appropriate strategic response may be to attempt retaliation in kind against the offending parties or their kin.

Even more frequent are instances of Remedial Dispersion. For this occurs when, given some convergence (consensus) on a singular event/problem definition, there are advanced two or more strategic response options, each of which is posed as having some prospect of ultimately proving most effective. The usual source of such is that different individuals or blocs may tend to advance utility orderings rooted in deep-seated a-prioristic preferences which --being merely subjective or speculative in origin-- will usually be defended with especially great vigor. Consider, for example, the four qualitatively-disparate outcomes that have been advanced as possible consequences of US military intervention in Nicaragua:

(a) On the basis of historical analogy, it has been argued that the net effect would be another Vietnam (e.g., the imposition of an all-out civil war on top of a contained revolution, and an ultimate defeat for US interest);

(b) Formal sociological analysis imposed a mediating model in terms of Social Cohesion theory; that is, the imposition of a US presence would merely serve to unite the Sandanistas and Contras against what is perceived by both to be an alien presence, and so ultimately serve to close not only Nicaragua but also the rest of Latin America to any US influence;

(c) Those fond of exegesis based on *realpolitik* precepts suggest that any US adventure in Nicaragua would have to be compensated for by giving the Soviets unchallenged access to some target that could be deemed as being within their domain of vital interest, say Pakhistan;

(d) And against these pessimistic scenarios stands what might be thought of as the *null hypothesis* of the current administration in Washington . . . the presumption that the Sandanistas are really just agents of the international Communist conspiracy, and unless stopped in Nicaragua will soon be knocking at the doors of Galveston.

And what makes dispersion of judgement or opinion in cases such as these especially troublesome is that all four of the positions may be said to be more or less equally a-priori plausible.

Finally, there is Conjunctive Dispersion, this perhaps the most pernicious of second-order confoundations. For what it implies is the existence of two or more recriminatory paradigms each seeking to have its advises serve as the exclusive inspiration for some strategic choice. What's most unique about paradigms is that they pose a cross-coupling of a particular state-event alternative with some singular strategic response option . . . with the former often conditioned by the latter. In the academic world, paradigmatic ambiguity arises as a consequence of the tendency of disciplines to divide themselves into contentious *schools*, each tending to define some problem/event so as to recommend treatment via that set of remedial tools it has made its own special province. Consider, for example, the quandary of those public officials trying to formulate a national policy to deal with --say-- inflation. When they turn to the academic community for advice, what they are likely to encounter are at three contradictory sets of event/response options:

a) a position inspired by Monetarist theory;
b) a position representing the Keynesian perspective;
c) a position premised on Supply-Side predilections.

For each *school* of economic theory will tend to define the phenomenon of inflation in terms that recommend treatment via constraints on the Money Supply, central fiscal initiatives or stimulants to capital formation, respectively. Moreover, as is characteristic of Paradigmatic platforms, all rest on assumptions that have not been (and indeed cannot be) subjected to formal objective validation. As such, any commitment actually taken by a policy authority must then be informed largely by rhetorical criteria . . . elect that particular paradigmatic option that best reflects his own a-priori predispositions. Or if boldness is not his nature, he might seek to define a policy platform that becomes intelligible as a crude political compromise, one giving some substantial presence to advises drawn from each of the contentious platforms (though the resultant negative cross-impacts might ultimately dilute net effectiveness to the point where the policy platform has virtually no real moment).

There are of course other variations on paradigmatic-driven state stochasticity we might consider. For example, in time of international stress, we tend to see this familiar scenario will tend to define the event in terms that recommend a Diplomatic response, the Pentagon will advance a definition that would favor a military remedy, with the CIA most likely advancing a causal option that would clearly be best addressed by a covert response of some kind. The classic corporate counterpart to the above is the New Product Planning process, where the priority properties being advanced by the Production, Finance and Marketing departments may all define what amounts to an *empty* intersect, i.e.: the production department stresses standardization, finance folk want minimal incremental capital investment and the marketers want *pizazz*.

But as imposing as these confoundations may appear at this point, their full significance cannot really be appreciated until we consider confoundations that might arise on another dimension altogether. For the confoundations we've considered thus far affect only Realization and Ordering operations, this as a consequence of the first of the characteristics of strategic decision exercises we just mentioned (the dominancy of alternatives in the form of idiosyncratic, paradigmatic or axiological constructs). And in the usual decision-making or problem-solving exercise, we'd look to initiatives in the Assessment phase to resolve any instances of closure or dispersion. But should anything now act to deprive them of this prospect, then even the most optimistic of strategic decision-makers may find themselves with cause for dismay. Hence our concern now with the second of the earlier-noted characteristics of strategic decision exercises . . . limitations on the objective data or intelligence that might be acquired via asessment operations conducted under either of the orthodox methodological protocols.

This concern is particularly pressing because of the susceptibility of strategic analysis efforts to two assessment-related confoundations:[12]

> EMPIRICAL INACCESSIBILITY: one or more of the alternatives that have been realized entail arguments whose validation depends on data or evidence that cannot be collected, or are defined over properties that cannot be directly observed.
>
> EXPERIMENTAL INTRACTABILITY: the subject or phenomenon of interest is one that will defy any attempt to confine it within any sort of formal experimental design or otherwise attempt to subject it to bounded, controlled manipulation.

All the cases of dispersion we just cited were subject to one or more of these assessment-related confoundations.

For example, resolving uncertainty as to the real event associated with the hijacking of the TWA flight is likely to depend on the generation of information that is unlikely to be forthcoming in the absence of direct access to the hijackers themselves (and even then, the isolation of real vs. merely manifest intents would demand the employment of psychological interrogational instruments whose validity may not be universally accepted). The earlier-noted instance of remedial dispersion in terms of ambiguity as to the order of outcome that might follow from a US military initiative in Nicaragua is a clear case of experimental intractability. For there does not appear to be any opportunity for engaging in a limited field trial (invading just one region?) that would provide any objective data on which to make an empirically-validated or objective determination as to the utility of this course of action.

But perhaps the most dramatic example of an issue to which assessment-related confoundations might apply is the Strategic Defense Initiative (SDI) or, as it is more popularly known, the *Star Wars* program. To set the issue in some kind of formal perspective, we can take it to represent an instance of Remedial Dissensus, for which the following notation would apply:

$$Ei \rightarrow U[R1; R2],$$

where E1 is the problem of what is perceived to be too high a likelihood of a nuclear conflict. We'll thus let R1 stand for the SDI initiative, with R1 being the prevailing strategy, this based on the proposition that the best approach to preventing a nuclear confrontation is the maintenance of rough parity in terms of offensive nuclear capabilities between the US and the Soviet Union as per the MAD doctrine (Mutually Assured Destruction).

A typical mainstream management science approach to determining resolving remedial dispersion would be focused on the relative utility of R1 vs. R2. And as for what might underlie the assignments of a utility valuation to any strategic response option, a typical formulation would be the following:

$$U(Rj * Ei) = F[B], \text{ where:}$$

1) (Rj * Ei) symbolizes the imposition of Rj on Ei;
2) [B] = (B1, B2 . . . Bn) . . . a set of desired objectives;
3) V is an estimate of the effectiveness of Rj (the extent to which can be relied upon to obtain the objectives).

The primary basis for ranking strategic response candidates would thus be with respect to F (the effectiveness estimator), such that we would look for that particular response candidate that is expected to answer most completely for the demands posed by Bi. We could then move to a multicriteria assessment basis by introducing certain secondary factors, e.g.:

C: a cost factor indicating the asset/resource requirements with which Rj must be invested;

K: a risk deflator that would consider the extent to which certain potentially reusable resources --e.g., personnel, equipment-- might be expended during the execution of Rj.

At this point then we would have an assessment function of the following structure:

$$U(Rj) = w\{F(Bi) \times C \times K\},$$

where **w** is a weighting operator such that w1 would reflect the relative importance of F in the asessment function, w2 a weight assigned C and w3 a weighting for K.

The challenge then is to isolate that particular strategic option representing the *optimum at the margin* between the several criteria. We might consider an even more complicated case where a multicriteria assessment requirement is superimposed on a multiobjective decision situation:

$$U(Rj * Ei) = w\{F \times C \times K\} \times Q[B1, B2 \ldots Bn].$$

In this formulation, (w), F, C and K have the implications noted previously, with [B] being a set of objectives that have been established as criteria to be met by the various response options and Q a weighting factor that reflects the utility or relative importance of each of the objectives in [B], such that Q1(B1) assigns a value to objective B1, etc.

What the above formulation suggests then is that an assessment of the expected utility (U) of some response option Rj with respect to some event/problem Ei can be approached by assigning an expected value (via F x Q) index for each of the elements in [B], and then adjusting this result to reflect cost and risk considerations. Were we then to perform such assessments for all of the response options R1, R2, etc., that were advanced as alternative ways of responding to some event, then we'd have the basis for determining a strategic choice as follows:

$$U[R1, R2 \ldots Rn] \rightarrow U\hat{}(Rj).$$

And in the multicriteria/multiobjective case we just laid out, the maximal-utility strategic response option should emerge as that candidate which is taken to have the greatest likelihood of most completely meeting the most highly valued of the objectives while also enjoying the most favorable cost/risk profile.

The utility assigned any singular strategic option might be computed with respect to array of outcomes to which it might lead, i.e.:

$$Rj \rightarrow P[O1, O2 \ldots On],$$

where the elements of the set [O] represent alternative state-level outcomes that are taken to have some likelihood of following from the implementation of Rj. Each of these outcome states would, in its turn, be assigned some sort of utility valuation that would reflect the extent to which it entails consequences that are deemed desirable . . . the extent to which it reflects the objectives encoded in the set [B], above. We might then look to define one of the outcome possibilities as the *desired* or maximal-utility state, some U^(Oi) ∈ [O]. As such, all other members of [O] must then represent outcome possibilities that are either suboptimal (deemed somehow to be of relatively less positive value or utility than Oi), or entail consequences that are in some way taken to be undesirable or even *dysfunctional* in that they may actually exacerbate rather than solve the problem at hand or otherwise worsen matters (such that they would be assigned a *negative* utility).

To return now to the Star Wars example, the assessment-related task would then be to try to get some estimate of the utility of SDI (i.e., option R2) by considering the likelihood and desirability of the outcome states that it might author. We might then designate the desired functional outcome state as O#, such choreographed around the following:

> **O#**: SDI will prove to be an effective defense against Soviet nuclear missiles (and, if the US transfers SDI technology to the Soviets, the latter would then also be presumed to have an effective defense against US nuclear weapons). A presumed second-order consequence is that the Soviets will realize the impotency of their offensive nuclear arsenals, and so join the US in the dismantling or destruction of all nuclear weapons in their military inventory. The result is thus the reduction of the likelihood of nuclear war to zero. Presumably, state O# is superior to what we might take to be the currently prevailing state (say Ot).

Therefore, the expected utility of the SDi initiative (Rj) would depend on the extent to which it can be relied upon to effect the transformation from the inferior prevailing state (Oc) to the target state (O1): U(Rj) = f[P(Ot => O#).

But standing as alternatives to O# would be at least the following possibilities:

O1: SDI technology will not ever be able to reach the point where it can be assumed to be effective in completely neutralizing an attempted Soviet first strike. It will, however, render the US relatively more impervious to crippling injury from such a strike than is currently the case. We might then define O1 to represent the situation where there is an increase in the likelihood of the US being able to win any nuclear confrontation that might arise. This prospect might then, of its own accord, reduce the likelihood of the Soviet's deciding to initiate any confrontation. Hence, state O1 is superior to the current state (Ot), even though not as favorable as O#.

O2: SDI will ultimately prove to be technically infeasible . . . .i.e., it will not work at all to any appreciable extent. It's technical infeasibility may be assumed to be already known to --or soon to be made apparent to-- the Soviets as well as the US congress and the American public. Therefore, the Star Wars program will ultimately be abandoned, and the resources already committed to it written off as a sunk cost. The ultimate consequence will thus be the restoration of the status-quo or, alternatively, the emergence of a state that is in most critical respects merely an essential replicate of the current state Ot. In short, any strategic ambitions that we may have for SDI will be made gratuitous by virtue of the fact that we lack the tactical wherewithal to bring them to operative reality (much in the sense that many technicians tend to dismiss arms control as an interesting strategic option because of the absence of any tactical mechanisms that can be relied upon to provide real verification). As such, the likelihood is that SDI will simply prove ineffective (i.e., have an actual utility approaching zero).

O3: Far from reducing the likelihood of a nuclear confrontation, the SDI initiative will in fact increase the probability of a holocost. For SDI will be perceived by the Soviets as a potentially fatal threat. From their perspective, its primary strategic implication is not so much to protect the US against the prospect of a Soviet first strike, but rather to set up the conditions where a US first strike against the Soviets will be feasible. It thus is an initiative of distinctly destabilizing significance, one that will allow the US to evade the constraining influences of the MAD doctrine. Therefore, any demonstrable progress towards the technical feasibility of SDI must be assumed to increase the probability of a preemptive attack by the Soviets. That is, this state outcome possibility is postulated as the obverse of O#, in that here the probability of nuclear war edges not towards zero, but rather towards one.

A rational decision about whether or not to implement SDI would then depend on the utility value assigned SDI vs. the strategy currently in force (the MAD doctrine) as a deterrent to nuclear war, which would in turn mean trying to provide for some reasonably precise, objective assessment of the relative likelihoods of the several outcome states, O#, O1, O2 and O3.

And it may be clear that such would be a task well beyond the scope of authority of either of the orthodox protocols via both of the sorts of assessment-related confoundations we just discussed. For clearly, the information that would be needed to make any reasonably precise, objective determination of their relative probabilities will not be accessible to us short of some sort of extraordinary and fundamentally infeasible intelligence coup (and even then, different analysts may *interpret* any set of intelligence items as implying very different things). Moreover, as has been extremely well argued elsewhere, this is a classic example of a strategic initiative that cannot be meaningfully subjected to any sort of empirical field trial or attempt at pre-validation; rather, it must work right the first time out of the box![13] As such, there may not even be any objective basis to answer for the technical effectiveness of the program much less to answer for its strategic effectiveness vis-a-vis putative Soviet aspirations, fears or intents.

In virtually all its aspects then, SDI represents a subject that will not be accomodated well by orthodox methodological protocols. For consistent with the second of the earlier-noted peculiarities of strategic decision exercises, SDI is an example of a subject that imposes definite limits on the ability of assessment efforts to provide enough *hard* or empirically-validated data or empirical predicates to allow for any significant degree of objective discriminacy, such that a strategic choice would have to be made from among alternatives whose integrity cannot be decisively determined either by direct demonstration (the Positivist preference) or *normal* science experimental procedures of the sort called for by the Inductive protocols.[14]

In summary then, when we bring confoundations into the picture, we must hold out the prospect of strategic decision-making exercises being led to an unsatisfactory conclusion along either of two lines:

Indiscriminacy, this suggesting the case where we have come to the selection phase with too many contentious (or recriminatory) canidates, with no basis for a rational choice. In short, strategic decision-makers have gotten into a situation of severe state-stochasticity or *dispersion* and have no legitimate way out of it.

Unactionability, which refers to the case where we not only began a

> strategic decision exercise under a condition of state-indeterminacy or *closure*, but were forced to end it there as well. That is, we will have arrived at the point where a selection must be made and have no really acceptable choices.

These then are the situations we most want to avoid or, lacking that, find ways to work around. But this now brings us foresquare up against the all too apparent *shortfall* in contemporary strategic decision technology.

6.3 Symptoms of the "Shortfall" in Strategic Decision Technology

The net effect of the various confoundations we've discussed is to pretty much carry strategic management authorities beyond the bounds of traditional scientific rationality. Indeed, the combination of confoundations and limitations on technical instruments become the primary contributors to this grand paradox of modern American managerial practice:

> The most sweeping and significant of decisions taken within the confines of today's organizations --those of strategic import-- will usually be the least likely to benefit from any formal discipline or precision.

The general point here is this: While we have a considerable variety of management science tools and computer-based decision aids that can be relied upon to serve line (operational) and middle-echelon (tactical) organizational authorities, once we cross the boundary into the higher-management or strategic domain we enter something of a technical wilderness.

The defense of this assertion might perhaps best be structured by following a more or less neatly linear line of argument that rests on the following hopefully not too controversial propositions:

> 1) For the most part, what evolution there has been in science's instrumental capabilities has been restricted primarily to means for accessing and manipulating empirical data, and so for bringing discipline to decisions rooted in objective predicates.
>
> 2) So when we look at the repertoire of currently available decision aids, we find it dominated by instruments that are based on quantitative analysis methods that can neither accommodate nor comprehend qualitative arguments. But these could be considered to be appropriate as strategic decision support facilities only under the following assumption:
>
> > Strategic decision issues are really just tactical issues writ large, involving merely relatively more money, more risk, etc. Thus, an adequate Strategic decision technology already exists, particularly in terms of the wide range of deterministic and probabilistic that we

management and decision scientists have been wont to develop over the past several decades.

3) As a corollary, the so called *Executive* decision aids now being marketed so aggressively by computer vendors and software houses (e.g., the raft of spreadsheet systems) are almost always just traditional mathematical or statistical techniques converted to computer programs sporting some sort of supposedly user *friendly* interface provisions. But these would only represent sources of strategic support for those who believe the following:

> That, to all intents and purposes, information processing is the same thing as data processing.

But were any decision-maker having true strategic responsibilities to try to use such techniques, he will very likely be forced into some sort of ultimately self-defeating expedient. Most usually, he'd have to try to reduce his problem to a form that could be accommodated by quantitative mechanisms, usually by imposing simplifying assumptions that may merely mask the true level of complexity of the strategic subject. In short, he'd be asked to try to displace reason with computation, to displace precept with percept or possibilities with probabilities.

Thus, when the three above propositions are considered in concert, it is inevitable that much of the contemporary technical interchange between strategic management authorities and mainstream management and decision scientists would be orchestrated around attempts by the former to convince the latter that his problem can be brought within the scope of authority of some sort of *quantitative* technique.[15] And the exchange between computer vendors or software houses and executives must be of much the same sort. For the industry has little to offer the decision-maker who is reluctant to confine himself to perusals of historical data bases or statistical summaries. Computer firms and their allies must then try to sell what they have. And what this means, virtually without exception, are technically pedestrian data-processing programs that become *Executive* decision aids more by dint of merchandizing bravado than by virtue of any real advance towards the concept processing facilities that strategic decision-makers really require.

But to proceed, we might once again note that, for the technician, true strategic decision exercises are distinguished by the fact that they take place over alternatives that represent *qualitatively* disparate alternatives. And again also, this suggests that strategic choices must usually be made in the absence of sufficient empirical or objective data. That is, the strategic decision domain is the place where data are always in scarce supply. But decisions must still be made. So when an adequate empirical data base is denied us, our only choice is to make up for the sparsity of objective data by taking recourse to subjective predicates. And what this then leads to is the earlier mentioned need for those operating in the strategic decision domain to put the majority of their faith in decision aids that have been devised to help support judgement-driven decision exercises, particularly the two families of techniques we've mentioned so often in earlier chapters: a) Elicitive techniques that can be used to help realize and order event and response alternatives that are trans-empirical or notional in origin; b) The various modern decision Structuring techniques that, as highly sophisticated multicritera and multiobjective decision aids, can help users bring some discipline to ordering operations where subjective or judgemental predicates dominate over any hard or objective predicates.

And here's where we begin to feel the full effects of the shortfall in modern scientific capabilities. For when we consider the various strategic confoundations we identified, what we can clearly postulate is the demand for certain strategic decision support facilities that neither of the currently available families of judgement-driven decision aids can offer. Particularly, neither can provide any formal support to assist strategic authorities with respect to these two critical tasks:

1) Answer for the extent to which any set of elicited or user-supplied event and/or response alternatives exhausts the potential universe of possibilities. That is, neither has any mechanics for helping guard against premature a-priori *closure* of strategic search as a consequence of too little diversity of perspective or values among the parties to a strategic decision exercise;

2) Help strategic decision authorities drive towards a rationalized convergence or concensus on a singular causal and/or remedial alternative in the face of significant a-priori dissensus or *dispersion* of opinion . . . again, this likely to occur whenever the parties to a decision exercise (e.g., the members of a Delphi panel or executive committee) are operating under disparate ideological or axiological agendas.

For as advocates of the Delphi method are quick to point out, its purpose is basically to provide a measure of the extent to which there is a diversity of opinion about some issue, not to force a consensus. And for their part, most Decision Structuring protocols are designed to serve just a single user, such that the prospect of deep-seated dissensus is not really a matter with which they concern themselves.

Hence, from yet another direction, the prospect that confoundations -- particularly in their second-order guises-- might drive strategic decision authorities into a corner from which no technical facility can help them escape. For from all that was suggested earlier, the emergence of confoundations is more likely to be the rule rather than the exception in real-world strategic exercises. For without question, there is much practical merit to the popular position that sees strategic decision exercises as inevitably revolving around matters of values, opinion and perspective . . . all fertile spawning grounds for dissensus via second-order confoundations, and all effectively beyond direct technical resolution.

We thus arrive at yet another proposition: As things now stand, to the extent that real-world strategic decision practice rests on any academic advice at all, it is most likely to be studiedly counter-technical in implication, being oriented instead towards suggestions of essentially socio-behavioral implication. Such will have much to say about the context or climate in which strategic decision-making ought to take place, but little or nothing to say about how they should be made . . . about analytical procedures or instrumental matters. That is, the prescriptions that they provide are virtually all focussed on what we might think of as the cultural (vs. technical) aspects of strategic management. Many of these prescriptions are well-considered and are useful complements to any technical initiatives that might be evolved. Particularly, they stand as a viable alternative to crude autocracy, arguing against any tendency for senior executives to think that it's chic or proper to confine alternatives only to those of their own intimate fabrication. Rather, they urge strategic authorities to both solicit and actually consider advice from different sources, but most particularly their subordinates in some organization. Therefore, these schemes are usually defined around a particular consultant's vision of what constitutes a proper *climate* for collective speculation, or how best to break down bureaucratic barriers to free expression, invoke *whole brain* thinking or stimulate a meaningful exchange of perspectives . . . all in the interests of getting some sorts of creative consensus.**16**

Sadly however, there is altogether too much empirical testimony suggesting that the consequences of adventures in unstructured *brainstorming* may not be a consensus, creative or otherwise. For as some realist wit has noted: *The world is divided into people who think they are right!* This may very well be the best of all possible explanations not merely for the origin of second-order confoundations, but also for their extraordinary persistence. And the difficulty is that none of the free-form brainstorming schemes being marketed today has any mechanics that might be relied upon to bring us to any happy resolution of a-priori disputation. So the net effect of trying to conduct strategic decision exercises under a casual brainstorming scheme may be merely to evoke instances of judgemental dissensus --second order confoundations-- that it can then neither contain nor control . . . to reduce strategic deliberation to the erudite but ultimately inconclusive exchanges of hyper-parochial prognostications and recriminations seen each night on the McNeil-Lehrer Report in the United States or the popular debating forums on European television. In such a case, the only route to a working consensus may be for the senior man to impose it by fiat, take recourse to crude political compromise or to simply delay making any sort of strategic commitment at all.

But it must also be said that some management theorists arguing from the socio-behavioral perspective may perceive themselves to be not in a complementary relationship to technicians, but rather engaged in a competitive contest for the affections of real-world decision makers. And some of these may perhaps be a bit too aggressive in trying to preserve the strategic decision domain from any technical intrusions . . . a little too anxious to have strategic decision-making remain an *art*. For so long as this remains the case, then the strategic domain will remain pretty much the exclusive province of those whose influence is tied to this popular perspective:

> Organizations are to be appreciated as collections of individuals, and management at all levels -- the strategic included-- is best thought of as *the art of getting things done through people*. This, in turn, means that the most critical of all managerial skills are motivational and communicational in character.[17]

Given such a perspective, the understandable tendency is to go on to emphasize the motivational, human relations and communication-related aspects of executiveship. There's no denying that such are desirable. Yet equally desirable would be those analytical and technical capabilities that would allow an executive to make a reasoned determination of just what *things* it is that people should best be doing, or help him formulate ideas really worth communicating in the first place!

It's of course the natural vanity of the technician to want to pose the lack of such capabilities as a prime cause for the increasingly frequent and dramatic instances of strategic default that punctuate our times: Grand schemes that die aborning, or lead to effects that were never intended, because the assumptions on which they rest are subsequently proven by reality to have been ill-considered; Policy platforms consistently brought to ruin on the shoals of the unanticipated; Sweeping strategic initiatives that come to be defeated by the most pedestrian of *tactical* twists. As an equally dismaying counterpoint to this frenetic trial-and-error, there is the ever-widening list of issues that seem to throw authorities into a kind of strategic paralysis . . . Acid rain, illegal immigration, terrorism, arms control, human rights, the Budget and Trade deficits, the Middle East, irresolution about nuclear power. Too many fundamental things of this sort now remain essentially unattended, growing all the while in threatening momentum.

And there are then all those lesser dramas being played out in the commercial sector, particularly in the United States. More and more manufacturing enterprises are being edged towards dissolution by what appears to be something of an epidemic of competitive inalertness and industrial insularity. Attempts to recover from long-term lapses of judgement or discretion on the part of higher managements by quick-fixes that shift the penalty to others, the most notable of which is the increasingly popular recourse to bankruptcy as a way around civil suits or as a means of reneging on inconvenient labor contracts. Understandably enough then, many of our strategic decision-makers in all sectors --business, government, the military-- have come to think of themselves as trying to cope with a world gone perverse, one where national ambitions seem predestined to die of wounds inflicted by an apparently endless stream of aberrations to the laws of probability. The popular villains in this vision are variously the weather, the vacillating whims of consumers and voters, ungentlemanly foreign competitors, capricious third-world ideological and political agendas, etc. But for critics of modern American higher-management, the search for villains might also be directed elsewhere.

For they would suggest that at least some instances of strategic error and default have been wished upon ourselves. Particularly, in the minds of some observers, contemporary higher-management authorities as a whole are never so ingenious as when trying to find some way to convince us that the real cause of some strategic or policy embarassment lay with some factor over which they had no control, or with circumstances that no one could have reasonably been expected to foresee. Some also are offended by the typical American executive's happy --even boastful-- indifference to any technical aspects of executiveship. This is a kind way of reporting the fact that the vast majority of those now occupying the highest-order positions in enterprise have in fact been ill-schooled in the fundamentals of mathematics, statistics, formal logic and computer science. Moreover, there is every indication that, if given a choice, those now preparing for management careers will be content to emulate their elders in this respect, restricting their comprehension of the technical aspects of executiveship to those much-vaunted symbols of Executive *realism* or toughness of mind: the *bottom line*; the short-run; the hard facts of the matter; a refusal to consider any advises that cannot be reduced to a one-page memo, etc.

To the critic however, these are signals of neither realism nor toughness of mind, but merely more stuff to support the charge that we are seeing the accession of a generation of American managers that are *overinformed but underenlightened*; the world-class champions of the *non transcendent aim*. For to the critic, the bottom-line and the short-run are not signals of sophistication at all, but merely admissions of an inability to comprehend the more intricate and the more remote; and the preoccupation with hard facts nothing but a backhanded defense for one's ill-preparedness to deal with concepts or abstractions. And as for the one-page memo, it's often taken by critics to speak volumes about the contraction in the span-of-attention that apparently so often comes with the climb to the top . . . about the effects of long years of too many meetings and too little time spent in isolated analytical reflection.

Another frequently-voiced concern is the international tendency to endow top business and political executives with what amounts to a *prophetic* license. The effect is to allow the latter the luxury of making major organizational commitments on the basis of intuition, insight, speculation or other sorts of informal (idiosyncratic) decision criteria that lower-order managers are generally expected to avoid. What fuels this privilege is the assumption that, in any organization, the *cream will naturally rise to the top*, such that those at the apex of the managerial hierarchy may be safely presumed to have arrived there by virtue of superior judgement or functional skill. The practical corollary is that, the more senior the executive, the greater the likelihood that he will be able to effect commitment to some strategic decision solely on the basis of personal preference, without the bother of having to provide any formal defense or structured rationale for his choice. As such, a key feature of modern higher-management practice is the tendency for executive judgement to translate directly into organizational action, with the most desirable trait in subordinates thus being *loyalty* once the man in charge has made a decision.

But nothing more will be served by our continuing to dwell on such complaints. For they may merely distract our attention from this far more fundamental quandary: Even those top managers who are committed to making the absolute best use of what science has to offer --those who either by intellect or disposition are wont to cut no corners or countenance no expediencies-- are still going to be in a bind. For the lack of any truly adequate *strategic* decision technology basically reduces his choice to two equally unsatisfactory options: Use *no method* at all (take recourse to some catch-as-catch-can convention) or use some quantitative expedient that may ultimately prove to be a *bad method.* Indeed, given the clustering of modern technical support around quantitative instruments and data processing programs, working strategic managers may perhaps be forgiven for taking the need to rely on subjective decision premises as a license to forget science and go with gut feel or raw intuition.

But this is not really their only recourse. For there are prospects for developing a family of proper strategic analysis support facilities. The search for such prospects is the subject for final chapter of this book.

NOTES AND REFERENCES

1. c.f., the classical volume by R. A. Fisher, *Statistical Methods and Scientific Inference* (Oliver & Boyd, 1956).

2. The originally-formulated von Neumann-Morgenstern paradigm appeared in their *Theory of Games and Economic Behavior* (Princeton U. Press, 1947). For a discussion of Marshak's early refinements, see his "Rational Behavior, Uncertain Prospects and Measurable Utility," *Econometrica* (18, 2; 1950).

3. As used here, uncertainty is taken to reflect the level of ignorance --degree of stochasticity-- with respect to actualities, and so might best be measured as a function of the morphology of the preference functions (the configuration of a probability or utility density function). For its part, risk will derive from estimates of the cost/loss (real or opportunity) to which we might be subject should realities fail to align with whatever expectations underlay actual decision choices. This connotation for uncertainty and risk derive from the practicing decision scientist's focus on a composite criterion, the Expected Value of Decision Error as a basis for evaluating the peril associated with any decision exercise, this being a summary product of the probability that anything other than an anticipated event will occur and the penalty each such possibility would exact.

4. A very good discussion of this technique is given by Martin Beckman in his *Dynamic Programming of Economic Decisions* (Springer-Verlag, 1968), and also by Kamian & Schwartz in their *The Calculus of Variations and Optimal Control in Economics and Management* (North Holland, 1981). For a treatment of Bayesian-based learning protocols in general, see K. S. Fu, "Learning System Theory," in (Zadeh & Polak, eds.) *System Theory* (McGraw-Hill, 1969).

5. It's here that perhaps the most pragmatically telling of Maurice Allais' well-known criticisms of Objectivist computational conventions applies. For he posed the following prospect: "*If I am able to participate in a long series of games, but could be ruined early on, possibly even in the first round, it is obvious that the justification of the rule of mathematical expectation by the laws of large numbers is invalid.*" For more on this, see pg. 71 of Allais & Hagan (eds), *Expected Utility Hypotheses and the Allais Paradox* (D. Reidel Publishing Co., 1979).

6. Allais & Hagan, op. cit., pg. 104.

7. Notable among such formulation are those of Ramsey in his *The Foundations of Mathematics and Other Logical Essays* (Littlefield and Adams, 1965 reissue of 1931 work), Savage's *The Foundations of Statistics* (Wiley, 1954) and Edwards, Lindman and Savage, "Bayesian Statistical Inference for Psychological Research," *Psychological Review* (70; 1963).

8. At least one decision theorist, J. C. Harsanyi, has explicitly considered such a prospect, as per this statement from his paper, "Acceptance of Empirical Statements: A Bayesian Theory Without Cognitive Utilities," *Theory and Decision* (18; 1985): " . . . *it is one of the great virtues of Bayesian theory that it clearly recognizes the important roles played both by formal and informal decisions in human decision making. If a Bayesian decision maker wants to find the best policy in a given situation, he has first to choose a specific model for analyzing this situation. Then he has to choose his prior probabilities and his von Neumann-Morgenstern utility function. All these choices are largely matters of personal judgement. But once these choices have been made, finding the expected-utility maximizing policy is a matter of computation and, therefore, represents a formal decision."*

9. For an important critique of Bayesian epistemology, see C. Glymour, *Theory and Evidence* (Princeton U. Press, 1980), chapter on "Why I Am Not a Bayesian".

10. This fact has led W. B. Weimer to assert that mainstream Bayesian epistemological argument ultimately reduces to " . . . almost a word-for-word substitution for the *confirmation theory* of the inductive logicians" (see his *Notes on the Methodology of Scientific Research*; Hillsdale, N. J., Lawrence Erlbaum Assoc., 1979). It also leads to an obvious technical consequence for Subjectivist-Bayesian driven decision exercises. For it can always happen that a-priori arguments may have virtually no significant impact on the final formulation. As von Winterfeldt and Edwards put it in their excellent discussion of Bayesian-learning based decision processes (*Decision Analysis and Behavioral Research*; Cambridge University Press, 1986):

> " . . . *prior probabilities . . . frequently have but negligible impact on the conclusions obtained from Bayes theorem, although utterly unlimited vagueness and variability would have utterly unlimited effect. If observations are precise, in a certain sense, relative to the (continuous or dense) prior distribution on which they bear, then the form and properties of the prior distribution have negligible influence on the posterior distribution.* "

And so long as this is can be the case, one might always suggest that the key point in Allais' famous indictment of the Objectivist formulations of the American school -- their neglect of " . . . *the fundamental feature characterizing the psychology of risk, that is the dispersion of psychological values"* -- may often be of only negligible practical impact. Thus, while this criticism may be an axiomatically interesting foray in the Subjectivists' axiomatic struggle against the Objectivists, it is not a particularly telling thrust from the working decision scientist's point of view.

11. There have been attempts to put such matters in some sort of clinical perspective, a good example of which is the widely-cited essay by Tversky and Kahneman: "Judgement Under Uncertainty: Heuristics and Bias," in *Science* (Sept. 27, 1974). But while works such as this provide us with a description of the problem of a-priori prejudice, the tendency is to assume out-of-hand that such are part of man's natural condition, and so largely beyond removal or repair via any technical or scientific initiatives. However, as we'll try to suggest in the next chapter, this is hopefully not the case. For there is some promise of being able to devise technical initiatives that can bring matters of perspective, opinion and judgement within the purview of formal apprehension.

12. There are also at least three ancillary classes of assessment-related confoundations that we might mention:

SEMANTIC IMPRECISION, such that one or more of the factors addressed by one or more alternatives is a subjective concept for which there is no generally acceptable exerimentally-accessible or measurable counterpart or surrogate.

SYNTACTICAL DEFAULT, this concerned with the tendency for subjective or notional realization constructs (hypotheses) to represent *improper* hypotheses . . . e.g., they may rest on implicit or *transparent* assumptions, impose elliptical linkages among their component arguments or be enthymetic rather than properly syllogistic in structure (all examples of logical flaws we'll be looking at in the next chapter).

PRAGMATIC CONSTRAINTS, the most pertinent of which are time and resource strictures. Time constraints are an obvious concern because, outside the leisurely world of basic academic research, the point at which we assessment efforts must be abandoned is more likely to be determined by the pace at which exogenous circumstances are developing than the rate at which uncertainty is being exhausted. Similarly, real-world decision exercises are also generally likely to be faced by a consistent scarcity of analytical resources in terms of skilled personnel, information acquisition budgets, or funds to construct prototypes or establish experimental facilities, etc.

13. For a fascinating essay on assessing the technical integrity of the *Star Wars* vision, see Lin's article: "The Development of Software for a Ballistic Missile Defense System", in *Scientific American* (253, 6), 1985.

14. In fact, SDI is a prime example of one of the luxuries that strategic decision authorities often allow themselves. For as a practical matter, the execution of the Star Wars agenda was undertaken even though the *strategic* level debate about SDI had not been concluded (nor indeed, had those in power really joined in the debate at all). That is, it was a strategic choice wished upon the world as a matter of simple executive fiat. Therefore, at least so far as the Reagan administration and their Pentagon subordinates are concerned, SDI was immediately transformed into an issue of tactical rather than strategic significance. As such, virtually all of the research now being conducted into SDI are intelligible as assessment-related activities directed at evaluating different means to achieve an end that itself was never subjected to any kind of assessment . . . exercises aimed at the prospective merits of simple kinetic impact weapons vs. particle-beam lasers, etc.

15. One of the seldom-mentioned but most pragmatically important factors arguing for these kinds of exchanges has to do with a very disturbing tendency in the general technical community. For increasingly, both academic and professional careers in the technical sector are tied to some narrowly-defined specialty like simulation, game theory, econometrics, cybernetic, Expert Systems or one or another of the *programming* variants (linear programming, nonlinear programming, dynamic programming, goal programming, etc.). The peril here is obvious enough. For there is always some prospect that a technical specialist may be less interested in actually solving a problem, per se, than in trying define it in a way that will bring it within the

purview of the particular method of which he is most fond. And in such redefinitions, it may be that we often let our enthusiasm outstrip our technical discretion.

16. For an example of the speculative underpinnings of *brainstorming* schemes, see Ginter & White, "A Social Learning Approach to Strategic Management: Towards a Theoretical Foundation", *Academy of Management Review* (7, 2) 1982, or van Cauwenbergh & Cool, "Strategic Management in a New Framework", *Strategic Management Journal* (3) 1982. But there is another line of non-technical approach that has much merit, this the attempt to view higher-management from the perspective of the methodological requirements it might be thought to entail. This perspective began largely with C. West Churchman, c.f., his *Challenge to Reason* (McGraw-Hill, 1968), and sets a tradition that has been carried on most notably by Ian Mitroff and others. See, for example, Mitroff and Mason's paper, "Business Policy and Metaphysics," in *The Academy of Management Review* (Feb., 1982). Or see Mitroff and Turoff's, "Philosophical and Methodological Foundations of Delphi," in (Linstone & Turoff, eds.) *The Delphi Method: Techniques and Applications* (Addison-Wesley, 1975).

17. As might be expected, the more vocal and tireless exponents of this position are those who have a stake in the *Case Method* as the basis for executive education. See, for example, Theodore Leavitt's article, "A Heretical View of Management *Science*" in *Fortune* (December 18, 1978). For the case-method approach seeks to prepare budding executives to deal with future problems by exposing them to selected anecdotes describing how their predecessors dealt with situations in the past. The case-method emphasis is thus one tangible expression of the thesis that the essence of managerial training is the *distillation of experience* (the other popular expression being the *principles* of management school). There are however two troublesome aspects to this approach. First, it's not entirely clear how the emphasis on historical anecdotes is to help working executives cope with situations for which there is no appropriate historical analogy . . . how, that is, one is to go about generating an original solution to some effectively unprecedented problem? The second point of concern is that if past experience is to serve as the basis for managerial preparation, how does one go about providing for an evolution in managerial sophistication between different generations? Apologists for the case method can of course follow only one line of defense against these criticisms and that, predictably enough, is to insist that management is an *art*, not a science. Unfortunately, it appears that a great many of those most enthusiastic in making this point are also those least likely to know much about the reach of modern mathematical and statistical instruments, or technical initiatives in any guise.

CHAPTER 7

PROVISIONS OF A STRATEGIC DECISION PROTOCOL

Popular opinion has it that strategic decision exercises revolve around matters of perspective, values and opinion, all of which are taken to rest somewhere beyond the reach of formal decision technology. But we want now to pose this counterposition: While it is certainly true that strategic decisions will not lend themselves well to the quantitative analysis instruments that have for long dominated the management and decision science repertoire, it does not necessarily follow that they must remain entirely and forever outside the bounds of scientific rationality. For in this final chapter we want to define and defend a Strategic Decision Protocol, this intended to help extend the bounds of rationality to decision exercises where there are only limited opportunities for effecting objective or empirical discipline. Key among its provisions are based facilities to assist strategic decision authorities in carrying out the following qualitative-analysis based activities:

- *the parsing of notional constructs to make qualitative arguments (matters of value, perspective and opinion) accessible to formal technical apprehension;*
- *the exchange of mathematical and/or statistical inference for formal logical inference;*
- *the decomposition of original alternatives to isolate particularly critical points of qualitative contention as high-priority items for assessment;*
- *use of indicator-driven, Action Research initiatives where orthodox empirical experimental methods cannot be employed;*
- *the isolation of an extensive-Bayesian dominant decision choice and/or the generation of "syncretic" causal or remedial constructs.*

The focal ambition for the protocol is thus to try to do for strategic decision authorities at least some of the things that traditional quantitative decision-support techniques can do for their tactical and operational counterparts.

7.1 Exchanging Quantitative for Qualitative Discipline

An overview of the key provisions of the Strategic Decision Protocol is provided in **Exhibit 7.1**. When taken in concert, its provisions are intended to suggest how a retreat from empirical decision predicates might perhaps be prevented from degenerating into an uncontrolled retreat from reason. For the protocol recognizes that strategic decision execises will consistently be characterized by some sparsity of objective predicates.

Again, this condition may often arise as a consequence of the inherent intricacy and elusiveness of the sorts of issues that tend to be the subjects of strategic decision exercises. Yet strategic decisions must still be made. So when an adequately rich set of objective predicates is denied us, our only recourse is to make up for the objective deficit by introducing *soft* predicates . . . arguments rooted more in speculation than observation, more in exegesis than experience. In short, in the normal course of events, subjective predicates are brought into a decision exercise to compensate for any shortfall in the currently available empirical data base. We may also suggest that it is precisely this situation that makes strategic decision exercises so particularly vulnerable to the various second-order confoundations we discussed. For sparsity of hard data leaves a vacuum that judgemental or other a- prioristic artifices then move in to fill. But we must also hold out the prospect that second-order confoundations may themselves be responsible for sparsity of objective predicates . . . e.g., second-order confoundations may cause subjective arguments to *drive out* objective predicates.

Hence the legitimacy of the popular assertion that true strategic decision exercises tend to be rooted in matters of opinion, values and perspectives that must be expected to elude any attempt at quantitative comprehension. But this assertion is often followed by a corollary: That matters of opinion, values and judgements are stuff that can never be brought within the purview of science, such that strategic decision exercises not only currently remain beyond the reach of formal discipline, but are condemned to forever remain beyond its grasp as well. We object to this corollary. For while such matters will indeed evade quantitative treatment, this does not mean that they must elude all efforts at scientific appreciation.

For the reach of science in general extends beyond the reach of quantitative techniques. Thus, what gives us hope of being able to fashion some sort of escape from the various confoundations we noted in the previous chapter is the proposition that being forced to take recourse to subjective predicates or opinion is not necessarily the same thing as a license to let strategic decisions be informed merely by casual speculation or raw intuition.

The core technical challenge for the Strategic Decision Protocol is then to help guide decision-authorities towards rational conclusions that must perforce

EXHIBIT 7.1 : Provisions of a Strategic Protocol*

	Analytical Phases	Technical Facilities
Realization	Io → [M1, M2, . . .]: -allows/encourages the postulation of "notional" possibilities that are only weakly correlated with any historical/ empirical precedents	Employment of a parsing scheme that can formally differentiate between qualitative (structural) and quantitative components of causal/remedial alternatives conveyed as proper models . qualitative arguments accessible to technical treatment
Ordering	[M] → F[M1, M2, . . .]: -initial ranking is assumed dominantly subjective and hence a-prioristic in inspiration; ordinal functions using categorical criteria	Involves recourse to certain logical processing facilities (grammars) to assist in the exchange of causal for disciplined subjective or judgmental arguments . . . this to bring a-priori preferences
Convergence	F[M] → F#[M*] ⊂ [M]: -extraction of some limited, affordable subset [M*] of most "interesting" possibilities for more detailed treatment	Decomposition of constructs to help identify points of contention promising highest information "leverage" (F#), to help set priorities for allocation of Assessment efforts and resources
Assessment	F#[M] → F´[M*] | I@: -attempts a partial exchange of a-priori ("soft," subjective) predicates for "hard" a-posteriori data (I@)	Employment of variations on the Action Research approach (difference-oriented, indicator driven surrogative trials) to work around confoundations

* Where M is a generic notation which can stand for either a problem-definitional or response alternative (qua "model"), with F being a generic preference operator, which might then represent either a probability or utility index, as appropriate.

go way beyond any objective/empirical predicates, the effect of which is to put them pretty much beyond the pale of the essentially data- dependent, mathematical and/or statistically-rooted orthodox methodological platforms discussed in the previous chapter. For when taken in concert, the several provisions of the Strategic Decision Protocol lay out an avenue of approach to the transition from quantitative to qualitative decision discipline. It can be distinguished from its orthodox predecessors in the following ways:

1) It allows for --and may even encourage-- the realization of problem definitional and/or response alternatives that may be *notional* vs. empirical in inspiration.

2) Like the Subjectivist protocol, it allows for ordering operations to be informed by subjective or judgemental arguments, but would then impose any such arguments to certain tests as to their logical integrity as qualitative premises.

3) It introduces a Convergence operation to mediate between the ordering and assessment functions, this to account for the consistent scarcity of time and/or analytical resources under which real-world decision authorities must operate.

4) Perhaps most significantly, it anticipates some definite limitations on the ability of assessment operations (empirical testing/assessment initiatives) to provide the wherewithal for adequate objective discriminacy.

5) It has decision choices determined by extensive Bayesian valuation, this different from the traditional Bayesian approach in that a-priori predicates always taken to be essentially qualitative in nature and non-empirical in origin.

By way of a quick overview, what (1) above implies is that the Strategic Decision Protocol, in contrast to the Positivist platform's preoccupation with the directly observable or demonstrable, and the inductive platforms' (the Objectivist and Subjectivist positions) preferences for hypotheses well-anchored in the factual, is willing to entertain realization constructs that may be only very weakly correlated with any historical/empirical predicates.

Such would represent notional possibilities, the practical purpose of which is to allow decision authorities to consider problems or situations that may have no real empirical precedent, and which may then demand response options that are equally ill-precedented or beyond any initiatives with which we have direct previous experience. In short, notional constructs consider future event/problem possibilities --and hence response options-- that may represent radical departures (i.e., be qualitatively disparate) from anything seen or done in the past. As such, the postulation of such possibilities is pretty much beyond the capabilities of inductive inference initiatives, restricted as they are to the comprehension of event/response alternatives that are variations on historical themes. For notional alternatives will always owe some considerable proportion of their substance to transempirical (or even counter-empirical or deliberately fictional) predicates, and so tend to appear in one or another of the following guises:

IDIOSYNCRATIC: Alternatives that will appear to have arisen essentially ab-intra and so be conditioned strongly by personalistic recollectives or perspectives.

PARADIGMATIC: More or less formal propositional structures, but which rest on one or more premises that may be either tacit (transparent) or unvalidated (untested).

AXIOLOGICAL: Value-based positions that are products of informal reasoning and defended mainly via rhetorical argument designed to convey some moral authority or affective appeal.

While constructs of the above sort may be looked at as anathema by strict positivists and inductivists (including many in the Subjectivist camp), the simple fact is that when empirical predicates are insufficiently rich to allow for realization operations, then non-empirical predicates must fill the gap.

The special technical problem posed by notional constructs is implied by first of the expressions used in Exhibit 7.1. For what the operation Io → [M1, M2 . . .] connotes is that realization constructs may now represent qualitatively disparate alternatives, i.e., problem-definitional or response options that are better thought of as *different in kind* rather than merely in degree. That is, we're now looking at cases where alternative M1 might very well represent apples and M2 represent oranges . . . this is consistent with the key point of distinction for true *strategic* decision exercises that we have used throughout this volume.[1] There is then a need to examine any set of notional realization constructs (members of [M]) to isolate those properties that are qualitative vs. quantitative nature. For while the latter might lend themselves to resolution via one or another of the orthodox methodological protocols, the former argue that the major points of contention among alternatives may derive from empirically-elusive differences of perspective, values or opinion that could only be resolved via qualitative-analysis initiatives of some sort. It is the task of the first of the technical provisions of the Strategic Decision Protocol, the parsing facility, to provide some basis for systematically extracting the qualitative properties of notional constructs from their quantitative provisions, as a prerequisite for all later analytical initiatives.

So far as ordering activities are concerned, the Strategic Decision Protocol follows the lead of the Subjectivist platform in allowing for ordinal preference functions to be influenced by subjective predicates; indeed, subjective predicates must be assumed to dominate the ordering operation in qualitative decision exercises. But the Strategic Decision Protocol will then move somewhat beyond the traditional Subjectivist protocol and provide something in the way of instrumentation that can help answer for the integrity of the subjective predicates that are employed. For the pragmatic question here is not whether or not subjective predicates are legitimate, but rather the *quality* of qualitative arguments; that is, whether they are products of proper reasons or merely instances of raw rhetoric or causal intuition. It is the task of the logical (vs. data) processing facilities of the Strategic Decision Protocol to help answer this question and, beyond this, to suggest how any instances of flawed reasoning might best be repaired. Such a facility is required because idiosyncratic, paradigmatic and axiological constructs may often suffer from certain syntactical flaws (e.g., enthymetic structure) that might render them even more difficult to assess than is already the case. This is a particularly critical function in the confines of the Strategic Decision Protocol. For here, in contrast to classical Subjectivist or Bayesian contexts, subjective predicates are expected to have a significant or even decisive impact on the final selection of a problem (event) definition and remedial alternative.

Yet as an even more telling effect, subjective predicates arrived at during the ordering phase may be used to exclude from any further consideration any alternatives deemed to be *uninteresting*. That is, subjective predicates are the key inputs into the Convergence operation the Strategic Decision Protocol entails. As a general rule, the practical significance of this operation will generally increase with any increase in the number of alternatives in the realization (universal) sets and the severity of any time or resource constraints. The purpose of this operation is to try to make sure that whatever time and resources are available to support the subsequent Assessment-related activities will be employed to best effect. There may be no real counterpart for this operation in strict academic or scientific research exercises (and hence in the orthodox decision protocols), where it is generally expected that all hypotheses that have been realized will be subjected to more or less the sort of degree of empirical attention during the Assessment (qua hypothesis-testing) phase. But real-world decision-makers will routinely find themselves having to work within possibly quite severe constraints on budgets or staffing or access to information acqusition or processing assets and/or temporal strictures (as it may be that it's the pace at which exogenous circumstances are developing, not the rate at which uncertainty is being exhausted, that will determine when the committment to a definite course of action must be made).

In any case, constraints of either sort may make it either impossible or inadvisable to adequately investigate all the alternatives that might have been realized . . . all members of the original realization set [M]. Therefore, when the number of alternatives is relatively large (and/or time and resource constraints particularly severe), the conclusions arrived at during the ordering operation will be used to determine which of the alternatives is to be given what level of more detailed attention --in which order-- during the Assessment stage of a decision-making exercise, and which alternatives are to dismissed from any further consideration via triage-type initiative. Hence the reductive transformation shown as [M] → [M*], with the latter housing only a limited number of assumedly most interesting alternatives.

It's important here to note the precise connotation for the term *interesting* within the Strategic Decision Protocol. For the most interesting candidates may not always be merely those causal/explanatory alternatives assigned the relatively highest likelihoods of capturing the true properties of the problem at hand, or those options expected to have the best chance of being the ultimately most effective/efficient of the remedial candidates (those options carrying the highest a-priori utility valuations). Rather, in learning-oriented decision exercises, the most interesting alternatives may be those that promise to provide the highest degree of information leverage during the Assessment stage; i.e., those that pose issues that, when and if empirically resolved, will expectedly result in the largest reduction in aggregate uncertainty. Or from yet another perspective, the most interesting alternatives might be those that might be described as being of greatest *instrumental* (vs. substantive) utility.[2] It is the task of the decomposition initiative to help make information-leverage related considerations accessible, and in turn allow for the indicated exchange of criteria from the original operator (F) to F#, this latter used to incorporate expectations as to information leverage or instrumental utility as bases for isolating most *interesting* targets for attention during the assessment operation.

A set of tentative probability or utility rankings is then carried to the Assessment Stage, being tentative because:

- they may be based on empirical evidence that is either somewhat dated or that was originally collected with respect to subjects and/or under conditions that do not precisely match those of current interest (such that it's to be treated as *secondary* vs. direct evidence).
- they may owe at least some of their substance to subjective or judgemental (vs. objective or empirically supported) arguments, and hence constructed largely independently of even historical or secondary empirical predicates.

As such, the Strategic Decision Protocol would have assessment operations directed at the generation of additional information (I@) that is of greater currency --either in terms of timeliness or ostensible objectivity-- than that which was available in the starting-state information base (Io).

But the Strategic Decision Protocol must also consider dealing with alternatives whose integrity cannot be adequately determined either by direct demonstration (the Positivist preference) or traditional *normal* science experimental initiatives of the sort called for by inductivist positions. More particularly, given its concern with qualitatively-predicated causal and remedial candidates, the Strategic Decision Protocol is especially alert to the prospect of confoundations intruding to prevent a complete exchange of subjective for objective predicates. Again, as noted in the previous chapter, two basic types of confoundations might arise:

Empirical Inaccessibility, in that certain of the properties of the subjects or processes of interest are of such a nature as to prevent unconfounded observation, manipulation and/or measurement (as, for example, when it is the capabilities or intents of adversaries with which we are concerned).

Experimental Intractability, this a consequence of the practical infeasibility of structuring any sort of formal experimental design that can be expected to adequately accomodate and/or contain the subjects of interest (e.g., there can be defined no appropriate and safe basis for in-vitro testing of *Star Wars* technology).

And to here bring into the foreground a matter that was dealt with only in a footnote in the previous chapter, decision exercises conducted over qualitative alternatives or notional constructs may often find instances of empirical inaccessibility and experimental intractability amplified by one or another of the following ancillary confoundations:

SEMANTIC IMPRECISION, such that one or more of the factors included in one or more of the event and/or response alternatives is a concept for which there is no experimentally-accessible or measurable expression or surrogate.

SYNTACTICAL DEFAULT, concerned with the tendency for subjective realization constructs to emerge as (logically flawed) *improper* hypotheses (they may rest on transparent assumptions, impose elliptical linkages among their component arguments or be enthymetic rather than properly syllogistic in structure, etc.).

PRAGMATIC CONSTRAINTS, the most pertinent of which are time strictures and scarcity of analytical resources (skilled personnel, information acquisition assets, funds to construct prototypes or establish experimental facilities, etc.).

Should any of the above materialize to any significant extent, the most obvious and troublesome consequence would be to limit any opportunities to call upon orthodox analysis or investigatory procedures to provide the *hard* data sufficient to allow for objective evaluations.

This means that the attempt to effect an exchange of subjective for objective predicates may have to depend on something other than orthodox experimental methods. And the something other we have in mind here is what's come to be known as Action Research.[3] As the name suggests, it's mainly significant as a basis for directed learning-while-doing vs. casual trial-and-error. But the *action* aspect will differ depending on whether it is problem-definitional or response options with which we're concerned. With respect to the former, *actions* would be intended to secure information that might not be available otherwise. In this sense, the action-research approach addresses itself to the possibility that the empirical data required for assessment may not be forthcoming unless we take some provocative initiative designed to force a reaction. Intrusive medical diagnostic procedures and obtrusive psychotherapeutic procedures, etc., are familiar clinical instances of this information acquisition tactic. But perhaps the classic example is what is referred to in the military sector as tweaking (e.g., where one party will send airplanes close to the border of an adversary in the hopes of getting the latter to reveal air defense capabilities).

However, when it is response options that are to be assessed, the *actions* to be taken would be the provisions associated with some response option, whose real-world impacts are now to be assessed by being put into actual implementation (perhaps in prototypical or restricted form). It's thus that action-research poses the prospect of informal, only partially controllable in-vivo experiments to be conducted in real-world contexts vs. abstracted (in-vitro) laboratory settings. Because of the real-world rooting, an action-research exercise can usually test only one option at a time and, in contrast to orthodox approaches, cannot guarantee any consistency of experimental conditions for any subsequent options to be tested (this because the provisions of the prior options will expectedly have done something to irrevocably change the properties of the subjects and/or setting on which they were imposed). To this extent, action-research is viewed by strict epistemologists as more notable for its expediency than its elegance.

Yet undeniably, much that currently passes for assessment-related activities in actual managerial practice may often be even more expedient, i.e., little more than essays in selective validation, where empirical efforts restricted mainly to the search for anything in the way of empirical support for just one alternative . . . that particular problem-definition or response option that emerged from the ordering operation as the line decision authority(s) a-priori preferred candidate. That is, selective validation is a vehicle by which decision analysts will devote themselves to the generation of evidence expected to reinforce the subjective predilections of their superior(s). Thus, only in the case where no such support could be gathered --or where there was uncovered, inadvertently perhaps, evidence that would outright refute executive a-priori assumptions-- might there be any investigation of other alternatives. As such, selective validation is an analytical expression of the tendency for real-world decision exercises to be conducted under a criterion of *satisficing*. For the best it can promise is convergence on an adequate vs. optimal selection.

But again, recourse to unorthodox assessment initiatives would not be recommended except when the prospect of arriving at an objectively-based *optimal* choice is denied by virtue of time/resource constraints or the empirical inaccessibility or experimental intractability of the phenomena of interest. Therefore, the pragmatic problem for the assessment-related aspects of the Strategic Decision Protocol is to try to stay somewhere in the neighborhood of a best feasible compromise between expediency and exhaustiveness. The key here is that assessment activities may be not at the evaluation of alternatives as wholes (integral constructs), but rather only at certain points of qualitative difference. This should allow any given quantum of analytical resources to stretch across more alternatives than would otherwise be the case.

Finally, there is the expectation that those engaged is strategic decision exercises will arrive at the point where a selection must be made, and have to settle for an extensive (or third-order) Bayesian choice. There are several points at which extensive-Bayesian conventions differ from their more familiar first- and second-order counterparts (as conveyed, respectively, by the Objectivist and Subjectivist protocols):

1) In extensive-Bayesian operations, a-priori predicates are always *soft* or subjective in nature and a-posteriori predicates always *hard* or empirical in origin . . . irrespective of the point in time at which they were acquired! Therefore, some of the evidence acquired via assessment initiatives may be deemed *soft* or a-prioristic should it take the form of indirect (surrogative) data ,or interpretive intelligence items, etc. By the same token, certain elements of the starting-state or initial information base (Io) might be deemed to be a-posteriori vs. a-priori in significance . . . this one way of evading traditional Bayesian epistemology's problem with allowing old evidence to confirm a new theory.

2) Extensive-Bayesian mechanics should be able to operate at different levels of aggregation. This feature is important because, in the strategic decision domain, the significance of any individual informational item may not be able to be meaningfully assessed except when viewed in concert with some amalgam of other informational acquisitions (historical or contemporary).

3) Extensive-Bayesian operations should allow for the imputation of different degrees of *softness* or *hardness* to any collectivity of informational items. As such, the discrete categoricals used in traditional Bayesian operations (hard vs. soft data; a-priori vs. a-posteriori predicates) would now be taken to represent ideal-type boundary conditions on continuua of reliability, precision, etc.

4) Finally, extensive-Bayesian formulations should provide a formal

basis for cojoining a-prioristic and a-posteriori informational sets in a way that allows flexibility in how each is to be weighted in terms of the net impact they are allowed to exert on the final election of a decision choice (whereas it is the wont of traditional Bayesian mechanics always to give more weight to the latter than the former).

Overall then, extensive-Bayesian driven decision choices will always be informed by both precept and percept . . . in part by both conceptual and computational conclusions, this in light of the unlikelihood of being able to effect a complete exchange of soft for hard data in particularly complex decision exercises. And in certain cases, extensive-Bayesian operations may lead to a special kind of consensus construct, a syncretic model, that may be elected in lieu of any of the originally-realized alternatives.

So much then for this much abbreviated view of the basic role to be played by --and linkages among-- the key provisions of the Strategic Decision Protocol. It now remains to provide some indication of the sorts of procedural and instrumental facilities on which the provisions might be based.

7.2 Parsing Operations: Making Subjective Arguments Accessible

Again, the alternatives appearing for consideration in strategic decision exercises will often take the form of idosyncratic, paradigmatic or axiological constructs, such that much of the axis of contention has to do with empirically elusive matters of perspective, values and opinion. It thus falls to the parsing provision to try to bring such matters somewhere within the purview of formal apprehension. The particular parsing scheme we want to introduce here can be choreographed around the following set of technical assertions, beginning with a restatement of a by now familiar proposition:

1) Strategic decision exercises involve the need to generate, evaluate and elect from among qualitative disparate event (problem) and response (remedial) alternatives.

2) These qualitatively unique alternatives must ultimately be conveyed by causal/explanatory (event or problem definitional) or prescriptive (response or remedial) *models* that are themselves qualitatively unique.

3) Qualitative uniqueness between *models* can only occur when they are defined over unique sets of structural-level specifications.

4) Structural-level specifications mean the provisions associated with the first two of the following four levels of analysis over which any model must be defined:

- At the Determinant level, the task is to define an array of State-variables (factors; entities) expected to exhaust the substantive properties of the phenomenon of interest.
- Relational level specifications are used to establish which determinants are related to which others in what pattern of interaction and influence (causuality).
- Coefficient level specifications provide each relational aspect with a qualifier indicating its magnitude, e.g., were it determined that two determinants are positively related, a correlation *coefficient* would provide a measure of the degree of the positive relationship.
- Finally, at the Parametric or lowest-order of analysis, our problem is to assign each of the determinants and/or non-constant coefficients some specific point-in-time value.

Thus, we might think of any proper model (some Mi) as taking the following form: Mi = (({v} x [D]i) x (Zi x {c})),

where: [D]i = Determinant array
Zi = Relational configuration
{c} = Coefficient array
{v} = Parameter array.

It is specifications on the first two levels that define a model structure . . . i.e., the specifications for ([D]i x Zi) peculiar to a particular construct, Mi. Hence this additional and particularly critical technical proposition: For any two models (some Mi and Mj) to represent qualitatively disparate constructs, Mi and Mj must differ from each other in one or another of the following ways:

- they must be defined over non-equivalent sets of determinants (must have at least one state-variable that is not shared), such that [D]i ≠ [D]j.
- or, if they are equivalent at the determinant level (defined over the same state-variables), then each must impose a unique relational configuration, which means that if: [D]i = [Dj], then: Zi ≠ Zj.

For these are the only ways that two models can be allowed to express (as descriptive constructs) or author (as predictive constructs) qualitatively distinct alternatives.

To make all this somewhat less abstract, let's suppose that given some set of informational inputs (data in the form of observables or apparent *symptoms*), there have been advanced two different and at least partially contentious causal definitions of some event that might represent a potential problem. We'll let these alternative event/problem definitions be represented by Ei and Ej. And given what's just been said, for Ei to represent a true *qualitative* alternative to Ej, then Ei must have been generated by some underlying model Mi that is structurally disparate from some Mj driving Ej.

We'll let the notation Ei|Mi and Ej|Mj indicate these dependencies, and then indicate the four structural-level situations that might arise:

1) If $[D]i \neq [D]j$ .and. $Zi \neq Zj$, then $Ei|Mi \neq Ej|Mj$
2) If $[D]i = [D]j$ .and. $Zi \neq Zj$, then $Ei|Mi \neq Ej|Mj$
3) If $[D]i \neq [D]j$ .and. $Zi = Zj$, then $Ei|Mi \neq Ej|Mj$
4) If $[D]i = [D]j$ .and. $Zi = Zj$, then $Ei|Mi = Ej|mj$.

A brief more or less empirical example for each of these four situations might help firm up the distinctions we're after.

For an empirical example pertinent to (1) above, we'd be looking for a case where two models (Mi:Mj) will involve structural differences on both the determinant and relational levels. As an illustration, we might look to the most fundamental instances of paradigmatic contention in economics, this through the offices of the following two basic orders of normative constructs:

- models constructed around the determinants (e.g., autonomous enterprises and mobile labor and capital) and relational dynamics (via the *invisible hand* by which the collective economic welfare is maximized when individuals and enterprises are allowed to pursue their own best interests) that are used to give expression to aspects of free market philosophy.

- models expressing Marxian-inspired predilections for collective socio-economic systems, usually defined over determinants in the form of instutitions to support central planning and cojoin economic and political activities, and relational-level specifications expressing some variant on the following key allocative dynamic: *From each according to his capabilities; to each according to his needs.*

Clearly, each of the above would tend to recognize different sorts of economic problems, posit very different definitions of any problems they both recognize (e.g., the Marxian explanation for the phenomenon of inflation is materially different than that arrived at from the prototypical capitalist perspective, with the former viewing it mainly as a consequence of flaws in human nature and the latter as a symptom of market disequilibrium) and so urge recourse to radically different remedial strategies (e.g., re-socialization vs. some sort of technical correction).

Another example of this deepest form of subjective dissensus may be the Reagan administration's foreign policy misadventure with Iran in respect to the matter of the American hostages held in Lebanon. For what we might think of as the *null* hypothesis was formulated roughly as follows:

M1: There exist certain moderate elements in the Iranian power structure that are anxious to have better relationships with the United

> States. Iran needs military supplies in order to successfully prosecute its war against Iraq. If the moderate Iranian elements are able to deliver arms and ammunition, their influence (vs. radical elements) will be increased. This influence could then be used in the short-run to secure the release of hostages being held by agents responsive to Iranian control. Therefore, delivering military supplies to Iran via the moderates should result in the following: a) The release of the hostages as a short-run outcome; b) With respect to the longer run, some repair of the adverse relationship between the US and Iran and the consequent reduction in the likelihood of any Iranian : Soviet rapprochement.

Now of all the criticisms that were raised against this happy hypothesis, the most telling was perhaps this: There are no political moderates in Iran when it comes to the US . . . just radicals of mildly differing degrees of rabidity. We might then think of the counterhypothesis (M2) being formulated so as to exclude the determinant most critical to M1, or :

$$D' = ([D]M1 - [D]M2) \rightarrow \text{Iranian moderate elements.}$$

And in practice, this determinant-level disparity was then reinforced by what might be perceived as disparities in Relational-level disparities, such that the countermodel actually advanced by critics of M1 took essentially this form:

> **M2**: Any Iranian interest in any US-sponsored initiative must be examined for any opportunity for Iran to exact some revenge for what it perceives to be a long series of historical insults. So in the short-run Iran will try to get as much in the way of military supplies as possible while delivering the least possible in the way of hostages. The only possible long-run outcome from attempting to trade arms for hostages would be inimical to US interests via: (a) Validating the seizure of US hostages as a currency for realizing material ambitions; (b) Irritating all Middle-east states who fear an Iranian victory over Iraq, and retargeting of Iranian military aggression that might then follow; (c) Dismaying all US allies who we have been urging to stand fast against terrorism; and (d) Leading to the erosion of US credibility with respect to other international committments.

Thus, in terms of Relational-level specifications, M1 and M2 may be said to differ in terms of the direction of influence they postulate between two key model determinants, the Delivery of arms to Iran and US interests, where:

terrorism in the future because it will effect a secular transfer of authority from more to less radical elements in the Iranian regime.

Z1|M1 $\rightarrow$ E1: delivering US arms to Iran will reduce instances of terrorism in the future because it will effect a secular transfer of authority from more to less radical elements in the Iranian regime.

$Z2|M2 \rightarrow E2$: delivering arms to Iran will result in more hostage-taking in the future and a general increase in both short-run and long-run peril to US interests.

In turning to the second of the Structural-level situations (that defined as the case where $[D]i = [D]j$ .and. $Zi \neq Zj$) we might simply take a little different perspective on the US:Iranian example we've been dealing with. Particularly let us grant that there are indeed such things as Iranian political moderates (a point not entirely without real-world advocates). As such, there would no longer be any distinctions between the Determinant arrays over which M1 and M2 are defined. Therefore, for M1 to generate E1 and M2 to yield some qualitatively disparate E2, the disparities between M1 and M2 would have to occur solely at the relational level. We'll thus let $Z1|M1$ reflect the proposition that delivering arms to Iranian moderates will serve both short-run and long-run US interests along the lines just noted. An alternative relational dynamic might then be this:

> $Z2|M2 \rightarrow E2 \neq E1$: attempting to use Iranian moderate elements as a conduit for the delivery of US arms will actually result in a weakening of the influence of the moderates vis. a vis. the more radical elements of the Iranian regime.

That is, whatever moderates might actually exist will be perceived as willing to appease a hated adversary at the expense of the purity and moment of the fundamentalist revolution . . . i.e., as traitors to the cause, and as a factor acting to dilute the revolutionary zeal. As a result, if an Iranian moderate movement existed before the US arms deal, it is unlikely to exist afterward in the same strength (and may quite possibly be expunged altogether). This would leave the more radical elements more completely in charge, and US interests in even greater peril, than was previously the case.

Or as an even more familiar example of the case where qualitatively distinct (state) events can be authored by relational level differences, we might move to consider the more or less constant contention between the three grand schools of modern macroeconomic theory, the Monetarist, Keynesian and Supply-side paradigms. For it has been demonstrated in a fairly convincing way that the basic difference between these three paradigmatic platforms ultimately reduces to the particular patterns of causality and directions of influence --i.e., unique relational-level specifications-- that each imposes on essentially the same array of state-variables. For example, most members of the Supply-side school pose capital formation and investment as the main engine of economic causality, with all other factors subordinate to this. In contrast, Monetarist- inspired models generally pose causal chains initiated by the rate of change in the money supply. And for their part, traditionalist Keynesian models usually have the central role played by collective fiscal initiatives to stimulate or dampen general economic activities.[4]

There is then the third of the situations of structural disparity to consider: $[D]i = [D]j$ .and. $Zi = Zj$. And by way of empirical example, we might quickly consider a matter of some current policy-level dispute, the initiative aimed at the deregulation of the Airline industry. For there were clearly two contentious models defined from the very earliest days of the debate, with the case for deregulation being made as follows:

> M1: The greater the degree of concentration of economic power in an industry, the greater will be the probability of consumers being forced to pay generally higher prices. Deregulation is a means of encouraging competition and hence lowering price levels.

As far as it goes, this model is a reflection of generally accepted economic wisdom. But critics of the rush to deregulation proposed a model M2 that introduced a determinant that was absent from M1 . . . the prospect of mergers and acquisitions taking place among Airlines. And once we include this new determinant, we'd get the following counter-position:

> M2: Deregulation will increase competition among Airlines, which will in turn have the effect of decreasing the general price structure. But decreases in the price structure will have the effect of forcing some firms to exit the industry, and of increasing the interest in the creation of larger enterprises as a defensive manuever. If this tendency is left unchecked, the result would be a thrust towards greater concentration (in a fewer number of generally larger firms), and hence adverse pressures on the general price structure.

Note that both M1 and M2 have essentially the same core relational-level logic: Decreases in competition imply increases in price. In this sense, then, Z1 may be taken as equivalent to Z2. There is however a key difference at the determinant level:

$$D'([D]1 - [D]2) = \text{mergers/acquisitions},$$

and this difference is of course sufficient for them to author qualitatively disparate projective conclusions:

> M1 $\rightarrow$ E1: deregulation will yield to an increase in the general economic welfare via consistent pressures towards an effectively minimal long-run average price structure.

> M2 $\rightarrow$ E2: deregulation will ultimately lead to greater concentration of market power and hence to higher prices.

Once we move to the fourth situation --where $[D]i = [D]j$ .and. $Zi = Zj$-- we're left with models where contention is not at the structural level, but rather with respect to coefficient and/or parametric specifications. That is, it's now merely quantitative matters that are in dispute.

For example, differences among the projections authored by the various companies marketing econometric forecasts may be argued to arise primarily as a consequence of coefficient-level differences. For structural differences among the models are essentially trivial. Virtually all use the same set of state variables over which are imposed essentially the same set of relational specifications (particularly in terms of certain classical static-comparative assumptions serving to suggest the direction of influence among factors such as GNP, disposable personal income, the tax structure, demand-supply conditions, etc.). Thus, disparities in projections is pretty much a consequence of coefficient-related differences such as these:

1) the specific valuations allowed basic *rate-variables* such as the Multiplier or Acccelerator effect;

2) the categorical valuations (strong vs. weak) assigned certain correlations, such as interest rate movements as a function of changes in the money supply, etc.

A good example of disparity at this level is the variance between forecasts of the federal budget deficit that have been generated by the Executive and Legislative branches of government during the Reagan administration. The former acts through the Council of Economic Advisors which serves at the pleasure of a definitely Republican president, while the Congressional Budget Office is an adjunct of a Democrat-controlled House. Not unexpectedly, the forecasts prepared by the former have consistently generated lower deficit projections than have the forecasts prepared by the latter. But the general models employed by the Council of Economic Advisors and the Congressional Budget Office are merely clones in virtually all significant structural respects. Therefore, the variance between the projections they generate tends to be authored by the tendency for the President's economists to assign more optimistic *parameter* values to certain key variables (e.g., increase in real GNP; projected tax receipts) than is the wont of the Congress' captive econometricians. That is, each group of model-builders tends to employ sets of assumptions and valuations that are suspiciously coincidental with the interests of their respective employers.

By way of quick summary then, when the points of disparity between or among alternatives is restricted to coefficient and/or parametric level specifications, we can generally expect to be able to use traditional quantitative analysis instruments to evaluate them and inform a *tactical* decision choice (this because the alternatives are better thought of as being merely different in degree than in kind). In contrast, the three other structural situations we discussed all involve instances where the locus of contention among models is with respect to qualitative matters, now accessible via the isolation of structural (determinant and/or relational) level arguments. And this brings us to the role that might be played by logical processing facilities.

7.3 Prospects for Logical (vs. Data) Processing Facilities

Once we've struck upon some way to capture and concretize qualitative arguments, it's possible to consider the imnplications of the second set of technical provisions in the Strategic Analysis Protocol. For they are intended to support this key proposition: Being deprived of the opportunity to use mathematical or statistical decision aids necessarily mean being forced entirely outside the bounds of rationality that science can make available. Rather, the preferred option is to take whatever steps may be available to cause opinion to be informed more by rigorous reason than rhetoric. It is of course this option that we now want to consider. And when we reduce it to its technical essentials, what we find is the need for an exchange of traditional mathematical or statistical inference for its natural if more elusive complement, some sort of logical inference! Indeed, such an exchange has significant pragmatic as well as technical merit. For as has been implied, real-world strategic decision-makers must ultimately be more concerned with what is *logically possible* than what's merely statistically probable. They are thus to be applauded more for the richness of their conceptual sensibilities than for any computational skills they might have.

Again, there was the suggestion that strategic authorities are to be adjudged primarily for their conceptual or logical sensibilities. And central among such sensibilities would be the following:

- an ability to freely shift among different analytical frames-of-reference so as to maintain elasticity of perspective.
- a capability for being able to examine situations at different levels of abstraction . . . to move well between the more general and the more specific, between precept and percept.
- an ability to decompose (parse) complex constructs into any simpler constituents and then see the different ways that things might be resynthesized or fit together again.

These capabilities would lead to the generation of richer (and hence more likely *exhaustive*) sets of alternatives. The practical effect of this should be to reduce the likelihood of strategic authorities failing to include the true *cause* of a problem among a set of problem-definitional alternatives that were advanced, or failing to include the truly best remedy among the set of response options that were contemplated.

There are no doubt some individuals who have a great native gift with respect to these three capabilities. But most of us would probably welcome some help in these areas, even if only to hedge our bets. As a practical matter then, what we are led to is the recognition that modern strategic management support systems should be designed to include some logical (vs. data) processing facilities to help answer for the quality and completeness of any sets of user-generated causal and remedial alternatives in the confines of a strategic decision exercise. Such facilities would then take the next natural step beyond those already taken by Elicitive and Decision Structuring instruments. For whereas these now allow for the exchange of subjective for objective decision premises, what we would ideally want is to follow this with some way of effecting the shift from statistical to logical discipline. In any case, as for their main practical mission, logical processing facilities would thus be intended to address the first of the two critical aspects of the shortfall in strategic decision technology that were earlier identified. Hence the following mission statement:

> Help strategic decision authorities answer for the extent to which any set of user-generated qualitative alternatives exhausts the richness of *logical possibilities* pertinent to some phenomenon or process of interest. That is, we'd want to call on logical processing facilities to assess the completeness of any array of problem-definitional and/or response options introduced by the various parties to a strategic decision exercise.

But there are two different guises in which such logical processing facilities might appear, rote and syntactical.

7.3.1. Machine-Aided Realization of Logical Possibilities

When this general requirement is translated into specific instrumental demands, there emerges the need for facilities that would allow a computer to generate some problem-definitional or response alternatives in its own right. These machine-generated constructs would then serve as a basis for a more or less independent test of the completeness of any array of user-defined constructs.[5] Moreover, we'd also like to be able to look to machine-generated constructs as a possible basis for suggestions as to how sets of user-defined alternatives that have been adjudged *incomplete* might best be enrichened. As a starting-point for a discussion of what this might entail, it's well to recall this key convention from the previous section: The only two ways in which qualitatively disparate event/problem definitions or response alternatives can be generated is to have them defined over non-equivalent determinant arrays and/or relational level properties. And because the consideration of possible response options usually follows the event/problem definitions process, we'll deal at some length with this matter and then follow with a more abbreviated discussion of response formulation activities.

Consider then the challenge of defining pairs of qualitatively unique event/problem definitions along the following three lines:

i.	E´ = V[Di] [D] E" = W[Dj] [D]	ii. E´ = Z[Dk] E" = ~Z[Dk]	iii. E´ = Z[Di] E" = ~Z[Dj]

As per the notation used earlier, [D] would represent a universe of determinants pertinent to some application domain, with V, W and Z then being alternative relational-level specifications. Thus, under (i) above, E´ and E" are defined over complementary state-variable arrays, such that they have no determinants in common . . . i.e., $([Di] \cap [Dj]) = 0$. In contrast, under (ii) above E´ and E" are defined over equivalent determinant arrays [Dk], but have different relational structures via the Z and ~Z specifications. And to elaborate on earlier suggestions, for Z and ~Z to be able to author qualitatively disparate relational-level configurations, they must entail differences on one or more of the following subdimensions for at least one pair of state-variables shared by E´ and E", say some V1 and V2 $\in$ [Dk]:

a) Z must impose a different connectivity between V1 and V2 than does ~Z., e,g, If Z has V1 and V2 positively correlated, then ~Z might pose them as negatively correlated or perhaps even independent (not directly related).

b) Z must define a different dynamic causality than ~Z, this in terms of locus as well as direction of influence. For example, say that Z postulated that V1 drives V2 but that a change in V2 does not necessarily imply any change in V1. The referent ~Z might then propose that V2 influences but need not be influenced by V1.

c) Z must propose a different conjunctivity (logical or mathematical) than ~Z. For example, if Z imposes an OR relationship between the two state variables (such that we get $V1 \cup V2$), then ~Z might dictate an AND conjunction that would yield $(V1 \cap V2)$. Or if Z has V1 and V2 in an additive relationship $(V1 + V2)$, ~Z might pose $(V1 - V2)$.

Case (iii) would then be a conjunction of the above two, such that E´ and E" are constructs disparate on both the determinant and relational dimensions.

But before we consider the practical mechanics of constructing E´ and E" referents, there are two things to note. First, they would represent synthetic rather than realistic event (problem definitional) constructs. That is, they're intended to express *logically possible* vs. empirically probable possibilities and so may have little likelihood of occurrence in the real-world. Indeed, they may often be defined so as to be deliberately counter-empirical. For, by way of a second qualification, we want to do everything possible to ensure that E´ and

E" in fact represent maximally-disparate possibilities in terms of the determinant and/or relational level properties with which they are equipped, this because of the following rationale:

> To the extent that E´ and E" indeed represent the extremes of all logically-possible event/problem definitions, then the *true* causal properties must ultimately be located somewhere within the domain bounded by E´ and E".

Synthetic referents thus mark the extremes of a perhaps otherwise empty continuum of event possibilities: {E´ . . . E"}. In this sense, E´ and E" might then be suggested to set the feasibility limits for a domain-of-inquiry over which event/problem definitions for some class of phenomena might conceivably range.

This then also has the effect of suggesting the search-space over which strategic authorities ought to be prepared to wander if they were to try to think as broadly as possible about the matter at hand. That is, the charge to generate *limiting* synthetic referents is the opportunity for the parties to a strategic decision to put into practice the several key logical capabilities we spoke of (elasticity of perspective, moving among different levels of abstraction, etc.). Thus, for a typical strategic decision exercise, a useful convention may be to try to define E´ = V[Di] so as to represent the most tractable of all conceivable problem definitions, or that entailing that particular collection of causal attributes that are presumed to be the least demanding to treat. The other synthetic referent or E" = W[Dj] might then be defined so as to represent the feasible worst-case situation . . . i.e., constructed around a set of properties that promise to be the most difficult, most expensive or most risky to treat (perhaps via a *centrifugal* Delphi-type process that would, with each iteration, attempt to urge participants towards successively more disparate scenarios).

But our major interest is the role computers might play in all this. And the most obvious role is to help make sure that any E´ and E" pair are indeed maximally-diverse in terms of the qualitative attributes they entail . . . that they do indeed set the limits on the range of logical possibilities. Were it either case (i) or (iii) under which we are operating --both involving structural differences at the determinant level-- one test for maximal disparity between E´ and E" would be to see that the determinant arrays [Di] and [Dj] are in fact effective complements. And the most obvious basis for such a test is the simplest of all formal logics, which also happens to be that logic which computers can most easily comprehend, Boolean conventions (with more sophisticated logical grammars implying increased powers of machine discriminacy). For were we to provide a computer with the membership of [Di] and [Dj], it's comprehension of basic Boolean operations should then allow us to task it with making sure that there is an empty intersect between the two, such that [Di] $\cap$ [Dj] = 0. Yet such would be merely the most trivial of the tasks towards which a computer might be turned. For there are two somewhat more challenging assignments a machine might be given, both examples of simple rote realization (the unconstrained generation of all logically-possible variations on some theme):

- given [D] and [Di], the computer could be charged with the realization of some (or all) alternative [Dj]'s that would have no properties in common with [Di]. Or, given [D] and [Dj], the computer could be tasked to generate alternative [Di]'s according to the same criterion.
- a computer could be supplied only [D] and then asked to realize all [Di] vs. [Dj] arrays that would meet the criterion of mutual exclusivity.

In both the above cases then, a computer may be said to have the major responsibility for carrying out the model-generation responsibilities associated with case (i) and the determinant-level requirements posed by case (iii).

It's also entirely feasible to think of a modern computer being able to answer for the challenges posed by case (ii) and the remaining aspect of case (iii), where it is relational-level differences that are at stake.[6] We might then contemplate programming a computer to recognize and enforce certain basic relational conditions:

	Correlation		Mathematical		Logical
>> :	Strongly Positive	+ :	additive	$\cup$:	or/union
<< :	Strongly Inverse	- :	subtractive	$\cap$:	and/intersect
> :	Weakly Positive	/ :	division	~ :	not
< :	Weakly Negative	x :	multiplication	~/ :	nor
@ :	Unrelated	* :	exponentiation	'/ :	nand

Equipped with this simple vocabulary of relational possibilities, a computer could then be charged with generating the range of relational possibilities that might pertain between any two state-variables, say some V1 and V2 $\in$ [Dk]:

For example, suppose that Z were to pose a strongly positive correlation between the two state-variables, or V1 >> V2. Were we to look then for a most-opposite condition for ~Z, this might be V1 << V2 (or perhaps even the case V1 @ V2 which would imply no correlational at all). Similar considerations would hold for the various mathematical and logical conjunctions. Thus, given sets of categorical conditionals like those above, computers could conceivably be tasked with generating effectively polar-opposite relational specifications for all Vi and Vj pairs includable in [Dk], perhaps in simple tableau-form:

Z =

	V2	V3	. . .	Vz
V1	>>	<		+
V2		∪		
V3		etc.		
. .				
Vz	@			

~Z =

	V2	V3	. . .	Vz
V1	<<	<		-
V2		∩		
V3			etc.	
. .				
Vz	<>			

And as a next obvious step, we might of course then direct the machine to generate simple causal chains by combining various provisions drawn from the above lists into ordered strings.

For example, the expression V1 >> V2 < (V3 ∩ V4) would have a change in V1 excite a stongly positive change in V2 which would then effect a modest reduction in the value for V3 and V4. Indeed, it's clear that the categoricals represent *primitives* that could be employed to generate a virtually infinite variety of relational possibilities among any number of state-variables constituting a partition (a collection of three or more *connected* determinants).

We might then move to consider the prospect of computers being employed to generate synthetic event/problem definitions as composites of determinant and relational-level properties. Such would involve directing the machine to realize E´ and E" pairs as logically-possible aggregated or composite constructs includable within some {[D] x [Z]} domain. One way to allow for this would be to provide a computer with programs enabling it to perform basic operations defined under graph theory, constructive geometry, network theory (e.g., Petri Net conventions) and the various non-computational mathematics.[7] But there is another technical option that is much closer to our immediate technical reach, even if somewhat less elegant.

Particularly, we might consider providing a computer not with a repertoire of basic logico-mathematical operational capabilities, but rather acquainting it with some collection of ready-made, coherent (aggregative) constructional referents. And given the focus on generating constructs that are essentially maximally-diverse in terms of structural properties, the ready-made referents we'd be most interested in would be members of standing dichotomies developed by various disciplines. For such referents have been deliberately constructed so as to represent effectively polar-opposite referents. Consider, for example, the following pairs of generic structural ideal-types:

Hierarchical	vs.	Reticular
Reflexive	vs.	Linear-sequential
Segmented	vs.	Modular
Recursive	vs.	Associative, etc.

And there is an equally if not even more impressive set of dichotomies posing radically disparate dynamic referents, e.g.:

Negentropic	vs.	Entropic
Asymptotic	vs.	Oscillatory
Centrifugal	vs.	Centripetal
Homeostatic	vs.	Chaotic
Pendular	vs.	Equifinal

What makes such dichotomies so very attractive is that each specifies those definitive criteria sufficient to distinguish the respective members of each pair. That is, others have already provided the wherewithal for computers to both recognize and enforce polar-opposite ideal-types . As such, if only by way of a compellingly pragmatic expedient, a computer could clearly be expected to perform automated (rote) realization of essentially maximally-disparate qualitative constructs by defining E´ and E" around the properties associated with the contrasting members of any dichotomy. Or, as an even more appealing proposition, we might have the computer charged with realizing constructs as conjunctions of structural and dynamic referents when such might be appropriate (for example, we might let E´ = Segmented and Evolutionary and E" = Modular and Revolutionary).

But recall that the practical consequence of any synthetic referents is a continuum stretched out to reflect the range of logical possibilities, {E´ . . . E"}. And if, along the lines just suggested, we can conceive of a computer being employed to realize synthetic extrema, we can also contemplate having it generate some *interior* synthetic referents to start filling in the gaps between E´ and E". In certain cirumstances it might be possible to work at a disaggregated level of analysis. Particularly, if the determinant-level specifications for E´ and E" were originally generated as Boolean extrema, then a machine might be tasked with realizing a quasi-Boolean median determinant array or some construct we'll refer to as [D#] such that:

([Di] – [D#]) = ([D#] – [Dj]).

This would be appropriate when the determinants of interest represent intervals on an ordered continuum of numerical or *fuzzy* variables. For example, [Di] might be defined around those state-variables that might be taken to be most conducive to capital formation, say a high level of personal savings, a favorable interest rate structure, etc., with [Dj] then entailing essentially opposite conditions (an insubstantial or perhaps even negative savings rate); [D#] might then be defined to reflect conditions roughly midway between the two extremes. The same opportunity might hold for relational matters. For example, if Z were to pose a strongly positive correlation (>>) between two variables and ~Z a null correlation (@), a synthetic median (Z#) might then posit a weakly positive correlation (>).

The result would then be a synthetic realization structure having a median construct E# such that (E´ – E#) = (E# – E"):

	Z	Z#	~Z
[Di]	E´	-	-
[D#]	-	E#	-
[Dj]	-	-	E"

In terms of its substantive implication, had E´ and E" originally been defined so as to represent the best (most benign or favorable) and worst (most perilous) of all possible worlds, then E# might describe a state roughly midway between the two in terms of its potential for threats and opportunities.

By extending these operations, we could generate Boolean *quartiles*, etc., and so begin to develop perhaps fairly well-elaborated arrays of synthetic referents. Or, from a more general perspective, a machine might be tasked to perform the *rote* realization of some sample subset of (or perhaps all) logically possible alternatives available within a composite search space, [(Di; D#; Dj) x ({Z; Z#; ~Z)]. That is, we have it busy mixing-and-matching different determinant arrays with different relational configurations. At the very least, we might ask the computer to work to fill in the empty cells in the above matrix or to realize Z[D#], Z[Dj], Z#[Di], etc.

Even more appealing, however, is the prospect of a computer being directed to realize interior constructs in the case where the original synthetic referents (E´ and E") were defined over aggregated referents . . . members of a dichotomy. For what this would involve is an elemental dialectical capability. For again, the ideal-type referents would have been pre-defined so as to represent a *thesis* and *antithesis*, such that the task would be to converge on some E# as the synthesis. To illustrate, suppose that E´ and E" represented, respectively, a neatly hierarchical vs. reticular model structure. The essential difference between the two is that the latter allows for equipotentiality, such that any determinant can directly influence --or be directly influenced by-- any other. In contrast, a strict hierarchical configuration does not allow for direct interaction between state-variables belonging to different partitions or levels. We might thus want to define E# to impose a weakly reticular configuration (qua partial graph) allowing for cross-mappings among some subset --approximately half?-- of the determinants. Similarly, there would be readily realizable median states between any of the pairs of dynamic opposites (e.g., a dynamic midway between the entropic and negentropic extrema would allow more or less equal authority to cohesive vs. dissipatory factors).

But again, whatever and however synthetic referents are realized, their practical purpose is still to assist in assessing the *completeness* of user-generated constructs. Thus, the synthetic logical extrema (E´ and E") are significant mainly as a basis for testing for the breadth of the event/problem definition or causal constructs that were generated by the parties to a strategic decision exercise. For to the extent that it can be demonstrated that the domain of logical possibilities extends from E´ to E", then any set of alternatives that is distinctly narrower in terms of the range over which it extends might be a cause for some concern, most particularly those arrays then tend to be clustered somewhere in the neighborhood of just one of the extremes. At the very least, we would want to look for some sound pragmatic rationale for the a-priori exclusion of other possibilities. Any interior synthetic referents (logical medians and quartiles, etc.) would have a complementary role. Particularly, they would be the primary basis for attempting to assess the extent to which a set of user-defined alternatives is sufficiently elaborate in terms of the number/diversity of its membership (the test for which would involve examining the nature of the mapping between the members of the user-defined and machine-realized arrays). But the interior synthetic referents would also have another important function: To suggest where and how to best move to *enrichen* any set of user-generated alternatives that has been adjudged as somehow *incomplete*.

Turning now to response-side matters, the usual prerequisite is the convergence on a singular maximum-likelihood event/problem definition as some P^(Ei) = ([D^] x [Z^]), where [D^] represents the consensus as to the determinants thought to apply and [Z^] the particular relational configuration assigned the highest likelihood of occurrence. And as earlier suggested, any response option should be capable of being formulated as a model laying out the provisions for a plan of action to be directed against the problem at hand, and so might be expected to provide details as to at least the following:

- ACTIONS [C]: details the nature of the actions to be taken
- ASSETS [A]: dictates the type/level of resources to be committed
- ACTORS [U]: indicates the organizational units that are to carry out the various actions
- TARGETS [T]: specifies the agencies or conditions (problem aspects) against which the actions are directed

We might then express any strategic response option (some Rj) in terms of a proper model like the following:

$$Rj = Z[Dj], \quad \text{where } [Dj] = (A + U + C).$$

That is, we here take the determinant array [Dj] to collect the *substantive* aspects of the reponse option. As such, the expression Zj(A + U + C) would in effect prescribe the organizational structure that will be used to execute Rj . . . the particular allocation of responsibilities and resources that has been decided upon. But it is another sort of construct that is of more interest to us here, this being the impact structure, or Zj(C x T). This attempts to capture the practical essence of the imposition of Rj on P^(Ei).

This is because the array Tj indicates that particular subset of problem properties (substantive and dynamic) that Rj has elected to attack:

$$\text{if}: \; Ei = ([D\hat{}] \times [Z\hat{}]),$$
$$\text{then}: \; Tj = ([D^*] \subset [D\hat{}] + [Z^*] \subset [Z\hat{}]).$$

We may thus think of (C x T) as expressing a partial mapping between aspects of Rj and properties of P^(Ei). The operator Zj would then be used to display what we might think of as the *causal* characteristics of Rj, this by specifying the sequence in which the various actions are to be executed . . . which problem properties are to be attacked in what order or under what circumstances (any conditionals that apply for the undertaking of some specific Cj x Ti element).

Overall then, we've now a basis for the generation of a cross-impact model expressing the interaction between two other models:

$$M(Rj \times Ei) = Zj\,[D]j|i, \quad \text{where: } [D]j|i = (Cj + Tj).$$

We might then think of any other strategic response option, say some Rk, being expressable as follows:

$$M(Rk \times Ei) = Zk(Ck + Tk).$$

And given the conventions under which we've been operating, for Rk to represent a true strategic alternative to Rj, then one or another of the following conditions must hold:

$Tk \neq Tj$: Rk proposes to treat a different subset of problem properties than Rj

$Ck = Cj \;\&\; Tk \neq Tj$: Both Rk and Rj propose to treat the same set of problem properties but Rk proposes to treat one or more problem properties differently than Rj.

Etiher of the above is sufficient to make $(Ck \times Tk) = (Cj \times Tj)$, or to introduce what we might think of as determinant-level differences between the two options. But should neither of the above hold, then the following must apply:

$$Zk \neq Zj \quad \text{if } (Ck \times Tk) \neq (Cj \times Tj),$$

such that Rk would propose to array the same set of treatments against the same set of problem properties but do so in a different sequence. As such, rote realization facilities of the sort discussed earlier might be employed to generate a pair of synthetic response-side referents, R´ and R", such that either of the intersects at the determinant level are empty . . . i.e.:

$(C' \cup C") = 0$: R´ and R" have no actions in common; and

$(T' \cup T") = 0$: R´ and R" treat different problem properties

or relational-level specifications are effective inverses for any points of commonality: Z" = ~Z' for any/all C´ | T´ = C" | T" (e.g., if Z´ = +, then Z" = -; if Z´ = >>, then Z" = <<).

Given the ambition for synthetic referents in general, R´ and R" would be defined so as to represent the logically possible extremes --in terms of cost, risk, etc.-- of the range of strategic options an organization might conceivably be able to mount against some problem. Or, at the least, R" would be intended to represent the limits of feasibility . . . the most exotic of the options allowable within pragmatic and policy constraints. But while R´ and R" could be defined autonomously, the more usual situation would be that previously-defined synthetic event/problem definition referents would be available to inspire the realization of their response-side counterparts:

$$\begin{array}{ccccc} \{E' & \ldots & E\# & \ldots & E''\} \\ \downarrow & & \downarrow & & \downarrow \\ \{R' & \ldots & R\# & \ldots & R''\}. \end{array}$$

Thus we come to the prospect of computers being concerned not merely with the generation of event/problem and response alternatives, but with comprehending the cross-mapping possibilities among them.

But this is a prospect that really can't be accomodated well within the confines of the simple rote realization operations we've concerned ourselves with thus far. Rather, it would better be addressed by a more sophisticated class of machine-based facility, syntactical realization technology.

7.3.2 Towards Syntactical Realization Facilities

The need for an order of facilities above and beyond those for doing rote realization derives from an obvious equivocation: Some (if not most) of the alternatives that would be generated under rote realization are likely to be *uninteresting*. That is, though they will all be logically possible, not all will be plausible in any practical sense. It would thus remain for the human user to scan the set of machine-generated alternatives and extract those that have any realistic significance, discarding the remainder. But if [D] contained a relatively large number of members, then the set of rote realization alternatives may become so large that detailed human perusal becomes infeasible. To some extent, detailed perusal may not be of much significance anyway. For again, the primary role of the computer here is not to generate actual strategic choices, but rather merely to provide some referents against which the exhaustiveness of user-generated alternatives can be assessed. Towards this end, users might content themselves with extracting merely a few sample [Di] and [Dj] subsets to examine. But as a rule, it would appear that the better part of technical wisdom would be to reserve rote realization for instances where there are only a quite limited number of determinants to consider (as, for example, with the relatively few consensus state-variables pertinent to mainstream macroeconomic modeling).

In other cases, if computers are to have any meaningful role to play, it must be by virtue of our having found a way to allow them to endogenously distinguish between alternatives that are merely logically-possible and those that are truly *interesting* in light of some sort of normative criteria. And while such may seem a bit exotic, readers may recognize that this is by no means an unprecedented ambition. Rather, it is reflective of what's posed as the key contribution from a particularly interesting class of artificial intelligence constructs, Discovery Systems.[8] This is because such systems are specifically designed to provide computers with the wherewithal to do *automated realization* . . . to endogenously generate alternatives for subsequent consideration by men (rather than, as do their much more familiar artificial intelligence cousins, Expert Systems, having the man generate alternatives for subsequent consideration by the machine). To be sure, Discovery Systems as yet remain more a matter of potential than tangible promise. For actual essays in machine-driven modeling have been at best only sporadic and restricted mainly either to applications where it is merely coefficient and/or parametric level alternatives that are being generated or to various set-piece qualitative cases where the alternatives to be realized are all products of strict deductive inference (where, in effect, conclusions derive from a reordering of programmer-provided premises).

Programs capable of doing restrictive or discriminate vs. merely rote automated realization thus rest a bit beyond our immediate technical grasp. And while there is no reason at this point to discount the possibility of their eventually being brought within our technical reach, there is some reason to argue for a line of approach somewhat different than that which has been followed previously. For the tendency has been to impose situation-specific *substantive* criteria as a basis for a-priori discrimination. Substantive criteria pose constraints in terms derived directly from the properties of the phenomenon or subject at hand and so tend to reflect users' expectations about what will be interesting constructs. Recall however, that one of the primary purposes of machine-driven realizations is to guard against premature a priori closure via user-inspired biases. Therefore, whatever a priori constraints we impose on Discovery System programs might best be studiedly non-substantive in nature . . . deliberately disassociated from any direct empirical, experiential, paradigmatic or idiosyncratic content, etc. What this suggests is having automated realization operations informed by abstract or generic (vs. situation-specific) constraints of some sort. Hence the concept of syntactical realization operations, where a-priori discriminacy is to be effected via methodological rather than substantive constraints.

For under syntactical technology, a computer would be programmed to recognize a set of rules in the form of a grammar (syntax) allowing it to distinguish legitimate from improper constructions. What makes this at all plausible is that formal logical systems (any many orders of mathematics as well) will already have a more or less elaborate set of syntactical provisions in terms of the axiomatic conventions on which they rest. These will not only specify operations permissible in the singular (as, for example, with the sets of relational categoricals introduced earlier), but also set out provisions for generating proper concatenative or complex constructs via their interpretations of universalisms such as transitivity and commutativity, etc. One might then concieve of syntactical realization facilities as mechanics to effect endogenous discriminacy by proscribing the generation of any alternatives other than those that conform to whatever a-priori syntactical or criteria are in force. But here we want to propose a more immediately accessible expedient. For rather than trying to program a machine to constrain itself, somewhat the same end might be obtained by a much less demanding technical trick:

> Direct the machine to refrain from forwarding --for consideration by users-- any alternatives it may have generated (by rote) that it can subsequently recognize as illegitimate or non-normative.

Yet once we have a computer that can recognize improper or uninteresting constructs of its own authoring, we might then consider a prospect of even greater pragmatic significance in the confines of strategic decision exercises. Particularly, a computer that can comprehend normative criteria might also, if we wished, be allowed to enforce them by:

- failing to corroborate (for further consideration) any user-generated alternative that does not reflect proper syntactical discipline or otherwise conform to normative criteria;
- suggesting a basis for the modification or repair of any logically flawed user-defined alternatives.

Here would be a key to meeting the second of the critical contributions we'd like to see from logical-processing facilities: Helping decision authorities drive towards a working consensus in the face of a-prioristic dispersion. For such facilities should be able to provide some basis for examining axiolgical (subjective or value-driven) constructs for their axiomatic attributes, and so be able to isolate instances where an alternative's rhetorical appeal may have been purchased at the price of logical integrity. Hence the compelling prospect of logical/conceptual processing facilities being deployed to help drive out bad *soft* arguments in favor of good subjective predicates. The pragmatic consequence would then be to see that whatever dissensus remained in a strategic decision exercise would be due more to the natural complexity (stochasticity) of the subject at hand than to any irrationalities . . . to contention arising merely from ideological, affective, paradigmatic, academic or bureaucratic vanities.

There are at least two different sorts of syntactical conventions that might be used to examine qualitative constructs for their logical quality, constructive and canonical. As for the former, the most obvious source of normative criteria would be the various standards used to adjudge the quality of formal scientific constructs qua *hypotheses*:[9]

Explication (vs. transparency) of first premises;
Syllogistic (vs. enthymetic) argumentation;
Expressed (vs. eliptical) linkages, etc.

Programs to comprehend such criteria might possibly be developed by encoding procedures defined under one of the approaches to Confirmation Theory developed as an aspect of formal epistemology.[10] Such are of interest in that they involve the deliberate abstraction of any arguments or constructs from empirical or semantic --i.e., substantive-- attributes, with assessment thus restricted to their conformity with logical vs. reality-based requirements for rationality (rigor).

While such may provide a basis for machine-recognition of flawed or contra-logical constructs, the question arises as to sources of scientific suggestion as to how computers might possibly be programmed to assist in their repair. As for the matter of programming mechanics, work being done in the area of genetic algorithms and rule-structures would be a valuable source of technical suggestion.[11] As for what would be programmed, we'd be looking for schemes useful not merely for flagging violations of logical standards, but at the same time able to indicate what's required to convert logically-flawed or incomplete constructs into proper hypotheses.

Fortunately, there are at least three sources to which we might turn:

1) Ackoff and Emery's work on elucidating the structural elements of qualitative models, this especially useful as a basis for identifying *transparent* premises and hence for indicating where elaboration would be required.[12]

2) Provisions in Seadler's *Ideotopology* or other approaches to the systematic parsing --and hence the possible reconstruction of belief-structures or axiological (vs. axiomatic) constructs.[13]

3) Any of the schemes designed to effect Replacement Programming as a basis for coverting constructs into fundamental logical consitituents.[14]

For their part, canonical criteria are best thought of as generic rather than abstract because thay are not so much creatures of analytical philosophy as ideal-type system properties defined by various technical disciplines (e.g, system engineering). Particularly interesting would be those canonical standards that relate to *reachability*. This is because they might serve as a basis for programming computers to bring some degree of formal discipline to the task of mapping between problem-definitional (event) and strategic response alternatives, or $Rj \rightarrow Ei$. Among canonical reachability criteria that might be employed are:

> COMPLETENESS: is there an aspect of Rj (some action, C) that can be relied upon to reach --directly or indirectly-- each and every salient target problem-property (T) of Ei?
>
> ELEGANCE: the extent to which Z(Cj x Tj) appears to take advantage of any opportunities for *leverage* (instances where an action taken against one problem-property will concatenate to cause sympathetic changes in other problem properties).
>
> ECONOMY: is the sequencing of actions set up in such a way as to effectively minimize aggregate asset/resource requirements? Have all instances of fundamental similarity between alternative event/problem definitions been identified?

This latter is important for to the extent that some Ei and Ej have any qualitative properties in common, the incremental resources/assets required to treat both would be defined only over their complement.

As a final matter relating to logical processing facilities, it should be stressed that the computer's ability to recognize constructive and canonical criteria is made feasible by the fact that such criteria can generally be reduced to unambiguous graph-theoretic or mapping rules. And because, as implied earlier, properly *parsed* qualitative constructs themselves become intelligible as simple network or graph configurations, both the criteria for syntactical integrity and the constructs upon which they are to operate would at least be in the same language, as it were. To this extent, the technology required to actually implement programs to comprehend and enforce constructive and canonical criteria may then be too terribly far beyond the reach of the knowledge-engineering conventions that have been evolved to generate and operate on conceptual structures.[15] Note also this very important pragmatic consideration: The sorts of computer-based facilities described here should be of enormous assistance in actually carrying out the somewhat intricate manipulations of event and response referents called for under the two adaptive strategic platforms we discussed in Chapter 5.

7.4 Initiatives for Resolving Strategic Disputation

The remaining provisions of the Strategic Decision Protocol are directed mainly towards the second of the key missions for next-generation strategic decision support technology:

> Assist strategic authorities in working towards a *rationalized* consensus in the face of the dispersion of a-priori predicates (via second-order confoundations) to which strategic decision exercises are vulnerable.

For in the absence of provisions to help with this task, there is this problem: Encouraging the parties engaged in a strategic decision exercise to stretch their imaginations may merely invite second-order confoundations in the guise of deep-seated differences of perspective, values and opinion; and given either of the assessment-related confoundations we identified (empirical inaccessibility or experimental intractability), these differences cannot be properly resolved via either of the orthodox methodological protocols.[16]

Thus, the remaining provisions of the Strategic Analysis Protocol are all aimed at helping strategic decision-makers find some way of arriving at a *rational* conclusion in the face of a-priori dispersion, and despite some degree of empirical inaccessibility and/or experimental intractability:

1) Decomposition of qualitative models;
2) Difference-oriented, indicator-driven convergence via Action Research initiatives;
3) Isolation of a strategic choice in terms of an Extensive Bayesian dominant alternative or syncretic construct.

We'll now move to close this volume with a discussion of the conceptual and technical rudiments of each of the above.

7.4.1 Qualitative Decomposition of Contentious Constructs

Again, decision exercises may often be susceptible to both scarcity of analytical resources and temporal constraints, either of which may make it impossible to undertake an adequate empirically-oriented assessment of the full complement of alternatives that have been advanced. In such cases, the most familiarly argued approach would be to simply limit the number of alternatives to be subject to assessment attention by eliminating some n alternatives assigned the relatively lowest a-priori preference valuations. This would then generate some reduced, affordable subset of the original realization set, or $[M^*] \subset [M]$, with only the members of [M*] passed on to the assessment stage. But such a reduction poses some possibility that we will have a-priori eliminated the alternative representing the *true* explanation for the problem at hand or the remedial option that would have eventually proven to be most nearly *optimal*. At the very least, the elimination of any of the originally-realized alternatives would effect a sympathetic increase in the expected value of decision error (as a product of residual risk and uncertainty) associated with final selection. Therefore, it is desirable to try to find some basis other than crude triage for working around resource or time strictures.

The decomposition initiative is one possible ploy. For what it dictates is an exchange of units of analysis, such that it is not the original constructs (members of [M] or even [M*]) to be subjected to empirical attention, but rather only certain of the points at which they are in qualitative contention. Thus, it's now only the structural-level *differences* among the model alternatives that are the targets for assessment operations. The rationale is that, being more limited in scope and sweep than the integral models from which they were derived, difference-aspects should be both quicker and cheaper to assess at any given level of rigor, which should then reduce the degree of vulnerability to both temporal and resource constraints.

As for the technical mechanics, the Parsing process that opened the Strategic Decision Protocol would allow for operations that roughly parallel the sorts of decomposition exercises traditionally conducted by system engineers or mathematical or engineering-based artifices.[17] Or, they might mirror certain *knowledge engineering* conventions used to encode and manipulate referents for Expert Systems. To give some more or less concrete idea of how decomposition activities might be carried out in the confines of the Strategic Decision Protocol, we might briefly look a bit further into the matter of the contention between the several mainstream macroeconomic paradigms . . . the Monetarist, Keynesian and Supply-side schools.

As suggested earlier, with respect to any given problem, each would be expected to author a qualitatively unique reponse option. To illustrate, let's take the problem of interest to be what is perceived to be too high a rate of *inflation*, and assume (even at the risk of some oversimplification) that all three schools are content with a singular explanatory (problem-definitional) alternative: That inflation is caused by too many dollars chasing too few goods. Let's further assume that, from this common perception of the problem, that the paradigmatic peculiarities of these schools would lead them to pose the following response options:

> M1 (MONETARIST POSITION): Act to reduce available dollars by controlling the rate of increase in the money supply.
>
> M2 (KEYNESIAN POSITION): Act to reduce available dollars by imposing a Surtax that would have the effect of decreasing disposable personal income.
>
> M3 (SUPPLY-SIDE POSITION): Decrease general tax rates in order to stimulate both demand and available credit to both consumers and producers; the net effect should be an increase in demand which would then induce an increase in output levels which will mean more goods and hence a downward pressure on price levels.

Were we then to generate the simple static-comparative graphs for these three remedial options, we'd get something like this:

M1: $\downarrow$money supply $\rightarrow$ $\downarrow$dollars $\rightarrow$ $\downarrow$demand $\rightarrow$ $\downarrow$price level

M2: $\uparrow$taxes $\rightarrow$ $\downarrow$dollars $\rightarrow$ $\downarrow$demand $\rightarrow$ $\downarrow$price level

M3: $\downarrow$taxes $\rightarrow$ $\uparrow$dollars $\rightarrow$ $\uparrow$demand $\rightarrow$ $\uparrow$production $\rightarrow$ $\downarrow$price level

As originally stated then, the determinant-level differences among the three positions would be these:

[D1] – [D2] : Money-supply; Tax structure
[D1] – [D3] : Money-supply; Production
[D2] – [D3] : Production.

The most pertinent of relational differences would then be a causality posed by M3 that is the inverse of that proposed by M1 and M2, i.e.:

Z(M1 & M2) : $\downarrow$dollars $\rightarrow$ $\downarrow$price level
Z(M3) : $\uparrow$dollars $\rightarrow$ $\downarrow$price level

Other points of relational disparity would be excluded by virtue of the following: a) The relational aspects of M1 and M2 are identical for all determinants they share; b) All three alternatives have the determinants Dollars and Demand treated equivalently, i.e.: the condition dollars $\rightarrow$ demand is technically equivalent to the provision dollars $\rightarrow$ demand.

Were these positions subjected to even the most cursory scrutiny for logical integrity, each can be shown to be incomplete. For none explicates any condition(s) that would lead to its defeat. But such are evident and might inspire the formulation of counterhypotheses (~Mi's):

~**M1**: the Monetarist position generally fails to include the possibility that a decrease in the Money Supply might force an increase in domestic interest rates, which would in turn act to increase the level of imported funds and so actually increase available dollars:

Money $\downarrow$Supply $\rightarrow$ $\uparrow$Interest Rates $\rightarrow$ $\uparrow$Imported Funds $\rightarrow$ $\uparrow$Dollars

~**M2**: the Keynesian construct fails to include expectations as a state-variable. But once explicated, the following counter- hypothesis could be advanced: The attempt to control inflation by imposing a surtax may reinforce consumer's expectations that prices will continue to rise, and so lead them to make major purchases sooner rather than later . . . purchases financed not from income but by *dissaving* or drawing on credit, either of which would increase the upward pressure on price levels:

$\uparrow$Taxes $\rightarrow$ $\downarrow$Expectations $\rightarrow$ $\uparrow$Dissaving $\rightarrow$ $\uparrow$Price level

~**M3**: the Supply-side thesis omits the possibility that an increase in demand might merely provoke producers to raise price levels, leaving production (supply) level the same:

$\uparrow$Demand $\rightarrow$ $\emptyset$(Production) $\rightarrow$ $\uparrow$Prices

Were such *tacit* provisions to be made explicit, there would be an increase in the number of structural-level differences to work with. For in addition to any determinant/relational disparities among the original candidates (M1 : M2 :

M3), we'd now have certain points of contention for each hypothesis vs. its counterhypothesis (M1 : ~M1), (M2 : ~M2) and (M3 : ~M3).

To generalize then, one consequence of the parsing convention earlier recommended is the straightforward approach to decomposition that it allows. For as might be inferred from the example just given, we might take decomposition to involve a series of successive qualitative subtractions to be performed over the members of any set of alternatives qua models:

$$[M] \rightarrow \{M1([D1] \times Z1),\ M2([D2] \times Z2),\ \ldots,\ Mn([Dn] \times Zn)\}.$$

And again, for any Mi and Mj to represent qualitatively unique models, the following must hold: $[Di] \neq [Dj]$ and/or $Zi \neq Zj$. Therefore, determinant-level differences would involve any state-variables appearing in Mi but absent from Mj. An array {D´(i:j)} would then be used to contain such differences, e.g.:

$$\begin{aligned} \text{if}: &\quad [Di] = (d1, d2, d3) \\ \text{and}: &\quad [Dj] = (d1, d2, d4, d5) \\ \text{then}: &\quad \{D'i{:}j\} = (d3, d4, d5). \end{aligned}$$

Next would follow the attempt to recognize any instances of relational-level disparity between Mi and Mj. And again, such would become apparent in terms of any differences in the relational specifications the two models impose on any pair of determinants they have in common . . . say some d1 and d2. Such differences might best be looked for on any of the following basic relational subdimensions:

- Zi might impose a different connectivity between d1 and d2 than does Zj, e,g,: If Zi has d1 and d2 positively correlated, Zj might pose them as negatively correlated.

- Zi could define a different causality than Zj, this in terms of locus as well as direction of influence. For example, Zi might dictate that d1 drives d2, with Zj perhaps allowing d2 to influence d1 but not the reverse.

- Zi may propose a different conjunctivity (logical or mathematical) than Zj. For example, if Zi imposes an OR relationship between two determinants ($V1 \cup V2$), then Zj might dictate an AND conjunction ($V1 \cap V2$). Or if Zi has d1 and d2 in an additive relationship, Zj might impose a multiplicative, subtractive or exponential relationship, etc.

An array to collect and house all such instances of relational-level disparity between Mi and Mj might then be constructed as:

$$\{Z'i|j\} = \text{all}\,(zi - zj) \quad \text{for all } \{d\} \in [Di] \cap [Dj],$$

where {d} is any array (partition) of interlinked state-variables existing as a point of intersection between Mi and Mj.

Were the above difference extraction operations to be performed for all pairwise combinations of models in [M], the following aggregate difference arrays could be generated:

> {D^}, this containing a mention of all determinant level differences among all (Mi|Mj) ∈ [M].
>
> {Z´}, this collecting all relational-level differences among all the members of [M].

These might then be used to construct a *master difference array* containing a mention of all points of qualitative contention among all alternatives, or the set {S^} = {D^} + {Z^}.

Thus, as a consequence of the above decomposition operations, there must be at least one difference-aspect --at least one element of {S^}-- available as a basis for *discriminating* between every possible pair of alternatives (all Mi vs. Mj combinations) in [M]. And this, in turn, can allow for the setting of priorities that would direct subsequent assessment activities towards those particular difference-aspects presumed to have the potential for exerting the greatest aggregate information leverage. The simplest approach is to first direct attention towards the resolution of those difference-aspects pertinent to that pair of alternatives assigned the highest a-priori preference valuations.[18] Suppose that the ordering at this point were as follows:

$$F(Ma > Mc > Md > Mb > \ldots Mz);$$

In such a case, the first of the difference-aspects to be subjected to assessment attention would be those pertinent to the Ma|Mc confrontation. The next focus of attention would then be on assessment efforts designed to resolve the points of contention between the winner (dominant survivor) of the first round and the next most favored candidate, which means directing assessment activities at those difference-aspects pertinent to either Ma|Md or Mc|Md, etc.

But there is also a second level at which opportunities for allocative efficiency must be considered. For there may often be two or more points at which any two alternatives are in qualitative contention, and hence two or more difference-aspects that might be subject to assessment-related attention . . . e.g., Mi : Mj → (S^1, S^2, . . . , S^k) ∈ {S^}. Again, considering the nature of the decomposition exercises that were conducted, any of the above has the potential to be *sufficient* as a basis for discriminating between Mi and Mj. But at the same time, each of the difference-aspects must also be expected to imply some differences in the level of time and/or resource committments required to resolve them. Therefore, when operating under temporal/resource constraints, it may be necessary to limit attention to some limited number (perhaps even just one) of the difference-aspects pertinent to any Mi|Mj pair. And when such a convergence of attention is required, the interests of information-leverage would dictate that the relatively highest priorities be assigned those difference-aspects best meeting criteria such as:

- those posing information acquisition requirements that can expectedly be met most economically;
- those for which appropriate data/intelligence can be acquired in a more timely way (sooner rather than later);
- those whose resolution can be based most completely on evidence that is objective and direct vs. interpretive or surrogative in nature, and hence likely to be most conclusive or convincing to those responsible for making actual selection committments.
- those posing information collection requirements which are least likely to set off any adverse second-order consequences (such as causing a change in the behavior of the phenomena of interest, being perceived as a threat by some adversary worthy of an aggressive counteraction or closing the door for later evidence collection efforts, etc.).

There is, however, still another level at which information-leverage considerations might be addressed. But this requires considering the definition and use of indicators, a subject better discussed in the confines of assessment activities as they may be carried out under the Strategic Decision Protocol.

7.4.2 Indicator-Driven Action Research Assessment Activities

The concept of an *indicator* was first introduced as an aspect of intelligence-driven strategic planning/positioning. We'll now generalize a bit, defining an indicator as a variable posing certain information acquisition requirements expected to provide a more or less objjective basis for resolving a particular point of qualitaiive contention in favor of one or another member of any pair of candidates. Indicator-driven assessment operations would be oriented not towards validation of any particular alternative, but rather towards attempts at successive elimination of all other possibilities (an orientation that might be defended either with reference to Sherlock Holmes' pragmatics or modern epistemology's skepticism about conclusively proving any hypotheses).

In any case, as a consequence of the decomposition operations just noted, any of the difference-aspects that were isolated --any $\hat{S}k \in \{\hat{S}\}$-- could now inspire the definition of one or more indicators: $\hat{S}k \rightarrow [I1, I2, \ldots, In]$. If there are two or more indicators available for some singular difference-aspect, then the interests of efficiency would dictate that priority go to that particular indicator deemed to best meet the sorts of information-leverage criteria introduced just above. Just to give some idea of what indicator-selection processes might involve, we might return to the several contentious macroeconomic remedies for inflation we worked with in the previous section.

From what was done in terms of the decomposition initiative, it's clear that M1 and M2 (the Monetarist and Keynesian options) are essentially equivalent as qualitative constructs. Indeed, their dispute is mainly at the coefficient level, revolving around whether it is more *efficient* to reduce dollars by dampening the increase in the money supply or imposing a surtax of some kind. We've also suggested that so far as Dollars and Demand are concerned, all three of the candidates impose an equivalent relational specification; it's just that the triggering condition for M3 (the Supply-side position) is opposite that of M1 and M2). Therefore, what we are left with as the apparently most critical difference-aspect among the three options is that provision of M3 arguing that an increase in Demand will translate into an increase in Supply. And set against this provision we have the counterproposition from ~M3, this postulating a tendency for producers to meet increases in demand by increasing prices vs. increasing ouput (or, more continently, that the rate of increases in prices will exceed the rate of increase in supply). The problem however is that neither M3 nor ~M3 --when taken in aggregate-- lend themselves well to any bounded empirical field-trial . . . i.e., any test that might serve to validate M3 would involve actually putting the policy advice in place as a kind of grand, uncontrolled experiment wished on the world.

But the key point of difference between M3 and ~M3 might perhaps be subjected to indirect a-posteriori investigation via a typical variant on the Action-Research approach, a Two-Way Surrogation Experiment. Such would be aimed at assessing the behavior of subjects that may be substitutes (surrogates) for real-world actors who are being engaged in a simulation of (surrogate for) the real-world setting of interest. For example, an experiment might be choreographed around groups of students engaged in playing a business game, with demand increases of two sorts being introduced as simulated *action* elements:

a) Increases in demand that are a consequence of potentially rescindable alterations in tax rates;

b) Potentially self-sustaining increases in demand given demographic, productivity or other structural factors.

Game-players' reactions would then be recorded with respect to these indicators:

I1(M3:~M3): The ability/willingness of subjects to distinguish between the two different categories of demand increases.

I1(M3:~M3): For those subjects making the distinction called for in I1, any differences in the extent to which the two types of demand increases evoked decisions to increase levels of output or, ultimately more significantly, to increase the level of capital investment in productive facilities.

The greater the frequency with which game-players distinguished between the two sources of increased demand --and the greater the extent to which increases via (b) above were followed by supply-expanding decision, the greater the level of a-posteriori support the experiment would provide for ~M3 vs. M3. For such an outcome would suggest that if students are unwilling to increase investment in productive capacity on the bases of artificially-induced demand increases, real-world businessmen might be expected to be equally reluctant. Hence the more credible the counterhypothesis that increases in demand following from decreases in tax rates may be more likely to provoke increases in prices than increases in supply. But while surrogative assessment schemes have the advantage of being economical, quick and safe, their disadvantage is that indicator-related evidence they offer is merely of imputational authority.

As for the basic mechanics of indicator-driven assessment, whatever evidence is obtained would be used to assign a value **v** to an indicator **I**, which would then be used as the basis for the assignment of an a-posteriori preference index **F´** to the models in contention:

$$v(I) \rightarrow F'(Mi) \text{ and } F'(Mj),$$

where v can represent either a numerical, categorical or *fuzzy* value. As a quick illustration of what this might involve in practice, it might be useful to reconsider an earlier mentioned case, airline deregulation.

Recall that what was in effect the *null* hypothesis (as per model M1) argued that deregulation would increase competition and thereby lower prices, while the counterhypothesis (M2) posed the prospect of deregulation inviting mergers/acquisitions that would ultimately lead to greater concentration of economic power and escalation of prices. As is the case with so many policy platforms, M1 --when taken in aggregate-- did not lend itself well to attempts at empirical pre-assesement via bounded field-trials or other traditional hypothesis-testing procedures. As such, the committment to M1 was taken largely on the basis of a-prioristic arguments, and then wished upon the airline industry as something of a grand, basically uncontrolled experiment.

But there are some apparent opportunities for at least partially objective pre-assessment when that target is not M1 or M2, but rather the key point of qualitative contention between them . . . or S^k(1:2) = the prospect of mergers/acquisitions. For any evidence of any significant tendency for deregulation to be followed by an interest in effecting mergers and/or undertaking acquisitions might be construed as a-posteriori evidence against the outcome postulated by M1 (or, alternatively, as some degree of objective support for M2). And as to the matter of the indicators that might be defined with respect to this difference-aspect, there are at least three to be considered. The first might be associated with a surrogation-type experimental effort such as that described earlier.

Particularly, we might again involve a group of students in a business game, this time acting as substitutes for airline executives. The starting-state condition for the game would be the conditions applying prior to deregulation. Prospective deregulatory provisions would then be introduced as simulation arguments and evidence collected with respect to this indicator:

> **I1** = the relative frequency with which subjects took recourse to merger and/or acquisition as a response to deregulation, with higher frequencies resulting in higher v(I1) values.

There is however an entirely different class of indicators that might be available from another and more distinctly provocative variant on action-research. Particularly, the *action* to be imposed might take the following form: The judicious seeding of rumors as to an imminent shift in government policy from regulation to deregulation! This then would be followed by the search for any reactions via either of these two indicators:

> **I2** = Credit Take-Downs: attempts by airline companies to sequester financial support geared to the prospect or promise of an attempted take-over of one or more competitors. The greater the number/amount of any take-downs, the higher the magnitude assigned v(I2).

> **I3** = Contact/Contract Intelligence: an acceleration of contacts among airline executives with counterparts in other firms and/or mediational agents (investment bankers); increase in intensity of and activity among members of interlocking directorates; reporting of extraordinary contract arrangements such as any arrangements whereby one firm undertakes the lease of assets owned by another, etc. More intense levels of such activities would lead to higher v(I3) valuations.

In sum then, higher values for v(I1) and/or v(I2) and/or v(I3) would be used to impute a greater likelihood of deregulation triggering significant (vs. trivial) levels of merger/acquisition activities, which would in turn translate into lower a-posteriori assessments of the attractiveness of alternative M1 vs. M2. On the other hand, lower values for all indicators would not necessarily validate M1, but would certainly be taken as an occasion to reduce it's a-posteriori valuation F′(M2) relative to that for F′(M1).

It's important to note, however, that the F′ values assigned the respective members of any pair of confrontational alternatives are not independent. In this one sense, indicator-based assessment operations are roughly akin to conjoint ANOVA type experimental designs where two or more hypotheses are being evaluated simultaneously in a single frame of analysis. But here, the focus on indicators as the arbiters of a-posteriori preference --given their derivations from difference-aspects-- may be interpreted as involving any pair of contentious alternatives in what amounts to a constant-sum game situation, where whatever advantage one gains is at the direct expense of the other. This, again, is entirely consistent with the basic strategy that emphasizes convergence via *successive elimination* vs. selective validation. But this poses something rather special, but certainly obvious, in terms of the mechanics for indicator-driven preference valuations:

$$F'[Mi:Mj] = \Pi\,(w * c * v\{I \times S\hat{}k\}),$$

where the expression {Im x S^k} is used to collect all the indicators for all of the difference-aspects tested with respect to some particular Mi : Mj confrontation, and *v* is again a valuation for a specific indicator with respect to a specific difference-aspect (with this valuation being a more or less objective measure of the level-of-activity and/or tendencies that were actually observed, adjusted for instances of variance and/or metric imprecisions). The operators *w* and *c* are new here.

For *w* is a weighting factor used to reflect the relative significance assigned each S^k. This is useful because, while each difference-aspect may be taken as a route to a-posteriori discriminacy, not all will be created equal. That is, some difference-aspects may be imputed to have relatively more authority than others. For example, in attempting to resolve the conflict between two different diagnostic hypotheses with respect to some medical patient, certain points of disparity between the two sets of symptoms may be taken to be generally more conclusive than others, and so be assigned relatively higher weights in making a committment to a problem-definition).

The qualifier *c* is then a confidence index employed to adjust the valuation (v) assigned any indicator, with indicator valuation perhaps being undertaken along any of the lines shown in the following table.

Confidence criteria differ depending on the category of observables, with the degree of confidence assigned any indicator-driven evidence a reflection of the following:

REMOTENESS: The extent to which the condition being tested is incidental rather than integral to the original point of argument. For example, in the exercise trying to get some measure of the integrity of the Supply-side reponse platform with respect to inflation, evidence as to the extent to which subjects can distinguish between two different sources of demand refers to a secondary predicate; it's authority with respect to the validity of the alternative itself (hypothesis M3) must thus be mediated by some estimate of the extent to which such recognition is a sufficient condition for that hypothesis to be true (or false).

RELEVANCE: Reminiscent of its use in orthodox inductive hypothesis testing, this factor would refer to the extent to which the

Observables Type	Inference Methodology	Confidence Basis
Hard, objective data obtained via direct observation	Deterministic valuation or directed resolution	Effective certainty via Positivist procedures
Current intelligence or partial empirical data base/Sample (primary or secondary data)	Statistical inference methods for arguing from the specific to the more general/ Cross-sectional inference generation	Confidence is a function of values for experimental tests (e.g., means tests for ANOVA)
Historical data base, usually arrayed as a Time Series	Extrapolative/ projective Statistical methods (longitudinal inductive inference)	Confidence is a function of degree of Variance in empirical data set
Iterative observations on some parameter(s) of interest	First-order Bayesian inference, assigning more weight to most recent observations	Confidence tied to asymptotic closure on a "stable" value
Combination of Hard (positive) and Soft (interpretive) observations	Extensive Bayesian inference methods to cojoin objective and subjective arguments	Confidence is a function of "net" reinforcement between the two sets of predicates

context/conditions under which the a-posteriori evidence was obtained aligns with the context/conditions to which it is to pertain. Consider, for example, that the authority of evidence collected via the sorts of two-way surrogation experiments earlier described might best be deflated to reflect the degree to which business school students are imperfect substitutes for real-world executives and the degree to which a laboratory simulation is an imperfect expression of actual environments.

RELIABILITY: Having to do with the integrity of any evidence obtained, this would reflect matters such as the extent to which results obtained for one indicator and/or difference-aspect tend to be corrobated (reinforced) by results for other indicator/difference-aspect junctions; the extent to which the a-posteriori evidence was directly observable or imputational (subject to some sort of interpretive mediation); the credibility of the authors of a-posteriori evidence or those actually conducting the assessment activities (their technical competence or assumed freedom from bias, etc.).

Depending on how all the above matters actually resolve themselves, there may be four basically different sorts of outcomes from any a-posteriori assessment effort directed at any Mi|Mj pair of alternatives:

1) Elimination of one member of any pair of contentious alternatives were indicator-related evidence to cause the preference valuation for either Mi or Mj to approach zero;

2) The emergence of strongly-dominant preference, such that one of the candidates is now deemed significantly more preferable than the other, e.g.: $v(I) \rightarrow F'(Mi) >> F'(Mj)$;

3) Less satisfactory would be the case where v(I) would lead to only weakly-dominant discriminacy, such that one alternative is deemed only marginally preferable to the other;

4) Least useful would be the situation where the indicator-induced information failed to inject any degree of a-posteriori discriminacy, such that $F'(Mi) = F'(Mj)$.

And finally, when there had been conducted an indicator-driven assessment of all Mi|Mj combinations definable within the universe of alternatives [M], the wherewithal would be at hand for the attempt to isolate an extensive-Bayesian dominant choice.

7.4.3 Isolating Extensive-Bayesian and Syncretic Choices

There are, however, two different tacks that might be taken towards the determination of an extensive-Bayesian choice, the Aggregated and Disaggregated modalities. Of the two, the first is the more conventional. For the extensive-Bayesian valuations (F") over a set of alternatives would emerge as composites of the a-priori (F) and a-posteriori (F′) preferences assigned the various members as a consequence, respectively, of the ordering and assessment operations, i.e.:

$$F'' = [W1(F) * W2(F')] \times [M1, M2 \ldots Mn],$$

where W1 is the weight assigned the a-priori preferences and W2 is the weighting for a-posteriori derived preferences.[19]

In the interests of strict rationality, it cannot generally be dictated that W2 is to be greater than W1. For there is no necessity within the transempirical protocol that logically-grounded conclusions (when disciplined according to the formal deductive or inductive conventions noted earlier) be deemed inferior to empirically-based arguments (given their anchoring in what must perforce remain imperfect experimental situations).

In any case, under the aggregated approach, the alternative expected to be selected for implementation would be that member of [M] assigned the maximal composite valuation. If the alternatives represent problem-definitional alternatives (re: contentious causal/explanatory models), then the extensive-Bayesian dominant choice --F''max (Mi) $\in$ [M]-- would be isolated as the maximum-likelihood candidate or that Mi assigned the highest conjunctive probability of best answering for the structural and dynamic properties of the phenomenon at hand determined at the conjunction of both the personalist (subjective) and frequentist (objective) interpretations of ordinal probabilities. Were it response options being considered, then the extensive-Bayesian dominant choice would be taken to represent the ostensible maximal-utility option . . . that particular course of action which is assumed to most closely approach the upper limits of potential effectiveness and efficiency, determined as a hybrid of both cognitive (subjective) and cardinal (empirically-predicated) bases for defining and measuring utility.

But while the aggregated approach just described has the advantage of reflecting the way Bayesian evaluations are usually performed, it may often be that a disaggregated approach may be superior in precision. For following the parsing conventions earlier recommended, it would be possible to represent any alternative (Mi) in matrix form:

	d2	d3	. . .	dn
d1	z(1,2)	z(1,3)	. . .	z(1,n)
d2	-	z(2,3)	. . .	z(2,n)
d3				
. .		etc.		
dn				

Where : Mi = [Di] x {Zi} such that each d $\in$ [Di] is a determinant over which Mi is defined, with each z(di $\cap$ dj) $\in$ Zi being a relational provision

And as a consequence of the difference-oriented/indicator-driven assessment exercises that would have been conducted, it may be that one or more of the provisions for Mi would have been assigned an a-posteriori preference valuation . . . had it been the subject of one of the difference-aspects investigated with respect to one or more Mj alternatives.

We might then extract any such d and z aspects and include them in two subsets, say [d*] $\subset$ [Di] and [z*] $\subset$ Zi. The members of these subsets would then carry only their a-posteriori or F′ indices, such that the only model constituents that are still equipped with a-priori (F) indices would be the *residual* provisions, i.e., [d#] = ([Di] – [d*]) and [z#] = ({Zi} – [z*]).

Under the disaggregated approach, we'd thus get the following basis for an extensive-Bayesian valuation:

$$F''(Mi) = W1(F([d\#] + [z\#])) + W2(F'([d^*] + [Z^*])).$$

It is then the disaggregated approach that best answers for the exchange of a-posteriori for a-priori predicates that was the primary mission assigned the assessment operations in the transempirical protocol. Moreover, it is the disaggregated approach that opens the door to the possibility of passing over any of the originally defined problem-definitional or response options in favor of a Syncretic selection alternative.

For a syncretic construct would be contrived around what are deemed the best aspects drawn from among some set of competitive or contentious alternatives.[20] A syncretic construct might then be viewed as something of a technical imperative for decision-exercises following a failure to arrive at a satisfactory extensive-Bayesian dominant selection (where the degree of composite discriminacy is of low order). For in such cases, the only other alternatives are not terribly attractive:

- Delay any sort of committment, this perhaps taken in conjunction with a demand for further study;
- The senior executive might impose a consensus by fiat by commanding acceptance of whichever alternative aligns best with his personal (a-prioristic) predilections;
- A crude compromisive construct might be developed that gives some presence to each of the contentious positions, even at the risk of including provisions that will set-off negative cross-impacts or work against each other (as has been suggested is the case with the current national economic policy platform, it being intelligible as a casual amalgam of basically incompatible Supply-side, Monetarist and Keynesian planks).

Syncretic constructs may be seen to offer a possible avenue around these popular but also perilous decision default options. A syncretic construct becomes practicable because of the sequence of prior provisions of the Strategic Decision Protocol. For such would have already provided us with at least some of the constituents for a syncretic construct via the following:

> Those particular specifications that, via whatever a-posteriori assessment exercises were conducted, were determined to be the preferred member of any set of mutually-exclusive provisions with respect to the model aspect at issue . . . i.e., around those provisions that may be taken to have won the empirical trials aimed at resolving difference-aspects.

But the above may not exhaust all the points at which structural specifications would be required in order to generate an adequately elaborate or complete causal/explanatory or prescriptive model.

That is, there will likely be some determinant/relational levels gaps that will have to be filled. And what appears to be the technical key to filling them properly would be a shift in focus away from the difference-aspects (mainly in terms of mutually-exclusive provisions) with which the previously-discussed technical initiatives have been preoccupied. Rather, the center of attention would now be on any instances in which they are not in contention. These may be of two sorts:

- points of complementarity, whereby one model contains provisions that have no direct counterpart in another . . . such being points of difference that are not points of contention.
- points of equivalency or essential qualitative similarity, such that two or more models share certain determinants and/or relational specifications.

Complementary provisions may prove very valuable, for they may most often arise as a consequence of specialization --technical, professional, functional or disciplinary-- among the parties to a decision exercise. Specialization may allow certain individuals or subgroups to recognize certain factors (some state-variables or dynamic possibilities) of which those operating from other backgrounds or areas of expertise might simply be unaware. And to the extent that such provisions do not directly contradict or threaten any other parties' interests or preferences, there may be no objection to their inclusion in a syncretic model. In short, any instances of complementarity may represent a valuable source for the enrichment of a syncretic model . . . for injecting diversity and breadth without engendering controversy.

As for points of equivalency, these would be accessible as a natural side-effect of the parsing/decomposition initiatives that would have been conducted over the original alternatives. In particular, for any Mi vs. Mj pair, the following would hold:

Let: [D] = [Di] + [Dj], such that [D] is the union of the determinants over which Mi and Mj are defined;

and: {D^i|j} = ([Di] – [Dj]), this extracting all determinants not shared by Mi and Mj;

thus: {D@i:j} = ([D] – {D^i:j}, which is the array of all determinants belonging to both Mi and Mj.

A similar set of considerations could be used to extract the set of relational-level similarities, such that [Z] = ({Zi} + {Zj}), with {Z^i:j} then being a difference set and {Z@i:j} a set containing all shared relational-level specifications. A rough measure of the degree of complementarity between Mi and Mj is thus given by {D@i:j}/[D] and {Z@i:j}/[Z]. These similarity extraction operations might then be performed for all pairwise combinations of Mi vs. Mj alternatives in [M], and the aggregate results encoded in two master similarity sets, {D@} and {Z@}.

The master similarity sets might then each be inspected to ascertain the frequency with which any given determinant or relational specification appears among the entire population of alternatives. The resultant frequency distributions, in their turn, might be taken as a crude reflection of the degree of subjective/judgemental or a-priori consensus associated with any determinant or relational provision viewed in isolation . . . this distinct from the a-priori preference indices generated during the ordering operation, these reflecting the collective affection for one integral model relative to all others in some set. Therefore, we might look to complete a syncretic construct by filling in the gaps left among the a-posteriori preferred provisions by including those determinant and relational specifications assigned the highest frequency of mention via the above similarity-related operations. And to make now a final technical assertion, certain of these consensus provisions might become obvious targets for empirical efforts intended to still further reduce the a-prioristic residual in a syncretic construct . . . even if practical constraints dicate recourse to that most expedient of transempirical tricks, selective validation. As such, a syncretic selection is simply another avenue towards an extensive-Bayesian conclusion to a decision exercise.

Overall then, the Strategic Decision Protocol is intended to speak more or less directly to this proposition: Even though true strategic decision exercises will be strongly rooted in subjective and judgemental predicates, they are not irrevocably condemned to remain forever beyond the pale of scientific discipline and precision.

NOTES AND REFERENCES

1. This, again, is in contrast to the orthodox protocols' earlier-mentioned general restriction to the treatment of alternatives that are all basically intelligible as members of the same general class of phenomenon or [m1, m2 . . . mn] $\in$ M1, where m1 and m2, etc., are thematic rather than state-level alternatives.

2. See, for example, Harsanyi's concept of instrumental significance in his paper, "Acceptance of Empirical Statements: A Bayesian Theory without Cognitive Utilities," *Theory and Decision* (18; 1985).

3. The key sources of suggestions about mainstream Action Research procedures are the articles in (Clark, ed.) *Experimenting with Organizational Life: The Action Research Approach* (Plenum Press, 1976).

4. These distinctions may be derived from the analysis conducted by J. L. Stein in his *Monetarist, Keynesian and New Classical Economics* (Oxford: Basil Blackwell, Ltd., 1982).

5. There are of course certain techniques that might be used to assist users in systematically arraying alternatives. The simplest of such are passive graphic constructs such as Influence Diagrams, etc. Secondly, there are the various approaches to computer-based Structural modeling, c.f., A. Geoffrion, *An Introduction to Structured Modeling* (UCLA: Western Management Science Inst. Working Paper No. 338, 1986). There are also certain other formal grammars that allow for interactive scripting, e.g.: Bisschop & Meeraus, "On the Development of a General Algebraic Modeling System in a Strategic Planning Environment", *Mathematical Programming Study* (20), 1982 or Brodie's, *On Conceptual Modeling* (Springer-Verglag, 1984). But none defines model *structure* as we've done here, and so may not recognize the difference between what are qualitative provisions and what's merely mathematical mapping provisions.

6. One choice would be to pick up where existing simulation systems leave off. For these permit the generation of *statistically probable* possibilities by varying the input parameters supplied to a given model structure. In such cases, a surrogate test for exhaustiveness (or, more properly, representationality) can be had by having input arguments generated randomly, say via a Monte Carlo front-end. Or we could direct a simulation program to generate the consequences for the extreme values of some probability density distribution fitted over inputs, and then work with the mean or median input arguments, etc. The problem however is that traditional simulation programs all require a *stationary structure* during any iteration. And structure, of course, is exactly what we here would want to be able to alter during any iteration.

7. See, for example, Michel & Miller, *Qualitative Analysis of Large-Scale Dynamical Systems* (Academic Press, 1977). Or, with respect to statistical-type relational structures, consider the sorts of tests recommednded by J. W. Tukey in his *Exploratory Data Analysis* (Addison-Wesley, 1977).

8. The ideas of Doug Lenat about discovery technology are particularly interesting . . . e.g., D. B. Lenat, "The Ubiquity of Discovery", *Artificial Intelligence* (9), 1977 or "The Role of Heuristics in Learning By Discovery: Three Case Studies", in (Michalski, et. al., eds.) *Machine Learning* (Tioga, 1983).

9. For a general view of the role of logical formalisms, see Mario Bunge's *Epistemology and Methodology-II* (Boston: D. Reidel, 1983) or Carl Hempel's classic book, *Aspects of Scientific Explanation* (Free Press, 1965). Other interesting examples and discussions are given by R. Tuomela in his *Theoretical Concepts* (Springer-Verlag, 1973) and by J. H. Holland in *Induction: Processes of Inference, Learning and Discovery* (MIT Press, 1986). It's important here to note that one consequence of the parsing convention just discussed is to open a door whereby a-priori ordering operations might perhaps be subject to some sort of formal logical discipline. One potential source of such discipline are the formal symbolic logic systems (grammars)

now available, most evolved to support essays in analytical philosophy. And what might make their employment possible is that, following the parsing process, determinant-level model properties would be intelligible as *nouns*, with relational-level specifications comprehensible as *verbs*. And much as with any linguistic grammar, a logical grammar could then be employed to test for the syntactical integrity of any model once it's been properly parsed. This is of considerable practical interest because of the natural tendency for the authors of idiosyncratic, paradigmatic or axiological constructs to let rigor be subordinated to rhetorical enthusiasm.

10. See W. Craig's "Bases for First-Order Theories and Subtheories", *Journal of Symbolic Logic* (25; 1960). Or J. A. Winnie, "The Implicit Definition of Theoretical Terms", *British Journal for the Philosophy of Science* (18), 1967.

11. Recent advances in the construction of genetic algorithms are reported in (Grefenstette, ed.) *Genetic Algorithms and Their Applications* (Lawrence Erlbaum, 1987).

12. See their approach to operations on value-based constructs in *On Purposeful Systems* (Chicago: Aldine, 1972).

13. Seadler's approach is outlined in "Ideologic Essentials of Public Administration", in *The Management Handbook for Public Administrators* (Van Nostrand Reinhold, 1978). For another approach, see R. F. Saltz: "Searching for Structure in Beliefs", in Harris, ed., *Rationality and Collective Belief* (Ablex Publishing Co., 1986).

14. Though the matter of *replacement* programming is still in some dispute, its notational and basic logical conventions are of extreme interest as a basis for parsing complex models and for examining them for *syntactical* confoundations. For more on this, see W. Craig's paper, "Bases for First-order Theories and Subtheories", *Journal of Symbolic Logic* (25), 1960.

15. A very fine survey of knowledge engineering concepts is J. Sowa's *Conceptual Structures* (Addison-Wesley, 1984). See also D. E. Shasha, *Knowledge-Based Systems Design Using Conceptual Graphs* (IBM Research Institute: #TR 73-023), 1983.

16. For an indication of the on the tribulations to which causal collective decision-making schemes are subject, see Diehl & Stroebe's paper: "Productivty Losses in Brainstorming Groups", in the *Journal of Personality and Social Psychology* (55; 1987), H. Tajifel & J. Turner, "An Integrative Theory of Intergroup Conflict", in (Austin and Worchel, eds.) *The Social Psychology of Intergroup Relations* (Monterey, CA; Brooks/Cole, 1979), or D. G. Meyers & H. Lamm, "The Group Polarization Phenomenon", *Psychological Bulletin* (83), 1976. Also interesting is Janis' book, *Victims of Groupthink* (MIT Press, 1986) and T. J. Bouchard's essay, "Whatever Happened to Brainstorming" in the *Journal of Creative Behavior* (5; 1971). There are of course a number of rather elegant traditional Bayesian-based techniques that might be employed to try to discipline collective decision exercises, e.g.: D. A. Seaver, *Assessing Probability with Multiple Individuals: Group Interaction vs. Mathematical Aggregation* (University of Southern California, Social Science Research Institute, Research Rpt 78-3, 1978); D. A. Schum, "Current Developments in Research on Cascaded Inference," in Wallsten, ed., *Cognitive Processes in Decision and Choice Behavior* (Lawrence Erlbaum, 1980); Schum & A. W. Martin, *Assessing the Probative*

Value of Evidence in Various Inference Structures (Rice University, Dept. of Psychology; Tech. Report #81-02, 1981). But the general problem is that most such techniques demand more in the way of hard data or empirically-validated arguments to drive them than is likely to be available in true strategic decision exercises.

17. The decomposition initiatives discussed here are variations on themes that have some mention in the literature on qualitative analysis as it applies in the domain of academic research, e.g.: Michael Patton, *Qualitative Evaluation Methods* (1980); John Van Maanen (ed.), *Qualitative Methodology* (1983); Van Maaner, Dabbs and Faulkner, *Varieties of Qualitative Research* (1982); David Silverman, *Qualitative Methodology and Sociology* (1985); Anselm Strauss, *Qualitative Analysis for Social Scientists* (1987); Robert Walker (ed.), *Applied Qualitative Research* (1985). But understandably enough, such sources have more to say about qualitative analysis procedures for leisurely learning than decision-making under stress. In particular, they tend to be long on general procedural advice but short on instrumental recommendations (or, when instrumental suggestions are made, these will most often involve a scheme to convert qualitative arguments to a form comprehensible to quantitative appreciation via a scalar transmogrification scheme of some kind). Therefore, a better source of suggestion about the mechanics of decomposition in the Strategic Analysis Protocol is theory based, engineering or system applications, c.f.: Himmelbau (ed.) *Decomposition of Large-Scale Systems* (American Elsevier, 1983).

18. Another approach would be to impose a frequency distribution over all members of {S^}, and then elect to give earliest and/or most complete assessment attention to those particular difference aspects having the highest frequency-of-mention.

19. The algorithmic mechanics for effecting extensive-Bayesian conjunctions would not be materially different from those used to aggregate ordinal probabilities (c.f., Laine, et. al., Group Decision Making Under Uncertainty: A Note on the Aggregation of "Ordinal Probabilities", *Theory and Decision* (21; 1986) or for working with second-order probabilities, particularly as explicated by Baron in his Second Order Probabilities and Belief Functions, *Theory and Decision* (23; 1987).

20. For an example of a somewhat crude attempt to develop a *syncretic* construct, see Chapter 1 of my book: *Societal Systems: Methodology, Modelling and Management* (Elseveier-North Holland, 1978).

Index

THEORY AND DECISION LIBRARY

SERIES A: PHILOSOPHY AND METHODOLOGY OF THE SOCIAL SCIENCES

Already published:

Conscience: An Interdisciplinary View

Edited by Gerhard Zecha and Paul Weingartner

ISBN 90–277–2452–0

Cognitive Strategies in Stochastic Thinking

by Roland W. Scholz

ISBN 90–277–2454–7

Comparing Voting Systems

by Hannu Nurmi

ISBN 90–277–2600–0

Evolutionary Theory in Social Science

Edited by Michael Schmid and Franz M. Wuketits

ISBN 90–277–2612–4

The Metaphysics of Liberty

by Frank Forman

ISBN 0–7923–0080–7